k

D1016410

IN PUBLIC HOUSES

IN PUBLIC HOUSES

DRINK & THE REVOLUTION
OF AUTHORITY IN COLONIAL
MASSACHUSETTS

David W. Conroy

Published for the Institute of Early American

History and Culture, *Williamsburg, Virginia,*

By the University of North Carolina Press,

Chapel Hill & London

The Institute of Early American History and Culture is
sponsored jointly by the College of William and Mary and
the Colonial Williamsburg Foundation.

Manufactured in the United States of America
Library of Congress Cataloging-in-Publication Data
Conroy, David W.
    In public houses: drink and the revolution of authority in colonial
Massachusetts / by David W. Conroy.
        p. cm.
    Includes bibliographical references and index.
    ISBN 0-8078-2207-8 (cloth : alk. paper) — ISBN 0-8078-4521-3
(pbk. : alk. paper)
    1. Popular culture—Massachusetts—History—18th century. 2. Popular
culture—Massachusetts—History—17th century. 3. Bars (Drinking
establishments)—Massachusetts—History—18th century. 4. Bars
(Drinking establishments)—Massachusetts—History—17th century.
5. Massachusetts—Social life and customs—To 1775. 6. Taverns (Inns)—
Massachusetts—History—18th century. 7. Taverns (Inns)—
Massachusetts—History—17th century. I. Institute of Early American
History and Culture (Williamsburg, Va.) II. Title.
F67.C756   1995
394.1'2'0974409033—dc20   94-32658
                                                                      CIP

The paper in this book meets the guidelines for permanence and
durability of the Committee on Production Guidelines for Book
Longevity of the Council on Library Resources.

This volume received indirect support from an unrestricted book
publication grant awarded to the Institute by the L. J. Skaggs
and Mary C. Skaggs Foundation of Oakland, California.

99   98   97   96   95   5   4   3   2   1

FOR MY PARENTS,

Richard and Alice Weir Conroy

Acknowledgments

It is a pleasure to acknowledge the help and guidance I have received from many people and organizations while researching and writing this study. A grant from the University of Connecticut Research Foundation helped to finance initial research. My search for sources of evidence took me to a number of institutions and government offices in Massachusetts, including the Massachusetts Historical Society, the American Antiquarian Society, the Massachusetts State Archives, the Massachusetts State Library, and the repositories of records at the Suffolk, Middlesex, Worcester, and Hampshire county courthouses. I appreciate the assistance that I received at all of these places in finding and retrieving documents and printed materials. At the Massachusetts Historical Society, Peter Drummey was particularly helpful in searching for references and finding appropriate maps and illustrations. Celeste Walker of the Adams Papers found a valuable reference. John Hench of the American Antiquarian Society guided me in the identification of shorthand titles of books mentioned in tavernkeepers' inventories. I have also benefited from the presentation and discussion of papers on related topics in seminars in early American history sponsored by both of these institutions. Joan Bines of the Golden Ball Tavern Museum in Weston drew my attention to material on that tavern's history. Elizabeth Bouvier, archivist of the Judicial Archives, helped me to negotiate the problems involved with the transferal of records from county repositories to the new Judicial Archives at the Massachusetts State Archives.

Throughout the research and writing of this book the Boston Public Library has been a critical source of resources and references. I made extensive use of the published town records and the town histories painstakingly collected by its librarians over the years. Despite budget cuts and the problems of coping with austerity, the staff unfailingly rendered me interested, informed, and professional assistance. I am particularly grateful to the librarians of the Humanities Reference Department and the librarians and staff of the Microtext Reading Room. The latter's prompt and efficient service day after day eased and speeded my examination of diverse sources.

I have also benefited from the criticism of papers that I have presented at various conferences and meetings. In 1984 I delivered a paper at the international conference "The Social History of Alcohol" at the University of California at Berkeley. I wish to thank Susanna Barrows and Robin Room of Berkeley for this opportunity to meet scholars from around the world doing research on related topics. This paper was later selected for publication with a collection of papers drawn from the conference edited by Susanna Barrows and Robin Room. *Drinking: Behavior and Belief in Modern History*, published by the University of California Press, has been a valuable guide to recent research on alcohol studies. Over the past few years my affiliation with the Alliance of Independent Scholars in Cambridge has been a great source of pleasure and instruction. Members of the Alliance listened to and commented on three papers I presented. I owe special thanks to Polly Kaufman and Gillian Gill for their comments. I have also been stimulated by the interest expressed by my students at the University of Massachusetts at Boston and Northeastern University in lectures on related topics.

My adviser, Richard D. Brown, first suggested to me that the tavern's role in colonial society, especially in communication, deserved more attention. I am grateful for the several close, critical readings he gave this study in its origins as a dissertation under his supervision, for the valuable references he drew to my notice, and for his instruction in lectures and seminars. Readers for the Institute of Early American History and Culture at Williamsburg, Christine Leigh Heyrman and an anonymous critic, made stimulating suggestions. Fredrika J. Teute, editor of publications at the Institute, helped me to refine conceptualization, argument, and organization. She has been a patient editor and thoughtful critic. I am equally indebted to Gil Kelly, managing editor, for his meticulous editing of the manuscript and advice on a countless number of details from wording to maps. I have also benefited from critical readings of all or part of this study by John Brooke, John Greene, Karen Kupperman, Ted Margadant, Norman Pierce, and John Travers. Marcia Conroy and Eugene Gallagher helped in many ways. If I have not followed every suggestion or agreed with every criticism, this book is certainly better for the many I received.

My greatest debt is to my parents for their encouragement and support. This book is for them.

Contents

Illustrations and Tables

Abbreviations and Note on the Text

ACM: Archives of the Commonwealth of Massachusetts, Boston

MHS: Massachusetts Historical Society, Boston

WMQ: William and Mary Quarterly

Transcriptions of colonial sources have been modernized.

Introduction

I n April 1721 blows were struck in Richard Hall's tavern just across the street from the Town House in Boston. The incident involved two prominent gentlemen. Elisha Cooke, Jr., Boston selectman and representative, said or did something that provoked John Yeamans, a supporter and associate of royal governor Samuel Shute, to strike him. News of the fight spread quickly, and one mariner's reaction to it was recorded. Christopher Taylor became outraged that his hero Cooke, the leader of opposition to the royal establishment in Boston, had been assaulted. "Damn [Yeamans]," Taylor cried, "why don't he come out to me, I wish I could see the dog come out— 'a God I would have some of his blood." Taylor was so incensed that he insulted Governor Shute by refusing to bow to him when he rode up King Street in his coach.[1]

This incident illustrates the pitfalls of any effort to open the doors of public houses of the colonial period to investigation and analysis. First, the context of this particular altercation is lost. There are no surviving records that allow us to picture the structure and contents of Hall's tavern. We don't know what words passed in this politically charged atmosphere to stir such feeling. And the currents of conversation that passed between other patrons amid this confrontation are unknown. Nor do we know whether Taylor heard the news of the fight in another King Street tavern

1. Court of General Sessions of the Peace, Suffolk, Record Book, 1719–1725, Apr. 4, 1721, 80–81, Judicial Archives, ACM.

1

or whether liquor contributed to his "menacing" walk on the street and his daring insult to the governor. In comparison to that other prominent gathering place, the meetinghouse, taverns have left a meager paper trail. The rich yield of sermons, diaries of ministers and pious laymen, devotional tracts, and manuals of instruction all open up the religious life of Sabbath assemblies to view. But the conversations and activities inside taverns are largely lost to us. Indeed, the more strictly oral culture of taverns does not invite·investigation.

But if there are pitfalls to such an investigation, there are also tempting possibilities. This altercation in Richard Hall's tavern suggests the informality, the spontaneity of interaction in public houses. For a moment the records reveal colonists in a setting where authority is lax, where the sale of drink might prompt more open and unguarded expression. News of the incident affected Christopher Taylor so much that he aired his sentiments to anyone who would listen. In taverns men did not ordinarily sit according to their place in the local social hierarchy or merely listen to sermons and exhortations. Here there was at least the possibility for greater assertion in posture and conversation. And in drink men might abandon the constraints that governed interaction in most public situations and thus make taverns a fertile breeding ground for new possibilities in social and political relationships.

Thus it is important to probe this dimension of colonial society as much as evidence will allow, to catch colonists in more informal public situations, in order to develop a fully rounded portrait of the character and progress of that society. The tavern was the most numerous public institution in colonial New England, but little is known about it. The overriding purpose of the following study is to bring this shadowy institution into focus and reveal its place in the evolving public life of colonial and Revolutionary Massachusetts. Conceived more broadly, this study presents the tavern as a public stage upon which men, and sometimes women, spoke and acted in ways that sometimes tested—and ultimately challenged—the authority of their rulers and social superiors in the hierarchy of Massachusetts society.

Such a study has few precedents. The commentaries and histories touching on tavern life in colonial Massachusetts are sketchy at best. Much of what has been written about taverns has focused on the degree to which inhabitants practiced temperance in their drinking. A brief survey of the existing commentary on taverns and drink in colonial Massachusetts reveals conflicting perspectives and suggests the need to dig deeper into this dimension of social life and weigh the evidence more carefully.

Over the course of the colonial period contemporary observers present a confusing picture. Each generation tended to revere the previous one as a model of temperate behavior in comparison to the tavern haunting and intemperance it condemned in its own time. For Increase Mather, writing in the 1670s, the founding generation of colonists became symbols of exemplary virtue. Mather's generation assumed that mantle of superior virtue and piety for the preachers writing and exhorting in the early eighteenth century. For the Revolutionary generation, temperance, self-discipline, and industry represented ancestral virtues recently lost but that must be restored.[2] Declension from a virtuous past would seem to have been the text for each generation in turn.

In the eyes of a new generation writing in the early 1800s, all of the colonists over the span of the entire colonial period came to possess a temperate reputation. In 1820, for example, the Board of Counsel of the Massachusetts Society for the Suppression of Intemperance contrasted a temperate colonial past, in which taverns were strictly regulated, to a lax and imperiled republican present. Members of the board had studied "ancient and modern laws enacted on this subject" from the conviction "that laws must be one of the powerful instruments in reforming the intemperate." If their "Christian ancestors were for ages" under a monarchy "extremely anxious" to suppress drunkenness and taverns "when the means of intoxication and persons intemperate were but few," how much more important it was for a Republic to enforce regulation! Colonial officials, the board believed, had possessed "much more influence" than their republican counterparts in respect to law enforcement, perhaps because "they had less fear of the vicious in popular elections."[3] To members of the society looking back in 1820, colonial officials enforced strict control over public houses.

Other commentators on drinking habits and taverns, especially those who espoused the more radical promotion of total abstinence, were more skeptical of the temperate quality of colonial society. Taking a more critical view, these reformers concluded that colonists as a whole had remained

2. Increase Mather, *Wo to Drunkards* . . . (Cambridge, Mass., 1673); Cotton Mather *et al.*, *A Serious Address to Those Who Unnecessarily Frequent the Tavern, and Often Spend the Evening in Publick Houses, by Several Ministers* (Boston, 1726); L. H. Butterfield *et al.*, eds., *Diary and Autobiography of John Adams* (New York, 1964), 190–192; Edmund S. Morgan, "The Puritan Ethic and the American Revolution," *WMQ*, 3d Ser., XXIV (1967), 3–43.

3. Massachusetts Society for the Suppression of Intemperance, *Report of the Board of Counsel to the Massachusetts Society for the Suppression of Intemperance, June 2, 1820* (Boston, 1820), 1–11, MHS.

trapped within the constraints and customs of a more backward age. Thomas Herttell, writing at the same time as the board of the Massachusetts Society, believed that law had never been a truly effective deterrent against intemperance. In a rudimentary way, he adopted a sociological approach to drink and taverns. From time immemorial, he argued, the offering of drink had been the medium universally adopted by society for manifesting friendship and good will, one to another. "Not to offer drink" would be deemed "unfriendly, mean or unmannerly." And the visitor to whom it was offered must drink "to reciprocate good will for the proffered kindness." Such a time-honored custom in "hospitality," Herttell explained, had been "the growth of successive ages, and has hence become a kind of second nature." Thus in order for laws to become effectual, "they must be bottomed in public opinion." If not, "they are either successfully opposed in their passage, soon repealed or rendered inoperative." Such had been the "fate of all, or most of the laws passed, or attempted to be passed, with the view of limiting the number of taverns to the public requirement."[4]

Shorn of its messianic fervor, Herttell's historical perspective on taverns and drink has much to recommend it. For Massachusetts and other colonies, it suggests the importance of balance in the analysis of tavern assemblies. One must weigh reform ideals as expressed in sermon and law in the early modern era against the traditional values associated with consumption by individuals and tavern companies. Only through an understanding of how the sale and distribution of drink helped to define social relations in ways sanctioned by the populace at large, Herttell implies, can the importance and impact of drink regulation be assessed. For the historian, such an approach identifies the public house as not just an anathema of the clergy, an obstacle to temperance, but a vital institution where the customs Herttell describes were acted out. Such an approach also invites investigation of the tavern as an institution that might be important in the political culture of colonial America.

But no scholar developed such an approach to the study of taverns and drink in colonial society in the nineteenth and early twentieth centuries, as is evident from the paucity and quality of those few studies that included any discussion of taverns or drink. Those published at the turn of the century tended to be nostalgic, misty-eyed idealizations of the preindustrial past. Books like Alice Morse Earle's *Stage-Coach and Tavern Days*

4. Thomas Herttell, *An Expose of the Causes of Intemperate Drinking, and the Means by Which It May Be Obviated* (New York, 1820), 11, 13, 21, 34. See also William Ellery Channing, "Public Opinion and Temperance," in J. G. Adams and E. H. Chapin, eds., *The Fountain: A Temperance Gift* (Boston, 1847), 51–54, MHS.

contain valuable information and insights, but they tend to treat colonial taverns as unchanging, uncontroversial parts of a more pristine and harmonious era.[5] In the hands of these writers, colonial taverns assumed the character of picturesque artifacts associated with benign folkways, with no connection to the modern-day saloon that temperance reformers sought to eliminate in the twentieth century. And there they largely remained after the end of Prohibition and through the 1950s.

The rediscovery and elucidation of Puritan theology by Perry Miller and his students during these years—a watershed in the historiography of New England that defined its conception and study for more than a generation—also tended to reinforce the temperate image of Puritan colonists.[6] By uncovering the intricate web of ideas in covenant theology and its subsequent evolution in New England, Miller more than anyone else relegated the tavern and related aspects of community life to the periphery of scholarly interest merely by the force and majesty of his analysis. The masterful manner in which Miller traced the evolution of theological belief and practice became for many a blueprint for the evolution of Massachusetts and New England society as a whole.

Since 1960, however, scholars have begun to investigate colonial Massachusetts from a variety of different perspectives. The advent of what is generally called the New Social History has altered our understanding of colonial history in general and is now an established genre of historical inquiry. Intensive studies of local communities such as those by John Demos, Philip Greven, Kenneth Lockridge, and Robert Gross (to name a few) have indirectly challenged the historiographic tradition founded by Miller through the exploitation of sources other than literary documents.[7] Insights into the values, behavior, and activities of colonists as they lived and worked from day to day in port towns and small agricultural commu-

---

5. Alice Morse Earle, *Stage-Coach and Tavern Days* (New York, 1900); Edward Field, *The Colonial Tavern* . . . (Providence, R.I., 1897); Samuel A. Drake, *Old Boston Taverns and Tavern Clubs* . . . (Boston, 1917).

6. Perry Miller, *The New England Mind: The Seventeenth Century* (Cambridge, Mass., 1954); and *The New England Mind: From Colony to Province* (Cambridge, Mass., 1953).

7. John Demos, *A Little Commonwealth: Family Life in Plymouth Colony* (New York, 1970); Kenneth A. Lockridge, *A New England Town, the First Hundred Years: Dedham, Massachusetts, 1636–1736* (New York, 1970); Philip J. Greven, Jr., *Four Generations: Population, Land, and Family in Colonial Andover, Massachusetts* (Ithaca, N.Y., 1970); Robert A. Gross, *The Minutemen and Their World* (New York, 1976). Kym S. Rice surveys tavern life in the colonies in *Early American Taverns: For the Entertainment of Friends and Strangers* (Chicago, 1983).

nities, and from one generation to the next, have been gleaned from birth and death records, land transactions, wills, town meeting records, court cases, and gravestones. What had hitherto been deemed almost inconsequential has now become vital evidence toward a more complete reconstruction of the past. In such a scholarly climate, the high incidence of public houses in Massachusetts merits more thorough investigation.

As with several of the above community studies, such an inquiry must necessarily draw on the insights of social scientists. Clifford Geertz's seminal essays on the interpretation of ritual ceremonies and behavior have stimulated a wealth of studies of colonial America that seek to uncover aspects and dynamics of the familiar face-to-face village societies in which most colonists lived. Anthropologists observing village and tribal societies in this century have concluded that drinking customs can help to integrate a social unit in certain circumstances and possess a symbolic importance in the vertical and horizontal social relations of pre- or semiliterate societies.[8] Such perspectives form a useful counterweight to the emphasis on temperance regulation and the pathology of alcoholism in modern industrial societies. They encourage the historian to conceive of gatherings to drink in colonial America as occasions at which an entire range of values of social, economic, and political significance was acted out or acknowledged and reaffirmed. The mounting wave of criticism by Puritan leaders of English drinking customs in the seventeenth century is an indication that for some segments of the population these customs no longer integrated society in a manner considered beneficial. In other words, the "functional" value of these customs and habits had come to be considered "dysfunctional" as new value systems were articulated, sanc-

8. Clifford Geertz, "Thick Description: Toward an Interpretative Theory of Culture," in Geertz, *The Interpretation of Cultures* (New York, 1973), 3–32; Erving Goffman, *The Presentation of Self in Everyday Life* (New York, 1959); Goffman, *Behavior in Public Places: Notes on the Social Organization of Gatherings* (New York, 1963); Goffman, *Interaction Ritual: Essays on Face-to-Face Behavior* (Chicago, 1967). A pioneering study of alcohol use in traditional societies is Audrey I. Richards, *Land, Labour, and Diet in Northern Rhodesia: An Economic Study of the Bemba Tribe* (London, 1939), 76–87, 135–143, 366–380; Clarence H. Patrick, *Alcohol, Culture and Society* (Durham, N.C., 1952), chap. 2; Thomas W. Hill, "Ethnohistory and Alcohol Studies," in Marc Galenter, ed., *Recent Developments in Alcoholism*, II (New York, 1984), 313–337. Historians of public gatherings who have been directly influenced by Geertz, Goffman, and other social scientists include Rhys Isaac, "Dramatizing the Ideology of Revolution: Popular Mobilization in Virginia, 1774 To 1776," *WMQ*, 3d Ser., XXXIII (1976), 357–385; and A. G. Roeber, "Authority, Law, and Custom: The Rituals of Court Day in Tidewater Virginia, 1720 to 1750," *WMQ*, 3d Ser., XXXVII (1980), 29–52.

tioned by religious creed, and promoted. Thus an important part of the investigation of the public life of taverns in this period is to trace the course of negotiation between old and new value systems in community life.

Social scientists also underline the importance of the material context of public life. Probate records allow us to picture some public houses as well as provide us information about their contents. Boston taverns were humble, modest institutions in the seventeenth century, judging from surviving inventories. Even the more prominent taverns were simply two-story substantial frame houses open to the public. Furnishings were simple. Presumably, country taverns were even more spare. Still, enumeration and interpretation of the contents of public houses can tell us much about the character of gatherings there as opposed to the formality of the meetinghouse. Tracing how these furnishings change over the course of the eighteenth century and discovering when new beverages like rum began to be sold in volume provide a foundation for understanding the burgeoning critical commentary on "luxury" and "dissipation."[9] The development of a hierarchy among public houses in eighteenth-century Boston can tell us much about social stratification and differentiation in the growing port town. The appearance of the "genteel" tavern may be discovered and contrasted with houses kept by the poor for the poor. Inventories can also help to determine the extent to which proprietors of public houses owned books and how such books might begin to influence and change their interaction with patrons. To what extent did the print culture penetrate the traditional oral culture of taverns in the colonial period?

Modest though they might have been in the seventeenth century, public houses were a source of controversy in the new colony. Whereas for centuries it had been customary for figures of authority to distribute drink often to those under their care and government, Puritan rulers made it their duty to suppress drinking to excess, drunkenness, and the number of taverns. Chapter 1 of this study delineates the Puritan assault on traditional drinking habits. At the behest of the clergy, the colony's government placed taverns and drink under greater control as the seventeenth century progressed. Through numerous laws the ruling elite reached ever deeper into public rooms to regulate behavior, even stipulating how much time could be spent in taverns and how much patrons might drink. These laws, together with a close examination of magistrate Samuel Sewall's use of taverns and drink, provide definition to the words "temperance" and "in-

9. For a discussion of this commentary, see Drew McCoy, *The Elusive Republic: Political Economy in Jeffersonian America* (Chapel Hill, N.C., 1980), chap. 1.

temperance" in the seventeenth century. They show to what lengths Puritan leaders went to change traditional uses of drink and with what success.

The regulation of taverns also possessed political implications. The elaborate, rigid social order of England had been simplified and relaxed in New England by circumstance and design. Annual elections were instituted. Puritans still believed in a society organized by rank and degree, but the principle of hierarchy had been modified in practice. Behavior began to be the measure of a man's status. Elected leaders became open to some measure of scrutiny of their fitness for high office. By the same token, leaders became obsessed with controlling public behavior. It became more imperative to control the use of taverns, lest they begin to influence a political system and culture that permitted broader participation. Voters were expected to defer to a select group of rulers at town and provincial levels. Thus Puritan rulers sought to suppress traditional drinking habits while preserving traditional notions of hierarchy and deference. Ideally, voters must soberly recognize and reward rulers for their piety, education, and social distinction. Tavern crowds might undermine this process. The regulation of taverns was thus part of the maintenance of a deferential political system.

Chapters 2 and 3 measure the success of these efforts to suppress taverns while preserving hierarchy. An alarmist note to legislative initiatives after 1680 suggests that the resistance to drink laws was widespread. The tenor of the laws together with licensing records is assessed to reveal whether a popular culture of drink in defiance of the clergy and lawmakers existed in colonial Massachusetts. The term "popular culture" is not used here to minimize the importance of the writings and publications of the clergy in defining cultural values. One modern study of popular religious practice describes how thoroughly some Calvinist precepts influenced common belief and frames of reference. But it also shows that even devout Puritans held ambivalent feelings about some doctrines and could be selective about what they chose to accept and follow.[10] Were the inhabitants of Massachusetts towns ambivalent about the teachings of the clergy in respect to drink? Indeed, taverns might have contributed to community cohesion in ways that the clergy failed to understand or refused to accept. One must be careful to evaluate clerical criticism of taverns in light of the rivalry they might have felt toward the institution. An investigation of

10. David D. Hall, *Worlds of Wonder, Days of Judgment: Popular Religious Belief in Early New England* (Cambridge, Mass., 1990), 18–20, 156–165.

tavern life can provide fresh perspective on the sometimes delicate relations between clergy and populace.

If taverns were public spaces over which the ruling elite and the populace at large contested for control in the seventeenth century, their role in public life in the eighteenth century becomes still more problematic. A cursory examination of licensing records reveals that taverns and retail houses selling drink multiplied dramatically after 1720 in Boston and the country towns. Indeed, by 1737 Boston had 177 drinksellers, or roughly 1 for every 100 inhabitants.[11] Chapter 3 provides further explanation of the origins and consequences of this sharp increase in public houses. Is it simply popular pressure for more access combined with population growth, or are other forces at work? Does the popular culture of drink overwhelm the mass of Puritan restrictions? A high proportion of those granted licenses were women. Their place in this increasingly competitive trade in drink can shed light on the problems women faced when they stepped out of the confines of prescribed female roles to enter business. The difficulties that they and other drinksellers as a whole confronted in earning a living provide insight into the instability of many households in Boston in the eighteenth century. Under such circumstances, amid the increasing availability of rum at low prices, traditional village drinking habits could and did lead to abusive, self-destructive behavior among some inhabitants. In urbanizing Boston, there was a sinister side to the popular culture of drink.

In the eighteenth century, clergymen continued to call on all elected officials to act against intemperance. The suppression of traditional drinking habits and the number of public houses had become a sacred duty of office. Almost annually ministers prompted magistrates to these duties in election sermons delivered before the governor, Council, and Assembly in the eighteenth century. But to what extent did selectmen, justices, and representatives heed the clergy? Two chapters on the politics of taverns in Boston and the countryside explore the use of drink and taverns in the changing political culture of Massachusetts. Despite the rapid multiplication of public houses in Boston and country towns after 1720, the Assembly enacted no new major laws to regulate the drink trade. The laws on the books might have been deemed sufficient. Or perhaps representatives were more cautious in their approach to this issue, more accommodating to constituents who frequented taverns. Indeed, some tavernkeepers began

11. The Names of Persons Licensed in the County of Suffolk, James Otis, Sr., Papers, MHS.

to be elected to the House. Was the popular culture of drink beginning to influence the tenor of relations between rulers and ruled?

One must also take into account the controversial presence of royal authority after 1692 in measuring any shift in the balance of reform and indulgence in respect to drink. Did native-born colonial leaders turn to tavern crowds to recruit support in their conflicts with royal governors? These chapters place the fight between House leader Elisha Cooke, Jr., and John Yeamans in Richard Hall's tavern in perspective. Public houses become a stage upon which one may trace changes in Massachusetts political culture in the eighteenth century.

Finally, this study uncovers the role of taverns in the Revolution. In the half-century prior to 1765, the colony seemed to be drifting further and further away from fundamental ideals and values while no alternative set of values was gaining full articulation and acceptance. Uneasiness over the quality and direction of Massachusetts society is reflected in the wave of reform sentiment touched off by the outbreak of conflict with England. Why did the reform of drinking habits and related behavior seem so essential as the crisis of authority in Massachusetts deepened? Tributes to Puritan virtues were much in evidence in public appeals to the populace, and these virtues now began to be extolled as a necessary foundation for a republican society and government. Rum became the focus of new criticism of imported luxuries held responsible for the decay of the rustic virtues of simplicity, industry, and discipline. But did rhetoric transform public life? These new calls for reform must be measured against the social reality of Revolutionary mobilization. Were taverns a point of reception for republican ideology, a means of diffusing the messages of pamphlets, or a context for acting out new principles? Uncovering the role of taverns and drink in the Revolution can provide a ground's eye view on the impetus, activities, and goals of leaders and followers as they faced a critical juncture in political affairs. An epilogue sketches the continuing use of taverns by the new citizens of the Republic in the decades that follow; but it also shows how the multiplication of voluntary organizations after 1790 and the modern consumption of print affected the importance of public houses in defining public life.

This study devotes particular attention to the changing texture of tavern life in populous Boston, an important crucible for the formation of New England culture between the years 1680 and 1776. Here public houses were most numerous and controversial. Licensing records are incomplete for Boston, and very sporadic after the year 1732, but enough have survived to establish the direction of change in the eighteenth century. For country towns, Middlesex County licensing records are complete, and some records have survived for Worcester and Hampshire counties. These records reveal the operation of the licensing system, the cornerstone of regulation, in which a hierarchy of officials approved and granted licenses. Theoretically, applicants for licenses or renewals humbly sought approval from selectmen and justices and on some occasions submitted petitions to the governor, Council, and House. Licenseholders must also submit to inspection and regulation by tithingmen, excise collectors, grand jurymen, and sheriffs. But licensing records also reveal subtle shifts in the relationship between licenseholders and this hierarchy of regulators, changes that affected the very faith in and practice of hierarchy itself.

Thus public houses provide a window into much more than the drinking habits of colonists, important as that topic remains. Revealing their place in Massachusetts society also illuminates related topics, such as changing consumer taste, gender roles, urbanization, and the expanding use of print. The rigor and impact of regulations concerning public houses enacted by the Assembly over time can tell us much about the nature, location, exercise, and limits of political power in colonial and Revolutionary Massachusetts. From the first years of settlement, public houses were controversial gathering places. Rulers perceived them to be a threat to order and suppressed their number and use as much as possible. Nevertheless, taverns became a public stage upon which colonists resisted, initiated, and addressed changes in their society. Indeed, in these houses men gradually redefined their relationships with figures of authority.

Chapter 1

The Puritan Assault
on Drink and Taverns

At the time of the Great Migration of Puritan colonists to America in the 1630s, the consumption of drink at taverns had long been entwined with public gatherings in English society. In New England echoes of these traditions reverberated on various public occasions, as Massachusetts colonists regularly converged on public houses to meet and conduct civic affairs in the seventeenth century. On some occasions the voters of an entire town might assemble in these familiar rooms to transact town business. Still more august assemblies convened in taverns in public pomp and ceremony when selected taverns hosted meetings of the courts. In public rooms, the justices presided over the adjudication of offenses ranging from unpaid debts to murder, and on such days taverns could be the settings in which the most fundamental values of Massachusetts society were exhibited and reaffirmed. Here the hierarchy of governors from king to constable was announced, upheld, and made partially visible; here the "best men" at the top of the social hierarchy sat in judgment of the people called to court; here those who had violated the order and harmony of community life were condemned and humiliated.[1] On such days colonists witnessed and

1. The term "best men" comes from a sermon by Increase Mather, *Wo to Drunkards* . . .

acted in a vital tableau of community life, a physical assembly integrated in part through the sale and exchange of drink.

Yet the generous drafts of liquor consumed at these and other assemblies had also become a source of contention. A transformation in public life was under way. In the seventeenth century the habitual use of drink in taverns came under severe censure and greater regulation. In first Old and then New England, Puritan leaders became the most vocal critics of customary drinking habits. Their vision of a godly commonwealth owed much to tradition, revering as it did the principles of hierarchy and consensus in community life. But they simultaneously sought to establish a reformation in public and private behavior by compelling conformity to the nascent modern value of temperance.

This was not just an attack on idleness and dissipation. At the time of the Puritan migration, public houses had come to be viewed as potential sources of challenge to England's ruling hierarchy. Such houses had multiplied dramatically in previous decades, and many harbored growing numbers of the transient and unemployed poor with no secure place in the social hierarchy. The mounting concern for the preservation of order through the enforcement of temperance informed the establishment of New England. By the end of the century the officers of the courts who convened in taverns had become responsible for the enforcement of a number of drink regulations and laws. Taverns continued to be indispensable gathering places in Massachusetts towns, but Puritan leaders were determined to purge many of the customary uses of them from community life.

I

The character of public life in Massachusetts taverns is not easy to unveil, but the diary of Superior Court justice Samuel Sewall between 1674 and 1729 provides glimpses of court meetings and other official gatherings in taverns in Boston and other towns. The settings for the courts were modest. Few communities possessed buildings designed to host civic functions, and none of these buildings exceeded the size of a substantial house, public or private. Deputies to the General Court (more commonly called the Assembly after 1691) and the governor's Council gathered in Boston's Town House in the seventeenth century, a simple wooden structure built in 1657 with an open ground floor used for a market and chambers above.

(Cambridge, Mass., 1673), 13: "When drink is got into the brain, then out come filthy songs, and scoffing at the best men, yea at godliness itself in the power of it."

As a member of the Council, Sewall most often attended meetings in the Town House chambers. Nearby taverns, however, appear to have been the favored site for court sessions. In 1690, for example, Sewall and other justices decided the guardianship of the son of an Indian sachem at a session held in George Monk's Blue Anchor Tavern. Monk hosted so many sessions of this and other courts that the appraisers of his estate in 1698 designated one chamber of his tavern as the "court chamber." Before Monk, John Turner had kept tavern for the courts in Boston.[2]

In Salem, Charlestown, Cambridge, and other county seats, the courts also assembled in taverns. At Charlestown in 1700 the justices of the Superior Court heard cases in "Sommer's great room below stairs" until seven at night. The court once convened at a Cambridge meetinghouse only because the town house was situated too near a house with smallpox, and tavernkeeper Sharp—also afraid of the disease—refused "to let us have his chamber." All five of those licensed in Salem in 1681 became obliged to "provide for the accommodation of the courts and jurors, likewise all matters of a public concern proper for them."[3] In Massachusetts there continued to exist a close affinity between the provision of drink and public gatherings.

2. Walter Muir Whitehill, *Boston: A Topographical History* (Cambridge, Mass., 1968), 14; M. Halsey Thomas, ed., *The Diary of Samuel Sewall, 1674–1729* (New York, 1973), I, 253, 421, 477, 609 (hereafter cited as *Diary*); Suffolk County Probate Records, Record Book, IX, 47, XIV, 3–4, Judicial Archives, ACM.

The virtually autonomous government of the colony of Massachusetts evolved out of the Massachusetts Bay Company, a joint stock company chartered by James I in 1629. Originally the General Court was a meeting of the governor, assistants, and freemen who owned stock. In 1630 Governor John Winthrop admitted more freemen and permitted them to vote on issues before the Court. By 1632 this expanded General Court was granted the right to choose the governor and deputy governor, and the expanding number of freemen in the towns received the right to elect deputies (or representatives) to the Court. Though styled a court, the General Court also legislated laws. The crown revoked the 1629 charter in 1684 and eventually replaced it with a royal charter in 1691. After this date the term "General Court" began to be eclipsed by use of the terms "Assembly" and "governor's Council," the constituent parts of the General Court under the new charter.

3. Joseph B. Felt, *Annals of Salem*, I (Salem, Mass., 1845), 419; *Diary*, I, 521. On Mar. 10, 1752, the Court of General Sessions of Middlesex County "ordered that the sum of two pounds two shillings be allowed and paid by the county treasurer to Mr. Nathaniel Brown, taverner, in Charlestown in full for firing and candles provided for Superior Court of Judicature 1750, 1752 sittings, January [and] two [pounds] for firing and candles provided for Inferior Court of Common Pleas, December." Court of General Sessions, Middlesex, Mar. 10, 1752, Judicial Archives, ACM.

Plate 1. Samuel Sewall. *Courtesy, Massachusetts Historical Society, Boston*

Even after the erection of the new and more imposing Boston Town House in 1713, taverns continued to host the courts. Sewall lectured the grand jury at the first session held in the new building, telling them, "You ought to be quickened to your duty" to detect and prosecute crimes because "you have so convenient and august a chamber prepared for you to do it in." At this very session, however, the court adjourned and reconvened at a nearby tavern. Sewall himself later waited "on the court at the

Plate 2. The Town House. *Drawn from the original specifications by Charles Lawrence, 1930. Courtesy, the Bostonian Society / Old State House*

Green Dragon" to testify against a defendant.[4] Thus colonists were accustomed to associating taverns with that most paramount of Puritan concerns—the maintenance of law and order—because public rooms were so often the settings where the judicial hierarchy of the province made itself visible and decided cases.

The ready resort to taverns by court officials undoubtedly owed much to the convenience of heat and light provided by tavernkeepers during the winter against the expense of duplicating these services in town house or meetinghouse. Court sessions—Superior or lesser courts—could last anywhere between a few hours and several days, depending on the docket or

4. *Diary,* II, 711, 713.

the weather. When justices traveled on circuit to Plymouth, Springfield, Salem, or Bristol, they often did not arrive on time or together. In 1707 Sewall reached Plymouth about ten in the morning after a day and a half of travel from Boston, but two other justices did not arrive until six at night, so they "could only adjourn the court."[5] To heat and light the town house or meetinghouse to no effect for such an expanse of time was costly. Tavernkeepers could also provide lodging, food, and drink to justices riding on circuit as well as to their escorts and servants.

It is not clear whether justices consumed alcohol while court was in session. Sewall frowned when tavernkeeper Monk brought in a plate of "fritters" during one session, and was pleased that only one justice ate them. Between sessions, however, justices probably dined in the "court chamber." In Hampshire County the justices, constables, jurors, and other court officials probably all dined together, since each of their meals cost the same amount in the accounts of tavernkeepers.[6] Rather than move back and forth between tavern and town house (if one existed) and duplicate fires and other services in less convenient chambers, Massachusetts judicial officers simply made public houses into their seats of authority.

Taverns could be suitable sites for the administration of justice because men of high social rank expected and received deferential posture from ordinary men in any setting, at every occasion of meeting. Though Sewall betrayed a desire for "august" settings for court proceedings, the authority of the court rested much more in the personal status of the individuals who presided over it than in the chambers in which it took place. Social status and hierarchy differentiated members of Massachusetts society in a marked way, far more intricately than the size and scale of public and private houses suggest. The dress, speech, and bearing of individuals readily signaled their status and how they should be addressed. Sewall and fellow justices expected and received expressions and postures of deferential regard not only from people attending the courts but on all other occasions of meeting. When justices traveled to distant towns to convene courts, sheriffs and deputy sheriffs greeted and escorted them not just to ensure their safety but to honor their persons and offices. On Sewall's way to Springfield in 1698 a guard of twenty men met him at Marlborough and escorted him to Worcester. There a new company from Springfield met him to bring him the rest of the journey. This group saluted the justices

5. *Ibid.*, I, 253, 563.

6. *Ibid.*, I, 253. Sylvester Judd, *History of Hadley* . . . (1863; rpt., Somersworth, N.H., 1976), 93.

with a trumpet as they mounted their horses. Sewall often treated these attendants with food and drink, a gesture symbolic of his own role as protective and nurturing patriarch. In the case of a journey to Plymouth in 1716, he gave the sheriff and deputy sheriffs a dozen copies of one of Increase Mather's sermons, a more explicit gesture of a Puritan patriarch.[7]

Such honorific displays were also customary at militia musters meeting outside taverns and at formal state dinners in taverns. At a training dinner at Newbury, "Mr. Tappan, Brewer, Hale, and myself are guarded from the Green to the tavern," and "Brother Moodey and a party of the troop with a trumpet accompany me to the ferry." In Boston a processional display often announced a dinner or meeting at a tavern by government officials. In 1697 the Company of Young Merchants treated the governor and Council to food and drink at Monk's tavern. The company escorted the councillors from the Town House to tavern in formation and after dinner escorted them back, finishing with "three very handsome volleys."[8] While these processions were far less elaborate than analogous English ceremonies, they nevertheless served their purpose by announcing and reinforcing the magistrates' superior social status, judgment, and authority to those waiting for the court and spectators observing the scene. Such men could command deference in any situation in or out of court and could conduct the most solemn proceedings in any tavern.

Inside a tavern where court was in session, the authority of visiting justices influenced everyone's behavior. The chambers set aside for the courts in Boston in the 1680s had simple furnishings, but gradations in the furniture enhanced the authority of the presiding magistrates in subtle ways. John Turner's court chambers contained eleven chairs, presumably for justices and distinguished spectators, and three benches and a stool, where defendants and witnesses probably sat. Four tables made the chamber conducive to dining by the justices between sessions. George Monk accommodated the courts with a chamber containing a dozen leather chairs and one oval and three long tables. There was also a bench, again probably for litigants. Plaintiffs, defendants, and witnesses gathered more indiscriminately in the other public rooms of Turner and Monk. In one of Turner's front rooms they grouped around three tables and sat on benches. In another there were four tables, three benches, and only two chairs.[9] What appears to distinguish the court from other chambers is the

7. *Diary*, I, 396, II, 813.

8. *Diary*, I, 379, 546.

9. Suffolk County Probate Records, Record Book, IX, 47, XIV, 3.

number of chairs made available (perhaps considered necessary) for the magistrates who gathered there. When drinkers left the public rooms to enter the court chamber, the eminence of the men seated there, perhaps in a row, invested the room with a gravity absent in other parts of the tavern. On court days in public houses, the hierarchy of governors above and beyond the familiar model of family government became more visible to the people called to or visiting the house to ask for justice or receive punishment from the assembled magistrates.

Sewall's diary also reveals his personal habits of drink consumption. While he might not have consumed alcohol while hearing cases, he can be glimpsed making use of it on a variety of occasions. He regularly drank wine and cider in his home, when traveling, and at such events as weddings and barn raisings. In 1700 he invited several men he met by chance on Boston Neck into his home to drink. On another occasion he gave "a variety of good drink" to the governor and Council. He brought with him "a jug of Madeira of ten quarts" to a barn raising and gave a relative in prison eighteen pence "to buy a pint of wine." When traveling from Sandwich to Plymouth, Sewall dined at one tavern, fed his horse at another, and stopped to "drink at Mills."[10]

Sewall also consumed alcohol at funerals. The provision of drink at funerals was customary, even if the deceased was poor. In settling one Boston widow's estate, the appraisers allowed for payment from the estate for a quart of wine for themselves and seven and a half gallons for the widow's funeral, despite the fact that the estate could not meet the demands of the creditors, who received only nine shillings and twopence for each pound of debt.[11] At such a gathering honoring the deceased, the distribution of drink was considered indispensable. It held more importance than the creditors' demands on the estate.

Such use of drink and taverns remained within the bounds of temperate behavior in Puritan Massachusetts. At marriages, funerals, and barn raisings as well as court days the purchase, provision, and consumption of alcohol did not disrupt or violate Puritan precepts. Absence from labor was justified, and, if disorder did develop, such as drunkenness or profanity, magistrates or other figures of authority could take steps to quell it. Even the most rabid critics of intemperance admitted the necessity of public houses for the provision of alcohol so necessary for the conduct of social relations as well as the refreshment of travelers. In 1673 Increase Mather

10. *Diary*, I, 433, 466, 625, 693, II, 905.
11. Suffolk County Probate Records, XXVI, 704.

allowed that in such "a great Town" as Boston "there is need of such [public] houses, and no sober minister will speak against the licensing of them." Benjamin Wadsworth, another Boston minister, also conceded that "the keeping of taverns . . . is not only lawful but also very useful and convenient" for the "accommodating of strangers and travelers." Town dwellers "may sometimes have real business at taverns" and so may purchase "what drink is proper and needful for their refreshment."[12]

Yet, as these statements imply, what magistrates and ministers considered "proper and needful usage" continued to be an issue in Puritan Massachusetts during the first decades of settlement, provoking alarm by the last quarter of the seventeenth century. While Puritan leaders and their constituents continued to gather in taverns for a wide variety of purposes in the 1680s, even for the airing and adjudication of capital offenses, leaders at the same time increased their efforts to control and restrict patronage. A closer inspection of Sewall's diary reveals a distinct pattern of restricted patronage that exemplifies a model of behavior that clerical and secular leaders sought to impose on the populace as a whole in the seventeenth century.

Although Sewall might have spent hours in a court chamber over several days of court sessions, he rarely visited Boston taverns for other purposes. His diary of daily contacts and conversations between 1674 and 1729, including thousands of entries, shows a very low rate of patronage by any standard of measurement—only thirty-odd visits in fifty-five years. Almost all of these occasions involved private dinners with the governor's Council or other officials. For example, in 1709 the governor hosted a dinner for the Council and deputies to the General Court at the Green Dragon. The importance of such gatherings in promoting cooperation between members of the ruling elite is apparent in the careful manner in which Sewall recorded the order in which toasts were proposed and drunk. Yet, in a diary in which he noted minutely his activities, there is virtually no record of indiscriminate patronage.[13]

The same held true when Sewall traveled on the Superior Court circuit. In contrast to the low rate of local patronage, he recorded 313 stops at taverns outside Boston, mainly taverns at Lynn, Scituate, and Roxbury, staging points north, south, and west. But he rarely recorded lengthy conversations with tavernkeepers or their patrons. Usually, local officials

12. Mather, *Wo to Drunkards*, 29; Benjamin Wadsworth, *An Essay to Do Good* . . . (Boston, 1710), 2.

13. Rates of patronage compiled from *Diary*, I–II; I, 627.

or clergymen welcomed or sought him out to serve attendance. As when he was in Boston, the pages of his diary are filled with conversations and contacts with individuals of high social rank. Of the twenty-five individuals most often mentioned in the diary outside members of his family, six were ministers, and fourteen held high provincial offices, of whom thirteen graduated from Harvard.[14]

Sewall's infrequent, specialized patronage exactly corresponds with the ideals enunciated in pulpit and law that sanctioned assemblies of men only for religious edification or public business like militia training. The use of taverns must be limited to those "right ends and uses for which they are designed; namely, for the refreshment and entertainment of travelers, and to serve public occasions."[15] In contrast to his sparse visits to taverns, Sewall regularly attended Thursday lectures and private prayer meetings as well as Sabbath services. Moreover, he continually exerted himself to enhance the ability of ministers and secular officials throughout the province to preach and govern from a greater fund of scriptural knowledge and interpretation. Habitually he carried bundles of sermons lately printed to individuals he met by design or chance. Most of these gifts went to ministers, members of his extended family, and other officials. His conduct on January 30, 1725, was typical: "Dined at the 3 Cranes, and finished the court there, so as to reach home comfortably a little before sunset." He left "3 election sermons and 3 of Mr. Mayhew's lecture sermons with Capt. Phips; viz. 2 for Col. Phillips, 2 for Col. Lynde, and 2 for himself."[16] By this prodigious circulation of texts, Sewall exercised his faith in the study of the Word as the overarching guide to the conduct of public affairs and the government of the people. From the founding of the colony in 1630 it had been expected and intended that community harmony would spring from instruction in these texts from an educated ministry and their secular counterparts, not from habitual gatherings of neighbors to drink. Only within certain limits could church and tavern coexist peacefully in a well-ordered community. Religious instruction had become the foundation for defining and enforcing new boundaries of acceptable and unacceptable use of drink and taverns in Massachusetts towns. Sewall's diary reveals that he continued to practice and uphold these ideals after 1680 as alarm over drink and tavern usage mounted.

14. *Ibid.*, I, 627.

15. Massachusetts, *The Acts and Resolves, Public and Private, of the Province of the Massachusetts Bay . . .* , I (Boston, 1869), 679 (hereafter cited as *Acts and Resolves*).

16. *Diary*, II, 1026.

II

It is this commitment by the first and second generations of Puritan rulers to the enforcement of temperate behavior among the populace at large that underlay the development and elaboration of legislation to regulate taverns in the seventeenth century. To place Puritan antipathy toward tavern haunting and drunkenness in perspective, it is useful to contrast regulatory initiatives in the seventeenth century to the traditional drinking habits deeply woven into the fabric of village life in Tudor-Stuart England, vital customs at the time of the Puritan migration. Here anthropological studies can be a useful guide in understanding the emergence of conflict between advocates of temperance and habitual tavern patrons. Used with caution, these studies can help to illuminate the social functions of collective drinking in the Anglo-American world of the seventeenth century.

Such studies reveal that the ritual use of drink was part of a vocabulary of gesture and oral exchange used to express social relations. In traditional village societies where the manufacture of alcoholic beverages is indigenous to the culture and economy of the locality, the distribution and consumption of drink within groups can not only serve as a source of recreation but also play a vital role in establishing and maintaining communal bonds. In communities where kinship ties are the primary relationships shaping loyalties, where society itself is conceived and organized in terms of dozens of families at most, and where a subsistence economy defines group endeavor, the giving and receiving of drink has often been invested with emotional and symbolic significance. The particular sequence, manner, and frequency with which food and drink are given and received can serve to define loyalties, obligations, contractual bonds, and status. The gift of drink, or the ability to provide drink, can become a token of esteem and trust in these societies where gestures, informal or part of elaborate ceremonies, are an important means of publicizing or affirming agreements.[17] This is not to say that drinking always contributed to har-

17. A classic study of a village society in which drink possessed an elaborate ritual significance is Audrey I. Richards, *Land, Labour, and Diet in Northern Rhodesia: An Economic Study of the Bemba Tribe* (London, 1939), 76–87, 135–143, 366–380. More recent studies of the use of drink as a means of defining social relations are included in Mary Douglas, ed., *Constructive Drinking: Perspectives on Drink from Anthropology* (Cambridge, 1983); Clarence H. Patrick, *Alcohol, Culture, and Society* (Durham, N.C., 1952), chap. 2; Thomas W. Hill, "Ethnohistory and Alcohol Studies," in Marc Galenter, *Recent Developments in Alcoholism*, II (New York, 1984), 313–337. Also relevant is Mark A. Tessler, William M. O'Barr, and

mony and order within traditional communities. It could help to inspire and release aggressive behavior. Ideally, however, it could possess a symbolic meaning in particular cultural rituals that helped to perpetuate the cooperation of each member of a community in collective endeavor from season to season and year to year.

Judging from the context, level, and manner of consumption of alcoholic beverages in England during the sixteenth and seventeenth centuries, drink possessed such a ritual significance in the localized society of parish and village. Approximately three-quarters of the population lived in hamlets and villages of five hundred or fewer people. National administrative structures were being developed, but only a small proportion of the total population—the nobility, gentry, and professions—had extensive contact or personal experience with the king's government in London. Within the close-knit society of village and market towns, alcohol "played a role in nearly every public ceremony, every commercial bargain, every private occasion of mourning and rejoicing." Estimates of consumption drawn from excise figures indicate a rate of forty gallons per capita annually, a rate that does not include beverages manufactured privately.[18]

Drink helped to define the relationship between the material and supernatural worlds. An ecclesiastical calendar of festivals and holidays integrated collective drinking with religious observance during slack periods of the agricultural cycle. The churchyard as well as public house often became the site of feasting and dancing at Candlemas, Shrovetide, Mid-Lent, Easter, May Day, Whitsuntide, and Midsummer. In the market towns the officers of craft guilds financed "drinkings" for their members. In almost all trades it was expected that apprentices provide drink for their masters and coworkers when they commenced work in a shop. In the

---

David H. Spain, *Tradition and Identity in Changing Africa* (New York, 1973). For connections to late-medieval and early modern English society, see Keith Thomas, "Work and Leisure in Pre-Industrial Society," *Past and Present*, no. 29 (December 1964), 50–66. Marianna Adler discusses traditional symbolic functions of drink exchange in preindustrial England in "From Symbolic Exchange to Commodity Consumption: Anthropological Notes on Drinking as a Symbolic Practice," in Susanna Barrows and Robin Room, eds., *Drinking: Behavior and Belief in Modern History* (Berkeley, Calif., 1991), 376–398; Richard D. Brown defines "traditional" social, economic, and political characteristics in his *Modernization: The Transformation of American Life, 1600–1865* (New York, 1976), chaps. 1–2.

18. Brown, *Modernization*, chap. 2; Peter Laslett, *The World We Have Lost: England before the Industrial Age* (New York, 1973), chaps. 1–3; Keith Thomas, *Religion and the Decline of Magic* (New York, 1971), 17 (quote).

countryside landlords sponsored celebrations for their tenants and laborers that symbolized reciprocity.[19] Indeed, drunkenness was acceptable behavior on certain days and weeks when community observances interrupted the pace of work and allowed an entire community to indulge in Brueghelian excess.

Drink was a medium for the expression of trust and dependence in a society in which everyone defined himself in relation to others. After the characters Pistol and Nym quarreled in Shakespeare's *Henry the Fifth* about money owed to Nym, Pistol sought reconciliation by saying, "A noble shalt thou have, and present pay; And liquor likewise will I give to thee, and friendship shall combine, and brotherhood." Pistol will "live by Nym, and Nym shall live by me." In *The Merry Wives of Windsor*, Thomas Page invites a quarreling company to eat and drink with him with the words, "Come, gentlemen, I hope we shall drink down all unkindness." One customarily made gestures of tribute and respect by offering drink. To gain an audience with Sir John Falstaff, Master Brook "sent Your Worship a morning's draught of sack." In *Henry the Fourth, Part II* the landlady of a tavern reminded Falstaff, "Thou didst swear to me upon a parcel-gilt [partly gilded] goblet, sitting in my Dolphin chamber, at the round table, by a sea-coal fire, upon Wednesday in Wheeson [Whitsun] week . . . to marry me and make me my lady thy wife."[20] One did not casually break an oath made with alcohol.

To similar purposes, health drinking was a popular custom. An English tract critical of this practice published in 1682 reveals the extent to which this ceremony celebrated personal bonds and obligations structured by patron-client, master-servant relationships. The author condemned the assumption that men who did not drink a series of healths to the king

19. Peter Clark, "The Alehouse and the Alternative Society," in Donald Pennington and Keith Thomas, eds., *Puritans and Revolutionaries: Essays in Seventeenth-Century History Presented to Christopher Hill* (Oxford, 1978), 47–72; Adler, "From Symbolic Exchange to Commodity Function," in Barrows and Room, eds., *Drinking: Behavior and Belief*, 382; Charles Phythian-Adams, "Ceremony and Citizen: The Communal Year at Coventry, 1450–1550," in Peter Clark and Paul Slack, eds., *Crisis and Order in English Towns, 1500–1700: Essays in Urban History* (London, 1972), 57–85; David Underdown, *Revel, Riot, and Rebellion: Popular Politics and Culture in England, 1603–1660* (New York, 1985), 13–17.

20. William Shakespeare, *The Life of King Henry the Fifth*, ed. Alfred Harbage (New York, 1971), II, ii, 103–107; *The Merry Wives of Windsor*, ed. Louis B. Wright and Virginia A. LaMar (New York, 1965), I, i, 185, II, ii, 143–144; *The Second Part of King Henry the Fourth*, ed. Allan G. Chester (New York, 1970), II, i, 81–88.

should be "suspected" of disloyalty to their sovereign or their fellows, for "loyalty and respect to others is not proper to be shown in so absurd method." Repudiating the symbolic link between drink and life, he asked, "How can any man drink another's health?" Or, by "what new kind of transubstantiation can his health be converted into a glass of liquor?" All of the "modes and ceremonies in drinking" described and condemned here, including the postures of "prayer standing up, standing bare, sometimes kneeling upon their knees," suggest the extent to which drink was a medium by which commitment and belief were acted out in English communities.[21]

In the myriad latticework of social relationships that constituted the English social hierarchy, the consumption of drink customarily performed an integrative function. Falstaff conceived of drink as uniting the body of the kingdom by stimulating all parts to work together: the wine "warms it and makes it course from the inwards to the parts extremes" and "illumineth the face, which as a beacon gives warning to all the rest of this little kingdom, man, to arm, and then the vital commoners and inland petty spirits muster me all to their captain, the heart, who, great and puffed up with this retinue, doth any deed of courage, and this valor comes of sherries."[22]

Yet, as the 1682 tract also indicates, the habitual use of drink in almost every aspect of public and private life—and particularly to the point of drunkenness—had also begun to come under concerted attack by the clergy and secular authorities by the seventeenth century. Drunkenness and idleness had of course long been subjects of moral censure within the Christian tradition. But such censures assumed a new urgency in the seventeenth century amid the pressures of population growth, commercialization, and the rise of Puritanism. The population of England nearly doubled between 1540 and 1650, from fewer than three million to more than five million. The capacity of village communities to feed and employ their members regularly came under severe strain. The migration of servants and laborers no longer took place mainly within established kinship networks or between neighboring communities. Laborers more often searched for work among strangers further afield. People were set adrift. The Elizabethan Poor Laws, providing for the return of poor vagrants to

---

21. *A Warning-Piece to All Drunkards and Health-Drinkers: Faithfully Collected from the Works of English and Foreign Learned Authors of Good Esteem, Mr. Samuel Ward and Mr. Samuel Clark, and Others* (London, 1682), preface, 3–5.

22. *Second Part of Henry the Fourth*, IV, iii, 98–109.

their parish of origin if they required relief, are testimony to the strain that population growth and migration placed on village relationships. It had become necessary for the state to intervene in order to establish responsibility for the migrant poor and pressure communities to care for them.[23]

At the same time, the local gentry less readily held open house for their tenants and seasonal laborers—a symptom of the continuing dissolution of feudal ties of protection and service. Gentlemen became the objects of criticism in print for virtually abandoning their local obligations in order to pursue interests at city and court. Many landlords also moved to enclose their lands and evict their tenants as they maneuvered to pursue profit and individual advantage in a more commercial economy.[24] The high visibility of groups of unemployed transients underscored the fact that relationships between patron and client, landlord and tenant, and master and servant within the network of personal bonds and loyalties constituting local society had become more tenuous and more easily disregarded.

The simultaneous multiplication of alehouses serving the poor (numbering thirty thousand in England and Wales by one report in the 1630s) began to be perceived as a threat to the king's order. Alehouses had only begun to emerge as a significant center of recreation and ritual life—and an institution requiring regulation—in the late fourteenth century. By 1552, when Parliament ordered that all alehousekeepers have a license, the institution had become a center of social life rivaling the church and the

---

23. Peter Clark, *The English Alehouse: A Social History, 1200–1830* (New York, 1983), chap. 1; Clark, "The Alehouse and the Alternative Society," in Pennington and Thomas, eds., *Puritans and Revolutionaries,* 47–72; Clark, "The Migrant in Kentish Towns, 1580–1640," in Clark and Slack, eds., *Crisis and Order,* 117–163; Phythian-Adams, "Ceremony and the Citizen," in Clark and Slack, eds., *Crisis and Order,* 57–85. Keith Wrightson and David Underdown synthesize studies of the multiple sources of social strain in Tudor-Stuart England. Wrightson contrasts the "enduring structures" of English society with "the course of social change," in *English Society, 1580–1680* (New Brunswick, N.J., 1982). For the strain of population growth on resources and village life, see chap. 5; Underdown, *Revel, Riot, and Rebellion,* 18–20, 28, 34–40. Underdown demonstrates how the "vertically-integrated society" of "paternalism, deference, and good *neighbourliness"* weakened under the impact of new efforts by the gentry, yeomen, and manufacturers to dissociate themselves from "their poor, less disciplined neighbors, and to use their power to reform society" (40). For an acute discussion of labor and work ethic issues in England, see Edmund S. Morgan, *American Slavery, American Freedom: The Ordeal of Colonial Virginia* (New York, 1975), chap. 3.

24. Lawrence Stone, *The Causes of the English Revolution, 1529–1642* (New York, 1972), 67–76; Underdown, *Revel, Riot, and Rebellion,* 23–25.

guilds. But as the social and institutional fabric of English society was rent asunder, alehouses came to be associated with crime, disorder, and potential rebellion.[25] More and more of their customers no longer occupied a settled niche within the local hierarchy. Some alehouses harbored a clientele with only a tenuous hold on subsistence or men moving in search of it. Collective drinking in mean alehouses, kept by men and women living on the fringes of society, no longer integrated the social structure in the customary ways. During times of dearth, groups of idle, masterless men languishing in disreputable alehouses posed a threat to constituted authorities. Parliament and local justices became preoccupied with the problem of restoring them to employment and patriarchal control.[26]

Drinking now possessed a more sinister edge to it in more ways than one. As greater numbers of Englishmen drank as strangers outside the familiar social networks and accustomed rhythms of an agricultural society, consumption probably began to have more serious effects on physical and mental health. To drink to someone's "health" even came under question.[27]

James I made the regulation of alehouses a priority. In a speech to the Star Chamber in 1616 he declared the "abundance of alehouses" to be one of the most serious "offenses" in his realm. He complained of alehouses as places of "receipt" for "stealers of my deer" and of horses, oxen, and sheep from the country at large: "So there would be no thieves, if they had not their receipts, and these alehouses as their dens." He issued a command to all justices of the peace that diseputable houses be "pulled down." On this issue James and his Parliament could agree. The Parliament of 1604 had already introduced and debated eleven bills concerning the regulation and reduction of alehouses. In 1599, 1604, 1609, and periodically thereafter the Privy Council ordered local justices responsible for granting licenses to purge the poor and disreputable from the ranks of drinksellers under their jurisdiction. Parliament also tightened licensing procedures and in 1603

25. Clark, *The English Alehouse,* 23–48; Harris G. Hudson, *A Study of Social Regulations in England under James I and Charles I: Drink and Tobacco* (Chicago, 1933), 12. Twenty-four Essex townships surveyed in 1644 had 55 licensed and 52 unlicensed houses; 30 Lancashire townships in 1647 had 83 unlicensed and 143 licensed. Essex villages had 1 alehouse for every 20 households, and Lancashire had 1 for every 12. Wrightson, *English Society, 1580– 1680,* 168.

26. Underdown, *Revel, Riot, and Rebellion,* 34–37; Wrightson, *English Society, 1580– 1680,* 166–170; Morgan, *American Slavery, American Freedom,* 65–68.

27. *A Warning-Piece.*

made drunkenness a crime.[28] Dens of drinkers outside the personal purview and control of local gentry had made alcohol an issue to a king not noted for his temperance.

The alehouse never became as potent a source of disorder as its most virulent critics feared. The expansion of administrative controls over the drink trade during the first decades of the seventeenth century did make drinksellers more subject to inspection and removal, and Parliament adopted a policy of creating work for surplus laborers. Masters of crafts came under pressure to hire unemployed laborers even if they were unneeded and to take responsibility for their daily sustenance for bonded periods of time. The erection of workhouses and houses of correction also became an antidote to gatherings of the unemployed in alehouses. Yet no matter how many local purges of the ranks of drinksellers took place, no matter how thinly employment was scattered, the readiness of the poor to turn to the sale of drink, legally or illegally, ensured that the incidence of drinksellers remained high. Alehouses continued to be viewed as flashpoints of disorder, especially during grain shortages. Then, a full century after the demise of James I, the notorious Black Act made poaching a capital offense in 1723: the use of alehouses and inns on the edges of royal forests and private parks as points of rendezvous and sale for poachers had helped inspire this act.[29]

Puritans in positions of authority at the local and national levels had no sympathy for James I, whom they viewed as a fountain of corruption. But, like James, they sought to establish greater control over drinksellers. For Puritan spokesmen, however, agitation on this issue represented but one aspect of a program for more comprehensive reforms of church and society. The Reformation stimulated still more harsh criticism of a wide array of traditional customs related to drink and public houses. Puritans believed the Sabbath to be the only legitimate day of rest. On every other day, men must rigorously apply themselves and their dependents to the

28. Hudson, *A Study of Social Regulations*, 11; Underdown, *Revel, Riot, and Rebellion*, 48. As with the king, many members of the expanding number of gentry no longer tolerated hunting by inferiors and adopted strict proprietary rights to all game (Underdown, 22).

29. Clark, "The Alehouse and the Alternative Society," in Pennington and Thomas, eds., *Puritans and Revolutionaries*, 61–64; Underdown, *Revel, Riot, and Rebellion*, 35–37; Morgan, *American Slavery, American Freedom*, 67–68. The continuing connection between alehouses and poaching is apparent in E. P. Thompson, *Whigs and Hunters: The Origins of the Black Act* (New York, 1975), 157–158, 163; and Douglas Hay, "Poaching and the Game Laws on Cannock Chase," in Douglas Hay *et al.*, eds., *Albion's Fatal Tree: Crime and Society in Eighteenth-Century England* (New York, 1975), 189–253.

pursuit of their callings. The Puritan work ethic and the sanctification of the calling became the basis for criticism of aristocratic disdain for labor, rent-supported idleness, and conspicuous consumption among the upper ranks. In their agitation to define traditional festivals as sinful and disorderly, Puritans groped toward a new definition of community relations that might better equip them to cope with the acute instability of their age. They sought to distance themselves from their neighbors and the wandering poor by demonstrating sobriety, diligence, and piety. Further, their leaders believed that they must organize to protect their position and hold forth their values and prescriptions for reform as exemplary.[30]

Puritan leaders even went so far as to attack the Anglican ecclesiastical hierarchy. Belief in the cultivation of a reasoned understanding of the Scriptures under an educated ministry became the foundation for criticism of the established church as a vast repository of ritual and magic. Anglican prelates defended or promoted many of the old, drink-related customs such as saints' days, church ales, and Sunday sports.[31] Thus while Puritans remained as concerned as their Anglican counterparts with the threat that alehouse crowds might pose to constituted authority, they simultaneously pressed to reform the structure and ethics of church and state in ways that challenged the standing order. Idle, dissolute aristocrats and uneducated churchmen as well as laborers haunting alehouses became targets of religiously inspired criticism. For Puritans, alehouses were a leading symbol of a society and state choked by corruption and impiety from top to bottom.

Whereas once the drinking of healths to patrons and masters and at religious celebrations had been a universally accepted expression of loyalty to and membership in community and kingdom, Puritans now considered it a provocation of God's wrath. The authors of the 1682 pamphlet condemning prevailing drinking customs in England collected more than 120 instances from "reliable" sources of God's showing his great "abomination" of and "declared vengeance against drunkards and health drinkers." A drunken woman at "Whitsun Ale," for example "fell a cursing God" until "at last the devil came, and hoisting her into the air, threw her down

---

30. Wrightson, *English Society, 1580–1680*, 222–227; Underdown, *Revel, Riot, and Rebellion*, 40–43. For overviews of the various ways in which Puritans attacked and undermined traditional values and beliefs, see Christopher Hill, *Society and Puritanism in Pre-Revolutionary England* (London, 1961); and Thomas, *Religion and the Decline of Magic*.

31. Thomas, *Religion and the Decline of Magic*. During the reign of Charles I there were systematic attempts to preserve the old festivals in recognition of their value in upholding the vertical structure of authority. The Laudian church defended the old customs. Underdown, *Revel, Riot, and Rebellion*, 63–65.

again in a place not far remote." Near Mauldon a group of men "plotted a solemn drinking at one of their houses" and drank healths "in a strange manner." All died within a few weeks. One of a group of gentlemen drinking healths to their "lords," on whom they owed "dependence," laid hold of a pot full of Canary-sack wine, swore a deep oath, and asked, "What, will none here drink a health to my noble lord and master?" He drank it to the bottom and died two hours later.[32] Puritans still believed in a supernatural world in which God and devil constantly battled for men's souls and might act directly on them. But drink had become a controversial medium for expressing or affirming relations between man and God. Now it was a device and enticement of the devil.

The authors condemned those who continued to drink to the health of the duke and king. Such "customs" should now be replaced with prayer to preserve the king from "the danger of all popish and sham plots," the best way to show "true love to the king."[33] According to the new codes of Puritan worship, drink interfered with the rational use of mental faculties to discern and preserve reformed practice and therefore must be purged from religious observation along with the expression of tributes to men of authority. The use of drink could now be a disrupting agent in the social relations of superiors and inferiors, not a means of reinforcing them.

A more demanding religious code of behavior later reflected in Sewall's diary—the restraint in the use of alcohol and public houses—crystallized amid this milling confusion and occasional chaos of community life in the first decades of the seventeenth century. To be temperate in drink, one must never drink to excess or drunkenness or visit public houses without any specific need or purpose. If one consumed drink to the point where mental and physical faculties became impaired, or beyond the basic need of refreshment, one became guilty of excessive drinking. At specific occasions like a wedding, celebrants might consume a series of drinks, but never to the point of drunkenness. Consumption must never delay or interrupt labor.

Puritan ministers defined the new restrictions on behavior. To be accepted as members of the reformed church, first in Old and then in New England, men and women must withdraw from habitual tavern associations, shunning the old rituals now considered a corruption of true Christian worship, or face public censure by their fellow communicants and spiritual leaders. The redefinition of pious behavior and the reorganization of church government also entailed the redefinition of legitimate, accept-

32. *A Warning-Piece.* The 120 instances begin at p. 5 and continue through p. 45.
33. *Ibid.,* 46.

able uses of drink and taverns. Puritan leaders in effect called on English-men to enter voluntarily into communities dedicated to the scholarly inter-pretation of the Word and shed associations now considered a corruption of true Christian practice. Public houses might still host the courts and other public occasions but must be prevented from becoming places of habitual resort for such customs as health drinking. Alehouses, which catered to the poor, could have no legitimate place in community life. The Puritan migration to New England to found dissenting churches free of state harassment invested the ideal of temperance with new purpose. In Massachusetts, Puritan leaders believed, ministers could more vigorously enjoin their congregations to practice restraint in the use of alcohol. In the new commonwealth, leaders assumed that the tavern would be limited to certain prescribed functions.

III

For Massachusetts colonists, migration did resolve many of the re-ligious and social conflicts related to drink in England. For in Massachu-setts towns, the social landscape of drinking changed. Many of the social and economic conditions that had made intemperance an issue requiring action by the state were absent. The configuration of community life changed.[34] No groups of idle, hungry, and masterless men congregated in alehouses and constituted a threatening "alternative society" separate from the personal control and overseership of the governing hierarchy. Exaggerated fears that the alehouse was a seedbed of revolt and disruption disappeared. With the exception of Boston, most towns had only one or two public houses through the first fifty years of the colony's existence. In Middlesex County, only the towns of Charlestown, Cambridge, and Woburn had more than two in 1688. Only Plymouth and Scituate in

34. David Grayson Allen and David Hackett Fischer both emphasize the transferal of English customs, folkways, and institutional life from East Anglia to Massachusetts. I accept this argument insofar as the broad foundation of society is concerned. But removal from East Anglia also radically changed the social landscape. The upper and lower tiers of society were suddenly absent from view. The problem of public houses was reduced in scale and severity. The social environment was less controversial because there were no crowded alehouses. Some English customs had even been eliminated, and a variant of East Anglian society could take root. David Grayson Allen, *In English Ways: The Movement of Societies and the Transferal of English Local Law and Custom to Massachusetts Bay in the Seventeenth Century* (Chapel Hill, N.C., 1981); David Hackett Fischer, *Albion's Seed: Four British Folkways in America* (New York, 1989).

Plymouth County had more than one. The low density of population initially helped to sustain personal contact between those of high and low status, rulers and ruled, masters and servants of society. Rather than illicit drinking assemblies, it was the sectarian challenges to the Congregational establishment posed by Antinomians and other radical splinter groups that preoccupied magistrates concerned with stability and order during the first decades.[35]

Moreover, in Massachusetts Puritans no longer had to fear the immediate consequences of challenging English church and state policies by denouncing such customs as saints' days. The powerful influence of tradition as embodied in the Anglican ecclesiastical calendar had been weakened by the act of migration. Colonists voluntarily abandoned religious holidays that continued to have vitality in England. Even Christmas passed unnoticed. On December 25 Sewall often noted with satisfaction in his diary that "shops [are] open as at other times" and "provisions, hay, wood, brought to town." Sewall once chided two boys for playing tricks on April 1, because New England men "came hither to avoid anniversary days, the keeping of them, such as the 25th of December."[36]

True, a number of efforts to revive such observations occurred in the 1680s when the colony lost its charter and the first royal government was installed. Sewall noted on Christmas 1685, "Some somehow observe the day; but are vexed I believe that the body of the people profane it, and blessed be God no authority yet to compel them to keep it." Sewall also became alarmed by the appearance of a procession in the streets of Boston in 1687 in honor of Shrove Tuesday, the day before the beginning of Lent.[37] But only a few men participated, and the procession was a pale imitation of

35. Court of General Sessions, Middlesex, Record Book, 1686–1688, Licenses Granted, 39–40, Judicial Archives, ACM; Court of General Sessions, Plymouth, Record Book, 1686–1727, 12, Plymouth County Courthouse; Edmund S. Morgan, *The Puritan Dilemma: The Story of John Winthrop* (Boston, 1958), chaps. 8–10. Virginia DeJohn Anderson demonstrates that the high proportion of families, the predominantly spiritual motivations for migration, and the modest material expectations for a "competency" among the founding generation contributed to the stability that Massachusetts enjoyed compared to other colonial undertakings, in *New England's Generation: The Great Migration and the Foundation of Society and Culture in the Seventeenth Century* (New York, 1991); see esp. chaps. 3–4.

36. *Diary*, II, 736, 920–921; see also I, 481, 502, 588, for Sewall's aversion to the celebration of anniversary days.

37. *Diary*, I, 90, 133. Never repudiated by a majority of Englishmen, the calendar of drinking festivals underwent a revival in Restoration England. See Underdown, *Revel, Riot, and Rebellion*, 280–283.

what had once been customary. Such observances and rituals did not regain the sanction of popular support.

Sewall possessed such confidence in the lapse of devotion to the old ecclesiastical calendar that he proposed to the Council in 1696 that the days Tuesday, Thursday, and Saturday be renamed the third, fifth, and seventh days of the week because "the week only, of all parcels of time, was of divine institution."[38] The motion did not pass, but the fact that such a radical repudiation of traditional nomenclature could be seriously considered indicates the distinct break that colonists as a whole had made with the pagan-Christian observations of centuries' vintage—and with the customary use of drink on these days. Although the vast majority of colonists continued to labor according to the irregular dictates of season and weather, religious observance had been separated from the agricultural cycle without conflict.

Public houses, however, must still be established to accommodate approved gatherings and to shelter travelers. And the regulation of these houses remained a priority of the ruling elite. The exacting personal standards of the first generation of clerical and secular rulers, the vision of reformed churches becoming the spearheads of reformation, the messianic impulse to found communities distinctly more pious than those left behind—all contributed to the close attention given by the General Court to regulation once the first, difficult years had passed. When the Court outlawed health drinking in 1639, it stated that such a "useless ceremony" should be abolished "especially in plantations of churches and commonwealths wherein the least known evils are not to be tolerated by such as are bound by solemn covenant to walk by the rule of God's word in all their conversation."[39] Puritans sought not just to purge community life of alehouse gatherings or merely establish greater control over the sale of drink but to reform behavior, speech, and attitude rigorously, especially in a public setting like a tavern.

The regulation of the few public houses in each town assumed a still greater importance when it became apparent that popular participation in institutions of church and state would be broader than in England. Puritan leaders faced the difficult task of establishing the prerogatives of leaders in church and state in a society in which distinctions of rank and status had become less marked and entrenched than in England. In the social and in-

38. *Diary*, I, 351.

39. Nathaniel B. Shurtleff, ed., *Records of the Governor and Company of the Massachusetts Bay in New England, 1626–1686*, 5 vols. (Boston, 1853–1854), I, 271.

stitutional context of England, Puritan congregations had been embattled subcultures despite the wealth and prominence of many of their members. Theoretical arguments concerning how much power ministers should share with the laity drew on Calvinist doctrines, but they were also influenced by the immediate need of dissenting clergy for support from the laity against harassment from the state.[40] Communicants had assumed a new measure of power and influence in these churches.

Once established in Massachusetts, however, ministers sought to moderate the trend toward "democratical confusion" by investing the pulpit with more formal powers. The Cambridge Platform, drawn up in 1646, delegated certain prerogatives involving the definition of doctrine and the admission of new members to the clergy; but crucial powers, including ordination and dismissal, remained in the hands of individual congregations. Lay church leaders also determined clerical salaries.[41] As long as a minister could inspire his congregation to piety, he occupied a commanding position. But by stripping the church of the power and majesty of the ecclesiastical hierarchy, of rich ornament and distinctive architecture, Puritans had also divested the ministry of the accoutrements, emblems, and symbols of power and authority. The adherence of colonists to ministerial injunctions to practice temperance thus became an important measure of a minister's influence over his congregation, of the success and failure of his preaching. Puritan ministers had made it their mission to purge community life of ritual folk practices involving the extensive use of drink, but at the same time they had become more dependent on their congregations for financial support and continuance in office than their Anglican counterparts. Unrestrained, uninhibited conversation in taverns respecting the style and content of a minister's preaching could have serious consequences for his position in the community. Oral communication must be closely monitored.

Regulation also possessed a new urgency in a colony in which local and colonywide government allowed for wider participation by the adult male population in the choice of rulers. The opportunity to acquire property opened up the traditional restrictions on the franchise. In the society that Massachusetts colonists had abandoned, only a tiny proportion of the patrons of the more than thirty thousand public houses possessed any for-

40. David D. Hall, *The Faithful Shepherd: A History of the New England Ministry in the Seventeenth Century* (Chapel Hill, N.C., 1972), chaps. 1–4, esp. 102–120.

41. *Ibid.*; Stephen Foster, *The Long Argument: English Puritanism and the Shaping of New England Culture, 1570–1700* (Chapel Hill, N.C., 1991), 170.

mal right to participate in the government of their communities. English justices and members of Parliament in the seventeenth century feared possible crowd actions instigated in alehouse assemblies, not their influence in elections. But in Massachusetts, voters composed a large share of the patrons of the two-hundred-odd public houses in the colony by the end of the century. Boston had a population of approximately one thousand adult males as of 1683, and about one hundred of them were elected to some type of office. By one estimate about 70 percent of free adult males in Boston were eligible to vote in town elections in 1687, although only a minority regularly did so.[42]

Elections in the seventeenth century were never characterized by open competition between rival candidates. Rather, they were a way for voters to renew their confidence in and subjection to rulers who possessed the wealth, education, piety, and leisure time commensurate with their offices and responsibilities. Still, the structure of political power had become more decentralized than in England.[43] If popular behavior became corrupted in taverns, if rulers did not conform to the "character of the good ruler," the consequences could be more serious for the conduct of public life than in England. The mission of the colony might be entirely thwarted by the elevation of impious men. Thus while migration resolved some conflicts respecting drink by opening up opportunities for owning land and creating a demand for labor, it also presented potential new problems for a ruling elite trying to preserve a hierarchy of superiors and inferiors.[44]

42. B. Katherine Brown, "The Controversy over the Franchise in Puritan Massachusetts, 1959 to 1974," *WMQ*, 3d Ser., XXXIII (1976), 212–241; G. B. Warden, *Boston, 1689–1776* (Boston, 1970), 31–32; Gary B. Nash, *The Urban Crucible: Social Change, Political Consciousness, and the Origins of the American Revolution* (Cambridge, Mass., 1979), 29.

43. T. H. Breen, *The Character of the Good Ruler: A Study of Puritan Political Ideas in New England, 1630–1730* (New York, 1974), chaps. 1–3. Haverhill town records reveal the way in which the franchise could expand according to the circumstances beyond what law allowed. In 1681 a complaint was made that a motion to build a new meetinghouse was defeated because of the "additional and willful votes of many prohibited by law from voting." George W. Chase, *History of Haverhill, Massachusetts . . . to 1860* (Haverhill, Mass., 1861), 136, 168, 204.

44. Michael Walzer has argued that Puritans in England attacked the traditional political order. Clerical intellectuals "dissociated themselves from the three crucial forms of traditional relationships: hierarchy, organic connection, and family." There were also shifts in the imagery, style, and mode of argument. Among Puritans "it was behavior rather than being that determined status." I agree that Puritan discourse often subverted traditional political and social configurations. See *The Revolution of the Saints: A Study in the Origins of*

Magistrates implemented controls over the sale of drink during the first decades, but not in any alarmist fashion. As in England, Puritan magistrates acted to restrict the sale of drink to those given "license," or permission by their rulers, as the chief method of control. Massachusetts procedures through the seventeenth century drew on English practice in many respects but were engrafted to institutions that departed from English models in significant ways. In 1633 any person wishing to sell wine or distilled liquors simply asked permission of the governor or deputy governor. The growth and dispersal of population and the formation of new towns and county courts brought more systematic procedures. In 1639 the General Court ordered every town "to present a man to be allowed to sell wine and strong water" to the Court for approval. Those who sold other beverages such as cider presumably could do so with the permission of local selectmen. In the 1640s the Court delegated the authority to grant licenses to the quarter courts, staffed by appointed justices. Participation by local selectmen appears to have remained vague until a law of 1681. For the future it was stipulated that "the selectmen of all the towns shall approve of all persons to be licensed before licenses be granted to any of them by the county court."[45] By this time those selling any alcoholic beverage needed a license, and by this law licenses must also be renewed annually. Continuance of a license became conditional upon

---

Radical Politics (New York, 1973), 149, 163, chap. 5. Later studies, however, have revealed the sheer variety of postures and stances within English Puritanism and persistent efforts to reconcile the Puritan agenda with the standing order. Puritans often backed away from the radical implications of their ideas. See Foster, *The Long Argument,* 9, 20, 26–27, 165–170. In New England, leaders reemphasized hierarchy. In 1679 clergymen denounced the tendency of servants to embellish their dress and "go above their estates and degrees thereby transgressing the laws both of God and man" ([Increase Mather], *The Necessity of Reformation* . . . [Boston, 1679], 2–3). For an acute discussion of the alteration and preservation of rank in Massachusetts, see Fischer, *Albion's Seed,* 174–180.

45. Sidney Webb and Beatrice Webb, *The History of Liquor Licensing: Principally from 1700 to 1830* (1903; rpt., Hamden, Conn., 1963), 1–48; Shurtleff, ed., *Records,* I, 106, 140, 279–280, II, 100, 188, 276, 277–278, III, 427–428, V, 305. For the development of county government, see George Lee Haskins, *Law and Authority in Early Massachusetts: A Study in Tradition and Design* (New York, 1960), 32; For the increasing importance of law as an instrument of mediation in community life, see David Thomas Konig, *Law and Society in Puritan Massachusetts: Essex County, 1629–1692* (Chapel Hill, N.C., 1979), 124. The reorganization of the courts under the new charter is covered by Hendrik Hartog, "The Public Law of a County Court: Judicial Government in Eighteenth Century Massachusetts," *American Journal of Legal History,* XX (1976), 282–291.

annual review of conduct. By including selectmen in the licensing process, the General Court recognized the fundamental importance of the town (as distinct from the county) as the primary administrative agent of colony laws and orders.

The impetus to restrict licenses to those carefully screened by selectmen and justices originated in part in concern over the increasingly diverse and potent beverages available in these years when intemperance emerged as an issue. Changes in drink manufacture, distribution, and consumer taste are difficult to trace. At the time of the Puritan migration, beer had gradually begun to supplant ale among the populace at large; people of means and distinction more commonly consumed wine and distilled liquors. This division is reflected in English distinctions between drinksellers, roughly defined by the terms "inn," "tavern," and "alehouse." The inn was a large establishment that sold wine and distilled liquors as well as more common beverages; it catered mainly to the gentry. Taverns also sold wine to a fairly select clientele but did not have the extensive accommodations of the inn. Almost anyone could set up the much more numerous alehouses, where ale and beer could be bought for consumption inside or outside the premises.[46] The mass of the English population patronized the local alehouse.

In seventeenth-century Massachusetts, distinctions between establishments were less marked, as reflected in the simple furnishings of benches and tables in the public rooms where courts were convened. The terms "tavern" and "inn" described almost any public house where food and beverages could be consumed and lodgings were available. The more important distinction to emerge was that between "tavernkeepers" and "retailers." The latter could sell for consumption only "out of doors" or at the purchaser's home. During the seventeenth century licensing officials restricted each licenseholder to sales of certain beverages. In 1677 only seven of the twenty-seven people approved by the Boston selectmen could sell wine. The rest sold mainly beer and cider. The General Court sought to ensure that beer brewed for sale was of good quality and to promote beer and cider as the staple alcoholic drinks. Price controls ensured that cheap and affordable drink was always available, and indirectly controlled the alcoholic potency of a brew. By law of 1637, no individual could sell any beer, wine, or other drink for more than one penny per quart. The Court hesitated in 1679 to outlaw the sale of alcohol at public outdoor gatherings

46. Clark, *The English Alehouse*, 6–14.

such as militia musters despite reports of drunkenness, but it did order that only weak, watered beer be sold, presumably to inhibit drunkenness.[47]

Lawmakers considered alcohol a staple of every person's diet and in no way wished to interfere with the customary use of it at meals and on occasions such as when Sewall consumed and distributed it. But magistrates did wish to prevent the populace from purchasing high-priced, potent beverages for use beyond basic dietary needs. In effect, Puritan leaders opposed the commercialization of the drink trade, that is, the introduction of beverages produced outside the colony for which colonists might trade their goods and currency.[48] This policy became increasingly difficult to pursue, because the seventeenth century witnessed an expansion in the trade of alcoholic beverages and the raw materials for their manufacture. By the end of the century rum and molasses had emerged as vital commodities in the Atlantic trading network developed by Boston merchants.[49]

These licensing restrictions formed the foundation of Puritan policy on drink. Lawmakers, however, supplemented this system with a host of other laws, because license restrictions alone proved inadequate to the task of suppressing intemperance. The English alehouse, the ubiquitous magnet for laborers in the English countryside, was not so easily abolished in Massachusetts. In spite of the laws prohibiting consumption on the premises, retailers continued to permit patrons to drink in their houses. Laws enacted in 1639, 1654, 1661, and the 1690s testify to the importance of retail houses as illicit gathering places. The office of tithingman, created in the 1670s for purposes of general moral policing, became specifically responsible for the discovery of unlicensed houses and houses violating the terms of their licenses.[50] No matter how carefully screened, licenseholders appear to have done little to restrain consumption.

47. Boston, Record Commissioners, *Boston Records from 1660 to 1701*, Report of the Record Commissioners of the City of Boston (Boston, 1881), 109; Shurtleff, ed., *Records*, I, 213–214, 258, II, 100, 286, IV, pt. 1, 59, pt. 2, 344, V, 211.

48. For an example of this sentiment, see [Cotton Mather], *Sober Considerations, on a Growing Flood of Iniquity* . . . (Boston, 1708).

49. Fernand Braudel, *Capitalism and Material Life, 1400–1800*, trans. Miriam Kochan (New York, 1973), 162–178; Bernard Bailyn, *The New England Merchants in the Seventeenth Century* (New York, 1964), 129–130, 187; John J. McCusker, "Distilling, the Rum Trade, and Early British America," paper presented at MHS, Oct. 17, 1991.

50. Shurtleff, ed., *Records*, I, 279–280, IV, pt. 1, 203, pt. 2, 37, V, 448; *Acts and Resolves*, I, 190–191, 328, V, 448. Through 1700, Massachusetts officials made distinctions between establishments in various ways. In 1682 licenseholders were classified into three catego-

In licensed houses, drink continued to be sold in quantities that magistrates considered excessive and intemperate. In 1645 lawmakers forbade any tavernkeeper from serving a person more than one-half pint of wine at a time. This constituted a drastic reduction in common consumption. The 1682 pamphlet published in London cited instances of individuals carrying "pails full of drink into the open field," of alewives serving "pots" of drink, of a vintner "standing in his door with a pot in his hand to invite customers," of a man drinking a "pot full of Canary-Sack." Judging from inventories of Boston tavernkeepers in the 1680s and 1690s, all beverages continued to be sold in pint or quart pots more often than any other quantity. John Turner did have three quarter-pint and four half-pint pots, but he served wine and other beverages more often in his six wine quarts, four beer quarts, and eleven pints. Witnesses waiting to be called into Turner's court chamber violated the 1645 law even as justices sat in the other room. Nicholas Wilmot had only eight pint pots, as opposed to twenty-one quart pots; Captain William Hudson only five pots under a pint and eighteen of a pint and above; George Monk four half-pints as opposed to sixteen pints and quarts.[51] Two of these taverns hosted court sessions. The majority of other tavernkeepers might have possessed a narrower range of vessel sizes of more than a pint. True, drinkers often passed pots of drink around or used them as punch bowls would be later. But customers did not always drink with company. The 1682 pamphlet speaks of individuals drinking a full pot. The inventories suggest that generous allotments were the rule. The consumption of a quart by one person might also lead him to spend more than the one-half hour allowed in public houses by the same law of 1645.

The General Court encountered the same problems in enforcement when it legislated against health drinking and the use of drink to pay laborers. In 1639 the Court decreed that any person who "directly or indirectly by any color or circumstances drink[s] to another" would be

---

ries: taverns, alehouses, and retailers. The two basic distinctions in use by the 18th century were (1) between those tavernkeepers who could sell wine and distilled liquors, and those limited to beer, ale, and cider; and (2) between those allowed to sell for consumption on the premises, and those forbidden to. By 1700 the categories had been simplified to innholders or tavernkeepers and retailers. What appears to distinguish Massachusetts from England is the effort to restrict a large proportion of licenseholders (all retailers) from allowing consumption in their houses. *Boston Town Records from 1660 to 1701*, 76, 156, 207, 215; Court of General Sessions, Suffolk, Record Book, 1702–1712, 8.

51. Shurtleff, ed., *Records*, II, 100; *A Warning-Piece*, p. 8, nos. 14, 16, p. 20, no. 17; Suffolk County Probate Records, IX, 47, 74–75, 374, XIV, 3–4.

fined. Health drinking was not just an occasion for the consumption of a series of drinks but a custom associated with pagan ritual. Written covenants and "sober" conversation must now define loyalties. Colonists so universally flouted this law, however, that it suffered repeal in 1645.[52]

Efforts to purge the exchange of drink from labor contracts and payments met the same fate. A decree in 1633 ordered all laborers to work the entire day, an indirect reference to the practice of drinking at intervals during the day as a respite from labor. When William Whyte, who probably lived near the ironworks north of Cambridge, was fined for selling beer without a license, he defended himself by saying that his intentions had only been to brew beer for the colliers. Without beer the workmen "would not so comfortably proceed in their works." By a law of 1645 the General Court forbade masters from paying laborers in part with drink. Yet consumption continued to punctuate the course of labor. In 1672 the Court deemed it necessary to forbid the allowance of liquors or wine to workmen every day "over and above their wages," even though some "refuse to work" without it.[53] Throughout the seventeenth century, laborers continued to expect and demand the provision of drink by masters as a condition of employment.

The laws enacted between 1630 and 1680 are, of course, an imprecise means of describing drinking behavior by the populace at large in the seventeenth century. Perhaps evasion was characteristic of only a minority of colonists during the first decades of the colony's existence. Certainly a number of statutes targeted particular age and occupational groups, such as mariners, servants, apprentices, laborers, and youths—groups that probably sought tavern fellowship or covert drinking as a release from subordination in other settings. In 1651 the Court complained of diverse "corrupt persons . . . who insinuate themselves into the fellowship of the young people" and encourage them to drink "to the grief of their parents, masters, teachers, tutors, guardians, [and] overseers."[54] Such laws do imply that the elected representatives of a temperate majority mainly acted to discipline an intemperate minority. It is difficult to draw a profile of the most frequent offenders, because a majority of drinking offenses could have been heard by individual justices who left no records of their actions.

Yet a consideration of the laws as a whole indicates that excessive drinking occurred among a broad spectrum of society, not just particular

---

52. Shurtleff, ed., *Records*, I, 271, II, 121.

53. *Ibid.*, I, 109–110, II, 100, IV, pt. 1, 59–60, 347, pt. 2, 510; William Whyte to General Court, May 15, 1646, Taverns, 1643–1774, LXI, 13, ACM.

54. Shurtleff, ed., *Records*, IV, pt. 1, 59–60.

groups. Magistrates and deputies repeatedly resorted to the enactment of new laws probably because they could not rely on heads of households and employers to discipline those under their government to the degree desired. The series of laws suggests a growing gap between Puritan standards of temperate conduct and actual conduct. What leaders like Sewall defined as intemperance, a majority of patrons might have considered traditional and necessary levels of consumption. In any case, the Court by its own admission could not restrain consumption to approved levels. In 1648 the deputies admitted that excess drinking continued despite all of the laws devised to contain it. In a preface to a 1651 law the deputies to the Court explained the need for more legislation by stating that, "notwithstanding the great care" the Court had taken to suppress drunkenness, "persons addicted to that vice find out ways to deceive the laws." Again, in 1664, the Court became "sensible of the great increase of profaneness among us." A critical visitor to Boston in 1682 noted the widespread evasion of the laws respecting drink and taverns. He asserted that "all their laws look like scarecrows" when one observes their habits, for "the worst of drunkards may find pot companions enough, for all their pretenses to sobriety."[55]

IV

Popular evasion of the most restrictive drink laws enacted by the first generation of leaders does not reflect a general failure of the mission and goals of the colony. The focus of community life for the founding generation was the establishment and support of gathered covenanted congregations. The private exercise of literacy, particularly the use of the Bible, underlay this reform of religious life. The spiritual motivation and preoccupation of the founding generation of colonists is reflected in the fact that many colonists chose to buy religious books if their finances permitted the purchase of any item beyond necessities. Of the inventories of seventy emigrant households, a full 74 percent list books. Other surveys of probated estates later in the century reveal a lower incidence of book ownership; most families probably owned only a Bible, a few other books, or none at all. Even so, churchgoers were encouraged to read the Bible and catechisms intensively. Colonists conceived of reading as mainly an aid in the

55. Shurtleff, ed., *Records*, II, 257, IV, pt. 1, 203, pt. 2, 100; *Acts and Resolves*, I, 679; J. W., *A Letter from New-England concerning Their Customs, Manners, and Religion Written upon Occasion of a Report about a Quo Warranto Brought against That Government* (London, 1682), 3, 7.

transformation of a person into a pious communicant by the repeated return to the same familiar sacred texts. One turned to these texts as a weapon to withstand the temptations of tavern haunting and excessive drinking.[56] To the extent that reading and instruction persuaded colonists to abandon all the old drinking holidays, print coupled with learned preaching did triumph over the popular culture of drink.

Still, the conception of printed matter as primarily an extension of preaching by a learned ministry, qualified to discover and display religious truth, limited the impact of print as an agent of social transformation in general—and as a weapon against the oral culture of collective drinking in particular. In contrast to the few books owned by most households, ministers on average owned one hundred books each.[57] There existed a gulf in levels of literacy between clergymen and most colonists that preaching only partially bridged. Ministers and pious members of the governing elite absorbed in study could not expect the same of most of their fellow communicants, who did not possess the resources or were not sufficiently literate. Moreover, ministers qualified their encouragement of private study by their concern over preserving the prerogative of preaching in their own voices. Thus Sewall distributed sermons mainly to other rulers and ministers in the course of his travels.

Limitations on the exercise of literacy by ordinary colonists are also reflected in the restrictions on the use of print to publicize events and news of provincial importance. Throughout the seventeenth century no one considered it necessary or advisable to establish a newspaper designed to inform everyone of extralocal events. Print must be restricted so that local and provincial leaders could receive information of extralocal importance first and, at their discretion, make it generally known by formal announcement. Members of the elite conceived of themselves as gatekeepers responsible for screening information and deciding what might be transmitted to the general population. Sewall acted in this tradition when he became manager of the official state press in 1681. He saw print as a form of speaking, a specific relation between persons in which considerations of status—patriarchal speaker to deferential listener—were always present.[58]

---

56. Anderson, *New England's Generation*, 173–175; David D. Hall, *Worlds of Wonder, Days of Judgment: Popular Religious Belief in Early New England* (Cambridge, Mass., 1990), 24–39, 51. Hall summarizes studies of book ownership by Clifford Shipton, Gloria Main, Anne Brown, and David Hall (248–249).

57. Hall, *Worlds of Wonder*, 44.

58. Richard D. Brown, *Knowledge Is Power: The Diffusion of Information in Early America*,

This constricted conception of the use of print, in part to uphold and preserve hierarchy, reinforced the importance and primacy of face-to-face relations among most colonists. Their primary identification lay with the limited number of households with whom they had regular contact. However much Puritans had turned their backs on the rich and varied ritual life of the late-medieval era, they still clung to traditional conceptions of community life in important ways. They exalted the values of consensus, harmony, and cooperation and accepted the principle of hierarchy as the foundation of government. Formal Sabbath and lecture meetings alone could never sustain the networks of face-to-face contact that embodied community in its most immediate sense for most inhabitants. On the Sabbath the community came together to listen and pray. On the other days of the week conversations, gestures, and professions of reciprocity in public houses interlaced community bonds mainly among men; the fact and content of these encounters could be selectively transmitted by men to their wives, thus helping to uphold the patriarchal control over the flow of news.[59] Indeed, the abandonment of the seasonal religious celebrations and

---

1700–1865 (New York, 1989), 28–33. The first attempt to publish a news sheet in 1690 was suppressed by the government (*Diary*, I, 267). Brown notes that some "contagious diffusion" of information occurred, but usually required certification by a figure of authority before it became credible; David Hall suggests that print was liberating for some individuals in the 17th century by discussion of instances in which colonists used their knowledge of Scripture to challenge clerical instruction. Moreover, popular religious works dramatized the lives of ordinary men and women (*Worlds of Wonder*, 57, 69–70). In contrast Michael Warner emphasizes that the Puritan ideology of print was not generally emancipatory because print was not an instrument of public mediation. In an important ideological way Massachusetts remained an oral society despite the high value attached to literacy. Warner, *The Letters of the Republic: Publication and the Public Sphere in Eighteenth-Century America* (Cambridge, Mass., 1990), 19–23, 31.

59. There is evidence of women's using taverns, but mainly for specific purposes such as shelter while traveling. Overall the evidence suggests that the vast majority of casual patrons were men, a pattern which reinforced patriarchal control of the diffusion of information as far as communication through taverns is concerned. Women of course could hear formal announcements at church at the same time as men, a factor that may account for the higher premium they would attach to membership among succeeding generations.

Theodore Dwight Bozeman has emphasized the "primitivist" thrust of much of Puritan reform and colonization as a caution to those scholars who see the Puritans as harbingers of modernization. Puritan leaders did repeatedly repudiate the "new" in an effort to recapture and implement the quality of biblical society as well as specific scriptural laws and teachings. Ironically, the intense identification with local communities and the premium placed

the restrictions on any kind of activity on the Sabbath except Sabbath meetings themselves invested informal tavern patronage with a new importance. Here also a collective mentality could be nurtured.

Thus while figures of authority increasingly used print to attack tavern haunting and related sins during the seventeenth century, the limited use of print itself by ordinary colonists could not begin to displace or weaken the functions of fellowship and communication that public houses continued to fulfill. When ministers and lawmakers more absorbed in the culture of print attempted to make reformed worship into a vehicle for the near elimination of collective drinking between 1630 and 1680, they confronted boundaries to reform. The stubborn persistence of a popular culture of drink in early Massachusetts, in defiance of law and printed entreaties, is a measure of the limits of bonding by instruction and study of the Word (particularly among men) and an index of the continued vitality of more traditional means of establishing and maintaining collective life.[60]

Despite Sewall's infrequent use of taverns, the tavern's importance as a source of news and fellowship for more common men throughout the seventeenth century stands out in his diary. Court days, for example, brought individuals throughout a county to taverns not only for legal purposes but for the exchange of local news from one part of the county to another, including the airing of criminal cases. At one Superior Court session in Plymouth, Sewall dined with the sheriff and deputies at the tavern. While the group ate, another justice arrived and "brought the news of Maccaty's [a ship captain] arrival [in Boston] and the bulk of the news."[61]

On court days the number of people traveling the roads increased, and

---

on consensus could also help to sustain the public house as a vital institution. *To Live Ancient Lives: The Primitivist Dimension in Puritanism* (Chapel Hill, N.C., 1988), 131–139, 344–351.

60. David D. Hall has argued that printed religious tracts formed the foundation of collective mentality in Puritan Massachusetts and that terms such as "popular culture" obscure the subtle continuum between print culture—as exemplified by clerical preoccupation with the study of the Word—and the "oral culture" of face-to-face communication. I agree that a continuum existed but would also assert that there were definite limits to the influence of print and preaching. The popular culture of tavern assemblies was in direct and persistent conflict with printed religious appeals, and the influence of the clergy receded by the last quarter of the 17th century. The worlds of print and of oral exchange were never completely integrated into a "Puritan culture." Hall, "The World of Print and Collective Mentality in Seventeenth-Century New England," in John Higham and Paul K. Conkin, eds., *New Directions in American Intellectual History* (Baltimore, 1979), 166–180.

61. *Diary*, II, 947.

the flow of news into local taverns through travelers moved more rapidly. Coming home from a Plymouth session, Sewall met an acquaintance in Braintree. Sewall immediately asked, but the traveler "told me no news." A little farther on his way, however, "Major Walley overtook me, and told me the dreadful news of Mr. Cotton's sudden death." Then he stopped to feed his horse at Mill's tavern, "where I hear of Cousin Quinsey's being about and that morning brought to bed of her son Joseph."[62] Because travelers and public gatherings converged on taverns, much of the news—whether of local births and deaths or of the outside world—was transmitted gradually through taverns. The more frequently the ordinary farmer or artisan visited the tavern nearest his home, the more informed he could become of the world beyond his immediate neighbors.

Taverns also served as a setting for the sifting, discussion, confirmation, or discrediting of rumors. Since the flow of news from person to person could be slow and erratic, colonists often heard startling rumors of events beyond the boundaries of a day's travel (about thirty miles by horse). It might require several visits to a tavern in one or more days for a townsman to sift fact from rumor, especially in rural towns. Numerous entries in Sewall's diary concern news heard, then confirmed or discredited. On his way home to Boston, Sewall once heard in a Dedham tavern that a member of his household had died while he had been away, but he returned to find him alive though still ailing. While leaving a militia muster (usually held outside a tavern), Sewall met a friend who asked "if I had not heard the news." He told Sewall that Louis XIV of France had broken his neck in a fall from his horse. The source of the news was a ship captain "who comes from New Castle, and had it at sea from Commodore Taylor." But two weeks later Sewall recorded the arrival of a ship from Dublin, seven weeks at sea, which "brings no news of the French king's death, so that conclude he is alive."[63] It would take still longer for the contradiction of earlier reports to filter through the countryside from Boston.

Sifting fact from rumor, or dismissing entire accounts, made it necessary for ordinary colonists to attend to their most reliable sources regularly. Ministers were one of the most important sources of news, because they often corresponded or had personal contact with people outside the community. But tavernkeepers, accessible every day of every season and receiving travelers seeking respite from the heavy exertion of travel over difficult roads, also occupied an important place in the chain of oral trans-

62. *Ibid.,* I, 258, 552, II, 626, 635.
63. *Ibid.,* I, 258, 492, 552, II, 626, 635, 947.

mission of news. A Concord minister speaking retrospectively of colonial social habits talked of "the supposed needfulness of collecting at taverns to learn the news of the day," which induced "the practice of tavern haunting, and the temptation to needless expense and injurious drinking."[64]

Since taverns received travelers, they often became settings where local inhabitants negotiated relations with the outside world by deciding how to react and respond to newcomers. The infrequency and unreliability of news coming from the outside world strengthened the identification of inhabitants with each other, and distinctions between familiar members of a community and strangers living beyond the community were very clear and rigid. If legitimate travelers, strangers were welcome as news carriers; but if shabbily dressed or traveling by foot, they became objects of suspicion and even apprehension. In either case, local inhabitants routinely interrogated strangers of middling rank or below arriving at taverns as to their identity and what news they could convey. Even in Boston, which had a population of more than six thousand people by the 1690s, residents noticed the presence of strangers on their streets. They might quickly become the subjects of official inquiry and be "warned out" if they possessed no means to support themselves.[65]

During winter snows and the mud of spring, when weather reduced the flow of travel and news between communities, neighbors became still more dependent on each other for news and fellowship. At the same time, farmers and mariners entered a slack period of labor and had more time to gather in taverns. Samuel Clough's *New England Almanack* for 1702 captures the contraction of social interaction into local drinking companies in verse:

> The days are short, the weather's cold
> By tavern fires tales are told
> Some ask for dram when first come in
> Others with flip or bounce begin.

64. Brown, *Knowledge Is Power*, chap. 3; *The Centennial of the Social Circle in Concord, March 21, 1882* (Cambridge, Mass., 1882), 60.

65. Sewall was too important and well known a personage to receive inquiries from common men, but Dr. Alexander Hamilton later became the subject of constant questioning (Carl Bridenbaugh, ed., *Gentleman's Progress: The Itinerarium of Dr. Alexander Hamilton* [Chapel Hill, N.C., 1948], 121, 124). Allan Kulikoff tabulates the increasing numbers of strangers in "The Progress of Inequality in Revolutionary Boston," *WMQ*, 3d Ser., XXVIII (1971), 400. Just as in England, Massachusetts poor laws mandated that individuals in need of relief be returned to the last community in which they had been accepted as inhabitants, usually the place of their birth.

In January,

> Ill husbands now in taverns sit
> And spend more money than they get
> Calling for drink and drinking greedy
> Tho' many of them poor and needy.[66]

Such verses suggest how drinkers in taverns collecting and sifting through news and rumors, or simply telling tales, might spend more than one-half hour in taverns and drink more than one-half pint of wine—both stated limits by law. And in renewing ties with neighbors drifting in at different times, it is easy to imagine how consumption by patrons might become excessive or even result in drunkenness. The latter had become a punishable crime, but drunkards usually drank in company with extended family members or longtime neighbors, people willing to shield them from the law. Prosecutions created ill feeling among neighbors dependent on each other for news and disrupted the chain of transmission. Indeed, the practice of collective drinking among neighbors created bonds between members of a company that might effectively transcend and nullify law.[67]

V

The interiors of taverns in the seventeenth century provide more clues to the quality of collective life in public rooms. At midcentury few people sat in chairs when visiting a tavern. Even the prominent King's Arms Tavern in Boston, where courts often convened, had only four chairs in the entire house in 1651, as opposed to more than two dozen forms and benches spread throughout thirteen rooms. Patrons most often shared seats, especially at night, reinforcing a sense of membership in a company. By the 1680s, chairs had become more numerous, but not so many that every patron could have one. Boston tavernkeeper John Turner had ten benches as well as twenty-three chairs. Nicholas Wilmot had almost as many stools as chairs. The introduction of chairs did subtly enhance the importance of the individual, but not at great expense to the traditional notions of interdependence associated with tavern patronage.[68]

The little differentiation between public and private space, or drinking

---

66. Judd, *History of Hadley*, 67.

67. The problems of law enforcement are discussed at greater length in Chapter 2.

68. The inventory of the King's Arms in 1651 is reproduced in Alice Morse Earle, *Stage-Coach and Tavern Days* (New York, 1900), 17–18; Inventory of Nicholas Wilmot, Suffolk County Probate Records, Record Book, IX, 374; John Turner, IX, 47.

and sleeping quarters, created an immediate intimacy between hosts and patrons. The Court Chamber at the King's Arms contained a closet with a bedstead in 1651. In Turner's "parlor" in 1681, customers could inspect and perhaps use his four pounds worth of books, four guns and other weaponry, and one of his beds. Almost all of the rooms appear to have been public, because the limited number of chairs, benches, and stools were spread throughout the house. There was no separate dining space. Although the drinking of healths could inject ceremony into drinking, the simple drinking and eating utensils did not encourage the conception of dining as a domestic or private assembly or act. These taverns had little or no glassware, and forks had not yet come into use to encourage refinement and differentiate one patron from another. Wilmot and Turner both owned some silver plate, but they usually served beverages in pewter pots and flagons, which might be shared, depending on their size. No mirrors or pictures on the walls provided any visual stimulation. Patrons focused on their drink and each other.[69]

When the courts assembled in these taverns, visitors must know and acknowledge their place and rank in the visible hierarchy of superiors and inferiors. But on most days the exchange of drink relaxed or eliminated this consciousness of rank, also omnipresent in the seating of the meeting-house. The exchange of news and information at taverns invested every new arrival, however humble, with the potential of being a news-carrier. The tenor of social relations in taverns is reflected in the name given to one of the rooms in the King's Arms—the Exchange. A variety of exchanges, from news to goods, might take place, but patrons all had a common purpose in availing themselves of drink. Men at the bottom of the social hierarchy could purchase access to a company of drinkers for a few pennies. On occasion this sense of communality would be formalized by a collective health drunk to the king or some other figure of authority. The conviviality of tavern companies is reflected in the names by which Wilmot designated his various rooms, suggesting warmth, sociability, and fancy. Two of his lower rooms he called the Rose and the Sun, and other rooms he christened the Cross Keys, the Anchor, the Castle, and the Green Dragon.[70]

Taverns offered men not only a respite from labor but a temporary escape from the anxiety over this life and the next. Worshipping a Calvinist God could be an intimidating experience. One was never sure of salvation, and it could be frightening when this awful uncertainty was empha-

69. *Ibid.*
70. *Ibid.*

sized in a sermon. With constraints on conduct eased, in taverns this fear could be temporarily softened by drink and raillery. In the meetinghouse the intricacy of Puritan beliefs and ideals was expressed and inspired collective anxiety; in the public house a less complicated and judgmental pattern of fellowship offered immediate gratification and allowed for some measure of self-assertion for men in so arbitrary a world. The tavern could be an antidote to the forbidding powers of the supernatural world, even though excessive drinking had come to be defined as the devil's lure and a provocation of God's wrath. The disorder of drinking companies denounced by the clergy still provided a release, a temporary escape, from the hierarchical order of God. Indeed, for ordinary men, as opposed to ministers, taverns and churches served complementary purposes in the integration of community life.

VI

Whether as a respite from labor or anxiety or as a means to acquire news and conduct transactions, men gathering in public houses continued to subvert the growing number of legal restrictions during the first half-century of the colony's existence. This persistence of traditional drinking habits certainly irritated rulers and clergy, but did nothing more. The stability of local and colony government during the first fifty years of the colony's existence, together with high levels of church membership in the various towns, helped to offset the stubborn popularity of taverns. If the laws continued to fail their purpose, the vitality of the gathered churches of the colony mitigated somewhat the violation of the colony's covenant with God that intemperance had come to represent. But, beginning in the 1670s, just as Sewall was becoming active in a series of appointed posts, concern over prevailing drinking habits began to mount into alarm.

Gatherings in taverns became a source of alarm, because Sabbath assemblies seemed a less compelling force in controlling behavior. Ministers wielded less influence over the second and third generations of colonists. Diminishing numbers of applicants for church membership, especially among men, weakened the position of clergymen not only as religious leaders but as arbiters of social and political issues and questions. In Salem only 17 percent of ratepayers had chosen to undergo the examination to become members of the congregation by 1683. Moreover, a minister of the second generation confronted more contention in his church, faced increasing difficulties in securing an adequate salary from his congregation, and consequently less often continued as minister to one church for the duration of his career. The polarization of some towns over the location of meetinghouses contrasted with the easy multiplication of taverns to accommodate the dispersal of population over a wider land base. Even the addition of one public house in a town could alter local ties and allegiances, because during the winter months voters and church communicants might gather in different houses at varying distances from the meetinghouse.[71]

The clergy increasingly resorted to jeremiads, scathing denunciations of intemperance and related sins with the promise of God's awful judgment if colonists did not uphold their covenant with him. Increase Mather warned his congregation in 1673 that they might drink the "conscience into a deep sleep, but when their souls shall awake in the midst of eternal flames, all the wounds received by this sin will be felt with a witness." But such threats could undermine a minister's authority, for, if a minister elicited no response from his congregation, no change in habits, the jeremiad might be turned against him in mockery of his claims. Samuel Danforth did succeed in stimulating a revival and a renewal of the church covenant in 1676 (at a time of crisis) and again in 1705 in Taunton. The possibility of a backlash, however, was implicit in the provision of the covenant renewal, namely, the reform of unnecessary tavern patronage, and restrictions on the expressions of "contempt" for the "magistracy and ministry" that presumably received airing in these houses.[72]

The narrow line that ministers walked between inspiring reform and inspiring resistance is also implicit in the conciliatory words of Benjamin Wadsworth, a Boston minister, in his introduction to a later sermon. Wadsworth went so far as to enumerate the "useful" functions of taverns, "lest I should be misinterpreted, or be thought to run into extremes."[73] Ministers increased their attacks on intemperance but also had to tread carefully in doing so. They had an obligation to reform their errant congregations, but they also risked alienation by asking for more from men in their congregations than they would or could give.

71. Konig, *Law and Society*, 91, 99–101, 107; Hall, *The Faithful Shepherd*, chap. 8. For example of different houses, see Chase, *History of Haverhill*, 136, 168, 204.

72. Mather, *Wo to Drunkards*, 11. The weakness of church membership as an influence against tavern patronage is apparent in the question put to Mather by a neighbor, namely, "Whether it be lawful for a church member among us, to be frequently in taverns." Mather responded that it was not lawful, but the question itself reveals the ambivalent attitude among the public at large toward admonitions like these. Samuel Danforth, *Piety Encouraged* ... (Boston, 1705), 23; Danforth, *The Woful Effects of Drunkenness* ... (Boston, 1710), 25–26.

73. Wadsworth, *An Essay to Do Good*, 2.

Colonists reacted with the same ambivalence to the literature of wonders and portents popularized by the clergy as a weapon against sins like intemperance. Most colonists readily believed that God revealed his wrath or pleasure through omens, portents, and remarkable occurrences. Sewall's diary is full of efforts to divine messages from heaven through the studied interpretation of different phenomena, from rainbows to sudden deaths. Stories of men and women seemingly punished by God for sins involving drink formed a prominent part of this literature drawn on by New England clergy. Churchgoers read or listened to stories like the following. An English cavalier drank a health to the devil while carousing in a tavern, where constraints on speech were often relaxed. The drinker proclaimed, "If the Devil would not come, and pledge him, he would not believe that there was either God or devil." His companions fled the room at such a shocking declaration: the cavalier disappeared through a window with a hideous noise, a terrible smell, and blood. Such stories might have inhibited colonists from casually invoking the devil's power to any purpose, but they did little to wean men from the controversial context of this event, the tavern. Nor did the gesture of health drinking diminish as a form of salutation. In 1679 ministers complained of the continuing popularity of "that heathenish and idolatrous practice of health drinking" and of the use of "oaths and imprecations in ordinary discourse." Moreover, Mather observed in 1679 that some colonists stood staunchly in "opposition" to "reformation." Indeed, "sins and sinners" now had "many advocates," and those who were "zealous" against sin have been "reproached" and "discouraged."[74] Ordinary colonists were selective in what habits they would abandon and in what behavior they would persist.

The implications of a robust drinking culture for secular governing institutions also worried officials by the end of the century. "When drink is got into the brain," Mather complained in 1673, "then out come filthy songs, and scoffing at the best men, yea at godliness itself in the power of it." The preservation of the colony's political culture hinged on the regular recognition and elevation of the "best men." Danforth spelled out the implications of such verbal defiance in a later sermon published in 1710. He warned that if the "drinking party is so potent as to prevail over the small number of sober men, that are the remnant of God's people in the land, then none shall be improved in offices of trust but such as work at, favor, and countenance this vice."[75] Massachusetts still remained relatively free of the social and economic conditions that had provoked alarm over ale-

74. Hall, *Worlds of Wonder*, chap. 2, 74; [Mather], *The Necessity of Reformation*, 4–5.
75. Mather, *Wo to Drunkards*, 13; Danforth, *Woful Effects*, 25–26.

house crowds in England. But failure to limit tavern patronage at a time when religious fervor, even common observance, appeared to be ebbing could have telling effects on the character of the governing hierarchy because so many men possessed enough estate to be eligible to vote. Puritan leaders had begun to confront the ramifications of the issue of alcohol control in an American setting.

As Sewall and other magistrates and the hierarchy of officials beneath them exercised the powers of their offices in town and public houses across the province, they still received the humble expressions of deference and esteem such as had always been offered to those who presided over court sessions and other public gatherings. The sheriffs and their deputies still escorted the Superior Court justices from town to town, and justices still publicly condemned and shamed lawbreakers before crowds attending court days. And town inhabitants continued to acknowledge place and rank when they gathered every Sabbath in meetinghouses where the seating arrangements reflected the social hierarchy of their communities. But popular tavern assemblies now more flagrantly undermined these public manifestations of a Puritan social order. It was not just the vitiation of piety that worried magistrates like Sewall. The lawmakers and justices who presided over court sessions at selected taverns perceived the need to strengthen the influence of the governing hierarchy over ordinary assemblies in taverns to make the force of law more evident on occasions other than court days. Oral attacks on men of authority by drinkers at informal gatherings in taverns must not be allowed to alter or undermine a public sphere carefully confined and orchestrated by pious men like Sewall to exclude the majority of men from assertive participation in public affairs.[76]

Devastating warfare with New England tribes beginning in 1675 exacerbated social tensions within the colony. Massachusetts ministers interpreted the outbreak of war as punishment levied by God for the creeping corruption of public life. The General Court agreed and made these "provoking evils" the justification for the passage in 1675 of new and more stringent measures to control behavior. The Court's concern over how individuals conducted themselves in relation to their superiors and how they acknowledged their subjection and dependence in both family and public settings is reflected in the statutes enacted. There existed, the depu-

---

76. Lawmakers acted to prevent the development of discourses in taverns independent of the operation of formal institutions of church and state. For an introduction to the expansion of the "public sphere," see Jürgen Habermas, *The Structural Transformation of the Public Sphere: An Inquiry into a Category of Bourgeois Society*, trans. Thomas Burger (Cambridge, Mass., 1989), 1–26.

ties to the Court observed, "a great neglect of discipline in the churches." The new generation had failed to "acknowledge" their "relations to God and to his church." Youths created "disorder" in many congregations, and they must now "sit in where they may be most together and in public view." A "grave and sober person" must be appointed by the selectmen to inspect them and report transgressors to the magistrates. Such officials could even impose a fine on their parents or governors or order the children to be whipped or sent to a house of correction. The Court also complained of numerous instances of "contempt of authority" in both civil and ecclesiastical settings and ordered that the hierarchy of officers from justices to grand jurors "take strict care that the laws already made and provided in this case be executed."[77]

The General Court also issued directives to the hierarchy of officials beneath it and heads of households to act against the "sin of excessive drinking, tippling, and company-keeping in taverns." Selectmen in each town must choose individuals to take responsibility for the discovery of unlicensed houses and for the "inspection" of ten to twelve families in their neighborhoods. Those selected must report the names of offenders to the selectmen and magistrates of their respective towns, who in turn would deliver the names to the county courts for prosecution. The county courts received instructions to refrain from licensing any more houses than was "absolutely necessary." Moreover, such houses must be used "for the refreshing and entertainment of travelers and strangers only," not town dwellers. Offenders could be whipped five stripes if unable to pay the fine of five shillings.[78]

These acts and orders all reflect the traditional faith in a social order of descending hierarchies of men reaching down to inspect social units as small as ten to twelve families. In England the distribution and exchange of drink had once contributed to the integration of such a structure of social relationships, from the apex of authority in the king to the common laborer. Now, in Massachusetts, the General Court acted to purge drink of its function in social integration, to reduce and channel its flow in tightly prescribed ways. The customs that had once helped to sustain a hierarchical order now came under attack for their potential to undermine constituted authority. Rulers and ruled were at odds over drink, because the former had adopted a code of behavior that they sought to impose on society at large with new vigor. In renouncing drinking custom, they

77. Edmund S. Morgan, ed., *Puritan Political Ideas, 1558–1794* (New York, 1965), 226–233.

78. *Ibid.*

assumed new authority to control behavior, but simultaneously put their customary authority at risk by provoking criticism and resistance.

The 1675 laws and orders had little impact, even after the disruption of the war had receded—especially in Boston, now crowded with refugees and harboring an increasing number of mariners, laborers, and other inhabitants with little or no identification with Puritan social ideals. By 1679 the General Court acknowledged that the laws had not "effected the ends intended." More drastic measures were needed. Thus the deputies ordered a reduction in the number of public houses in the entire colony. Boston had twenty-six public houses in 1675; now the deputies voted to limit the town to ten. Moreover, the Court moved to curtail patronage more rigorously by prohibiting every inhabitant in the colony from drinking in houses in "the town wherein they dwell" upon penalty of five shillings for each offense for both tavernkeeper and patron. The deputies allowed exceptions for the courts, military men, jurors, committees, magistrates conducting official business, commissioners, townsmen conducting public affairs, and merchants and shipmasters engaged in private business.[79]

This drastic measure would have compelled every inhabitant to conform to the pattern of restricted patronage practiced by Sewall in the 1670s. The order suggests that most lawmakers also restricted their patronage to travel and official business. The "temperate" men who composed the General Court both loathed and feared intemperance among the lower ranks. But, while the deputies had become sufficiently alarmed to take these drastic steps, the governor's Council declined to concur with them, perhaps because the councillors considered the orders to be unenforceable.[80]

The ministers of the colony, however, continued to half demand and half plead for further action by the General Court. The synod held at Boston in 1679 reviewed all the "evils" that had provoked God "to bring his judgment on New England." Sabbath breaking and nonattendance at churches, coupled with intemperance and tavern haunting, were prominent on the list. Even church members, the ministers declared, frequented public houses. The synod concluded by asking for more laws and better enforcement. In the aftermath of the very destructive and frightening war with the Wampanoags and their allies, the clergy never occupied a better position to ask for legislative actions designed to restore God's favor. The number of public houses in Boston had risen from twenty-six in 1675 to

79. Proposal to reduce the number of public houses in the colony referred to the Council, Oct. 31, 1679, Towns, 1632–1693, CXII, 307a, ACM; *Boston Records from 1660 to 1701*, 95.

80. Proposal, Towns, 1632–1693, CXII, 307a; *Boston Records from 1660 to 1701*, 95.

forty-five in 1681.[81] A growing proportion of the inhabitants and refugees living in Boston patronized public houses other than those where official business was conducted. Men of authority and substance had become less and less visible in Boston's growing number of public spaces. Public houses, of course, routinely accommodated strangers. But the sight of so many refugees drinking in new establishments probably added weight to the injunctions by Mather. Pressure for some action on the issue mounted.

In 1681 the action came. The Council reversed itself when it agreed to a second proposal by the House to seize the licensing system in all the counties in order to reduce and fix the number of public houses in each town.[82] Drastic measures had come to seem necessary. The colony poised itself for a new assault on intemperance and taverns.

By this action the government of the colony reaffirmed its commitment to and new emphasis on the cultivation of the virtue of temperance in Massachusetts towns. In the chaos of Tudor-Stuart England, Puritan leaders had become the most vocal critics of traditional English drinking customs and habits and supported parliamentary efforts to reduce the number of public houses throughout the kingdom. In effect, they sought to draw new boundaries in community life, enjoining their followers to withdraw from habitual collective gathering in order to enter voluntarily into covenanted churches founded on Calvinist principles. Favor in God's eyes became contingent upon the rational appreciation and study of the Word. Drink dulled and inhibited this intellectual quest. In Massachusetts, it was believed, reformed churches would become the basis for the development of new communities in which public houses would be limited to prescribed functions such as court days. The English cultural baggage sanctioning the extensive use of drink could be jettisoned.

To some extent the colony's founders and their successors realized their objectives in respect to drink regulation in the seventeenth century. Puritans purged the calendar of Christian faith of the excessive use of drink by the elimination of customs like saints' days. Leaders successfully established English licensing procedures, with some alterations, in the new colony. By 1681 every tavernkeeper in the colony must submit himself to the judgment and review of town selectmen and county justices once yearly. Temperance had become a principle of law and religion, a standard by which society must be constantly measured lest it be allowed to spin irrationally out of control.

Nevertheless, Puritan colonists, particularly men, continued to patron-

---

81. Mather, *The Necessity of Reformation*, 3–6; Shurtleff, ed., *Records*, V, 305.
82. Shurtleff, ed., *Records*, V, 305.

ize taverns beyond the prescribed limits, chiefly because public houses contributed so much to the formation and perpetuation of a collective mentality in the various towns and performed important functions in a still predominantly oral communication system. Community life continued to converge on taverns as well as churches, and the giving and receiving of drink remained a means by which social relations were expressed, maintained, and renewed. Tavern crowds became perhaps the most visible and chronic contradiction of Puritan social ideals by the 1680s, ever more disturbing because of the decline in applicants for church membership. More ominous to leaders like Sewall, popular tavern assemblies now possessed the potential to affect the outcome of the annual elections of town selectmen and representatives to the General Court. The issue of taverns and drink regulation lay at the center of the delicate balance between the prerogatives and discretionary authority of the few, and the wider participation in government now enjoyed by the many by virtue of their status as owners of property. To what degree could the hierarchy of rulers in the colony enforce temperance without jeopardizing customary deference by the many to the few? Would new restrictions only stimulate more open scoffing at the best men?

Despite the defiance of popular resistance, the General Court continued to increase the pressure on all officials—elected selectmen as well as appointed officials—to reduce their approval of licenses and enforce all the drink laws vigorously. The General Court's new orders answered clerical pleas for new restrictions and renewed the colony's commitment to a social order defined in part by temperance. The covenant with God must be restored. But the orders also placed law and law officials on a collision course with an entrenched and still thriving popular culture of drink.

Chapter 2

Law versus Popular Culture

When Samuel Sewall entered William Wallis's tavern in the South End of Boston on the night of February 6, 1714, every member of the group assembled there professed eagerness, perhaps in jest, to have him join in celebrating the Queen's Birthday. On this occasion they had gathered to drink to the queen's health; when Sewall entered, they rose to drink to his health, and then the queen's health with him. Sewall, however, became more angry with each new gesture. Summoned by a constable, he had come to exert his authority in quelling a tavern "disorder" and now insisted that the company of drinkers disperse immediately. But the drinkers refused to leave, replying that they "must and would stay upon that solemn occasion." After almost an hour of argument during which Sewall's associate, Justice Edward Bromfield, threatened to raise the militia to oust them forcibly, they finally departed. But they left only to rendezvous at the home of one of the group, and only after demonstrating contempt for one of the highest-ranking officials in the province. As Sewall would later recall in his diary, the company had defied his order to disperse by calling for more drink, and one man had actually put on a hat to "affront" him directly. Others mockingly helped Sewall to spell their names for future use in court. One cursed the constable for refusing to drink a health. But perhaps the most memorable insult for Sewall was the string of reproaches to the provincial government, including the comment that it had not made "one good law."[1]

Although a mixed group of visiting English officers and Boston residents provoked this particular incident, it reflects the more acute conflict that accompanied the greater efforts of the Assembly to control the sale and consumption of drink. Order and disorder hung in a new, more tenuous balance. Directly and indirectly, members of the Massachusetts judicial and law enforcement hierarchy confronted resistance to old and new restrictions. As leaders pressed the populace to reform, their increased efforts to impose a more temperate social order actually served to undermine the personal authority of the members of the governing hierarchy.

I

When the General Court took direct control over the licensing system in 1681, it ordered the reduction of the number of public houses in Boston from forty-five to twenty-four, and to one per town elsewhere in the province except for the seven seaport towns of Charlestown, Ipswich, Salem, Gloucester, Lynn, Hingham, and Newbury. The incidence of public houses in Boston (taverns and retail houses) dropped from one for every 133 inhabitants to one for every 250 inhabitants, according to the number of polls in the town in 1687.[2] By this action the Assembly moved to centralize control of collective drinking in each town and enhance the prospect that those keeping their licenses would restrain consumption. Tavern patrons in each town would be more likely to come under the personal view and government of magistrates and other officials invested with responsibility for enforcement. By reducing the number of places where colonists could legitimately gather to drink, the Assembly acted to make "governors" or "masters" more visible where drink was sold.

This reduction in houses, however, interfered with customary patterns of collective life to such an extent that the number of unlicensed sales increased. Three years after the 1681 order took effect, George Monk (the

1. M. Halsey Thomas, ed., *The Diary of Samuel Sewall, 1674–1729* (New York, 1973), II, 741–743 (hereafter cited as *Diary*).

2. Nathaniel B. Shurtleff, ed., *Records of the Governor and Company of the Massachusetts Bay in New England, 1628–1686* (Boston, 1853–1854), V, 305; population figure taken from Gary B. Nash, *The Urban Crucible: Social Change, Political Consciousness, and the Origins of the American Revolution* (Cambridge, Mass., 1979), 55.

Superior Court's favored proprietor) and four other Boston tavernkeepers who had survived the purge, and who presumably had tried to conform to the laws, complained about unlicensed sellers. In their petition to the Assembly they observed that "a great number" of Bostonians "presumed openly in contempt of authority to violate and break the wholesome laws established among us." These unlicensed sellers "do daily and frequently draw and sell by retail wine, cider, and all other liquors at their pleasure without control" and without paying excise taxes. They also allowed drinkers to "set and drink, play and revel in their houses at any time and as often as they please."[3] Thus the 1681 order resulted chiefly in an increase of the number of illicit, ungoverned companies of drinkers in open defiance of the law.

In answer to this complaint the deputies to the General Court reiterated demands for better enforcement. They ordered all officials to exert greater efforts to prosecute offenders. Tithingmen, grand jurors, and constables must "inspect all disorderly houses" and "prosecute the wholesome laws made against all such disorders." The Court also encouraged inhabitants to inform on the unlicensed by granting informers half of the fine imposed on any individual so convicted. But they were not confident that such actions would contain the demand for houses that the petition had revealed. Thus the deputies also decided to permit five more houses to be licensed in Boston the same year.[4]

They made more concessions to popular drinking habits in the following years. By the end of the 1680s the legal number of public houses had crept back up to forty-three, though Boston's population probably remained stable during this decade. By 1696, seventy-four people held licenses. Meanwhile, the direct supervision by the General Court (now more often called the Assembly) of the licensing system had lapsed; control had reverted to local selectmen and the county sessions courts. The incidence of legal drinksellers rose to its former level. Boston now had one public house (taverns and retailers) for approximately every one hundred people, or one for about every twenty adult males. Deputies also let lapse the ceiling on licenses in country towns, limited to one per town by the 1681 order. By 1688, four Middlesex County towns besides Charlestown

3. Petition of tavernkeepers to the Assembly, July 9, 1684, Taverns, 1643–1774, CXI, 48, ACM.

4. *Ibid.*; Shurtleff, ed., *Records*, V, 414, 448; Boston, Record Commissioners, *Boston Records from 1660 to 1701*, Report of the Record Commissioners of the City of Boston (Boston, 1881), 171, 203–204.

had more than one.[5] The Assembly gradually retreated from the standards set in 1681.

Yet the members of the Assembly remained uneasy about the number and character of public houses, especially in Boston. Sentiment among them and members of the judiciary to impose and enforce new restrictions did not diminish. Rulers continued to be reminded of their duties in this respect by the clergy. Moreover, the clergy and secular rulers confronted a series of jolts to the political stability of the colony in the last two decades of the century that made many more concerned with the maintenance of order. The crown had been hostile to the colony's defiant claims to autonomy since its founding. Only after the Restoration, however, did the Stuart monarchy take steps to abridge self-government in all the colonies and, particularly, in Massachusetts. James II voided the 1629 charter in 1686 and replaced it with the government of the Dominion of New England under the hated Edmund Andros. Leaders and people overturned the Andros regime in 1689 when news of the Glorious Revolution in England reached Boston. The interim government, which never possessed official legitimacy, was replaced by a new charter making Massachusetts a crown colony. A royal governor arrived in 1692 to rule together with an elected Assembly and Council. In all, Massachusetts experienced six major changes in the structure and personnel of government at the provincial level between 1686 and 1694. The new charter abolished the restriction of the franchise to church members. Now all adult males with twenty-four pounds sterling or a freehold valued at forty shillings per year could vote for representatives to the Assembly.[6] This action did not result in any

5. *Boston Records from 1660 to 1701*, 171, 203–204; List of licenseholders in Boston, Mar. 30, 1696, Taverns, 1643–1774, CXI, 57. The population figure used here is an estimate taken from Nash, *The Urban Crucible*, 407. He estimates that Boston had 6,000 people in 1687, of whom 1,330 were taxables; Court of General Sessions, Middlesex, Record Book (1686–1688), Sept. 4, 1688, 39–40, ACM.

6. William Pencak, *War, Politics, and Revolution in Provincial Massachusetts, 1630–1730* (Boston, 1981), chap. 2.

In 1686 James II created the Dominion of New England, a new political entity, which eventually comprised all the colonies north of Pennsylvania. The king appointed Governor Edmund Andros and local councils to rule; they assumed all judicial and legislative power. In 1689 the Dominion was overthrown, and Massachusetts resumed its former government until a new charter was issued by William III in 1691. Now the king appointed the governor, who in turn appointed all judicial and military officials. The governor could also veto acts of the General Court, which consisted of the Assembly or House of Representatives elected by the towns, and the governor's Council, elected by the representatives and

dramatic changes in the composition of the Assembly or in voting behavior. But it did strip the structure of colony authority of its Puritan identity, and some observers interpreted events as punishment from God for such sins as intemperance.

Some ministers and secular leaders perceived a greater need than ever for initiatives against intemperance and related disorders. In a 1692 sermon Cotton Mather declared that the newly instituted liberty of conscience in the colony could not be permitted to become a "cloak for liberty of profaneness." It remained the duty of all magistrates "to punish all the vices which disturb the good order and repose of humane society." Mather reminded rulers that England also had laws to punish drunkenness and idleness. For Samuel Willard the overthrow of Andros had been a frightening experience that might have implications for the future order of the colony. In a 1694 election sermon he told the magistrates and deputies that "when there was no governor in Israel, but every man did what he would, what horrible outrages were then perpetrated." "We ourselves have had a specimen of this in the short anarchy accompanying our late revolution."[7] He also warned that a people divided into factions became prone to elevate unworthy men to office. Unwelcome though royal government might be, many clergymen perceived a greater threat in a restive, assertive, and intemperate populace. Even as the Assembly retreated from its 1681 order reducing the number of public houses, its members were stimulated anew to make the governing hierarchy more visible and respected in public assemblies throughout the province.

The political instability of the 1680s and 1690s coincided with the introduction of rum into the colony on a large scale. By the last quarter of the seventeenth century, Boston merchants traded foodstuffs and raw materials to the West Indies in exchange for sugar and West India rum. In the 1660s Boston distillers had begun to produce a lower-quality, "New England" rum, which quickly became a primary trade item in the multitude of

---

the outgoing councillors with the governor's consent. The Assembly took the lead in initiating legislation and gradually identified itself with the House of Commons. Hereafter the terms "Assembly" and "House" will be used to name the legislative component of the government, as opposed to "General Court," which falls into disuse as the Assembly's importance rises.

7. Cotton Mather, *Optanda: Good Men Described . . .* (Boston, 1692), 46; Samuel Willard, *The Character of a Good Ruler . . .* (Boston, 1694), 3; see also T. H. Breen, *The Character of the Good Ruler: A Study of Puritan Political Ideas in New England, 1630–1730* (New York, 1974), chap. 4.

exchanges across the Atlantic that allowed Massachusetts to import and pay for manufactured goods from England. Thus rum began to figure prominently in the lives of colonists, particularly Bostonians. Drunkenness and more unguarded expressions of opinion might have increased dramatically during these years, evidenced by the Assembly's eventual move to forbid its sale in taverns in 1712.[8]

To control and wrest revenue from the trade in rum, the Assembly levied excise taxes on it and other beverages in the 1690s. In 1698 the tax on rum was twelve pence for every gallon sold in taverns or by retail, twice the levy on wine. Beer, ale, and cider—beverages manufactured in the colony and promoted as the common drinks—had the much lighter tax of eighteen pence per barrel, or about half a penny per gallon. These taxes required a new set of officials responsible for collection and the prosecution of those who tried to evade payment. The taxes compounded the existing problem of regulation, because unlicensed sellers sought to undersell the licenseholders who paid the excise. In 1698, twenty-three tavernkeepers and retailers, eight of them women, complained to the Assembly of their loss of trade to illicit sellers.[9] Thus while the excise increased the price of rum, it also spurred the growth of illegal sellers, so much so that some licenseholders faced a significant loss of their trade.

Passage of a spate of new laws in 1693, 1694, 1695, and 1698 accompanied the periodic levying of excise taxes. Most of these laws simply reiterated or slightly amended previous statutes. Patrons who sat in a tavern for more than an hour could be fined; licenseholders who permitted a patron to become drunk in their houses must also pay a penalty; offenders who could not pay their fines might have their possessions seized or be committed to prison. Retailers who allowed consumption in their houses and unlicensed sellers continued to be a focus of attention. In 1695 the members of the Assembly complained about inhabitants who were "so hardy as to run upon the law, in adventuring to sell" without license. Retailers who allowed consumption on the premises or sold drink they were not licensed to sell could now incur the same penalty as those who sold without license. Once again the Assembly ordered all officials in the hierarchy of regulation to enforce all the laws "diligently." Officials even

8. Bernard Bailyn, *The New England Merchants in the Seventeenth Century* (New York, 1964), 129, 130, 187; Massachusetts, *The Acts and Resolves, Public and Private, of the Province of the Massachusetts Bay . . .*, I (Boston, 1869), 679–680 (hereafter cited as *Acts and Resolves*).

9. *Ibid.*, 344–346; Petition of licenseholders to the Assembly against the excise, 1698, Taverns, 1643–1774, CXI, 69, ACM.

received the authority to enter and search the house of anyone previously convicted of selling without a license.[10]

Deputies to the Assembly also declared their support for a new ceiling on the number of licenses in the 1690s. The incidence of public houses had risen so quickly after the lapse of the Assembly's direct control of licensing that some members of the Assembly proposed that they once again seize the power to determine how many licenses might be issued. Nathaniel Saltonstall, Haverhill's representative to the House, wrote to the Essex County justices in 1696 hinting that another takeover of the system might ensue if the justices did not reduce the number of public houses:

> I always thought it great prudence and Christianity in our former leaders and rulers, by their laws to state the number for public houses in towns, and for regulation of such houses. . . . But alas, I see not but that now, the care is over. . . . I pray what need of six retailers in Salisbury, and of more than one in Haverhill, and some other towns, where the people when taxes and rates for the country and ministers are collecting with open mouth complain of poverty and being rudely dealt with, and yet I am fully informed, can spend much time, and spend their estate at such blind holes, as are clandestinely and unjustly petitioned for, and more threaten to get licenses.[11]

Two years later a majority of the Assembly agreed to consider the imposition of new restrictions similar to those ordered in 1681. They proposed that the House "do set the number of innholders and retailers that shall be in each town." But while the House voted for this measure, the governor and Council rejected it, perhaps in recognition of the forces that had undermined the 1681 curtailment.[12]

All branches of government, however, did agree to tighten procedures to acquire a license. By law of 1698 the time when justices could review, consider, and issue licenses became limited to the first session annually of the courts of general sessions. Further, licenseholders must become bound for twenty pounds and take an oath to observe all drink-related laws. Justices also received new instructions from the Assembly to refrain from licensing any more houses than they shall "judge necessary for the receiving and refreshment of travelers and strangers" and for the "public

10. *Acts and Resolves*, I, 56–57, 154–155, 190–192, 327–330.

11. Nathaniel Saltonstall to Justices of Quarter Sessions in Salem, Dec. 26, 1696, Prince Collection, MHS.

12. Proposals for the Regulating of Innholders and Retailers of Wine and Liquors, June 8, 1698, Taverns, 1643–1774, CXI, 63, 67b.

occasions" of each town. By establishing a special licensing session where all renewals and applications could be considered at one time, the Assembly took back part of the power delegated to county justices in the 1640s; for at any other time of the year applicants must first petition the governor, Council, and Assembly for authorization to go before the justices to ask for a license.[13] Thus while the Assembly stopped short of seizing the administration of the licensing system in 1698, it did alter it so as to discourage applications throughout the year by making the provincial government the first seat of approval for such applications. For some licensing decisions, the selectmen and justices now shared authority with the governor, Council, and Assembly. In some ways these procedures made the acquisition and renewal of a license more rigorous than in England, where county justices almost alone controlled the issuance of licenses. Still, there existed at least a potential for popular input into the decisions made by licensing authorities. Applicants first sought approval from local boards of selectmen, who must stand for election annually before their townsmen.

II

Despite the painstaking efforts by the Assembly, the number of public houses remained at issue. In 1704 the governor, Council, and Assembly reminded the justices that "for many years last past the General Assembly, as well as the ministers in the several parts, have . . . labored to prevent the growth of intemperance and debauchery by all possible means and among others by abridging the number of public houses in Boston, Charlestown, and Salem, the principal seaports for the presence of seamen and strangers." For the future, the letter continued, the justices should take particular care that only "persons of good reputation be licensed"; further, that licenses be given to "men and no widows who cannot support the government of their houses." Once again the Assembly considered fixing the number of licenses, but there is no record of any action taken. The letter to the justices might have been a veiled warning that such an action might be taken if justices did not reduce licenses and enforce laws.[14] Pressure on licensing officials to contain the number issued continued.

13. *Acts and Resolves*, I, 329. This law does not explicitly state that applicants seeking licenses at times other than the licensing sessions must first apply to provincial authorities, but this must have been the intention because Taverns, 1643–1774, CXI, is full of such petitions asking for authorization to go before the justices for a license.

14. Order of General Court concerning Innholders, June 27, 1704, Taverns, 1643–1774, CXI, 76.

The 1704 letter to the justices reflects unanimity between members of the Assembly and the clergy in the prosecution of vice. Certainly there existed joint purpose and cooperation. But clergymen in particular agitated to pressure lawmakers to act, again and again. Clergymen had failed to persuade their congregations to alter their habits voluntarily. Now they turned to lawmakers to compel changes in behavior. In 1704 Cotton Mather chose to publish, not another sermon condemning drinking, but an abstract of mainly drink laws as a "faithful monitor" for law enforcement officials. He included guidance on how to level censures and rebukes, when to exercise discretion, and when to be firm and unyielding.[15] Mather had taken it upon himself to advise directly on law enforcement, to energize the hierarchy of enforcement through a pamphlet directed to them.

Clergymen could not make law; they could only urge it. But they urged it repeatedly, sometimes pleading and sometimes making dire predictions of divine retribution. In 1709, Mendon minister Grindal Rawson delivered an election sermon on the necessity of a "speedy and thorough reformation." In this oration before governor, Council, and Assembly he called for more laws against vice. If experience shows the "insufficiency" of previous laws, he declared, "must not others be contrived and established, which will offer a greater probability of success?" Lawmakers heard this refrain year in and year out. And they continued to act. One year after the Rawson sermon the Assembly ordered that only one tavernkeeper and one retailer be licensed in all country towns unless selectmen of the town judged that there existed a need for more to service travelers.[16] Selectmen retained some discretion in their exercise of their power of approval, but they came under pressure to justify each license. Thus did the Assembly continue to heed clerical injunctions.

With this series of new laws and excise taxes between 1690 and 1710, together with the renewal of efforts to reduce the incidence of public houses, the members of the Assembly mounted a more intensive attack on the popular culture of drink. They could do so within a political culture where questions of policy, particularly those concerning moral regulation, remained strictly within the province of the narrow segment of society considered qualified to rule over others. As minister Ebenezer Pemberton put it, "Rulers are gods," and "their character demands submission and obedience from a people." On the surface, colonists submitted to the pater-

15. Cotton Mather, *A Faithful Monitor, Offering an Abstract of the Laws in the Province of the Massachusetts-Bay* ... (Boston, 1704), 4, 8–10, 13–15, 19–20, 52–53.

16. Grindal Rawson, *The Necessity of a Speedy and Thorough Reformation* (Boston, 1709), 28; *Acts and Resolves*, I, 664.

nal guidance exercised by rulers, and rulers acted without fear of popular retribution. Elected representative Nathaniel Saltonstall did not hesitate to criticize the number of taverns in Haverhill despite their popular followings. When representatives enacted harsher restrictions on drinking, they implicitly revealed their confidence in their ability to maintain their elevated positions within society. The series of new laws in the 1690s is indirect testimony to the willingness of voters to reelect those men who had passed these widely evaded and unpopular laws. Elected representatives and voters alike remained conscious of the "character of the good ruler" in respect to drink regulation. Samuel Willard reminded the government in 1694 that the "liberties and rights" preserved by the rebellion of 1689 could never be safeguarded unless the government restrained vice and promoted virtue.[17] A government that gave free rein to vice was a government that would eventually be overwhelmed by vice. Virtue must be cultivated among the people so that they might recognize and submit to their superior rulers.

Yet, by the enactment of these new laws and by efforts to reduce the number of public houses, the Assembly began to strain the capacity of the law to achieve social reform and control. By repeatedly ordering all elected and appointed officials to enforce the laws vigorously, the Assembly came close to exposing the weakness of both law and the authority of elected officials in the face of popular resistance. This is implicit in the 1675 warning to tithingmen that, if they "neglect of their duty, and shall be so judged by authority, they shall incur the same penalty provided against unlicensed houses"—the houses they were supposed to discover and prosecute. Again, in 1695, the Assembly warned all officials that, if they were convicted of "taking any bribe, fee, reward directly or indirectly" or of conspiring to conceal or overlook violations of certain drink laws, then those officials would be required to pay three times the value of the bribe.[18] Such warnings narrowed the discretion that officials responsible for enforcement could exercise and moved them into the category of potential lawbreakers themselves. The Assembly sought to uphold the law by compelling the machinery of enforcement on which it rested—justices, selectmen, tithingmen, grand jurors—to use their personal and official authority

17. Ebenezer Pemberton, *The Divine Original and Dignity of Government Asserted . . .* (Boston, 1710), 85; Willard, *The Character of a Good Ruler,* 16, 24, 26; Breen, *The Character of the Good Ruler,* 202.

18. Edmund S. Morgan, ed., *Puritan Political Ideas, 1558–1794* (New York, 1965), 231; *Acts and Resolves,* I, 191.

to promote respect for the ordinances. But by so doing it also risked provoking confrontation between elected officials and the populace at large.

The problem of enforcement, or lack thereof, became most acute in Boston. Selectmen in particular came under conflicting pressures. The seaport towns—periodically a berth to mariners temporarily leaving the cycle of shipboard labor—had always been the seats of intemperance in magistrates' eyes. Boston's population increased from about six thousand in 1690 to more than ten thousand by 1720. With a growing proportion of its population consisting of mariners and laborers, the influence of the church over the populace weakened. By one estimate the churches of the town in 1690 could seat only about a quarter of the population, and by 1720 this proportion had dropped to one-fifth. Cotton Mather and other Boston ministers became so concerned over the eclipse of clerical influence that they published *Proposals*, measures to strengthen the ministry as an institution, in 1702.[19] In such a setting reformers encountered deeper-seated resistance.

Boston selectmen, together with Suffolk County justices, did make an effort to adhere to Assembly directives. The seventy-five houses licensed in 1696 dropped to a low of sixty in 1705 at about the same time as the Assembly considered seizing the licensing system once again. The number approved and licensed rose to seventy-two by 1708, but selectmen reduced the number once more to sixty-one in 1710, the year when the Assembly agitated again for reductions. The diligence of selectmen in holding licenses to a minimum is reflected in their refusal in 1705 to approve five applicants who had acquired the approval of the justices; the selectmen declared "it to be their opinion that there are more than enough of such licensed houses already, and that the new granting of more will be of ill consequence to this town." Later the same year the selectmen vetoed an applicant approved by the justices to keep the important Green Dragon Tavern. Two years later they denied approval to another applicant for the same tavern because of reports of disorder and gaming in his previous establishment. In 1709 the selectmen refused even to consider sixteen petitions for licenses because, they said, "there is more than enough" public houses in the town. The next year, responding to the act for "reducing the over great number of licensed houses," they decided not to renew

19. Carl Bridenbaugh, *Cities in the Wilderness: The First Century of Urban Life in America, 1625–1742* (New York, 1938), 264; [Cotton Mather], *Proposals For the Preservation of Religion in the Churches, by a Due Trial of Them That Stand Candidates of the Ministry* [Boston, 1702].

sixteen licenses. Again, in 1713, they denied renewal to nine licenseholders, and to ten more in 1714. Even though the population had increased from approximately sixty-seven hundred in 1700 to about ten thousand by 1720, Boston's selectmen allowed no increase in licenses and thereby reduced the incidence of public houses. As of 1718, seventy-four people held licenses in the town. This was one fewer than the number in 1696, twenty-two years earlier.[20] Thus between 1700 and 1719 the selectmen, elected annually at the Boston town meeting, heeded the orders and policies of the Assembly by taking the unpopular steps to reduce access to public houses.

Selectmen also had to confront the issue of rum as clergymen tried to prevent it from becoming a staple alcoholic drink in the colony. Cotton Mather registered his mounting concern over the introduction of rum for wide consumer use in a sermon devoted to the issue in 1708. Mather did not advocate a complete ban on the sale of rum; he could "readily allow, it's being of a manifold use, both as a medicine, and a cordial," and even for use by laborers at certain times to "fortify" them. But Mather feared that the unlimited use of rum might "overwhelm all good order among us." Secular leaders and church members must set an example if they would not "unqualify themselves" for their positions. If authorities did not curtail the consumption, the "votaries of strong drink" might "grow so numerous that they will make a party against anything that is holy, and just, and good." Although Mather hesitated to make specific suggestions how to dam the "flood of rum," he did ask "that our legislators would please to take the matter into their consideration."[21]

Boston selectmen responded accordingly. In 1714 they admitted James Pitson, a "ciderman" from London, as an inhabitant of the town and approved his petition to retail. The selectmen thought that the skillful manufacture of cider might prove a common benefit to the town. Presumably it might reduce the demand for rum. A year later they warned a distiller from London to leave, claiming there was no need for any more distillers in the town.[22]

Selectmen and lesser officials also participated in the visits and patrols of officials recommended by the Assembly to enhance enforcement in

20. Compiled from Court of General Sessions, Suffolk, Record Books, 1702–1712, 1712–1719, ACM; Boston, Record Commissioners, *Records of Boston Selectmen, 1701 to 1715* (Boston, 1884), 46–47, 52, 63, 91–92, 111–112, 187, 212.

21. Cotton Mather, *Sober Considerations, on a Growing Flood of Iniquity* . . . (Boston, 1708), 5, 15, 16, 18.

22. *Records of Boston Selectmen, 1701 to 1715*, 218, 227.

every town. In January 1707, councillors, justices, selectmen, and over-seers of the poor met and agreed to pay visits to every family in the town on a specified day in order to discourage disorderly conduct. They orga-nized eight teams of two or more councillors and justices, a selectman, a constable, and a tithingman. Officials made similar agreements regularly over the course of the next decade. Most of these visits took place during the day, after which officials gathered at the Town House to discuss their findings. By agreements made beginning in 1712, councillors and justices also walked and inspected at night.[23]

Some of the most prominent men in the province led these processions of lesser officials: Paul Dudley, attorney general and justice of the court of general sessions; Major John Walley, councillor and justice of the Superior Court; Colonel Elisha Hutchinson, councillor and justice of sessions; Ed-ward Bromfield, justice of the Superior Court and sessions; and Samuel Sewall, councillor and justice of the Superior Court. Even though ten watchmen patrolled the town from 10:00 P.M. until dawn, with the added assistance of constables and tithingmen commissioned to quell disorders, now leaders considered it necessary for judges and councillors to lend assistance so as to close the gap between law and enforcement.[24]

Constables and tithingmen had long been under pressure to enforce drink legislation. In 1690 Governor Simon Bradstreet, Sewall, Elisha Hutchinson, and two other councillors had personally composed warrants that required constables "to walk through the several parts of the town this day, and take effectual care to suppress and dissipate all unlawful assemblies, or tumultuous gathering together of people" for games and other "disorders." The order had come one year after the overthrow of Edmund Andros, when this act of rebellion had made many leaders anx-ious over "tumultuous gatherings." In 1712 shortages of grain also made local and provincial leaders nervous. Underlying these particular circum-stances, however, lay a chronic conflict between Puritan standards of social discipline and the popular culture of tavern assemblies. Thus in 1712 Sewall did not just bestow a warrant in the hands of Boston constables but on occasion personally led them through the streets of the town.[25]

Sewall and his associate justices and councillors expected that their presence would lend greater dignity and authority to the offices of consta-ble and tithingman and also place pressure on them as well as selectmen to

23. *Ibid.*, 55–56, 62, 67.

24. *Ibid.*; Boston, Record Commissioners, *Boston Town Records from 1700 to 1728* (Bos-ton, 1883), 3, 5, 7, 24, 43, 48, 61, 152, 176, 214.

25. *Diary*, I, 252–253; *Records of Boston Selectmen, 1701 to 1715*, 99, 106, 194.

pursue enforcement more aggressively. The personal involvement of men of Sewall's high status in these patrols became a means of closing the gap implicit in the 1690s legislation that repeatedly ordered "all officers" to uphold the law yet simultaneously categorized lower officials as potential offenders by threatening their prosecution for bribes. No one wished to be appointed or elected a tithingman. As early as 1679 two-thirds of the tithingmen chosen in Salem refused to take the oath required of them, presumably because they knew they would not or could not execute their duties according to the letter of the oath. The Assembly levied a forty-shilling fine on those who refused to serve.[26] By walking with tithingmen, however, justices and councillors hoped to infuse the office with new respect.

From the 1630s forward, Puritan magistrates and representatives to the Assembly had gradually constructed a hierarchy of regulation and enforcement from justices and selectmen down to tithingmen and paid informers. Now they urged this hierarchy of officials to make themselves more visible in processional display through the streets of Boston. In many respects it was a traditional display of authority, an impressive tableau of the social and political hierarchy in miniature. As Ebenezer Pemberton put it in 1710, "There are various degrees and orders of men engaged in the administrations of rule," and "each degree have their proper sphere to move and act in."[27] This principle underlay the processions of officials that visited families by day and walked the streets by night.

But the purpose of this traditional hierarchy was in part modern. These officials walked to suppress popular gatherings to drink, to purge Boston society of customs and habits of centuries' vintage—customs that had not long ago contributed to the cohesion of the English social hierarchy and order. Could a traditional society, a society of ranks and degrees, remake itself selectively? Could Puritan leaders preserve some aspects of traditional society and institutions, and purge others? Such was the difficult metamorphosis that leaders like Sewall sought to execute when they led lesser men to inspect the town for drink-related disorders.

To some extent, Sewall and his fellow magistrates succeeded. These inspections and tours did have an impact on the populace of Boston, judging from the small number of minor disorders that Sewall recorded when he participated. Even Guy Fawkes Day passed uncelebrated on November 5, 1709, when Sewall patrolled. In 1715 he dispersed a group of players at

26. William Hathourne *et al.* to the General Court, Nov. 30, 1679, Towns, 1632–1693, CXII, 311, ACM; *Acts and Resolves*, I, 190–191, 329.

27. Pemberton, *The Divine Original*, 13–14.

ninepins at "Mount Whoredom" (Beacon Hill), but he found that "gener-ally, the town was peaceable and in good order." At no time did he encoun-ter the degree of resistance he confronted at the Wallis tavern, when even a councillor and justice had difficulty in dispersing a group of men assem-bled to drink the health of the queen. These patrols, however, appear to have been well publicized and anticipated. Moreover, by agreement, Sewall and others deemed it necessary to extend the length of time they remained active. In 1712 leaders agreed that the councillors, justices, and selectmen should walk the town for a period of eight weeks.[28] Constables could not exert sufficient authority by themselves, or hesitated to do so at all.

Along with constables and tithingmen, the selectmen who walked through the town at night must also have had mixed feelings about the efficacy of their actions. Both selectmen and justices had ignored the Assembly's orders to refrain from licensing widows. When the visitation policy began in 1707, women operated twenty-six of the sixty-three legal houses in the town. For most, the sale of alcohol represented their sole means of support; they needed to move as much alcohol as possible in order to support themselves and their children. Moreover, the number of li-censes that the selectmen decided not to approve for renewal suggests that a majority of licenseholders routinely violated the spirit and letter of the drink laws. Between 1703 and 1718 selectmen objected to the renewal of more than seventy licenses. As of 1714, twenty-eight of eighty tavernkeep-ers and retailers had faced difficulties in renewing their licenses or would face them in the future.[29] Such a high rate of reluctance and refusal to renew licenses suggests widespread disregard for the drink laws, ulti-mately bringing them into question. Selectmen eventually withdrew al-most all of their objections to renewals after those denied approval repeat-edly pleaded for reconsideration of their cases. Acquiescence by selectmen suggests that they recognized the limits to their ability to compel confor-mity to the laws through their power of approval and renewal.

Selectmen wrestled with more difficulties than the problem of renewals. Holding the number of legal houses to a minimum also forced them to reject a growing number of petitioners who knew that the town could

28. *Diary*, II, 795; *Records of Boston Selectmen, 1701 to 1715*, 172, 185.

29. Petition of tavernkeepers in and around Boston against the excise, 1698, Taverns, 1643–1774, CXI, 69. Of the 23, 8 were women. All complained of the slim profit margin imposed by the excise. Court of General Sessions, Suffolk, Record Book, 1702–1712, 156–157; *Records of Boston Selectmen, 1701 to 1715*, 33–35, 46, 63, 91–92, 111–112, 166, 187, 212, 231; Boston, Record Commissioners, *Records of Boston Selectmen, 1716 to 1736* (Boston, 1885), 6, 20, 40.

support a higher number of houses. Between 1702 and 1715 they rejected more than 300 petitions (including those submitted more than once) while approving only 128.[30] The selectmen who refused so many applicants repeatedly confronted the pressure of the populace at large for greater and easier access to taverns and drink.

Crowd actions in 1711 to prevent the exportation of grain during a shortage probably helped to provoke new legislation from the Assembly in 1712, the Act against Intemperance, Immorality, and Profaneness, and for Reformation of Manners. Once again the hierarchy of regulators received orders to "exert their utmost zeal and vigor in seeing that the said several laws be duly observed and kept, and that the violators thereof be duly prosecuted and punished." In this law the Assembly recommended that night patrols be instituted everywhere: "The selectmen and other principal well-disposed persons in each town, desirous of a reformation, are hereby exhorted and directed to countenance, [ac]company, assist, and join with the justices, sheriffs, tithingmen, constables, and other officers, in their endeavors to discover and suppress all unlicensed houses and vice."[31] The Assembly urged processions of officials in every town to act.

The Assembly also seemed to acknowledge the failure of previous laws, because it saw fit to reiterate them. But this law also contained new provisions. It tightened licensing procedures by requiring written certifications of approval from selectmen; forbade fiddling, piping, and other music in taverns; renewed orders for the choosing of tithingmen; ordered the appointment of informers in every town; and provided that the names of "common drunkards" be posted in the houses of all retailers. The most important provision of this new law, however, was the radical decision to ban the sale of distilled liquors in taverns.[32] Colonists could still purchase rum and brandy from duly licensed retailers, but they could not consume it in tavern companies. In light of the recent crowd actions in 1711, members of the Assembly might have banned distilled liquors in taverns because they suspected that consumption of rum contributed to the coalescence of agitated crowds. Rum might have helped to inspire aggressive words and postures, a violation of the manners expected from common men.

Such a drastic ban, however, ultimately served only to expose further the underlying weakness of these new initiatives to control the trade in drink. Compliance with the ban on the sale of distilled liquors in taverns cannot be determined with precision. But excise levies and inventories of

30. Compiled from *Records of Boston Selectmen, 1701 to 1715*, 106, 151.

31. *Acts and Resolves*, I, 679–680.

32. *Ibid.*

drink can roughly reveal the proportion of drinksellers who continued to sell rum and brandy. Approximately 40 percent of the thirty-nine Boston tavernkeepers licensed in 1715, three years after the enactment of the ban, probably complied with the law, according to excise levies of that year. The low assessment of excise tax from these tavernkeepers suggests that they sold fermented beverages, mainly cider. David Copp, for example, had 105 gallons of cider in stock at the time of his death in 1718; Sarah Wormall, licensed from 1716 to 1721, had only 12 gallons of wine as opposed to 131 of cider. Neither had any rum or brandy, although Wormall owed money for spirits. Nathaniel Emons had 189 gallons of cider and only 1 gallon of brandy in 1721.[33] All three probably had licenses to sell only beer, ale, and cider. Beer and ale, however, do not figure prominently in any Boston inventories in the early eighteenth century. This infrequency suggests that, while cider had become the basic alcoholic drink, rum might have begun to replace beer as a popular alternative. Using Copp's excise as a measure, fourteen other tavernkeepers sold mainly cider.

Fifteen other tavernkeepers, or 40 percent, paid more than ten pounds excise in 1715, a strong indication that they sold distilled liquors in large quantities in defiance of the ban. Thomas Gilbert, for example, paid sixteen pounds excise. In 1719 he had 218 gallons of rum and brandy, 255 of wine, 735 of cider, and 54 of dead cider mixed with wine in his cellars. In 1717 Edward Durant had no cider at all, but did have 250 gallons of rum and other spirits. Samuel Mears, licensed from 1708 to 1726, drew on 320 gallons of rum and brandy, sixty pounds worth of wines, and only 16 gallons of cider. Thomas Selby, proprietor of the Crown Coffee House from 1714 to 1725, paid twenty-five pounds excise, the highest paid by a tavernkeeper in 1715. At his death in 1725 he had more than a thousand pounds worth of liquors in his house, almost all of it wine, rum, and brandy.[34] When the Assembly banned the sale of distilled liquors in tav-

33. Court of General Sessions, Suffolk, Record Book, 1712–1719, 93; Suffolk County Probate Records, Record Book, XXI, 351–352, XXII, 370, 528, Judicial Archives, ACM. Standards of measurement used were determined from the *Oxford English Dictionary*. For example, one pipe of port equals 115 gallons, but only 100 gallons of Tenerife wine.

34. Suffolk County Probate Records, XX, 388–399, XXI, 561, XXV, 530–536, XXVII, 269. A tavernkeeper like Thomas Selby, who was also a merchant, might have sold large amounts of rum to retailers in Boston and other towns. The law is not clear on this point. But most tavernkeepers with inventories of rum undoubtedly sold it for consumption in their rooms in violation of the 1712 law. If they had begun to sell it by retail (in violation of their licenses) to evade the law, duly licensed retailers of rum would have protested the

erns in 1712, it was reacting to a continuing shift in consumption toward more potent beverages. But almost half of the tavernkeepers licensed three years after the ban appear to have paid the law no heed. Even the excise officers proceeded as usual.

Perhaps the greatest index of shifts in consumption is the subsequent career of James Pitson, the London ciderman admitted as a resident in 1714 (two years after the ban on rum) in order to promote cider. Pitson, however, proceeded to acquire a license to sell distilled liquors in 1717 and moved to keep tavern on King Street near the Town House. At his death in 1737 he still sold mainly cider—530 gallons of it. Yet he also had in stock Canary wine and 161 gallons of West India and New England rum. Cotton Mather estimated in 1708 that Boston imported fifteen hundred hogsheads, or almost 78,750 gallons, of rum each year for consumption in this town of fewer than ten thousand and for distribution into the interior.[35] Whether it was the taste of rum that appealed, especially when mixed with limes and lemons in punch, or its capacity to induce intoxication more quickly, rum rapidly became one of the most desired drinks in Boston. Some tavernkeepers appear to have sold rum and nothing else, judging from their inventories.

It is perhaps because of the failure of the 1712 ban on the sale of rum in taverns that Benjamin Wadsworth adopted a more conciliatory tone in his sermon on intemperance in 1716. He conceded that town dwellers "may sometimes have proper occasions to go into taverns, and stay a while there," particularly if they have specific business to conduct. By previous laws town dwellers could be fined for sitting in a tavern. Wadsworth also conceded that the use of strong drink, including rum, "is not only lawful, but in some cases convenient." Many abuse rum and other beverages, but "it does not thence follow that 'tis unlawful to use them." Significantly, he did not mention or explicitly defend the 1712 ban, an indirect admission of its failure. Having made these concessions, however, he stated his conviction that drinksellers had become "more dangerous to the public, than so many Indians on the frontiers." The allure of Indian culture, together with warriors' skill in warfare, posed a challenge to the colony's social mores, goals, and stability from without. Unrestrained consumption in taverns threatened to subvert Puritan culture from within. After all the laws that had been passed, together with the continuing restriction of the issuance of

---

competition. Selby probably also ignored the law in his own tavern, since he owned eight silver punch bowls commonly used for rum punch.

35. *Records of Boston Selectmen, 1716 to 1736*, 27; Suffolk County Probate Records, Record Book, XXXIV, 360–364; [Mather], *Sober Considerations*, 2.

licenses, reformation seemed more elusive than ever. Wadsworth blamed intemperance for setbacks in the colony: "God is in various ways contending with us." He "has punished us by a long war," and "last summer we met with disappointment" by a "very severe drought." Therefore, rulers and ruled "should not only talk of a Reformation, but diligently and heartily endeavor it."[36] Ministers continued to press the Assembly to act despite the recent failure of the 1712 ban.

III

But the more efforts expended for reform in sermon and law, the more apparent the deeply embedded resistance to it. Wadsworth spoke in a far less conciliatory manner in a sermon he published three years later in 1719 on "vicious courses." Once again he denounced those town dwellers who spent hours, an entire night, or even entire days in taverns when only travelers should be there. He wondered why drink continued to be so important to hospitality, why persons "tempt and prompt others to drink to excess" and "think they can scarce make them welcome, if they don't make them drunk." To give the bottle to one's neighbor is deemed "good fellowship," Wadsworth lamented, but it is truly "damning wickedness." Colonists must avoid "fellowship" that undermined the rational pursuit of religious truth under the guidance of a learned ministry. Immersed in the world of print, Wadsworth could not understand the stubborn vitality of customs of drink distribution and exchange.[37]

Most colonists, however, continued to reconcile the use of drink, now including rum, with the patterns of fellowship so vital to the conduct of everything from the transmission of news to the execution of business transactions. "Is it not vile," Wadsworth asked, that scarcely anyone can make "a bargain, make up accounts, pay or receive a little money, but that they must needs go to a tavern, and solemnize the matter as it were by swallowing strong drink?" Colonists did this, although "neither the time of day, nor state of their bodies calls for any such thing." And why, he continued, "can't tradesmen finish or bring home a piece of work, but must almost think themselves wronged, if they are not treated with strong drink?" Every transaction must be ratified with drink. An advocate of the apprenticeship of women in retail trade later argued that women would purchase goods from wholesale merchants at less expense than men, be-

36. Benjamin Wadsworth, *An Essay to Do Good* ... (Boston, 1710), 2–3, 20, 22.

37. Benjamin Wadsworth, *Vicious Courses, Procuring Poverty Describ'd and Condemn'd* ... (Boston, 1719), 15, 17, 20, 21.

cause the latter "generally transact all business of this kind in taverns and coffee houses, at a great additional expense, and the loss of much time."[38] Wadsworth thereby described the ready adaptation of traditional drinking to the execution of agreements in emerging structures of commerce.

Wadsworth's criticisms, however, ignored the tensions and doubts inherent in the conduct of business that the exchange of drink helped to ease. Men chose to "solemize" transactions of the sort mentioned by Wadsworth with drink because so much depended on each party's faith in the other's forbearance. Like most colonists, Boston tavernkeepers routinely enmeshed themselves in a dense network of paper and book debts and obligations, agreements made particularly necessary by the chronic shortage of specie in Massachusetts.[39] For each of these debts individuals had to solicit the good faith of another. Once one had succeeded in getting credit, the debtor had to trust the creditor's willingness to allow the debt to be paid off gradually, according to the debtor's capacity. In turn the creditor had to be persuaded of the debtor's good credit, or the ability to meet obligations at some future time. The creditor had to trust that this debtor had not incurred so many obligations to so many unknown people that the debtor could not possibly meet them all. So much depended on a shrewd assessment of another's ability, assets, and character.

Cotton Mather devoted an entire tract to debtor-creditor relationships in 1716. After cautioning debtors on their behavior and attitudes, he besought creditors to "have as much patience with them as you can." If "debtors be honest, and struggle and wrestle for it, and have any merit in them," then treat them "with all the goodness and mercy of a brother." In the personal nature of money transactions, drink consumed at taverns helped to inspire the feelings and attitudes Mather advocated. Debtors and creditors exchanged drink as a token of acknowledgment by two parties to the mutual trust they had come to invest in each other. Drink helped to

38. *Ibid.*, 16–17; *Boston Gazette*, Mar. 24, 1740, no. 1052. The fact that so much business was conducted in taverns was an additional discouragement to women's entering commerce.

39. For an example of a creditor who loaned money on a large scale, see the estate papers of Thomas Selby, Suffolk County Probate Records, Record Book, XXV, 530–535, N.S., XIV, 72–76. For an example of a poor debtor who borrowed money from more than 10 people, see estate of John Smallpeice, XXII, 199–201. Gordon S. Wood suggests that such personal networks of debt might have been more extensive in the colonies than in England because of the lack of commercial institutions like banks and the relative backwardness of the colonial economies (*The Radicalism of the American Revolution* [New York, 1992], 66–67).

ease the deliberations necessary to receive and lend money. This was why individuals sat down with each other at taverns even to "pay or receive a little money" or "make up accounts."[40] Wholesale avoidance of taverns and drink had not yet become a significant measure of good credit, despite clerical efforts to link it with temperance.

Meetings at taverns to solemnize the execution of business normally helped to forestall situations where creditors made sudden demands on debtors, and provided an environment conducive to negotiation for more time or money. Of course, at various times creditors would call in debts. When Edward Lutwyche decided to give up the Crown Coffee House, which he rented, and move to the country, he put a notice in the newspaper asking all persons indebted to him to pay so "that he may be enabled to comply with his creditors."[41] Lutwyche must satisfy creditors before he moved, and so he placed pressure on those indebted to him. Death and the consequent settlement of estates also cut through myriad latticeworks of credit negotiated in taverns.

Occasionally the entire edifice of credit and debt came crashing down, as in 1720 when a shortage of specie and credit stimulated a large number of legal actions for repayment of debts in Boston. According to one commentator, creditors took harsh steps against "good honest housekeepers, who are willing to pay their debts, . . . and have the wherewith to pay, but can't raise money." Meetings at taverns helped to alleviate the anxiety and suspicion that accompanied the dispensation of credit and offered a means to avoid the courts. Even when in prison for nonpayment, debtors would commonly plead to work out some accommodation with all their creditors by arranging to meet with them as a group at taverns.[42]

As ministers like Wadsworth moved to condemn more and more dimensions of tavern life, popular resistance became more emphatic. Boston selectmen confronted it at town meetings when it came time to choose tithingmen. Back in 1676 the selectmen had chosen seventy-three such officials responsible for the discovery of unlicensed houses and the inspection of families. The number so chosen, however, steadily declined in

40. Cotton Mather, *Fair Dealing between Debtor and Creditor* . . . (Boston, 1716), 25; Wadsworth, *Vicious Courses*, 21. Solomon Stoddard also addressed the issue of relations between debtors and creditors in *An Answer to Some Cases of Conscience respecting the Country* (Boston, 1722), 1–2.

41. *Boston Gazette,* Jan. 15–22, 1739, no. 952.

42. John Colman, *The Distressed State of the Town of Boston* . . . (Boston, 1720), 1, 5; notices for creditors to appear at tavern meetings are in the *Boston Gazette,* June 5–12, 1727, no. 393, July 23–30, 1733, no. 708.

succeeding decades, especially after tithingmen began to be elected by town meeting in the 1690s. In 1701 Boston representatives to the Assembly were instructed by the town meeting to modify the strict oath required of tithingmen. By this date they numbered fewer than twenty, despite the fact that Boston's population had increased by several thousand.[43]

In 1704 Cotton Mather tried to encourage tithingmen to execute their duties by stating in his compilation of regulations that their oath of office did not oblige them to bring every offender before a justice. He set forth different "reproofs" and "Christian admonitions" that tithingmen might employ to warn some offenders. Although Mather believed that "all Christians must be informers," he did concede that tithingmen might exercise discretion by choosing from several options how to proceed. If the offense was not part of a chronic pattern, an oral reproof might be sufficient. Mather tried to soften and reinterpret the oath of these officials in the face of widespread reluctance to take up the office.[44]

But tithingmen were reluctant even to issue warnings or "reproofs" to their neighbors. To censure or disperse a group of men making each other welcome with drink invited hostile repercussions in the future. As Samuel Danforth lamented in 1710, some continued to "applaud and commend hard and long and frequent drinkings as being generosity and sociableness." Solomon Stoddard of Northampton also took notice of this conflict in values in 1722. "Drunkenness, Sabbath breaking, and other sins," he stated, "are seldom punished for want of information." Many persons "are bound by oath to inquire into disorders and give information," but informers "are obnoxious to themselves, and are afraid that if they bring out others, that they shall be brought out." Informers "are afraid that others will be disgusted, that it will be a foundation of ill-will and contention." In Boston, six men paid fines for refusing to take the tithingman's oath in 1710. While tithingmen continued to be members of the eight teams of officials visiting families in 1707, it is doubtful that they walked with other officials after 1710, because they were not mentioned in succeeding agreements. And in 1727 Boston and seven other Suffolk towns refused to elect them at all.[45]

To some extent excisemen took up the duties of tithingmen, especially

43. David H. Flaherty, *Privacy in Colonial New England* (Charlottesville, Va., 1972), 195–200.

44. [Mather], *A Faithful Monitor*, 26, 52–54.

45. Samuel Danforth, *The Woful Effects of Drunkenness* ... (Boston, 1710), 40; Stoddard, *Some Cases of Conscience*, 10; Flaherty, *Privacy In Colonial New England*, 195–200; Court of General Sessions, Suffolk, Record Book, 1712–1719, Oct. 31, 1727, 123, ACM.

the detection of unlicensed houses. But the functions of the two offices differed. Tithingmen had been appointed to assist in the regulation of behavior. Excise officers concerned themselves mainly with the efficient collection of taxes due the colony government; they did not seek to report and punish excessive drinking. The decline and extinction of tithingmen in Massachusetts towns reflects the waning force of Puritan morality generally and, particularly, the persistence of collective drinking. When not buttressed by the eminence of justices like Sewall, tithingmen risked isolation from the neighbors and associates that higher authorities ordered them to disperse and inform against.

Ultimately this series of moves by the Assembly from 1681 through the 1710s to close the widening gap between Puritan social mores and social reality only exposed the Puritan hierarchy of enforcement and its various laws to contempt by the populace at large. The 1712 Act against Intemperance—in some ways the most emphatic, alarmist, and severe of all the laws enacted from 1630 to 1720—was also the last major legislation passed on the subject until after the Revolution. Whether members of the Assembly realized the implications for law enforcement if they passed more legislation is not a matter of record. Yet it is clear that by progressively defining the popular use of taverns and drink as excessive and illegal—and by placing pressure again and again on all officials to enforce the laws—the Assembly had transformed the law from a tool to promote order into a spark to disorder. Laws became less an expression of their authority than a stark exposure of the limits of their authority. By the second decade of the eighteenth century, leaders invested with the duty of suppressing drink found themselves forced to accept more traditional and popular definitions of the legitimate use of taverns and drink. By one means or another they came to the same conclusion as a Marlborough minister in an election sermon in 1728:

> Without you [the people], all that our rulers in civil and sacred orders can do will not avail. Though our legislature enact never so many good laws for the regulation of the morals of the people, unless you do your part, and improve the power and liberty you are invested with, in your several towns, to make choice of such for your grand jurors, tithingmen, etc., as are men fearing God, men of truth and fidelity, men of wisdom equal to the trust committed to them, and have the interest of religion at heart—who will carefully inspect the manners of the people, and bring the transgressors to open shame and punishment. I say, unless you are careful and conscientious in this, all our laws for the reforming of the

manners and morals of a corrupt people are insufficient and our law-makers labor in vain.[46]

This country cleric suggests that voters consciously elected tithingmen and grand jurors who were reluctant to enforce the drink laws. Such voting undermined all the orders of the Assembly to the hierarchy of officials below to press enforcement. Legislators pursuing greater enforcement risked provoking even more open and emphatic defiance of their laws. Sewall had confronted such an outburst in the Wallis tavern in 1714, when gestures of respect and deference by a company of drinkers had turned into mockery—open affronts to his person and office—because of his determination to disperse them.

Seven years after the failure of the 1712 Act against Intemperance, the authors of the mounting restrictions on tavern and drink usage suffered a further reversal. In 1719 the number of licenses granted by selectmen and justices in Boston suddenly jumped from 74 to 88, and to 134 by 1722, an 81 percent increase in just four years. In the face of colony laws, Boston selectmen initiated a sharp change in policy, even as they were still obliged to follow higher officials on tours of inspection. Between July 1714 and July 1719 they had approved only 87, or 28 percent, of the 313 petitions for licenses put before them; but they reversed this low rate of approval in the five years after 1719, when they approved 245, or 80 percent, of the petitions received.[47] Some members of the Assembly surely felt alarm. Yet, significantly, they chose not to intervene. Indeed, never again would the Assembly move to seize the licensing system and fix the number of public houses in such a comprehensive manner as in 1681 and at the turn of the century. Despite all of the efforts of the clergy and the colony government, the incidence of public houses increased to the level common in English towns at the time of migration and characteristic of Massachusetts in the 1670s before the intervention of the Assembly.

In the countryside, the 1710 order to limit country towns to one tavern and one retailer did not inhibit their multiplication in the first quarter of the eighteenth century. Public houses multiplied more slowly in rural areas, but by the 1730s the towns of Braintree, Wrentham, Weymouth, Stoughton, Roxbury, Cambridge, and Hingham had five or more public

46. Robert Breck, *The Only Method to Promote the Happiness of a People and Their Posterity* (Boston, 1728), 41.

47. Compiled from records of the Court of General Sessions, Suffolk, Record Books, 1702–1712, 1712–1719; and *Records of Boston Selectmen, 1701 to 1715; Records of Boston Selectmen, 1716 to 1736.*

houses each.[48] Most of these towns had one to two thousand inhabitants. The easy access to, and popularity of, public houses, characteristic of Tudor-Stuart England at the beginning of the seventeenth century, also became true of the Massachusetts countryside.

To be sure, the popular culture of drink had changed. Puritan ministers had succeeded in divorcing drinking from the calendar of religious observance. The introduction of royal government had aroused concern that observances like saints' days replete with drunken carousing might take hold in the royal colony. Increase Mather even considered it timely to emphasize in 1687 that such celebrations had been an expedient to convert pagans, when early Christians "thought to bring the heathens over to them, by appointed festivals to the honor of martyrs and other famous saints." The first generation of colonists, Mather continued, had come "into this wilderness with hopes that their posterity here would never be corrupted with such vain customs."[49] And, despite Mather's fears, these festivals never revived. The Puritan calendar set aside no formal occasions for collective drinking, but, rather, specified regular Sunday instruction and the appointment of fast days. This was a major transformation of how colonists interacted with each other as well as with their God.

Puritan rulers had also succeeded in making the sale and use of drink subject to some regulation despite the chronic problem of illicit sales. To sell drink openly, one had to possess a license granted by authorities. The hundreds of people who petitioned for licenses in the 1710s tried to defer to the law before resorting to covert sales. Moreover, the body of laws and sermons on intemperance between 1680 and 1720 represent a cogent articulation, probably the furthest-reaching in the Anglo-American world, of the modern ethic of temperance. Ministers had defined excessive drinking and drunkenness as something Christians must constantly struggle against. The periodic religious revivals of the eighteenth century suggest that many colonists felt guilty about their habits. Colonists measured themselves against a new set of standards, which ministers never let them forget.

48. The Names of Persons Licensed in the County of Suffolk, 1737, Papers of James Otis, Sr., MHS. Peter Clark has estimated that the per capita incidence of alehouses in England in 1577 was 1 to every 142 people. By the 1630s it was 1 to every 89–104 (*The English Alehouse: A Social History, 1200–1830* [New York, 1983], 41–46). If retail houses are included in estimates of incidence in Massachusetts, the numbers are comparable.

49. Increase Mather, *A Testimony against Several Prophane and Superstitious Customs* . . . (London, 1687), 40–41.

Nevertheless, the custom of coming together to drink, such practices as distributing drink to laborers, and the exchange of drink to ratify agreements continued to influence social relations in ways that far exceeded the limits prescribed by the church and law. Indeed, colonists fabricated new customs in the face of clerical criticism. In 1705 Solomon Stoddard, a Hampshire County minister, lectured in Boston on the dangers of a "speedy degeneracy" by condemning the resort to taverns after training exercises, at court days, and even after Thursday lectures. The last, he observed, had become "market days" for tavernkeepers; and the others, occasions for "reveling" and "riot."[50]

In 1719, the year when Boston selectmen eased the tight restrictions on the number of public houses approved, three Boston ministers together published a pamphlet in opposition to these and other drinking customs. Cotton Mather, Benjamin Wadsworth, and Benjamin Colman here argued that "customs" of recent origin involving drink might become a sort of "tyranny" if left to continue. The most "unreasonable things," they declared, can become habits, no matter how dishonorable, simply because time had lent them legitimacy. Such "things claim the character of what may be done" and "of what must be done, when people have been used unto doing them." The rest of the world is "miserably perishing by evil customs, wherein people obstinately carry on a vain conversation received by tradition from their fathers." New England had initially liberated itself from the heathen residue of past ages. But now, they warned, "evil customs" had taken root. Besides the convergence in taverns at militia musters and on court and lecture days, these ministers condemned the use of drink at weddings, commencements, corn huskings, and harvests. When affairs like court days are over, they stated, the people attending should retire to their homes instead of assembling to drink.[51] And all those persons of authority present should order them to disperse. Ministers perceived— and tried to stop—modified and altogether new drinking customs such as consumption at militia musters. There is no greater testimony than this pamphlet to the self-conscious modernity of Puritan spokesmen in respect to particular traditions and customs still observed in England, especially those involving drink.

50. Solomon Stoddard, *The Danger of Speedy Degeneracy* . . . (Boston, 1705), 20.

51. Cotton Mather, Benjamin Wadsworth, and Benjamin Colman, *A Testimony against Evil Customs* (Boston, 1719), 1–4. Richard L. Bushman discusses the emergence of such "customs" in his "American High-Style and Vernacular Cultures," in Jack P. Greene and J. R. Pole, eds., *Colonial British America: Essays in the New History of the Early Modern Era* (Baltimore, 1984), 345–383.

But this pamphlet also suggests the gulf that divided clergy and populace as to the repudiation of custom, particular and general. The clergy could not persuade the populace to reject habitual drinking even as they exalted traditions like consensus, harmony, and interdependence, which drinking could help to promote. Massachusetts society as a whole continued to be influenced by traditions, frames of mind, and values brought from England—including close control of the press by a ruling elite. Within this general set of values and ideals, collective drinking still had its place, if only to facilitate the transmission of news. The Puritan assault on custom remained only partially fulfilled, because in many ways custom still guided the organization and structure of community life. The populace at large still employed drink to express and further a traditional community ethos.

Persistent attack on these traditions by ministers only further exposed their own parallel loss of influence over public behavior. In 1726, twenty-three ministers composed and subscribed to a brief pamphlet entitled *A Serious Address to Those Who Unnecessarily Frequent the Tavern, and Often Spend the Evening in Publick Houses.* Ten of these clerics filled or assisted in Boston pulpits; the other thirteen preached in towns from Truro on Cape Cod to Bristol and Rehoboth in Bristol County, to Sudbury and Newton in Middlesex County, and in Suffolk County towns. They decided to publish this brief pamphlet because "a transient oral discourse is apt to make but little impression" and because "we might in this way reach those whom we can't speak to from the pulpit."[52] These ministers seemed to have less faith in the efficacy of their own oral injunctions. They tried to employ the authority and prestige of print as a weapon against the oral culture of taverns and also to reach that increasing number of colonists who did not attend church, especially in Boston. Simple printed entreaties might con-

---

52. Cotton Mather *et al., A Serious Address to Those Who Unnecessarily Frequent the Tavern, and Often Spend the Evening in Publick Houses* . . . (Boston, 1726). The ministers who were signatories to this address, as authors or sponsors, were Samuel Checkley (Boston), William Cooke (East Sudbury), William Waldron (Boston), Nathaniel Cotton (Bristol), Joshua Gee (Boston), John Greenwood (Rehoboth), Cotton Mather (Boston), Benjamin Wadsworth (Boston), Peter Thacher (Boston), John Danforth (Dorchester), Nehemiah Walter (Roxbury), Eliphalet Adams (New London), Peter Thacher (Milton), Israel Loring (Sudbury), John Avery (Truro), Joseph Sewall (Boston), Thomas Prince (Boston), Ebenezer Thayer (Roxbury), John Webb (Boston), John Cotton (Newton), Nathaniel Appleton (Cambridge), William Cooper (Cambridge), and Thomas Foxcroft (Boston). Information on their respective pulpits at the time this address was published was drawn from, Sibley's *Harvard Graduates,* II–VI.

tain those fluid, open currents of oratory and speech springing up in public rooms.

Some ministers perceived taverns as competing centers of communication. In an earlier sermon published in 1719 William Williams of Hampshire County had observed that in "many places the minister has but few visitors to inquire the way of life: but the innkeeper is thronged with company." There "they are by day, and there they are by night." Amid the post-1719 expansion in the incidence of public houses, the twenty-three declared that "taverns are multiplied among us, beyond the bounds of real necessity, and even to a fault, if not a scandal." They denounced the tavern as a setting that encouraged men "to speak evil of the way of truth" and turn all "religion into banter." Sewall himself had prosecuted a man for delivering a mock sermon in costume at a Shrove Tuesday performance held in a Boston tavern in 1712. The sermon allegedly contained "monstrous profaneness and obscenity," and Sewall confiscated as many copies as could be found. By the 1720s the repression of such blasphemous sentiments had so lapsed that the ministers believed the people in danger "of being imposed upon by designing persons, and unwarily carried into false notions of men and things" or "of leading others into them, by making wrong representations."[53] Ministers competed with others for the attention of the populace, and taverns provided these competitors a forum.

Clergymen returned to the issue of tavern regulation repeatedly in the 1710s and 1720s perhaps because of the corresponding decline in the material support from their congregations. Generally, clergymen were paid in bills of credit, the amount fixed at the time a minister assumed his pulpit. During the first decades of the eighteenth century inflation steadily reduced the value of these bills. By 1725 financial distress among the clergy had become so pervasive that the House felt compelled to pass a resolution recommending that each parish increase payment to its minister to compensate him for inflation. The House ordered the resolve to be read from every pulpit and at the next election day.[54] It is no wonder that clergymen should focus criticism on consumption at taverns when so many faced declining support. The bargaining and the commerce negotiated in tavern exchanges—the mysteries of an economy becoming more commercial—seemed to produce economic consequences that reduced ministers to financial distress. Ministers looked to the House to make this

53. C. Mather *et al., A Serious Address,* 6, 8, 22; William Williams, *A Plea for God, and an Appeal to the Consciences of a People Declining in Religion* (Boston, 1719), 24, 27; *Diary,* II, 680.

54. The resolution is reprinted in Ellis Sandoz, ed., *Political Sermons of the American Founding Era, 1730–1805* (Indianapolis, Ind., 1991), 160–161n.

world subservient to spiritual values once again, to contain and channel the people's priorities into the meetinghouse.

But while the Assembly might resolve, it did not act. Legislators had heeded clerical pleas for coercive measures from the 1670s to 1719. Selectmen and justices had restricted the issuance of licenses in the 1680s and during the first two decades of the eighteenth century. But in the 1720s and 1730s the Assembly and the courts retreated from their aggressive policies against intemperance and the proliferation of taverns.

A pamphlet published anonymously in 1724, which quickly went through three editions, articulated not only the new tolerance of collective drinking but also the incorporation of rum as a staple alcoholic beverage. The author satirized the recent agitation and laws to restrict the use of rum by depicting a farcical trial of "Richard Rum," the personification of the potent and popular beverage. Motivation for bringing Rum to "trial" was the general acknowledgment that rum drinking had become one of the most prevalent sins of the times and that "rational methods" to check it were both "lawful and commendable." A number of "witnesses" gave testimony to Rum's crimes against them. John Vulcan, a blacksmith, told the court that Rum "catched me fast by the middle, tripped up my heels and laid me fast on my back so that I have not been able to get up or go to work for two or three days." A tailor, a weaver, and a miller gave similar testimony to the impact that Rum had upon them.[55]

Then the colonies themselves offered their testimony against Rum. Collectively they believed that if the "prisoner" could be kept "out of our countries but eight or ten years, we might have silver money plenty as in other countries, which would relieve trade." They held Rum responsible for the drain of hard currency from the colonies, because much of it and the ingredients for its manufacture came from the West Indies. Despite its emerging importance as a center of distilling, Boston blamed Rum for its distress, saying "the medium of exchange is gone, and we are in a sinking condition." In "a little time we shall not have the wherewithal to buy our daily bread." A few witnesses spoke in support of Rum. "Barbados and the Islands" told the court that he is "the best branch of our trade." What, they asked, "would New England do with their horses, refuse fish and lumber, and provisions" if it could not trade them for Rum? Indeed, they claimed, "upon us depends the prosperity of trade in many other countries." But the

---

55. *At a Court Held at Punch-Hall, in the Colony of Bacchus, the Indictment and Tryal of Richard Rum, A Person of Noble Birth and Extraction Well Known Both to Rich and Poor throughout All America* (Boston, 1724), 5, 9.

overwhelming drift of testimony condemned Richard Rum, blaming him for individual and colonywide distress and disaster.[56]

Nevertheless, the court acquitted Richard Rum, for it was also obvious from the testimony that few colonists could resist his appeal. The pamphlet underscored his popularity with all colonists. Rum had quickly become one of the most popular items for purchase by colonists, because the consumption of alcohol remained crucial to gestures of respect, liberality, and beneficence as well as the conduct of commerce itself. The trial was held in "Punch Hall," probably a reference to court use of tavern services. Court days had become drinking holidays. Moreover, all of the jurors deciding Richard Rum's fate possessed names denoting their pleasure in and frequent use of alcohol. Indeed, it is suggested that some were near drunkenness themselves.

John Vulcan testified to the distress that Rum had brought him, but he prefaced his remarks by saying, "Being liable to much heat, I have for many years had an unquenchable spark in my throat which I might quench with a pot of middling beer or cider." It was on this foundation that he had become a "lover of his [Rum's] company." Even Cotton Mather had allowed that the use of rum by laborers in times of extreme heat and cold was legitimate, echoing the dietary wisdom of the time. In a society accustomed to using alcoholic beverages at every turn, the development and diffusion of a commerce in rum represented a natural extension of custom. Thus, despite the more strident voices raised against rum, drunkenness, and taverns in the seventeenth and early eighteenth centuries and the development of religious principles exalting reason and rational thinking, the court of popular opinion acquitted Rum of his "crimes." Significantly, he and his well-wishers immediately retired to a "convenient place" (probably a tavern) and there composed a song:

> There's scarce a tradesman in the land
> that when from work is come
> But takes a touch (sometimes too much)
> of brandy or of rum.[57]

Although the pamphlet acknowledged the real problem that rum had come to pose for colonial society, the humor and farce that inform it also made a mockery of the entire body of Puritan teachings on intemperance. This secular, ironic, nuanced commentary deflated the jeremiads

56. *Ibid.*, 9–15.

57. *Ibid.*, 5, 22–23.

still launched by the clergy. The gap between ideal and real had here become ammunition for a satirical eye to observe the irony of human nature.

IV

Also ironic was the fact that, as the criticism of intemperance and taverns reached its height in the 1710s, tavernkeepers made their houses more comfortable, attractive, and even luxurious destinations for Massachusetts colonists. The changing material culture of public houses provides clues to their persistent popularity and the triumph of rum. Back in the mid-seventeenth century, benches and stools had been far more common than chairs in public rooms. After 1690, however, the reverse became true, judging from Boston inventories. George Monk had forty-seven chairs in his rooms and just nine benches. In private households considerations of status would limit the use of chairs, especially for servants and apprentices. But in taverns anyone could sit in them if he purchased alcohol.[58]

By the time that Boston selectmen lifted the limits on licenses in 1719, chairs had become common even in modest establishments. Sarah Wormall, a poor tavernkeeper who died in the early 1720s, had seventeen in her rented house. Of fifteen other taverns between 1709 and 1737, all had more than twenty; eight had thirty or more; and five had more than fifty. The important Sun Tavern in Dock Square near the public docks had ninety-three in 1727. These chairs varied in quality, from rush to leather seats, but all provided rest, particularly for that majority of patrons who performed manual labor for their livelihoods. And all provided a measure of comfort unknown to a previous generation. Moreover, the passage of time had not yet become an omnipresent concern in public rooms, despite the emphasis that ministers placed on its waste in taverns. Only four of sixteen tavernkeepers in Boston between 1709 and 1737 had clocks available for public view. Only the elite customarily used this luxury item.[59]

58. Laurel Thatcher Ulrich has found that only 56% of a sample of Essex County inventories had chairs in 1670. The proportion rose to 78% by 1700. See her *Good Wives: Image and Reality in the Lives of Women in Northern New England, 1650–1750* (New York, 1991), 69; Estate of George Monk, Suffolk County Probate Records, Record Book, XIV, 3.

59. Estate of John Winge, Suffolk County Probate Records, Record Book, XV, 233; William Endicot, XVII, 161; Edward Durant, XX, 388; Thomas Gilbert, XXI, 561; Jonathan Wardwell, XXII, 474; David Copp, XXI, 351; Thomas Thacher, XXIII, 63; Sarah Wormall, XXII, 528; Nathaniel Emmons, XXII, 370; Thomas Selby, XXV, 530–535; Samuel Mears, XXVII, 269; Ann Moore, XXV, 466–467; John Smallpeice, XXI, 684; Samuel

What made the passage of time in taverns attractive and easy was the fact that furnishings continued to promote interaction between customers. Individual comfort had increased, but not at the expense of the collective nature of gatherings. Only a minority of taverns had more than five tables. In 1719 Thomas Gilbert had more than twenty-three chairs in his four ground floor rooms, but only one of these rooms had more than one table. In James Pitson's Great Room in 1739 there were twelve chairs and only two tables.[60] Room by room, the furniture suggests fluid, integrated groups of drinkers rather than distinct subgroups. And during the winter months patrons naturally drew chairs close to the hearth.

The passing of long and late evenings in taverns is also reflected in the number of candlesticks that tavernkeepers generally had on hand. As early as 1681 John Turner had fifteen. The keeper of the Sun Tavern in 1727 had seventeen; Simon Rogers had nineteen in 1734. When all of them were burning, probably a majority of patrons found such public rooms to be better illuminated than their homes. As late as the 1790s a majority of households in central Massachusetts had only one or two candlesticks.[61] As few other houses did, taverns perpetuated day into night. And evening was a period when labor could not be performed well in ordinary households because of the limits and cost of candles. In contrast, taverns were inviting beacons of light.

Despite Puritan efforts to define the major purpose of taverns as providing services to strangers and travelers, it is clear that most Boston taverns rendered service primarily to local inhabitants day and night. The majority had only five or fewer beds. True, ordinary travelers expected that they might have to share a bed. Still, innholders furnished their establishments with the intention of seating customers much more than bedding them. For this reason ministers like Wadsworth complained of tavernkeepers' encouraging "their neighbors unseasonably and needlessly to spend their time and money with them."[62] That is to say, tavernkeepers invested in chairs rather than beds.

Of all the taverns in Boston during these years of official repression of

Tyley, XXII, 617; William Lowder, XXXIII, 415; Ann Coping, XXIX, 206; Simon Rogers, XXX, 278–279; James Pitson, XXXIV, 360–364.

60. *Ibid.*, Gilbert, XXI, 561; Pitson, XXXIV, 360–364.

61. Estate of John Turner, *ibid.*, IX, 47; Samuel Mears, XXVII, 269; Simon Rogers, XXX, 278–279; Jack Larkin, "From 'Country Mediocrity' to 'Rural Improvement': Transforming the Slovenly Countryside in Central Massachusetts, 1775–1840," paper presented at Boston Area Seminar at MHS, Apr. 18, 1991.

62. Wadsworth, *Vicious Courses*, 19.

public houses and intemperance, the Crown Coffee House possessed the most elaborate appointments. The emerging mercantile elite of the town made it their seat of rendezvous. Modeled after English institutions, it was a far more luxurious setting for gatherings of the elite than Monk's Blue Anchor Tavern had been in the 1690s. Standing on Long Wharf down King Street from the Town House, it was one of the first establishments in view of debarking passengers from across the Atlantic and thus an excellent place to gather news and ponder rumors. Thomas Selby, the proprietor of the Crown between 1714 and 1725, might himself have been an immigrant from England, since he was admitted as an inhabitant only in 1709. Whatever his origins, he came to personify style and elegance among tavernkeepers and the town at large in the 1710s. His establishment introduced the cosmopolitan tastes of the English gentry into Boston's public spaces. The Crown Coffee House set the fashion for those men of stature and wealth charged with setting an example for the populace at large and exercising paternal guidance of them.[63]

This tavernkeeper took elaborate care with his appearance, adorning himself with one of his two periwigs, in a society that not long ago had condemned such vanities. (Sewall had chastised the son of a minister for wearing one in 1701; he always noted their appearance with dismay.) Selby also owned a number of coats and waistcoats, one of silk damask and one with gold buttons. Twelve shirts, four stocks (neck cloths), and three pairs of silk stockings contributed to his sartorial splendor.[64] This tavernkeeper probably never toiled in house or yard, but relied on servants and slaves to perform labor.

Selby could also converse intelligently with the gentlemen patrons eager to avail themselves of current news and opinion. He owned thirty books and a Bible, more than the eighteen Monk had owned in 1698. He had the traditional penchant for religious literature, owning books on church government, the *Practice of Piety*, and *Beveridge's Sermons*. An Anglican, he probably attended King's Chapel. Gone were the days when Selby's religious affiliation and readings would have made him an outcast

---

63. *Records of Boston Selectmen, 1701 to 1715,* 2, 213. The following paragraphs are based on Selby's inventory in Suffolk County Probate Records, XXV, 530–535. My interpretation of Selby and his tavern has been influenced by Richard Bushman's survey of gentility in "American High-Style and Vernacular Cultures," in Greene and Pole, eds., *Colonial British America,* 345–383. Susannah Campbell kept a coffee house catering to gentlemen as early as 1704, but almost certainly not on the scale of Selby's. Petition of Nicholas Boone, Oct. 26, 1704, Taverns, 1643–1774, CXI, 77.

64. *Diary,* II, 732–733; Selby, Suffolk Probate Records, XXV, 530–535.

Plate 3. Boston, 1722. *Detail from* The Town of Boston in New England, *by John Bonner, 1722. Courtesy, Massachusetts Historical Society*

in Boston society. He also owned sixteen pamphlets, which were probably secular, since the 1720s witnessed an outpouring of political tracts on various issues.[65] Monk had not owned any pamphlets, mainly because such publications had been repressed.

This cosmopolitan gentleman and his wife Mehetable presided over a thirteen-room establishment staffed by four slaves. One ground floor room was dedicated to the new and just-becoming-fashionable drink of coffee. Selby had thirty-eight pounds of it at his death; Monk did not serve any in the 1690s, and in only one other tavern between 1709 and 1740 is there evidence of its use in any volume. The coffee was milled right there in the room, brewed in a copper coffee pot, kept on a special coffee stand, and served in thirty-two special "coffee dishes."[66] Tea and coffee equipment have been associated with a new sense of domestic ritual, but Selby also sought to attract coffee drinkers to his public establishment in the 1710s and 1720s. This stimulant had become an alternative to the array of alcoholic beverages colonists usually purchased when they purchased any drink.

This Coffee Room was elegant, compared to the plain rooms that Monk and Turner had set aside for the courts just a few decades earlier. It was decorated with ten painted panels and another sixteen prints hanging on the walls. Selby also had two paintings in gilt frames and four prints hanging in the Globe Room. Monk and Turner had possessed no such visual stimulation in the 1680s and 1690s. Selby's gentlemen patrons could also adjust their stocks in two mirrors in the Coffee Room or four others in the rest of the house. Most taverns had mirrors by the 1720s, but not in such numbers as in Selby's rooms. Patrons could also note the time by a "timepiece" in the Coffee Room or by an eight-day clock in a "japanned" finished case in the Crown Room.[67] Monk had not owned a clock.

Selby's table arrangements also set off this tavern. He owned more linen than was common in the past or among his peers. Thirty-eight table cloths

65. Selby, Suffolk Probate Records, XXV, 530–535.

66. *Ibid.*, James Pitson, XXXIV, 360–364. Coffee and tea equipment have been associated by scholars with a new sense of domesticity in the 18th century in ritual servings mainly orchestrated by women. Selby contributed to the promotion of the genteel use of tea and coffee by importing fine china and "tea tables." Carole Shammas, "The Domestic Environment in Early Modern England and America," *Journal of Social History*, XIV (1980–1981), 3–24; Gloria L. Main and Jackson T. Main, "Economic Growth and the Standard of Living in Southern New England, 1640–1774," *Journal of Economic History*, XLVIII (1988), 27–46; *Boston Gazette*, June 13–20, 1720, no. 27.

67. Selby, Suffolk Probate Records, XXV, 530–535.

covered his tables; Monk had owned only ten. (In only 50 percent of a sample of household inventories in Essex County in 1730 did table linen appear.) This linen covered five fixed tables and two oval ones in the Coffee Room, suggesting at least the capacity for privacy. Moreover, Selby's patrons could eat in the more refined fashion by the use of forks. Monk had owned none in the 1690s, and in only six of seventeen other taverns up to 1740 do forks appear. (Only a fifth of Essex County inventories had forks in 1730.)[68] The use of forks still distinguished genteel status in public houses in the 1720s.

In the Bar Room, the enclosed area set aside for drinking utensils, Selby kept forty-two drinking glasses, a quart decanter, glass cruets, and no fewer than eight silver punch bowls. Monk had owned some silver plate, as did most of Selby's peers in some quantity, but glassware was not common except for bottles. The number and quality of the punch bowls testify to the popularity of rum punches among Selby's patrons. At the Crown, gentlemen could treat each other to bowls of punch and also have access to individual glass vessels. Monk had owned only pewter. Selby could also accommodate larger groups. In his parlor were fifty chairs, thirty-five of them leather. Gentlemen's clubs probably convened here. All the rooms were smoky, because Selby had more than one thousand easily breakable clay pipes for sale; but the rooms were also well lighted by twenty brass candlesticks, two glass sconces, and a lantern for meeting customers in the yard at night.[69]

But it was not just the furnishings that set this tavern apart from its predecessors and peers. The astonishing variety and volume of wines and liquors sold by Selby in this provincial town made the Crown Coffee House distinctive among Boston taverns. Back in 1681 John Turner had in stock 145 gallons of Canary wine, 90 gallons of "ordinary" Canary wine, and some Madeira. By the 1720s Selby could entice drinkers with not only Madeira and Canary but also Fayall (a Portuguese wine from the Azores), Vidonia (a dry white wine from Tenerife), Red Jury (probably a French wine from the Jura region of eastern France), another superior variety of Canary, and port. He had 5,000 gallons of it stored in the tavern at his death in a town with a population between ten and fifteen thousand. Besides the wine, Selby of course offered rum (691 gallons), New England brandy (210 gallons), and still another "best" brandy (112 gallons). Drinks could be mixed with several varieties of lime juice. Selby possessed more than a thousand pounds worth of alcoholic beverages. Fashionable though

68. *Ibid.*; Ulrich, *Good Wives*, 69.

69. Selby, Suffolk Probate Records, XXV, 530–535.

the sale of coffee might have become, the Crown sold mainly wine and rum, and in great quantities. The volume is suggested by the number of bottles—1,760 of them—stacked in his yard. No other tavernkeeper had close to this amount. Selby paid the highest excise in 1715, probably making him the most flagrant violator of the 1712 law prohibiting the sale of rum and brandy in taverns.[70] Boston's emerging gentry formed part of the popular resistance to the drink laws.

This extensive patronage by genteel patrons is reflected in the numerous people who owed Selby money at the time of his death. Many of these debts were probably not "barbook" debts, since Selby lent money at interest. But gentlemen who treated others could incur substantial debts. One set of thirty-five men owed him a total of more than £94. Another thirty-seven had borrowed close to £300 from him. Another forty-three owed a total of £723. Selby might have been investing in merchant voyages, since there were a number of "captains" on the list. Situated on Long Wharf, the Crown Coffee House was well suited for such transactions. Selby also owed money, but the value of his estate exceeded £4,000 and could meet these obligations easily. Selby happily intermixed the sale of drink with capitalist enterprise.[71]

The attraction of this fashionable house is also suggested by the identity of the debtors. Merchant Thomas Amory, merchant and philanthropist Peter Faneuil, and Justice Anthony Stoddard all owed Selby money. Selby stood at the center of an extensive system of tavern-based finance and credit involving some of Boston's most illustrious inhabitants. The scale and extent of his tavern and finances made him more than just a tavern-keeper: a member and sponsor of Boston's emerging genteel and mercantile establishment. Well-heeled gentlemen who looked to London rather than local divines for models of deportment now had a tavern of their own. By 1731, Boston gentlemen even had a bowling green at the western edge of town in which to parade and divert themselves.[72]

Compared with its predecessors and peers, the Crown Coffee House offered refinements in every aspect of tavern entertainment—a feast to the

70. *Ibid.*, Estate of John Turner, IX, 47; Hugh Johnson, *Vintage: The Story of Wine* (New York, 1989), 207, 245; *Frank Schoumaker's Encyclopedia of Wine* (New York, 1968), 184; Court of General Sessions, Suffolk, Record Book, 1712–1719, 93.

71. Accounts of Selby Estate, Suffolk County Probate Records, Record Book, N.S., XIV, 72–76.

72. *Ibid.*; *Boston Gazette*, Oct. 18–25, 1731, no. 617. Richard L. Bushman describes the erection and refinement of similar taverns catering to the gentility in other colonies in *The Refinement of America: Persons, Houses, Cities* (New York, 1992), 161–164.

eye in its furnishings, room enough to seat almost seventy-five gentlemen, and enough beverages to create and satisfy new tastes. Selby's inventory of liquors speaks volumes about the subversion of Massachusetts drink laws by gentlemen who cultivated London styles and tastes rather than remained faithful to a Puritan legacy of strict regulation and temperance. Selby's patrons might still have condemned the drinking habits of the populace at large, but they set no example for them as Boston ministers repeatedly urged. Adorned with luxurious appointments, inviting habitual and lingering use, the Crown made silent mockery of the long efforts by members of the Assembly in the Town House just up the street to reduce tavern patronage. After 1710 the drink laws suffered reversal not just from below but from the ranks of the wealthy and influential. Georgian elegance and cosmopolitan tastes had come to storm Puritan Boston.

The refinement of the Crown in the 1710s anticipated a controversial consumer revolution in eighteenth-century Massachusetts. Public tables such as those at select taverns like the Crown became so laden with a varied display of liquors and food in expensive vessels that criticisms of the tastes and habits of the English and Continental upper classes began to be reprinted in Boston newspapers by midcentury. These criticisms were presented as apt lessons for Massachusetts gentry and those who aspired to gentility, but the taste for luxury would gradually infect the middling and even lower ranks. In 1748 one critic wrote, "The furniture and expenses of every tradesman now equal those of the merchant formerly, those of the merchant surpass those of the first-rate gentleman; those of the gentlemen, the old lords." For some, such social mobility was unsettling. It confused the badges of high, middling, and mean status. The taste for "luxury" had become so "universal" that "there is scarce a little clerk among us, who does not think himself the outcast of providence, if not enabled by his salary, fees, etc., to out live the rich man in the Gospel."[73] And of all the imported luxuries of the eighteenth century, none was in so much demand by all ranks as rum. The Puritan drink laws together with admonitions by the clergy tried to impede a consumer revolution, which nevertheless rendered all ranks eager for new tastes and sensations.

As the eighteenth century progressed, this criticism of the widespread demand for luxury in drink, dress, and material life would intensify into a distinct discourse predicting decline and ruin for the colonies as a whole if colonists did not restrain their appetites. Even the lesson of the Dutch burgomaster (probably reprinted from the Dutch through the English

73. *Boston Gazette*, Nov. 13–20, 1732, no. 672, Jan. 19, 1748, no. 1445; *Boston Weekly News-Letter*, July 12, 1750, no. 2513.

press) was borrowed to lecture Massachusetts inhabitants in 1748. This anxious social observer invited a group of Amsterdam magistrates and their ladies to a dinner and then shocked them by serving plain food and weak beer. Under each guest's plate the burgomaster placed verses relating "that such was the fare of their forefathers, when their city began first to thrive, and the states to have a name among the nations." But now "extravagance" and "intemperance" in food and drink threatened to destroy all that the forefathers had sacrificed to build. As with the Dutch, observers in Massachusetts and England believed that the Anglo-American world had begun to lose the stamina and fortitude necessary to keep a society strong and virtuous. Individual pursuit of luxury, many believed, weakened the vertical and horizontal social ties interlacing communities, and distracted individuals from devotion to the common good. What had once been defined as sin was now also symptomatic of a nation's slide into enervation and weakness. The Crown Coffee House signified simultaneously nascent yearnings for the cosmopolitan habits and tastes of London and a threatening invasion of the thirst for luxury that already afflicted the older, more mature societies of Europe. Amid the invasion of rum and other luxuries into the public and private houses of Massachusetts, the Puritan founders assumed the mantle of mythic forbearance, sobriety, and simple manners in the minds of their descendants. Critics believed that Massachusetts must not become too "mature," too much like England, or it would lose that youthful vitality, that virtuous simplicity, which distinguished its foundation.[74]

Critical commentaries on the enervating effects of luxury, however, inspired no new major laws in the decades after 1720. Rum had become a staple drink consumed by all ranks. After all the efforts of lawmakers between 1680 and 1720, the chief remaining deterrent to drinking was the

74. "The Prevalence of Luxury with a Burgo-master's Excellent Admonitions against It," *Boston Gazette*, Jan. 19, 1748, no. 1445. The burgomaster's admonition is said to have first been made in the reign of James II.

The ambivalent feelings that colonists possessed about the refinement of society and the spread of gentility are discussed in Bushman, *The Refinement of America*, 181–203, esp. 187–188; Drew R. McCoy, *The Elusive Republic: Political Economy in Jeffersonian America* (Chapel Hill, N.C., 1980), chap. 1. The second and third generations did distance themselves from the principles of the founding generation, who had emphasized the acquisition of a "competency" as a limit to material striving. Virginia DeJohn Anderson, *New England's Generation: The Great Migration and the Formation of Society and Culture in the Seventeenth Century* (New York, 1991), 166–176.

excise tax regularly levied on wine and spirits. But the revenue obtained from such taxes also tended to make rulers complacent about the still considerable volume of expensive beverages consumed. A commentator in Connecticut later expressed how consumption came to be a prop to government during the eighteenth century. "Drunkenness is decried from almost every pulpit," he declared; but, since it augments public revenue, "what justice of the peace punishes drunkenness"? "Though the divine may preach against it," intemperance will be "connived at by those whose business it is to put a check to it." It had become "necessary to countenance all the vices of drunkenness, extravagance, and debauchery; for from these the state derives its greatest help." No doubt merchants importing rum— and distillers producing it—also connived to relax official attitudes toward excessive drinking and drunkenness.[75]

Considering the official tolerance of excessive drink and tavern use in the decades after 1720, this observer perceived a kind of symbiotic relationship between government and vice whereby taxes on condemned but tolerated vices contributed to the government as a whole. Instead of enacting laws to prohibit or reduce consumption, and so ultimately undermine the authority of regulating officials, lawmakers now concentrated on skimming a percentage of the profits of drinksellers and keeping prices high enough to discourage mass drunkenness. As in England, Puritan preoccupation with limiting the number and use of public houses gave way to more relaxed and lucrative controls in the eighteenth century. Massachusetts legislators never had to wrestle with the great impact on popular behavior that the gin trade had in England, but they had come to terms with the comparable trade in rum.[76] The excise tax became a means of acknowledging vice, extracting some penance for it but also legally sustaining it. Rum continued to be a source of iniquity but simultaneously became the source of much-needed revenue. Legislators struck a delicate

75. Letter to the printer, *New-London Gazette*, Jan. 2, 1767, no. 164. John Adams wrote in 1761 that he was afraid "that some justices may be induced by lucrative motives, by mercantile principles to augment the manufactory or the importation of rum or molasses, without attending to the other consequences, which are plainly pernicious" (L. H. Butterfield *et al.*, eds., *Diary and Autobiography of John Adams* [Cambridge, Mass., 1961], I, 192).

76. Clark, *The English Alehouse*, 178–179, 185–187, 340. English authorities did wrestle with the upsurge in the consumption of gin at midcentury. They tried several methods of suppressing the gin trade until an act passed in 1751 brought the sale of gin into established public houses. Clark, *The English Alehouse*, 241–242; T. G. Coffey, "Beer Street: Gin Lane: Some Views of Eighteenth-Century Drinking," *Quarterly Journal of Studies on Alcohol*, XXVII (1966), 669–692.

balance, which acknowledged the power of the popular culture of drink. Only ministers, occasionally supported by a wave of reform sentiment, continued to dwell on the now mythic temperance of the founding generation in an almost ritualistic enunciation of an idealized past compared to a degenerate present.[77]

But the populace evaded or ignored these entreaties for the most part. While Thomas Selby and his gentlemen patrons sipped rum punch in the Crown in defiance of the law in the 1710s, other drinksellers and their patrons of low rank on the same street even more forcefully violated the spirit and letter of the drink laws. They and dozens more who sought licenses were more desperate. They lived on the edge of indigence and begged for licenses as a means to sustain themselves. In keeping with Puritan policies, licensing authorities tried to keep the poor out of the drink trade. By the 1710s, however, selectmen and justices became hard-pressed to refuse them.

77. Robert Breck, *The Only Method to Promote the Happiness of a People and Their Posterity* (Boston, 1728), 34–35.

Chapter 3

"To Sell What Drink They Can":
Liquor Licenses and Poor Relief

By the end of the seventeenth century, the poor had become a distinct pressure group within the popular culture of drink, especially in Boston. The pleas of the poor to selectmen and justices that licenses be granted to them as an act of charity brought Puritan policies on alcohol use into more acute conflict with popular traditions and mores.

The repeated entreaties by the widow Elizabeth Hawksworth to licensing officials in 1716 reflect the increasing tension between official policy and the needs of the poor. The selectmen did not want to approve her for a license. Just four years earlier the Assembly had enacted the severe Act against Intemperance, and in 1704 the deputies had specifically warned justices and selectmen not to approve widows. The pressure on these officials to curtail the number of licenses had become more intense. But Hawksworth contended with pressures of her own, most markedly her need to find some sort of livelihood. She first applied to sell drink as a retailer on July 13, 1716, at the annual licensing meeting of the selectmen but was refused. She returned to the selectmen's meeting eleven days later to ask for a license to sell food and alcohol as a "common victualer." Three days later she again returned, and after another three days she made a fourth request for a retail license. But her four appearances before the selectmen in 1716 were to no avail.[1]

The next year, on July 5, 12, and 26, she again presented petitions for licenses but met rejection each time. Upon a fourth try in August, however, she succeeded in persuading the selectmen to approve her to retail drink on King Street. But for some reason she did not take up the license. She might have been refused a license by the justices, the next tier of authority whose permission she needed. In any case, she came back before the selectmen the next year in 1718 at three different dates again asking for their approval and met rejection each time. But at some future unrecorded meetings, selectmen and justices finally approved and granted a license, which she held from mid-1718 to mid-1722, or until her death at about this time. She remained poor—her personal estate could not pay all her debts—but she had at least succeeded in supporting herself during these last years of her life.[2]

Hawksworth's persistence in seeking a license illustrates the increasing demands by the poor to grant them permission to sell drink after 1680. Under official warning from the Assembly and criticism by the clergy, selectmen and justices were supposed to refuse such entreaties. Ideally, licenses must be granted only to those who could exercise the type of "government" in their houses necessary to restrain consumption and inhibit antiauthoritarian speech and conduct. Throughout the seventeenth century, licensing authorities had generally excluded the poor or otherwise unqualified applicants as much as possible. But an increasing proportion of Boston's population needed relief at some point in their lives because of illness, widowhood, or unemployment. That need, together with the popular conception of a license to sell drink as a charitable gift by rulers to distressed inhabitants, gradually helped to weaken and finally break the policy of restricted licensing. By approving an increasing number of petitions from the poor, selectmen indirectly began to encourage rather than discourage intemperance. Poor applicants asked to sell not just cider but also rum and brandy. Rum was absolutely necessary, they explained, to keep the patronage of their friends and neighbors. In the Boston minister Benjamin Wadsworth's words, they would "sell what drink they can."[3]

1. Boston, Record Commissioners, *Records of Boston Selectmen, 1716 to 1736*, Report of the Record Commissioners of the City of Boston (Boston, 1885), 5–6, 7, 20, 23, 24, 41.

2. *Ibid.*, 20, 23, 24, 41. Hawksworth was licensed in 1718 through 1721. Court of General Sessions, Suffolk, Record Books, 1712–1719, 208, 248, 1719–1725, 95–97, 451–452, Judicial Archives, ACM; Estate of Elizabeth Hawksworth, Suffolk County Probate Records, XXII, 704, Judicial Archives, ACM.

3. Benjamin Wadsworth, *An Essay to Do Good* ... (Boston, 1716), 21.

I

In the England that the Puritans fled, the majority of those who held licenses to sell drink were poor, despite the increasing alarm in the government over the character of gatherings that poor drinksellers hosted. The Privy Council tried to make justices reduce the number of alehouses kept by the poor. At the beginning of the century the Council had issued the Articles of Direction touching Alehouses, requiring all judges of the Assize and justices to make sure "that the number of alehouses be not increased but diminished." Justices tried to execute the Council's instructions, but did not do so to the latter's satisfaction. The Council found it necessary to issue new, more drastic orders in the 1630s. During this decade authorities eliminated hundreds of alehouses—701 of 1,507 in London alone. But the repetition of the orders suggests that, no matter how many purges took place, the incidence of alehouses always crept back to the former level. Justices weighed instructions from the Council against the combined pressure of popular resistance to reduced access and the pleas by the poor for licenses. The numerous presentments in quarter sessions courts for selling drink without a license for which no action was taken are evidence of leniency from justices more attuned to the circumstances of individual households than was the Council. Justices were "inclined to ignore violations of the licensing laws where a little aleselling kept poor men from coming upon the parish."[4]

Liberality of this sort, however, came under more severe attack as English officials confronted a wide range of work and labor issues among the increasing numbers of wandering and resident poor and the rise of Puritanism. Now critics argued that numerous alehouses operated by the poor became breeding grounds for the poor by encouraging the lower ranks to expend what little they had on a temporary narcotic escape. Thus by granting a license to one poor household in order to avoid placing it on the poor relief rolls, justices might help to create more households in need of assistance. Hence the seesaw in policy between leniency and harsh rollbacks in licenses. The erection of workhouses to employ and house the poor, the antithesis of the alehouse, would become an increasingly popular

4. Peter Clark, *The English Alehouse: A Social History, 1200–1830* (New York, 1983), 72–74. Clark believes that the keepers of alehouses do become more substantial after 1660, and more so in the 18th century. But the poor were always present in the trade, a presence that Massachusetts officials tried to exclude more systematically; see Harris Gary Hudson, *A Study of Social Regulations in England under James I and Charles I: Drink and Tobacco* (Chicago, 1933), 4, 11–15.

alternative. Such an approach, however, demanded that officials consider the poor as an abstract sociological problem to be solved rather than personally extend charity to deferential supplicants in the form of permission to sell drink. Licensing officials wrestled with the conflicting demands of custom, exigency, and Puritan-inspired temperance reform.

In Massachusetts, licensing officials in the seventeenth century could more systematically attempt to exclude the poor from selling drink because of the low incidence of extreme poverty. At the very least, they could prevent the poor from obtaining licenses to sell wine and distilled alcohol. Such licenses must be limited to those who could best exercise authority over their patrons in keeping with Massachusetts' overarching commitment to the suppression of intemperance. Judging from the estates of John Turner, John Winge, and George Monk, the few licenseholders permitted to sell wine in the 1680s had to possess some means. Turner owned two plots of land in Boston, acreage in Concord and Dunstable, and one-sixteenth share in a merchant vessel besides his tavern. Winge, identified as a mariner in his inventory, probably captained a trading vessel before he undertook tavernkeeping. He owned three slaves and a farm as well as property in Boston. Monk, a vintner and tavernkeeper, inherited a small estate in England and added to that the Blue Anchor Tavern. Francis Holmes, first licensed in 1702 at the Bunch of Grapes on King Street, was probably the wealthiest tavernkeeper in Boston at the turn of the century. During the next two decades he transferred part of his assets to South Carolina; he eventually moved there and acquired five hundred acres, another eighty-acre plantation, a half-interest in a sloop, and various other lots of land in Charleston. In Boston he retained property on Long Wharf, lots of land in Dorchester, and the Boston tavern.[5] Since most country towns had only one or two public houses up through the 1680s, leading propertyholders and residents probably held the limited number of licenses. Given the wide opportunities for landownership and a shortage of labor, officials in Massachusetts could more readily deny licenses to those of low rank and few resources.

Massachusetts officials did grant some licenses to the "impotent poor," those who for one reason or another could not pursue their regular calling and had no other means of support. Indeed, Hugh March of Newbury

5. Suffolk County Probate Records, Record Book, IX, 47–48, XIV, 3, XV, 22, 233, XXV, 118–120. Winge and Turner were among the 10 allowed to sell wine in 1680. Monk does not appear in the 1682 list (after the purge), but he apparently continued to be licensed, because he petitioned against unlicensed sellers in 1684. Petition of tavernkeepers against those who sell illegally, July 9, 1684, Taverns, 1643–1774, CXI, 42, ACM.

claimed in his 1682 petition for a license, "It has been the usual practice of [the] Courts . . . to put ancient persons in to such places and callings [drinkselling] rather than turn them out after all their cost." Still, such licenses were not easy to procure in the colony. The poor and disabled always took pains in their petitions to explain that they sought a license because they could do little or nothing else. Michael Martyn emphasized in his 1670 petition that when he had possessed good health he had "been careful of my particular calling of a seaman" and had been "blessed in my undertakings" and so had earned "a comfortable livelihood for my family." Only after he had begun to be troubled by "the distemper of the stone" did he take steps to procure a license. William Norton, another poor petitioner, obtained approval from the Boston selectmen in 1673, but the selectmen asked Captain Oliver and Mr. Thomas Brattle to "move the Court to give him a license" because of poverty.[6] These and other petitions indicate that the poor and disabled could expect opposition from selectmen and justices if they did not prove their dire need. Some sought elite sponsors to testify to their character. As much as possible, licensing authorities wanted to keep licenses out of the hands of the poor, because they did not possess social status sufficient to exercise authority over companies of customers. They would naturally seek to sell as much alcohol as possible, for it was their only means of support.

For the same reason, Puritan licensing authorities tried to exclude women from the drink trade as much as possible. To some extent such an exclusion flew in the face of tradition and practice. In late medieval England, alewives had dominated the drink trade, and in some ways the operation of a modest public house represented a natural extension of the domestic duties and roles of women in private households in the seventeenth century.[7] The sale of drink and provision of lodging for travelers could be undertaken within the routines of a domestic economy, and it is highly probable that many of the licenses held by men masked operations managed by their wives and daughters, since so many widows of tavernkeepers in Massachusetts subsequently applied for their deceased husband's license.

Legally, a woman could hold a license only if she was a widow. Married

6. Petition of Hugh March to General Court, Oct. 11, 1682, Petition of Michael Martyn to General Court, about 1670, Taverns, CXI, 34, 42; Boston, Record Commissioners, *Boston Records from 1660 to 1771* (Boston, 1881), 72. Samuel Norden was approved a year earlier "upon petition of several of his neighbors and consideration of his necessitous condition" (63); see also petition of Thomas Ruche (8).

7. Clark, *The English Alehouse*, 30.

women could neither own nor acquire property, neither enter into contracts nor write a will. The law defined husband and wife as one person. Ideally, Puritan magistrates also wanted to exclude widows from the drink trade. As Puritans invested the suppression of intemperance with a new moral and legal urgency, pressure developed to have sober men preside over companies of drinkers and govern their houses in accordance with the new premium attached to temperance and with the new concepts of good order. To invest widows with the responsibility of regulating the drinking habits of mostly male customers could subvert Puritan precepts concerning female submission to patriarchal government. Whether licensed widows admonished men for their behavior or passively permitted men to drink themselves to drunkenness, they acted in violation of one or another Puritan stricture. Licensing authorities did not always require that an adult man be resident when they did grant a license to a widow, but the fact that widows Wardell and Franke had "to put a careful man to keep the house" in 1679 as a condition for their licenses suggests that this was a strong consideration.[8] Of course, if a widow remarried, her license did not travel with her. The license did not come up for renewal at the annual licensing session; rather, her new husband must petition for it as a new applicant.[9] Like the disabled and infirm, magistrates considered widows to be unwanted exceptions to a licensing policy designed to restrain consumption and patronage.

Between 1670 and 1680 the balance between the upholding of Puritan licensing policies, on the one hand, and the dispensation of charity to the poor through licenses, on the other, became more difficult to maintain. Refugees from inland towns escaping the havoc of King Philip's War flooded Boston. In 1675 the selectmen requested that the General Court assume responsibility for their support, and in 1677 it became necessary to distribute rations "to several poor families, of this town and such as came hither from eastern parts and places." These newcomers caused uneasiness among the craftsmen of the town. In May 1677, more than 120 of them complained to the Court about strangers' setting up shops even though they had not completed a full apprenticeship or been admitted as "inhabit-

8. Marylynn Salmon, *Women and the Law of Property in Early America* (Chapel Hill, N.C., 1986), xv, 14–18, 22–30, 56–57, 183–184; *Boston Records from 1660 to 1701*, 128.

9. This need for a new petition is evident from a comparison of Boston marriage records with the end of the terms of female licenseholders. A list of people licensed in Suffolk County in 1737 contains names crossed out or noted as "removed," or "dead" or "married" in the case of women. The Names of Persons Licensed in the County of Suffolk, 1737, Papers of James Otis, Sr., MHS.

ants" of the town. "Whereby it has already come to pass with many (and we fear if not prevented will much increase) that several inhabitants that have lived comfortably upon their trades and been able to bear public charges in a considerable degree, now cannot subsist, but stand in need of relief." By 1679 the town had asked for the power to eject all strangers, including lingering refugees, in order to defend itself from the "profaneness and charge too much growing upon us." Many established residents as well as strangers confronted disruptions in their livelihood. What employment strangers could find was probably only temporary. The war, one of the most devastating in American history per capita, left many widows. Amid these disruptions the number of public houses licensed by the selectmen and justices increased from fifteen to forty-five—more than doubling in one decade.[10] The problem of unlicensed sales had also become more severe.

The seizure of the licensing system by the Assembly in 1681 and the drastic reduction in the number of public houses ordered were not purely a response to the effects of the war. The drink laws had long been evaded and disregarded, and the order affected towns throughout the colony not flooded by refugees. But the war did increase the number of poor seeking licenses to support themselves and thus exacerbated the existing conflict between law and popular culture.

The pressure that the poor placed on licensing officials is evident from the flurry of petitions received by the Assembly after its order took effect. Samuel and Elizabeth Norden emphasized in their petition for restoration of their license that they were "unable to work." Widow Elizabeth Wardell had suffered losses from fire and also carried the burden of care for her daughter's children, whose estate had been destroyed in the war. Elizabeth Harris's husband had deserted her, leaving her with debts and two children. John Bull told the deputies of the Assembly that illness had rendered him "unable to follow his other calling." Joseph How went so far as to assert that the colony government had imposed an "impossible service" upon the county court by its "retrenchment" of the number of Boston taverns in order "to prevent drunkenness." The justices had been forced, How said, to "dismiss so many" petitions for licenses and "please [only] twenty-one." Moreover, he believed that his license should be restored to him because he had been an admitted inhabitant of the town for forty-four years and had suffered a series of calamities. He had followed his trade until

10. Petition of Handicraftsmen to General Court about intrusion of strangers, May 23, 1677, Rare Book Collection, Boston Public Library; *Boston Records from 1660 to 1701*, 101, 111, 135, 145.

his hand had been shot and injured; he had then tried to employ servants to carry on his trade, but this failed; then he lost his house and goods to fire. How could he be denied a license after such misfortune? These petitions suggest that most of those stripped of their licenses in 1681 faced indigence. In contrast to How, the well-to-do George Monk retained his license, even though he had been born in England and might have been a recent immigrant.[11]

The petition of Edward Wright in 1685 brought these conflicts over licensing policy into more acute focus. Wright had recently spent a year in service on the frontier in warfare against the Indians, during which time his health suffered to the extent that he now no longer could "follow his calling." Apparently in desperation, he and his wife began to sell drink without a license just after the 1681 reduction of public houses; he was discovered, prosecuted, and fined. Wright could not pay the fine, so the justices imprisoned him. At the time of his petition he had been in prison in Boston for eight months, during which time "he had not heard one sermon, nor had liberty to visit his family although [they] are in a lamentable distressed condition not having so much as a house fit to live in." Wright asked the justices not just to extend compassion to him and his family by releasing him from prison but to grant him a license to sell beer and cider so he could maintain his family and be less "chargeable to town and country." To Wright the policy of harsh fines and imprisonment for selling without license made less sense than the use of licenses to provide employment for the poor. The same year, Thomas Jones of Charlestown argued before the town's selectmen that "providence" had cast him into the calling of drinkselling because of ill health. The selectmen agreed that it would be an "act of charity" to approve Jones for a license.[12]

Albeit on a much smaller scale, licensing officials and members of the Assembly confronted the same problems that English officials had faced in the early seventeenth century when they ordered and executed a drastic reduction in the number of public houses. The granting of the privilege to sell drink and the dispensation of charity to the poor remained closely linked in popular opinion. There existed few alternatives to drinkselling for disabled men and women who could no longer do the manual labor that

11. Petition of Samuel and Elizabeth Norden, 1681, Taverns, CXI, 37, Elizabeth Wardell, 39, Elizabeth Harris, 39a, John Bull, 40, Joseph How, 38; Suffolk County Probate Records, Record Book, VIII, 295. William Monk left to his son George some property in England.

12. Petition of Edward Wright to Justices, Oct. 14, 1685, Judicial Records, 1683–1724, XL, 224, ACM; Petition of Thomas Jones, Nov. 18, 1685, Taverns, CXI, 52, 53.

the vast majority performed for their livelihood. But members of the Assembly did not modify their position respecting licenses in the next several years, despite all the petitions and the fact that Boston spent an increasing part of its tax revenues on poor relief (a total of nine hundred pounds for direct relief and the procurement of employment in 1700). Only after the complaints made in 1684 by Monk and Winge and other tavern-keepers about the pervasive incidence of unlicensed sales did the Assembly decide to permit more to be licensed. With the permission of the deputies, the selectmen approved six more licenses in September 1684. They included John Bull, Samuel and Elizabeth Norden, and Widow Wardell. The widow even obtained permission to retail distilled liquors.[13]

By 1690 the poor had again secured a place in the trade. Whereas seven of ten widows had lost their licenses in the 1681 purge, by 1690 widows held almost half of the forty-five licenses. When the number of public houses increased to seventy-five by 1696, widows presided over one-third of them.[14] In the aftermath of the reaction to the 1681 order, the Massachusetts licensing system operated in similar fashion to that of England, particularly in respect to Boston.

Puritan leaders, however, persisted in efforts to preserve the colony's religiously informed social ideals and policies. Just after the 1681 seizure of the licensing system, the town decided to rebuild its alms- and workhouse to provide relief to the sick, aged, and unemployed. Further, the town intended to house and reform any other "persons and families that misspend their time in idleness and tippling."[15] It is not known how many people entered or were placed in this workhouse, but it did not stop the issuance of licenses to the poor in the 1690s. Possibly the selectmen favored the sick and aged for licenses while placing the able-bodied poor in the workhouse. In any case, authorities conceived of the erection and expansion of workhouses, which had precedents in English poor laws, as an antidote to the issuance of licenses to the poor and a moral counterweight to houses harboring habitual drinking by the populace.

In 1698, when the Assembly again considered taking control of the licensing system and when the Boston selectmen did act to reduce the number of public houses, the town appointed a committee to consult on the best methods to prevent disorders. The committee, all of whom Sewall

13. *Boston Records from 1660 to 1701*, 171, 231, 241; Petition of tavernkeepers against those who sell illegally, July 9, 1684, Taverns, CXI, 48.

14. *Boston Records from 1660 to 1701*, 203–204; List of Licenseholders in Boston, Mar. 30, 1696, Taverns, CXI, 57.

15. *Boston Records from 1660 to 1701*, 157.

counted as friends and associates, recommended in 1700 that the town undertake to raise five hundred pounds in taxes to be used by the overseers of the poor to procure materials and tools "to set and keep the poor people and ill persons at work as the law directs."[16] Such steps undoubtedly bolstered the selectmen's parallel efforts to reduce the incidence of public houses in the town. Whereas taverns operated by the poor might undermine constituted authority, workhouses enhanced it and cultivated work discipline at the same time. Manufactures were not the objective, only the means.

Yet even as selectmen held licenses to a minimum between 1702 and 1719, rejecting more than three hundred petitions, they did make exceptions to the exclusionary policy toward the poor. True, Richard Hancock never received approval for a license, even though he applied for one nine times between 1704 and 1715. But Thomas Phillips, a disabled war veteran, received approval. Three times the selectmen refused to renew approval of his license because of disorders in his house, but each time they withdrew their objections after hearing pleas from Phillips.[17] Selectmen wrestled with pressures on them from above and below.

Exceptions also continued to be made for widows, despite the 1704 instruction from the Assembly that "licenses be given to men" and not to "widows who cannot support the government of their houses." Widows comprised fifteen of the thirty-seven tavernkeepers licensed in 1708, sixteen of the thirty-five retailers. A measure of disorder in the respective houses kept by men and women is whether the selectmen objected to the renewal of the license. Between 1710 and 1719 the selectmen made such objections against nineteen licenses held by women because of alleged disorders and thirty-three licenses held by men.[18] Since women held between one-third and one-half of all licenses in these years, they were only slightly more prone to be named as proprietors of disorderly houses. This near parity is surprising, since men probably drank with less restraint in houses kept by women, and any instance of disorder in a house operated by a woman only served to emphasize the disruption of male dominance that female tavernkeepers represented in a town and colony in which licenseholders were to govern their patrons. For a tavern to be disorderly—to be

16. *Ibid.*, 231, 241.

17. Boston, Record Commissioners, *Records of Boston Selectmen, 1701 to 1715* (Boston, 1884), 31, 35, 38, 51, 61, 75, 166, 187, 217, 229; Phillips, see 187, 212, 231.

18. Order of General Court concerning Innholders, June 27, 1704, Taverns, CXI, 76; Court of General Sessions, Suffolk, Record Book, 1702–1712, 176; *Records of Boston Selectmen, 1701 to 1715*, 111, 114, 142, 166, 187, 212, 231, *1716 to 1736*, 6, 20, 40.

the site of drunkenness and the mockery of religious teachings—was one offense. But when the proprietor was a woman, it became still more offensive to lawmakers and clergy, because women's presiding over male companies subverted the hierarchy of authority in the first place. Thus the continuing issuance of licenses to women is all the more striking during this period of tight restriction on the overall number of public houses.

The poverty of widows and the effort to avoid placing them on relief rolls help to explain their resilience in getting and keeping a place in the drink trade. Rebecca Fowle acquired approval for a license to retail in 1712 near Scarlett's Wharf. The selectmen refused to renew the license because of alleged disorders, but they withdrew their objections after reconsideration. When she remarried in 1717, the selectmen refused to approve the petition by her new husband to acquire the license in his name. Her marriage offered the selectmen the opportunity to get her out of the trade. By 1720, however, he had died, and she again sought a license. First she retailed "nigh the draw bridge," then at a new location in the North End, followed by an attempt to open a tavern, after which she returned to retailing.[19]

The selectmen also only reluctantly permitted Mary Willard to sell drink. They objected to the renewal of her license three times between 1713 and 1717, but each time she persuaded them to withdraw their objections. Although her house proved a chronic source of unspecified "disorders," the selectmen probably faced no other alternative except to place her and whatever dependents she supported on relief. Boston justices convicted Sarah Wormall of selling without a license, and the selectmen refused to approve her when she applied for one. Three years later, however, she did win approval because of need. Her estate at death suggests that she could not turn to her daughters for support, two of whom were single.[20] In responding to petitions from widows for licenses or for the restoration of licenses, selectmen listened to entreaties that proved difficult to dismiss.

Despite the continuing exceptions made for the poor and widowed, the status and wealth of licenseholders as a whole between 1700 and 1719 probably remained more substantial than for Boston's population as a whole. Although Queen Anne's War (1702–1713) fueled a growth in the

19. *Records Of Boston Selectmen, 1701 to 1715*, 168, 213, *1716 to 1736*, 23, 71, 102, 177, 197. Fowle's marriage to Ebenezer Tolman is in Boston, Record Commissioners, *Boston Marriages from 1700 to 1751* (Boston, 1898), 67.

20. *Records of Boston Selectmen, 1701 to 1715*, 187, 189, 231, *1716 to 1736*, 6, 20; Suffolk County Probate Records, Record Book, XXII, 36–37, 528.

town's economy, the war also left many widows and impoverished veterans, and the economy fell into a slump at the war's conclusion. The rate of real property ownership fell by 25 percent between 1685 and 1725. By the latter date, the bottom 40 percent of Boston society did not hold property and held a lesser share of the total wealth of the town than their counterparts had in 1690.[21] The strict limitation on the number of licenses granted, which in effect reduced the incidence of public houses with each passing year, would have tended to keep a majority of licenses in the hands of more substantial inhabitants. Selectmen and justices tried to prevent the wholesale entrance of the poor into the trade. The number of petitions for licenses increased from fifty-one in 1710 to eighty-one in 1718, but selectmen continued to disapprove far more than they approved (see Table 1).

They made enough exceptions to this strict licensing policy, however, to inspire criticism from minister Benjamin Wadsworth in 1716. Despite the continuing drop in the incidence of public houses, he perceived a "needless multiplying of licenses to sell drink, especially to be innholders." There existed so many of them, he believed, "that those who have [licenses] can get no tolerable gain by them, unless their neighbors prove wicked customers." Poor licenseholders were under greater temptation "to sell what drink they can." Wadsworth declared that licenses should never be granted to the poor as a means for their support:

> It may be a man has met with losses, or his trade fails, he's become low and indigent; the next thing, he seeks a license to sell drink; and when he has it, possibly many of his neighbors ruin themselves, by being his wicked customers. I fear that many are made poor, by being wicked customers to others, that were poor before them. If those really poor and low, would keep good conscience, I think they had better follow the hardest labor their bodies can bear, and be content to live very meanly, than to get a license to sell drink.[22]

Wadsworth defended the licensing policy brought to New England by the founders, renewed against threatened compromise in the 1680s, and now once again put in force by pressure of the Assembly. Wadsworth asked for still more restrictive policies, with no exceptions for the poor, who would not refrain from selling to those inclined to expend all their money on drink.

21. Gary B. Nash, *The Urban Crucible: Social Change, Political Consciousness, and the Origins of the American Revolution* (Cambridge, Mass., 1979), 62–65.

22. Wadsworth, *An Essay to Do Good*, 21.

Table 1. *Approval by Boston Selectmen of Petitions for Licenses, 1702–1718*

Year	Approved	Disapproved	Year	Approved	Disapproved
1702	6	2	1711	23	12
1703	12	15	1712	14	22
1704	1	11	1713	12	28
1705	2	18	1714	15	21
1706	4	18	1715	9	43
1707	6	25	1716	9	27
1708	16	20	1717	23	85
1709	5	35	1718	31	50
1710	13	38			

Sources: Compiled from Boston, Record Commissioners, *Records of Boston Selectmen, 1701–1715*, Report of the Record Commissioners of the City of Boston (Boston, 1884); *Records of Boston Selectmen, 1716–1736* (Boston, 1885).

Yet it is clear from the estates of poor licenseholders that they struggled to survive in Boston by operating under a different set of assumptions and priorities. For them, licenses could be a vital means to acquire the credit necessary to remain self-sufficient. When aged sailor John Smallpeice acquired a license to keep tavern in 1716, after first being refused, he and his wife had next to nothing behind them. They owned £60 worth of household goods and old nautical equipment. But on the strength of the license Smallpeice negotiated credit for 110 gallons of rum from John Ruck and Company worth £26. He considered this lifeline of credit vital, since he started to pay off the debt in £5 installments four months after receiving it. The license also probably helped Smallpeice to acquire loans or goods on credit from twelve other people totaling £157. Good times or bad, one could always sell rum in Boston, despite the law passed four years earlier prohibiting its sale in taverns. Some of the credit extended to Smallpeice might have been motivated by charity. Physician James Habersham rendered £13 worth of services, and another creditor extended £72 to this ailing and aged mariner.[23] Still, the tavern license opened up lines of credit to a man surely perceived as a poor credit risk. As Wadsworth

23. Inventory of John Smallpeice, Suffolk County Probate Records, Record Book, XXII, 199–201, N.S., X, 116–117.

angrily noted, such tavernkeepers and retailers could always sell to their neighbors. Creditors had some hope of receiving payment.

The accounts of other poor licenseholders in the first decades of the eighteenth century also reveal their capacity to negotiate credit on the strength of their licenses. Despite her conviction for illegal sales, the Widow Wormall finally received a license to keep tavern in 1716, which presumably helped her to negotiate credit from sixteen people by the time of her death. She owned only one hundred pounds worth of goods, a third of it in a few pieces of silver, but had acquired a total of one hundred pounds worth of credit by approaching a number of people for small amounts and borrowing from other widows when she could, since half of her creditors were women. Mrs. Shute lent her three pounds worth of beer, a rival drinkseller Sarah Bryant gave her nine shillings, and she acquired small amounts of spirits on credit.[24] Through the license she sustained herself, because the value of her goods, although just barely, covered her debts.

Elizabeth Hawksworth displayed particular skill in using a license to win credit, judging from surviving records of the early eighteenth century. She pursued credit with the same determination as she had the license, getting loans of money and goods from twenty-two people (almost all men). Some of her creditors probably granted loans out of charity, like Justice William Hutchinson's extension of thirty-five pounds worth of credit.[25] Still, Hawksworth was in business. A liquor license in hand made approaches to friends and neighbors easier and more successful. The hundreds of people who sought a license in the 1710s could wield it as a bargaining device with potential creditors. They asked authorities to grant them the indulgence to remain at least partially self-sufficient. Hawksworth had held on to half of a pew in the meetinghouse where Benjamin Colman preached, but, when he denounced intemperance from the pulpit, she no doubt ignored it. The popular demand for drink had motivated her long quest for a license, and she sought to use it to her best advantage.

The popular conception of the licensing process as an extension of charity to the needy is also evident in petitions for licenses. Few of the hundreds of petitions between 1700 and 1719 have survived, but those from the 1750s and 1760s reinforce the conclusions gleaned from probate records. The sponsors needed by the poor in the late seventeenth century appear to have become a formulaic requirement by mid-eighteenth century. Petitioners for licenses usually stated that their friends and neighbors

24. Inventory of Sarah Wormall, *ibid.*, XX, 528, XXIV, 36–37. See also Ann Moore, XXVI, 370–372.

25. Elizabeth Hawksworth, *ibid.*, XXII, 704, XXIV, 7–8.

promised to provide credit or patronage to them if they could obtain a license. Edward Blanchard hired a shop on Long Wharf with "the encouragement and help of friends." Hezekiah Usher told the selectmen that "his friends sensible of his present uncomfortable situation have put him upon applying for your approbation as a retailer promising him that if he procures the same they will assist him to furnish out a shop in the grocery way." Joseph Blake injured one of his legs "while at work on the new college at Cambridge which turning to a mortification had prevented him doing any sort of work since that time." He and his family had been supported "almost wholly by the charity of friends" after his medical expenses "swallowed up all the fruits of his former industry." Those friends now promised to "furnish out" a shop for him "provided he can obtain a license" to retail rum and other distilled liquors.[26] Some sponsors promised loans and patronage on condition of acquisition of not only a license but a license to sell spirits.

Widows also received encouragement from neighbors and friends. Rebecca Badger, a widow enfeebled by illness, had "friends" who "advise her immediately to open [a shop] at her house in Prince Street leading to the Charlestown ferry, provided she can obtain the privilege of selling strong drink to the country people who come into town by said ferry." Elizabeth Pittson had taught school since the death of her husband eighteen years before, but now her health forced her to leave that occupation. In order "to preserve life her friends urge her to the keeping of a grocer's shop provided she can obtain a license, as the only way she can hope for a livelihood under these circumstances."[27] Petitions by the poor, injured, and widowed—suggested, supported, and sponsored by neighbors and friends—formed part of the popular resistance to Puritan licensing policies in the eighteenth century. A growing proportion of the dozens of petitions rejected by the selectmen during these years undoubtedly evoked the same plea for the approval of a license as an act of charity.

Poor petitioners also stressed to selectmen that if denied a license they must become town charges, an indignity for them and a financial burden to the town. Jonathan Tarbox took in his son-in-law and his family after Tarbox had lost one of his hands in an accident. He bluntly stated in his petition that they "may all become a town charge" unless he acquired a license to retail rum and other liquors. Widow Badger told the selectmen that, if she did not receive their approval, she must become a "town

26. Petition of Edward Blanchard, July 12, 1769, of Hezekiah Usher, July 7, 1767, of Joseph Blake, Aug. 12, 1767, of Joseph Coolidge, July 9, 1765, Misc. Bd., MHS.

27. Petition of Rebecca Badger, July 20, 1768, Elizabeth Pittson, July 15, 1767, *ibid.*

charge." Moreover, the "indulgence" to sell rum, she stated, had been "frequently granted to the widows of such persons as have paid much less taxes than had been paid by her late husband for many years together."[28] The past rendering of taxes to the town by a petitioner must now, she claimed, be reciprocated by the granting of the indulgence to sell rum to neighbors.

As opposed to poor relief or placement in a workhouse, acquisition of a license allowed an individual and family to remain integrated in community and neighborhood life. Moreover, the license allowed some sellers to return the support from neighbors and friends by providing cheap and easy access to drink. Wadsworth was attuned to this inclination. He condemned those drinksellers "who allow ill practice in others, for their own gain." Drinksellers who owed money to neighbors should not "urge them to take it out in your way," that is, "to drink it out though they have no need of it." Indeed, "they had better lose their debt, then get it in such a manner." Wadsworth went on to condemn those drinksellers who permit their "poor neighbors, tradesmen, [and] laborers" to sit and drink in their houses and who act to "hide" their "wicked customers" and "deny that they are there" to constables. He condemned such drinksellers as guilty of conspiring to hurt the souls and estates of their customers. This reiteration of Puritan teachings on the use and sale of alcohol, however, increasingly came into conflict with the traditional conception of drink and licenses as mediums of charity from protective rulers to abject supplicants. Drinkselling continued to be perceived as part of a moral economy to relieve the poor, who in turn provided cheap drink to the populace at large.[29] The newfound emphasis on temperance interfered with these traditional assumptions.

Supported by the testimony of neighbors, petitioners brought these expressions of popular will, first, to the selectmen to condone and then to the justices for their legal sanction. Despite the growth of Boston's population from approximately six thousand in 1690 to more than ten thousand by 1720, selectmen often possessed some knowledge of the applicant's identity and circumstances, as reflected in the selectmen's records noting the location of public houses. They used street names, but often in reference to individual houses whose location was common knowledge. In 1717 the

28. Petition of Jonathan Tarbox, Sept. 30, 1767, of Rebecca Badger, July 20, 1768, *ibid.*

29. Wadsworth, *An Essay to Do Good*, 18. Opposition to temperance policies is akin to the mentality described by E. P. Thompson in "The Moral Economy of the English Crowd in the Eighteenth Century," *Past and Present*, no. 50 (February 1971), 76–136.

selectmen approved licenses for Mary Mayes "where Thwing was in Fish St."; to Richard Pullen "in the room of North in Hanover St."; to Sarah Tomlin "at Sales' in King St."[30] The licensing process continued to consider, case by case, the circumstances of inhabitants known to selectmen.

The increasing number of petitions from the poor and disabled cried out for a relaxation of the tight, restrictive licensing policy inaugurated at the turn of the century. During the 1710s selectmen visited families in the town with other officials in order to "prevent and redress disorders." But they continually confronted more traditional assumptions concerning order in the petitions of poor applicants and their sponsors for licenses: that is, the responsibilities of officials to those needing relief, the extension of charity through licenses.

Nevertheless, Boston ministers continued to exert pressure on selectmen to repudiate these appeals. In his 1719 sermon, Wadsworth reiterated his opposition to giving licenses to the poor and blamed intemperance for the poverty that afflicted so many Bostonians in the 1710s. Although new licenses were held to a minimum, Wadsworth remained upset with prevailing drinking habits: he warned selectmen and justices that they must "give an account to God" when making decisions about licenses. If officials should move to gratify "a particular friend or importunate petitioner" with a license, they would be judged "guilty before God for doing it." Failures in trade and business, he continued, must never be a justification for granting a license, for "this method of supporting one family too often ruin[s] several." Wadsworth also lamented the changing consumer tastes that caused so many petitioners to ask to sell rum. Bostonians sought to drink "the best" and "the most pleasant and delicious though the most costly." Licenseholders who thrust these liquors and mixed drinks on their neighbors, he declared, were guilty of "ruining" them and their families. The same year, William Williams preached an election sermon to the Assembly asking for additional legislation to regulate morals.[31]

Such sentiments received formal endorsement from Governor Samuel Shute the same year. In an address to the Assembly he applauded the message "so seasonably passed upon us from the pulpit" concerning the

30. Stella H. Sutherland, *Population Distribution in Colonial America* (New York, 1936), 22n. Boston's population is estimated to be 10,567 in 1722. *Records of Boston Selectmen, 1716 to 1736*, 21.

31. Benjamin Wadsworth, *Vicious Courses, Procuring Poverty Describ'd and Condemn'd . . .* (Boston, 1719), 12, 20–21; Wadsworth, *Faithful Warnings against Bad-Company-Keeping* (Boston, 1722); William Williams, *A Plea for God, and an Appeal to the Consciences of a People Declining in Religion* (Boston, 1719), 27.

promotion of virtue. And two Boston printers advertised copies of Wadsworth's sermon for gentlemen who wished "to give away a considerable number."[32] In the tradition of Samuel Sewall, gentlemen should distribute copies to those who might exercise an influence over the populace at large.

Boston selectmen, however, were ready to distribute licenses instead of sermons. In 1719 they succumbed to the pressures of poor petitioners for licenses. Just months after the publication of these sermons, selectmen began to approve a sharp increase in the number of public houses. Petitions for licenses won acceptance as never before. In every year but one between 1702 and 1718, selectmen had disapproved more petitions than they approved. A total of 470 petitions met rejection while only 201 received approval. After 1719 the reverse became true. They approved far more than they disapproved—596 as opposed to 394. The difference in policy is most marked in the five years before and after 1719, a decade when the pressure to grant licenses intensified and then was released. Between 1714 and 1718 selectmen approved only 87, or 28 percent, of 313 petitions; during the next five years 245 won approval, or 80 percent of the 305 received.[33]

The selectmen did not receive the full concurrence of the justices in their decision to change policy. In 1720 the Suffolk County justices granted licenses to only 18 of the 36 applicants approved by the selectmen. Still, the number approved and licensed rose sharply, from 74 in 1718 to 109 three years later. And in time the justices joined with selectmen in allowing an increase in the incidence of public houses. By 1730 most of those approved by selectmen also received approval from justices.[34]

The change in policy is also reflected in the higher incidence of licensed houses in the streets and alleys of the town. In 1718 there existed 75 houses serving a population of 10, 567 (1722 figure), or an incidence of 1 house for every 143 inhabitants. By 1737 a total of 177 public houses served a population of 16,975 (3,395 polls), making for a much higher incidence of 1 for every 96 inhabitants. While the population of Boston

32. *Boston News-Letter,* Feb. 16–23, 1719, no. 775, Mar. 9–16, 1719, no. 778.

33. Approvals by selectmen compiled from *Records of Boston Selectmen, 1701 to 1715* and *1716 to 1736.*

34. The difference between the number approved and the number actually licensed by justices was determined by comparing identities of those granted licenses in Records of the Court of General Sessions for Suffolk County with those approved by selectmen in *Records of Boston Selectmen.* Court of General Sessions, Suffolk, Record Books, 1712–1719, 207–208, 1719–1725, 41–42, 95–97, 1725–1732, 277.

grew by approximately 60 percent between 1720 and 1740, the number of licensed public houses increased by 103 percent.[35]

Retail shops selling alcohol for consumption "out of doors" multiplied at a much higher rate than did taverns. Whereas before 1719 the majority of licenses had been issued for tavernkeeping, the opposite became true by 1737, when justices granted only 34 licenses for taverns, against 120 for retailers. Legally, drinkers could sit only in the 34 taverns, for an incidence of 1 for every 471 inhabitants, or approximately 1 for every 100 adult males.[36] The expansion in the number of retailers may partially be explained by the increasing dependence on shops for foodstuffs instead of on home garden produce. Retailers also benefited from the increasing trade in rum, much of which was not produced locally. At least some Boston retailers supplied country residents with rum at prices cheaper than in country towns. Rebecca Badger planned to sell "strong drink to the country people who come into town by [Charlestown] ferry." But retailers cannot be regarded solely as shopkeepers purveying alcohol. Legislation enacted between 1680 and 1720, in keeping with laws passed during the previous fifty years, repeatedly tried to prevent retailers from permitting customers to sit drinking in their houses. But commentators still referred to retailers in the 1760s as "dramshops," where small amounts of rum and other beverages could be purchased and consumed.[37] Thus the total number of houses selling alcohol can be considered roughly as the number of places where inhabitants gathered to drink.

It is impossible to determine precisely the proportion of this increasing number of licenses that went to the poor, but evidence strongly suggests that they became the major benefactors of the relaxation in restrictions. The presence of widows in the drink trade—still controversial in the 1710s—continued to transform the licensing system into an extension or variant of poor relief. The proportion of all licenses held by women did not increase dramatically after 1719, staying between 30 and 40 percent, but the absolute number rose from 22 in 1702 to 71 by 1737. Between 1702 and 1732 (years when licensing records are available) a total of 253 women held licenses, 81 of them as tavernkeepers and the rest as retailers. The wealth possessed by twenty widows either at their death or at the begin-

35. Sutherland, *Population Distribution in Colonial America*, 22n; List of Licenses in Suffolk County, Papers of James Otis, Sr., MHS.

36. *Ibid.*

37. Petition of Rebecca Badger, July 30, 1768, Misc. Bd., MHS; L. H. Butterfield *et al.*, eds., *Diary and Autobiography of John Adams*, 4 vols. (New York, 1964), I, 204–205.

ning of their term as licenseholders (that is, their legacies from deceased husbands) between 1702 and 1780 strongly suggests that most obtained their licenses in situations of near or complete financial desperation. Of the 20, 11 possessed nothing more than rudimentary furnishings; 9 either died barely solvent or insolvent or were the widows of insolvent sellers.[38]

By the 1760s the association of the poor and widowed with the drink trade had become so well established that one writer to the *Boston Evening-Post* went so far as to assume that the licensing system had been instituted for the benefit of the poor and widowed and that they should be given preference over able-bodied men in licensing decisions:

> There seems to me, Mr. Printer, a piece of injustice that so many healthy young persons, and able-bodied men who have good trades, should have licenses granted to them; while the aged and decrepit, bowed down with grey hairs, and the poor widow, with perhaps a number of children, are forsaken and set to drift for themselves. It was for these objects of our charity that the granting of licenses was first instituted, and if only such persons were to have them, the town would not be so grossly imposed on and their expenses would be somewhat lessened, by this empowering the poor to get their living; therefore it is to be hoped some methods will be speedily entered into to prevent so gross an imposition, especially on the laborious part of our fellow subjects.[39]

Up through 1719, Puritan lawmakers and officials had attempted to prevent the licensing system from becoming a means of poor relief, in order both to suppress drinking and to exercise greater control over gatherings of the lower ranks more effectively. But, after 1719, relief of the poor became so pronounced an objective of licensing authorities that licenses given to "able-bodied men" represented a deviation from customary practice.

38. List of Licenses, 1737, MHS. The number of women has been computed from the Court of General Sessions, Suffolk, Record Books, 1702–1732. Many widows who held licenses lost them when they remarried and then held them under a different name when they became widowed again. Their marriages and remarriages have been traced to ensure that they are counted only once. The 11 who acquired licenses because of poverty are Hepzibah Alden, Elizabeth Lillie, Patience Copp, Katherine Thacher, Sarah Wormall, Mary Emmons, Elizabeth Hawksworth, Ann Moore, Olive Smallpeice, Isabella Caldwell, and Sarah Darby. Their estate papers are located in Suffolk County Probate Records, Record Books.

39. *Boston Evening-Post*, Dec. 21, 1767, no. 1675.

II

As the poor won more licenses after 1719, a distinct hierarchy of establishments became still more evident. Taverns like Thomas Selby's thirteen-room Crown Coffee House on Long Wharf stood at the apex of public houses in the 1710s.[40] Favored by well-dressed gentlemen accustomed to coffee, tea, a variety of liquors, and the special crockery and glassware used to imbibe them, this house set the standard for genteel entertainment.

Less refined but still busier was the Sign of the Sun in Dock Square, rented by Samuel Mears and his wife Hannah between 1708 and 1726. Mears owned less silver, 14 lbs., than Selby; the 148 lbs. of pewter served most customers. He did carry a silver watch, but had no clock for public view. There were forks available, but no coffee, tea, or the crockery for their use. The Sun stocked a less varied array of beverages, including parts of two pipes of Madeira (for Madeira, one pipe = 92 gallons) and Canary, 197 gallons of brandy, 123 gallons of rum, and only half a barrel of cider. As at Selby's, Mears's patrons valued taste. He had 4 gallons of cinnamon water and 85 gallons of lime juice to flavor drinks. Mears could seat more patrons, with ninety-three chairs in the house, thirteen of them "new," six of "Turkey work," and one "easy chair." Situated near the Town Dock not far from King Street, this tavern probably catered to seamen, dockworkers, and sea captains. They apparently demanded rum rather than cider, given Mears's inventory of beverages. The rooms were smoky, since Mears had more than fifteen hundred long clay pipes for sale; but seventeen candlesticks illuminated the rooms, inviting for sailors on leave from ships. Unlike Selby, Mears was not a gentleman. He and his wife had to labor in the tavern, but with the assistance of two slaves, Phillis and Jenny. But Mears owned a library almost equal to Selby's, thirty-one books plus his Bible.[41]

Ranking just below the Crown Coffee House and the Sun was the King's Head Tavern just up King Street from the Crown. The immigrant cidermaker James Pitson and his wife Hannah kept this modest, nine-room establishment, including a shop, which he rented from Lieutenant Governor William Dummer from 1717 to 1737. Pitson and his wife also labored in the tavern with the assistance of one slave, Prince. They could seat fifty-

40. Inventory of Thomas Selby, Suffolk County Probate Records, Record Book, XXV, 530–535. See Chapter 2, above.

41. Inventory of Samuel Mears, Suffolk County Probate Records, Record Book, XXVII, 269.

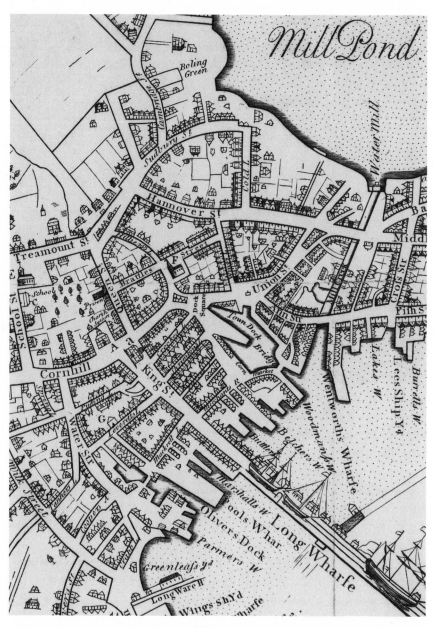

Plate 4. King Street and Long Wharf. *Detail from* The Town of Boston in New England, *by John Bonner, 1722. Courtesy, Massachusetts Historical Society*

eight customers and kept twelve "Turkey work" chairs in the Great Room. Pitson offered a slightly greater variety of drink than Mears. Besides West India and New England rum (152 gallons), brandy (9 gallons), Madeira (12 gallons), and Canary wine (10 gallons), he had on hand seventeen bottles of sherry, eighteen bottles of Dock Stevens (probably beer), some Bristol beer, and two bottles of bitter. Pitson had diversified his offerings of drink out of necessity but still possessed a greater quantity of cider (530 gallons) than anything else. Selby disdained to sell any cider, and Mears had little on hand. Pitson might have cultivated less discriminating, poorer, or thriftier cider drinkers. He also had a coffee mill but only two coffee cups. It was not a staple as at Selby's. In china rather than silver punch bowls, Pitson mixed drinks for companies and could flavor drinks with a variety of spices as well as with clove water (10 gallons) or mint water (12 gallons). Three dozen customers could be provided with individual knives and forks; eighteen wine glasses were also available. Pitson also helped to introduce refinements in drinking rituals by selling sixty-six glasses and twenty-nine punch bowls in his shop. Although considerably below Selby's number, the 432 empty bottles Pitson had on hand still suggest a high volume of sales.[42]

A prominent King Street establishment, Pitson's tavern probably catered to the middling ranks of tradesmen and artisans as well as travelers off ships. Country visitors who could afford a tavern where drinks came in glasses, wanted flavor, and knew how to use forks could also have contributed to business. So would those yearning for conversation with a well-informed tavernkeeper. Pitson owned a greater library than both Selby and Mears, eighty-eight books and thirty-one pamphlets.[43]

Several notches below the King's Head was the Widow Wormall's Marlborough Head Tavern, also on King Street. She kept tavern there from 1716 to 1721. Although her sign honored the victorious duke, she could offer barely the essentials in tavern entertainment, providing approximately nineteen chairs, napkins enough for seventeen customers, but no glasses, punch bowls, spices, or high volume or variety of beverages. At her death she had only 131 gallons of cider and 12 gallons of wine on hand. She did sell spirits, because she owed money for them, but she could not secure enough credit to buy in quantity. She had only twenty-eight pounds (by weight) of pewter altogether, so customers might have drunk from bottles or shared vessels on crowded occasions. Wormall had 120 empties. Only four candlesticks lighted the dim rooms instead of Pitson's ten and

42. Inventory of James Pitson, *ibid.*, XXXIV, 360–364.
43. *Ibid.*

Mears's seventeen. Still, there were a dozen forks for those who used them and one silver tankard available to help solemnize transactions and agreements among her humble clientele.[44]

Ranking below this establishment was the retail dramshop that Elizabeth Hawksworth had finally succeeded in getting licensed in 1718. A year before her death she moved to a house on Cornhill Street, a good location on the road leading from Boston Neck to King Street in the center of town. But she rented only three rooms in the house, two of them garret rooms to which it was necessary to climb at least one and probably two flights of stairs. Once customers had managed to get up to the shop, they were made comfortable enough. Three rooms contained twenty-nine cheap chairs. Hawksworth broke the law prohibiting retailers from encouraging customers to sit and consume beverages in their rooms. She had more drinking vessels than Wormall, owning ninety-one pounds (by weight) of pewter, some earthenware, and even a few glasses. She even had two tea tables, but not the crockery to go with them. Crammed into the back garret with these tables were sixteen barrels of cider—her major item for sale—and a barrel of sugar, thirty-two pounds of tallow, two pots of honey, and almost two cords of wood. She also sold rum, but had only three gallons in stock at her death. There were no forks. But, unlike Wormall, she had collected a few prints for her walls.[45] No doubt after climbing the stairs, customers could buy drink at rock-bottom prices.

Below Hawksworth's establishment was whatever Olive Smallpeice contrived to set up after the death of her tavernkeeper husband, John Smallpeice, the aged sailor, in 1719. When John had been alive, they had operated a tavern in rented rooms with twenty chairs, four tables, and some household equipment. The settlement of the estate left the Widow Smallpeice with only a bed, a few kettles and pots, four chairs, some hearth equipment, and sheets. Yet on this foundation the widow applied for and received a tavern license in her name, negotiated new lines of credit, and moved to a better location on Fish Street in the North End when it became vacant. She would later rent a tavern on King Street with a new husband.[46]

The possession of items like chairs and beverages like rum by drinksellers at the bottom of the social hierarchy reflects significant improve-

44. Sarah Wormall, *ibid.*, XX, 528, XXIV, 36–37.

45. *Records of Boston Selectmen, 1716 to 1736*, 86; Elizabeth Hawksworth, Suffolk County Probate Records, Record Book, XXII, 704, XXIV, 7–8.

46. John Smallpeice, Suffolk County Probate Records, Record Book, XXII, 199–201, N.S., X, 116–117. Olive Smallpeice is first licensed in 1720. Court of General Sessions, Suffolk, Record Book, 1719–1725, 41, 335; *Records of Boston Selectmen, 1716 to 1736*, 86.

ments in the standard of living of Bostonians. But it is also evident that greater gaps now existed between the material life of the upper and lower strata even in public houses. Differences in style and deportment accentuated by utensils, vessels, and linen now markedly distinguished the table manners and drinking customs of the upper and lower ranks. The popular culture of drink was becoming more differentiated as new mixed drinks, such beverages as coffee and tea, and the vessels used to imbibe them became available. Fundamentally, the popular culture of drink still served to forge and maintain relationships throughout the social structure, but specialized aspects of it also demarcated wealth, status, and exclusivity. The tone and tenor of tavern life in Boston became more complex as different clienteles distinguished themselves from each other. Most evident was the withdrawal of the genteel into select companies.[47]

But while gentlemen made establishments like the Crown Coffee House their own, it was establishments like those of the widows Wormall, Hawksworth, and Smallpeice that multiplied when the restrictions on licenses were eased in 1719. The poor staked out a claim to a large segment of the popular culture of drink, and drank with less restraint. Increasingly, licensing decisions revolved around an individual's ability to support himself or herself together with dependents rather than whether an applicant possessed a reputation for "sober conversation." As selectmen recognized and succumbed to this shift in priorities, they became less prone to refuse renewal or approval of a license because of reports of disorder. Objections to the renewal of licenses decreased rapidly after 1719; the number fell from sixty-six (against fifty-one individuals) between 1710 and 1719 to twelve between 1721 and 1730.[48] Even though the number of public houses had more than doubled, the number of objections plummeted. To be sure, the night and day visits and patrols by officials continued into the 1730s, but such inspections became less and less relevant to a population struggling with the faltering Boston economy and less intimidating to those licenseholders who had succeeded in making need a determining factor in the granting of licenses. The intemperate disorder that the Assembly had mobilized to quell from 1681 to 1719 had become an institutionalized feature of Boston society.

The relationship between licenseholders and those elected and appointed officials who had authority over them changed. Up through 1719,

47. James Thacher, *History of the Town of Plymouth* . . . , 3d ed. (Yarmouthport, Mass., 1972), 181.

48. *Records of Boston Selectmen, 1701 to 1715*, 111, 114, 166, 187, 212, 231, *1716 to 1736*, 6, 20, 40, 128–129, 166–167.

licenseholders had cause to be wary of the disapproval or wrath of select-men and justices. Those allegedly keeping disorderly houses had been forced to come before selectmen and justices in a ritual reacknowledgment of their subjection to their superiors, the "best men." They had to compen-sate for the behavior they had permitted or perpetrated in their houses by demonstrating due deference to the upholders of the king's peace. For ex-ample, John Lewes had "humbly beg[ged] pardon" of the justices who had fined him, saying that "since that time he had not presumed to disregard the law, or not to observe the same, so he hopes that it shall ever be a warning to him—to cause him to walk more orderly and inoffensively."[49] Such ritual displays of deference in word and posture by errant drinksell-ers in the chambers of selectmen and justices now almost ceased. Conse-quently, the concern of licenseholders over how much their customers con-sumed and what they said or did while drinking must also have diminished.

As a hierarchy among public houses catering to distinct clienteles distin-guished by wealth and deportment became more evident and demarcated, the control exercised by masters over servants and slaves became more tenuous because men of different ranks less often mingled in the same public space. To be sure, control was very much in evidence at taverns at the apex of the hierarchy, such as at the Crown Coffee House and the Royal Exchange. Here slaves could be periodically inspected for purchase. At least sixteen sales of from one to ten slaves took place in these and other taverns in the 1720s and 1730s. It is not clear whether they were auc-tioned, or offered at a set price, but either way such sales exhibited the structure and nature of racial authority in a stark manner. By midcentury, however, these sales appear to have ceased or were no longer advertised. The newspapers still offered slaves for sale, but notices instructed poten-tial buyers to inquire discreetly of the printer for the identity of the seller. This change suggests that the buying and selling of human beings openly in taverns caused enough social discomfort by midcentury to inhibit pro-prietors from hosting such venues.[50] Public sales of slaves also invited

49. Petition of John Lewes to the General Court, May 6, 1668, Taverns, CXI, 31.

50. *Boston Gazette*, Oct. 2–9, 1727, no. 411, Sept. 30, 1727, no. 418, July 8–15, 1728, no. 451, Apr. 21–28, 1729, no. 492, July 7–14, 1729, no. 503, Aug. 18–25, 1729, no. 509, Oct. 6–13, 1729, no. 516, Jan. 27–Feb. 2, 1730, no. 530, Mar. 2–9, 1730, no. 535, June 1–8, 1730, no. 548, Jan. 4–11, 1731, no. 576, Apr. 12–19, 1731, no. 590, Dec. 16–23, 1734, no. 781, July 8–15, 1734, no. 758, June 11–18, 1733, no. 702, Nov. 10–17, 1735, no. 828, Feb. 14–21, 1737, no. 893. Typical advertisements of the 1740s can be read in Nov. 13, 1744, no. 1185.

sellers and buyers of varying rank and civility. Boston gentry readily mixed with lesser men at court sessions and Sabbath meetings where rank was honored, but they preferred exclusively genteel assemblies when they visited taverns to drink, converse, and conduct business.

In a wider cross section of taverns throughout Boston, slaves were also visible as servants. In inventories of forty-one Boston tavernkeepers licensed between 1680 and 1780, nineteen owned at least one slave. These slaves worked on close terms and in close quarters with their respective masters, and some masters acknowledged their service by providing for them in their old age or manumitting them with support. John Winge, who kept a major tavern in the 1680s, stipulated that his wife not sell his slaves and that upon her death they be distributed among his children. Francis Holmes, proprietor of the Bunch of Grapes on King Street in the early eighteenth century, directed that his slave Prince not be sold, but either freed after his wife's death or placed with one of his children. But other tavernkeepers, simply indifferent to their slaves' fate or in financial straits, sold slaves without hesitation. William Lowder's slaves had to be sold because his estate proved insolvent. Thomas Selby's wealthy widow sold four slaves who had helped to operate the Crown Coffee House.[51] Thus in this substantial establishment, slaves witnessed their brethren sold and would themselves eventually suffer the same uncertain fate. In this house, blacks had to seek convivality furtively, out of view of the main rooms.

Outside the major taverns on King Street, slaves and servants fared better. Their efforts to meet together, however, periodically caused alarm. As early as 1705 constables received instructions to arrest any Indian, black, or mulatto servant on the streets after 9:00 P.M. In 1723, Boston selectmen ordered all burials of Indians, blacks, and mulattoes to take place at least half an hour before sunset because of the "ill tendency" of "great numbers" of the same attending funerals at night. In 1738 "Gentlemen in Authority" expressed new determination to prevent blacks, Indians, and mulattoes from meeting at night. In 1751 the Boston town meeting discussed the "great disorders and disturbances which have been frequently made" by black and Indian servants collecting into "companies at night" for drinking and gaming. Poor drinksellers, legal and illegal, undermined these efforts by their readiness to sell to blacks, Indians, and white ser-

51. Estate of John Winge, Suffolk County Probate Records, Record Book, XV, 22, 232, Francis Holmes, XXV, 118–120, William Lowder, XXXIII, 415, Thomas Selby, XXV, 530–535, XXVI, 468–469.

vants. In the increasing number of marginal, makeshift establishments after 1719, the opportunities for those at the bottom of the social hierarchy to buy drink expanded. There were always covert sellers. Boston justices indicted ninety-seven people for selling drink without a license from 1720 to 1728. William Cox, an unlicensed blacksmith, was convicted of keeping a disorderly house and entertaining blacks, servants, and women in 1727. The same year, James Habersham, an unlicensed boatman, paid a fine for entertaining blacks and servants. Joseph Coolidge, a gunsmith in poor health, promised the selectmen in 1765 that, even though he had suffered misfortune and must apply for a liquor license, he did not "intend to make the least profit in his new business by supplying negroes and other servants with liquor," unless permitted by their masters.[52] Such an explicit assurance suggests that poor sellers were inclined to do the opposite and that such sales were common knowledge. The *Boston Evening-Post* described one such drinking company in 1740:

> Last Friday a gentleman of this town went over to Roxbury to look for his Negro woman, who had been gone from him a few days, and hearing a noise in the tavern, he went in, past nine o'clock and found about a dozen black gentry, he's and she's in a room, in a very merry humour, singing and dancing, having a violin and a store of wine and punch before them. They all belonged to gentlemen in this town, and 'tis much to be wondered at, how they can be absent from their respective masters without their masters' knowledge.[53]

Some poor tavernkeepers tolerated or even welcomed slaves and servants, in their efforts to make a profit. Such covert gatherings for drink exchange no doubt helped to alleviate the despair and isolation that drove a female slave in Salem to "go into her own country" by taking a bottle of rum and some biscuits, burying them in a burial ground, and then taking her own life with a knife in 1733.[54]

---

52. Court of General Sessions, Suffolk, Record Book, 1702–1712, 111, 1712–1719, 76, 1719–1725, 66, 128; *Boston Gazette*, Mar. 26, 1751, no. 1619; Boston, Record Commissioners, *Boston Records from 1700 to 1728* (Boston, 1883), 176–177; indictments tabulated from record books of Suffolk Sessions; petition of Joseph Coolidge, July 9, 1765, Misc. Bd., MHS. For glimpses of Afro-American culture in New England, see William D. Piersen, *Black Yankees: The Development of an Afro-American Subculture in Eighteenth-Century New England* (Amherst, Mass., 1988).

53. Quotation from Kym S. Rice, *Early American Taverns: For the Entertainment of Friends and Strangers* (Chicago, 1983), 72.

54. *Boston Gazette*, May 21–29, 1733, no. 699.

III

The ability of slaves and servants to purchase drink from the growing number of poor drinksellers reflects the general relaxation of constraints on the drink trade after 1719. The governing hierarchy of province and town no longer aggressively inhibited the flow of drink, and particularly rum, but licensed those people most likely to sell in as great a volume as possible. The distribution of licenses to the poor and the flow of cheap alcohol through them to the populace at large seemed to reinvigorate drinking as a medium of good will and charity. To some extent this weakening of regulation after 1719 represents a signal triumph of popular culture over Puritan teachings, of traditional drinking habits over the newfound cultivation of temperance. Drink appeared to lubricate the operation of Boston society, to focus and channel social relations, in a manner that flouted sermons, laws, and regulations. Taverns continued to be the context for a variety of exchanges solemnized with drink, from simple agreements to commerce of greater scale.

Yet upon closer consideration, it becomes clear that participants in the drink trade suffered and confronted anxiety, desperation, and cutthroat competition, which belied and undermined the traditional association of the sale and consumption of drink with good cheer, cooperation, charity, and largess. The traditional village model of the local landlord of long standing selling drink to stable, familiar groups of relations and neighbors became less and less characteristic of Boston after 1719. Boston drinksellers and their customers lived in an increasingly unstable world in the eighteenth century, even as drinksellers competed to sell more potent liquors at the lowest prices for mass consumption. Conditions in the trade reflect the increasing dependence of propertyless Bostonians on the erratic twists and turns of commerce in the Atlantic trading community for their livelihoods. So many Bostonians turned to drinkselling as one source of sustenance during periods of need and unemployment that the trade became overcrowded, and many abandoned it readily if other work became available. The special problems that widows faced in the trade highlight the scramble for custom and how Bostonians in general often departed from tradition to maintain themselves and their dependents. Under a variety of pressures, Boston drinksellers gradually refashioned the popular culture of drink into something further and further removed from the traditions they clung to when they resisted reform between 1681 and 1719.

The instability of the popular culture of drink in Boston during the

Table 2. *Terms of Licenseholders in Boston, 1702–1732*

	No. of Licenses					Total of Licenseholders
	Term in Years					
	1–5	6–10	11–20	21+	Unknown	
Tavernkeepers[a]						
Women licensed independently	17	11	7	2		37
Men	52	23	14	7		96
Men followed by widows	6	14	7	6		(x2) 66
Total	75	48	28	15		199
Retailers[b]						
Women licensed independently	68	27	17	4		116
Men	82	34	30	6		152
Men followed by widows	13	16	21	1		(x2) 102
Total	163	77	68	11		370
Grand total	238	125	96	26	41	598[c]

[a]20 women (counted in table) lost licenses when they remarried.   [b]41 women would lose licenses when they remarried.   [c]Total deducts 12 women who served more than one term.

Sources: Court of General Sessions, Suffolk, Record Books, 1712–1719, 1719–1725, 1725–1732; List of Licenses for Suffolk County, 1737, Papers of James Otis, Sr., MHS.

eighteenth century is reflected most generally in how long Bostonians kept their licenses. Of the 569 tavernkeepers and retailers whose terms can be traced with some accuracy between 1702 and 1732, 257, or 45 percent, held their licenses for only one to five years. This proportion would be still higher if one counted the terms of widows who took up a deceased husband's license separately. Another 125 men and their widows kept licenses for six to ten years. Three-quarters of all men who retailed alcohol held their licenses for ten years or less (see Table 2).

One reason for the high turnover was the sheer number of people entering the trade and the extreme competition for customers. As early as 1704, when authorities still restricted licenses severely, Susannah Carter gave up her retail license because it did not meet her "expectation." Two years later John Cary did the same because of the "greatness of his rent and excise and losses." Robert Sanders found that the "profit of his draught would not so much as pay the excise" because of the "deadness of trade" and the fact that several others in the neighborhood held licenses. Sanders decided to go to sea. In 1716 Wadsworth claimed that public houses had multiplied to such an extent that "few who have them can get a gain answerable to their charge and trouble." After 1719 the drink trade became still more competitive when the restrictive licensing policy ended and poor drinksellers entered the trade in large numbers. People gave up their licenses not just because of death or remarriage but also when another opportunity presented itself. Joseph Goldthwait left tavernkeeping to start a trade in chimney sweeping. He laid out "all the money he had or could procure" to buy servants skilled in the work. But they died, and so again he sought a license.[55] Some drinksellers acquired licenses only to secure some type of subsistence until more lucrative work could be found.

The incidence of public houses became so high that many licenseholders moved around Boston to bolster their custom or reduce their rents. Each time a drinkseller moved, he must petition the selectmen for the renewal of the license in the new location. Approval might not be forthcoming. Still, a significant proportion of drinksellers moved around with their licenses. Of the seventy-four retailers (in seventy-seven terms) licensed from six to ten years, sixteen changed their residence at least once; of forty-eight tavernkeepers, fifteen chose to move.[56] Given the high incidence of tavernkeepers and retailers, even a move from one street to the next might require the establishment and cultivation of an entirely new set of customers and new relationships of credit and trust. The advantages and disadvantages of making a move had to be weighed carefully.

Many of those who moved attempted to establish themselves on King Street or Long Wharf at the bottom of the street. King Street was lined

55. Petition of Susannah Carter, Mar. 9, 1704, Taverns, CXI, 73, Petition of John Cary, June 8, 1706, CXI, 80, Petition of Robert Sanders, Mar. 17, 1703, CXI, 75; Wadsworth, *An Essay to Do Good*, 21; Petition of Joseph Goldthwait, Aug. 12, 1767, Misc. Bd., MHS.

56. Compiled from *Records of Boston Selectmen, 1701 to 1715* and *1716 to 1736*. Of 74 retailers licensed from 6 to 10 years, 16 make moves, 43 remain in the same place, and for 15 there is not enough information; of 45 tavernkeepers licensed from 6 to 10 years, 14 make moves, 20 remain in the same place, and for 11 there is not enough information.

with shops and taverns catering to government officials, travelers, seamen, and visiting country people coming to market. It was so busy that the din of hooves, tackle, and wheels reverberating through the Town House and the Court House became so great that in 1747 the Assembly voted to outlaw travel by coach, cart, and chaise on the street from 9:00 A.M. to 1:00 P.M., and from 3:00 to 7:00 P.M., when the House was sitting. It was in some respects the ideal place to sell drink, so much so that the government rented the cellars of the Town House to retailers. Twenty to twenty-five pipes of Canary wine, or about twenty-one hundred gallons, were advertised for sale there in 1737. Ten years later a fire in the Town House destroyed several thousand pounds worth of wines and liquors stored in the cellar.[57]

Yet if the brisk traffic on King Street made it the ideal place to sell drink, the houses on the street and wharf were also expensive to rent. And so many drinksellers located there, especially after 1719, that they faced keen competition. The Widow Wormall left the North End to take over the Marlborough Head on King Street. But she died there barely solvent: she owed seventeen pounds and three shillings to Mary Gibson for rent, her second-highest debt. Widow Sarah Tomlin stayed on King Street only one year, deciding to move back to her Ann Street location in the North End because of the high rent on King Street.[58] Even modest success in the drink trade required strategy and close attention to income and expenditure.

Edward Lutwyche moved almost every year in the 1730s. He first acquired a license in 1723 after marrying a retailer on Lyn Street at the furthest reach of the North End. Lutwyche was not satisfied with this location, for the next year he received approval to sell on King Street, and then he took over the prominent Crown Coffee House on Long Wharf. But this ambitious drinkseller apparently could not balance rent and excise with income, because he went back to retailing in 1734, then to the North End on Ship Street in 1735, and then to Clark's Square in the North End in 1736. He decided to try again on King Street, however, when he received approval to keep tavern there in 1738.[59] Competition on the more residential streets and on the more than one hundred wharves that jutted out into

<hr/>

57. Walter Muir Whitehill, *Boston: A Topographical History* (Cambridge, Mass., 1968), 26; *Boston Gazette*, Aug. 1–8, 1737, no. 917, Oct. 20, 1747, no. 1335, Dec. 15, 1747, no. 1343.

58. *Records of Boston Selectmen, 1716 to 1736*, 21, 44, 85–86; Estate of Sarah Wormall, Suffolk County Probate Records, Record Book, XXII, 528.

59. *Records of Boston Selectmen, 1716 to 1736*, 177, 192, 197, 234, 257, 258, 287, 314; Boston, Record Commissioners, *Records of Boston Selectmen, 1736 to 1742* (Boston, 1886), 129.

Boston Harbor compelled many to seek a King Street location when it became available. But the number of drinksellers already there, combined with high rents, forced some out just as quickly.

The increasing competition among more numerous drinksellers is also evident in the chain reactions of moves among a number of drinksellers. In 1717 alone, Stephen North moved from Hanover to Back Street; Richard Pullen took his place in Hanover Street; Joseph Everton moved to "where William Skinner was in North Street"; Mary Mayes to where Mary Thwing was in Fish Street; Thwing went to King Street; Edward Davice to Dorothy Hawkins's house on King Street; John Webb to Elizabeth Cravath's location on Mackrel Lane.[60] When Sarah Wormall rented the Marlborough Head Tavern on King Street, she replaced a man who had been there only one year. Olive Smallpeice immediately took her place on Fish Street and would later make a move to King Street when a spot opened up; Mary Smith had already petitioned to move her license to Smallpeice's former location. Jonathan Tarbox took advantage of the fact that "two retailers near him have lately dropped their licenses" on Salem Street when he petitioned in 1767. John Hibbins told the selectmen of "the removal of two or three persons from his neighborhood who were retailers."[61] Drinksellers jealously watched prime locations so as to make that move that might increase slightly the narrow profit margins in an ever more competitive trade. When news of a move reached drinksellers, they had to calculate quickly whether the spot that opened up might be more profitable.

In this constant quest for more custom and credit, widows faced several disadvantages. First, the settlement of their deceased husband's estate usually distributed resources to creditors and children—and sometimes revealed a licenseholder to be insolvent. As a rule, widows had fewer resources with which to continue the business or start it from scratch. David and Patience Copp had owned a tavern valued at five hundred pounds plus ninety pounds worth of personal goods while he held a license from 1714 to 1718. In the past Copp had encountered few problems in securing credit, since he borrowed from seventy people. But, when he died, his debts amounted to more than the value of the entire estate. His widow Patience was left with a small legacy with which to continue the business

60. *Ibid., 1716 to 1736*, 21–22.

61. *Ibid.,* 72, 84, 85, 86; Court of General Sessions, Suffolk, Record Book, 1719–1725, 335; Petition of Jonathan Tarbox, Sept. 30, 1767, of John Hibbins, June 15, 1767, Misc. Bd., MHS.

between 1719 and 1723.[62] She had nothing to invest and had become a poor credit risk. Widows had to settle the debts that their husbands had accumulated in the trade and thus were hampered in their efforts to operate independently.

A comparison of men's and women's excise levies in the 1710s (when excise records are available) also reveals the more fragile foundation on which widows entered and participated in the trade. When Thomas Selby assumed control over the Crown Coffee House, he quickly expanded its business. He paid twenty pounds excise in 1714 and twenty-five the next year. Two other male tavernkeepers paying high excise taxes increased the volume and quality of their trade between 1713 and 1715. But Francis Holmes, proprietor of the important Bunch of Grapes up King Street from the Crown, lost trade in the same years, probably to Selby. So did Mary Smith and Mildred Dorrell, also among the top ten in taxes. Widows composed 23 percent of the tavernkeepers licensed in 1715 but paid only 19 percent of the excise. Still, considering their disadvantages in estate settlement and the acquisition of credit, they held on to a respectable chunk of the tavern trade. Although Smith and Dorrell lost trade in the 1710s, they did not go under in decades when the trade became still more competitive. Smith held on to her license for at least twenty-six years. Dorrell had taken over from her husband in 1704 and would keep her license into the 1730s. And Anne Sword rented the Crown Coffee House and operated it successfully for nine years in the 1740s—satisfying the palates of Boston's most discriminating tavern patrons—until she was evicted.[63]

As with tavernkeepers, a few widowed retailers competed successfully. In 1713 three widows were among the ten retailers paying the highest excise. One of them, Deborah Man, paid the highest excise of all, amounting to twenty-five pounds—more than twice the amount paid by the next

62. Suffolk County Probate Records, Record Book, XXI, 351–352, N.S., VIII, 474–475. Even the wife of a substantial tavernkeeper like Samuel Mears, who operated the Sun Tavern between 1708 and 1726, could find herself with few resources to preserve the trade to which she had contributed so much. After all Mears's debts were paid and legacies distributed to two sons and a daughter, the widow Hannah was left with little but household goods to continue operating the establishment (XXV, 344–345, XXVII, 269).

63. Court of General Sessions, Suffolk, Record Book, 1712–1719, 26–27, 51, 93. Only the amount in pounds was used to tabulate gains and losses in taxes. Taxes measure not the volume of drink so much as the amount of distilled liquors sold, which is a measure of the quality of the trade of drinkseller because licenses to sell rum were in such demand. Petition of Anne Sword, September 1750, Taverns, CXI, 205–206.

retailer in rank and as much as tavernkeeper Selby paid. She probably helped to outfit ships' stores with liquor. She and sixteen other widows made up 39 percent of the forty-three retailers licensed in 1713, but paid 40 percent of the total excise. But if Deborah Man is excluded, the widows collectively paid only 28 percent of the excise.[64] The excise taxes paid by five widows had all dropped after these women succeeded their husbands as proprietors. With a few exceptions, widows generally sold less volume and operated more marginal establishments.

If they remarried, widows placed their licenses in jeopardy. Sarah Battersby began life as Sarah Clark; she married in 1703 but was widowed by 1706. She then applied for a license but was refused approval during these years of restrictive licensing policies. Her second husband, Thomas Phelps, however, did acquire a license in 1708 at an unknown location, and she received a license to sell after his death. In 1711 she married John Battersby, a seaman, but continued to keep the license in her name. This exception might have been allowed because he was at sea. She tried to move to Fish Street in 1713 and was refused permission. But the next year she was approved to keep a tavern at the lower end of King Street. She remained there a few years and did well, paying two pounds more excise in 1715 than she had in 1713. Then in 1717 the court voided the marriage to Battersby upon revelation that he had a wife in Ireland; the same year, she married fourth husband, Benjamin Bryant. Upon this marriage she almost lost the King Street location because the selectmen twice refused the license to Bryant when he petitioned for it. Bryant died in 1720, and Sarah moved to a new King Street location and sold drink there until she married John Battersby, presumably now free, a second time. But this time she lost the license because the selectmen refused to approve a license to Battersby the bigamist. For the next several years they might have been dependent on Battersby's wages (he left any outstanding wages to her in his will in 1725). By 1728 he had died. The new widow could not get a King Street location in 1728, but she did acquire approval to retail on Fish Street in the North End, where she sold drink until 1733. But she lost this license when she married Joseph Lowden. Eventually, however, Lowden got the license, since his name appears on a license roster in 1737.[65] Throughout most of

64. Court of General Sessions, Suffolk, Record Book, 1702–1712, 8, 23, 253–254, 1712–1719, 26–27, 51, 93, 215–216, 236–237. Shares of taxes paid were calculated using only the amounts in pounds; shillings and pennies were dropped.

65. *Records of Boston Selectmen, 1701 to 1716*, 42, 52–53, 179, 212; Phelps's name appears on the license rosters of 1708 and 1709. Court of General Sessions, Suffolk, Record Book,

her six marriages Battersby had managed to keep a license, but with interruptions and denials along the way. Each marriage had placed the renewal of the license under question. Still, she watched for and won a King Street location several times.

In their efforts to overcome their disadvantages and manage their houses to greater profit, widows sometimes came close to challenging the boundaries of prescribed female roles. Widow Ann LeBlond risked her reputation on a number of levels when she contracted with an itinerant physician from London for him to receive patients at her retail house on Treamount Street for several weeks. This physician promised to heal victims with cancerous growths, scrofula, leprosy, and other ailments. Arranging to have a stranger with dubious credentials operate out of her house was controversial, because men of authority often considered such visitors to be wandering quacks and confidence men. They were an insult to local physicians. This one promised, if he "miscarries of curing, that he will take no money." But they usually did not stay long enough to see whether their nostrums had any effect. Widow LeBlond risked incurring the wrath and retaliation of desperate patients suffering from serious illnesses. But she obviously hoped to make money from those coming to see him. This physician later operated out of Widow Storey's tavern in Portsmouth.[66] Opening her house to a male stranger making suspicious claims, aggressively pursuing trade, this widow placed herself in a vulnerable position in relation to male competitors and patriarchal authority.

In the same spirit, Widow Rebecca Holmes leased out space in her King Street tavern for a government function affecting all licenseholders in Boston. To her tavern in 1728 came licenseholders to reckon and pay their excise taxes over the course of two days. This was added business that male tavernkeepers on King Street would welcome. The crowds that assembled in taverns had to be satisfied but not allowed to get out of control. Widows must collect full reckonings from male companies. Widow Whyer across the river in Charlestown hosted a company "upon a frolic" at her tavern in 1727, going so far as to provide a fiddler for the company's entertainment (a violation of the law). But the group left without paying for all the drink supplied or compensating the fiddler to his satisfaction "for his trouble and wearing out his strings." She promptly put a notice in

1702–1712, 176, 193; *Boston Marriages from 1701 to 1751*, 14, 33, 69, 118, 185; *Records of Boston Selectmen, 1716 to 1736*, 39, 40, 42, 43, 85, 140, 166, 177, 233, 257, 314; List of Licenses for Suffolk County, 1737, Papers of James Otis, Sr., MHS; Will of John Battersby, Suffolk County Probate Records, docket no. 5300.

66. *Boston Gazette*, Oct. 10–17, 1720, no. 44, July 10–17, 1727, no. 398.

the *Boston Gazette* telling the members of this company to pay the "just reckoning" and give the fiddler more than the paltry twelve pence he had collected.[67] She did not name names, but the threat to was implicit. The fierce competition in the drink trade caused widows to hustle for more business and outmaneuver men in the same business. It was necessary to bargain closely in face-to-face deals with men who might resent their assertiveness and retaliate. In so doing, women in this cutthroat trade stepped out of the customary dependent roles women were expected to occupy.

Widows were also more vulnerable when rival tavernkeepers launched efforts to steal each other's trade. Such was the case with tavernkeeper Frances Wardell. As a widow she had married beneath her, bringing "considerable estate" to her new husband Jonathan while he brought "little or nothing." He obtained a license to keep tavern in 1711, but she operated the business because he was ill. Her trade dropped in the 1710s, according to excise payments, but, when Jonathan died, she owned and managed a middling-rank establishment on Cambridge Street near the bowling green. There were thirty-one old chairs, several pounds worth of silver plate, and eight feather beds. She had more than eight hundred gallons of cider in stock, but no wine or rum. Out of gratitude, her husband left her the entire estate instead of dividing it up among children; so she had a good foundation to continue the business. And as a widow she did well, even succeeding by the 1720s in attracting the custom of the Superior and lesser courts. They convened in her tavern, and thus she would be required to sell a greater variety of drink. And she put an addition on the house to provide more space for the courts. Then suddenly in 1726, after sixteen years in the trade, the selectmen refused to approve her for renewal of her license.[68]

It is probable that a rival tavernkeeper trying to capture her trade, including that of the courts, persuaded the selectmen to refuse her renewal. Wardell was "surprised" by the refusal. She immediately appealed to the governor's Council and House and won approval despite the selectmen. Then the next year it happened again. She went to the selectmen and asked for reasons for the refusal; they replied with only vague references to "misrule," a ready complaint against women governing male behavior. She appealed to the Council and House again, asserting that she had "conformed" to the drink laws "as much as any others of the same profession" (meaning not very much at all). She also recruited nine prominent men in

67. *Boston Gazette,* Sept. 11–18, 1727, no. 408, Jan. 15–22, 1728, no. 426.
68. Petition of Frances Wardell, Aug. 16, 1727, Taverns, CXI, 86–89.

her neighborhood to petition in her behalf. The Council and House over-ruled the selectmen again, and the attempt to terminate her establishment failed.[69] Ten years later she was still in business. Wardell had acquired enough political acumen to ward off jealous competitors and their allies from acquiring her trade, but it was a delicate business for a woman to assert herself before men and against men. Female assertiveness in busi-ness and before courts is a reflection of the variety of innovative actions required of all drinksellers to get and keep custom.

Mary Clapham faced a similar situation in 1758 in her effort to compete for trade in the commercial heart of the town. Fourteen years earlier her husband had acquired a retail license at a house on Queen Street leading up from the Town House toward Beacon Hill. By 1755 he had died, and Widow Clapham moved to a more lucrative location on Merchants Row off King Street near the wharves. But some individual or group did not want her there and accused her of "misrule" to the selectmen despite her total of seventeen years in the drink trade. Refused renewal, she was furious and desperate. Having no success with the selectmen, she presented a petition to the justices of Suffolk Sessions, saying that "the information" given to the selectmen against her "was without the least foundation." Further, this charge "was raised and promoted with a malicious intent to ruin her, and bring her and her family to extreme poverty." Stirred to consider the case carefully, the justices sent a letter to the selectmen asking them to attend the next session of court to answer Clapham's bold assertion that they had "no evidence to support such a charge" of misrule.[70]

But the selectmen defied the court by, first, refusing to attend it and, second, sending a letter to the justices stating that the justices were bound by law not to license anyone whom the selectmen had refused to approve and that it would be a dangerous precedent for them to overrule the selectmen. The selectmen wished "to pay all due deference to your honors" but still "pay the greatest deference to the laws and constitution of our country." The selectmen refused even to answer Clapham's allegations, tersely stating that they would not "go into an altercation with her before your honors or elsewhere." This arrogant reply affronted the justices, because they had a "long debate" about the issue. But they were faced with upholding the word of a poor widow against the judgment and authority of

69. *Ibid.*

70. *Boston Marriages from 1700 to 1751*, 329; Boston, Record Commissioners, *Selectmen's Minutes from 1742–3 to 1753* (Boston, 1887), 78; *Selectmen's Minutes from 1754 through 1763* (Boston, 1887), 29, 93–95.

the selectmen, suspect as their motives appeared. In the end a "very great majority" of justices voted to dismiss the widow's plea for renewal. Clapham did not possess the kind of connections that Frances Wardell had cultivated with the Superior Court justices by serving them. But Widow Clapham might have persisted and eventually rewon a license, for a "Mrs. Clapham" kept a house on King Street in 1773.[71]

In the accounts and endeavors of widows like Deborah Man, Rebecca Holmes, and Frances Wardell, one glimpses women successfully competing against men (and their wives) in an overcrowded trade. Deborah Man became the most successful retailer in Boston in the 1710s, paying as much excise as Thomas Selby. Rebecca Holmes presided over the bustling Bunch of Grapes on King Street. Frances Wardell had captured the trade of the Superior Court. These and other widows might have relished their independence so much that they hesitated to marry again and suffer interference from patriarchal authority—or have property willed out of their hands. Deborah Man continued sixteen years a widow in the business. Frances Wardell must have been courted by men seeking a wife with property in the 1720s and 1730s, but she did not marry a third time. Marriage was an economic partnership, a pooling of resources under exclusive male control, which these widows chose not to enter again. Only twenty, or about one-third of, female tavernkeepers took new husbands while they held licenses between 1702 and 1732. In 1740 the *Boston Gazette* reprinted an essay by an Englishwoman advocating that the daughters of lesser gentlemen and tradesmen be apprenticed in "genteel" trades rather than pressured into making bad marriages. If a woman was "trained up to business," the essay stated, she would not have to "submit to be a slave, and fling herself away as many are forced to do, merely for a maintenance."[72] Although drinkselling was less reputable than the retail trades advocated here for women, and probably closed to young and never-married women, some female licenseholders enlarged their options in life through engagement in the trade. For some, success might have made marriage less attractive.

Of those female tavernkeepers who did take new husbands, almost all

71. *Selectmen's Minutes from 1754 through 1763*, 93–95. Clapham was not on a 1765 licensing roster, but there is a reference to a group of Whig patriots meeting "at Mrs. Clapham's in King Street" in a newspaper in 1773 (*Massachusetts Gazette Extraordinary*, Mar. 11, 1773 [supplement to the *Massachusetts Gazette: and the Boston Weekly News-Letter*]).

72. *Boston Gazette*, Mar. 24, 1740, no. 1052.

made it clear that they wished to continue in the drink trade after the marriage, because their new husbands applied to get the licenses. These men most likely moved in with their wives so that their wives would not have to give up the custom they had developed on the streets where they lived. Of course, it was always possible that the new husband would not get the license. As had happened to Sarah Battersby, this was a real risk. But most of the new husbands eventually got their wives' licenses, perhaps because selectmen grudgingly recognized the established trade of the women they had married.[73]

But it would be a mistake to conceive of the drink trade as a liberating outlet, a means of transcending restrictive gender roles, for most women in the eighteenth century. The trade was just too crowded after 1719. Most widows in the trade retailed liquor in low volume. Of the forty-one widows holding retail licenses who took new husbands between 1702 and 1732, only thirteen of these new husbands tried to get their wives' licenses.[74] These women did not seek to combine the retail trade with marriage, another indication that the trade was so crowded that it rendered small returns. Selectmen and justices approved and granted so many licenses to the poor that marriage offered poor women a better position—companionship in misfortune at the very least as well as a sexual partner—than the license ever had.

More typical than Deborah Man and Frances Wardell was Adrian Cunningham. She had difficulty getting into the trade. Approved for a license by the selectmen in the place of Widow Sarah Hunt on Scarlett's Wharf in 1721, she apparently was rejected by the justices. The next year, however, she did get a license when she rented the Castle Tavern on Fleet Street in the North End in partnership with her sister. She did business there for two years. But this arrangement ended in 1725, when she married Elisha Odling. Odling could not offer much. He had been moving in and out of the drink trade from one location to the next for fourteen years. In all he had filed seventeen petitions for licenses and had been rejected eleven times. In 1712 the selectmen had ordered him to move out of the Salutation Tavern or lose his license. At one point he had rented the Marlborough

---

73. The number of female tavernkeepers whose new husbands applied for their licenses was determined by comparing the year in which a woman's license ended in the Court of General Sessions, Suffolk, Record Books, 1702–1732, with marriage records in *Boston Marriages from 1700 to 1751,* and then noting whether the new husband applied for the license in *Records of Boston Selectmen, 1701 to 1715* or *1716 to 1736,* and whether he was actually licensed (Court of General Sessions, Suffolk).

74. *Ibid.*

Head on King Street but could not make a success of it, since he stayed there only one year. Significantly, he did not have a license when Adrian agreed to marry him, and had little prospect of getting one. When he applied for Adrian's license, he was rejected by selectmen and justices for two years running. Finally, in 1728, he acquired a license to keep tavern in the North End on another street. Adrian Cunningham might have traded her Castle Tavern license in hand for marriage with the unstable Odling because now, at least, she would have a partner with whom to face the stress of subsistence in Boston. Men, even men like Odling, had more options for labor. But Odling died several years later, and Adrian acquired a license in her own name. She lost this license, however, when she was deemed "unfit" to be a drinkseller even in these years when disorderly houses received more toleration. She was back where she started. Another marriage, in 1737, might have improved her circumstances.[75] Drinkselling had never been anything more than a strategy for survival for this woman with few choices; it had never been a vehicle for independence.

With so many people like the Odlings selling drink after 1719, many of the popular assumptions that underlay the distribution of licenses to the needy came under strain and question. So many acquired licenses that numbers of them could not make a success of the trade even after receiving credit. Odling could not make it even on King Street. Not enough people climbed the stairs to sit drinking in Elizabeth Hawksworth's shop to come even close to enabling her to meet her debts. Although Ann Moore held a license to keep tavern for seventeen years, she did not bring in enough income to pay off debts to eighteen creditors at her death. Insolvency was common among drinksellers. Of twenty-four drinksellers who died between 1703 and 1758, ten proved insolvent or just barely solvent when all goods were sold.[76] The sale and consumption of drink remained intricately

75. Odling: *Records of Boston Selectmen, 1701 to 1715,* 92, 93, 110, 113, 130, 141, 142, 166, 168, 169, 235, *1716 to 1736,* 38, 39, 72, 87; Adrian Cunningham (Odling): *1716 to 1736,* 55, 98–99, 210, *Boston Marriages from 1700 to 1751,* 128, 227.

76. The 10 were William Endicot, Benjamin Johns, David Copp, Sarah Wormall, Nathaniel Emmons, Elizabeth Hawksworth, Ann Moore, John Smallpeice, William Lowder, and Samuel Wethered (Suffolk County Probate Records). It was not just marginal drinksellers like Hawksworth who could not pay their debts; proprietors of elite taverns also encountered problems. Samuel Wethered set out to compete with establishments like the Crown Coffee House in the 1730s and 1740s. By 1741 his tavern was a fashionable gathering place near the Town House. It was in Wethered's tavern that the new governor Shirley

entwined with the negotiation of credit among male colonists. But in the final reckoning, those dozens of people who had extended credit to these drinksellers might have lost most of their money.

Inevitably, the multiplication of drinksellers and the failure of many of them to sustain themselves revived arguments made decades earlier by critics like Wadsworth that the distribution of licenses to the poor only exacerbated poverty in the town. In the 1730s, when the number of public houses rose to close to two hundred, town authorities again took steps to get the poor out of public houses and put them to work. But, like previous efforts to make work for the poor, this initiative had uneven results. Selectmen and overseers of the poor did not compel those needing relief to enter the workhouse, and few chose to enter. A new program to employ the poor launched in 1748 initially met more success. This plan involved the recruitment of private investors to finance a linen manufactory to employ mainly women and children. By the 1750s the manufactory did employ several hundred spinners, offering an alternative to drinkselling to the widows of Boston. Ultimately, however, the project failed, mainly because of low-priced imported linen.[77]

The failure of these programs juxtaposed to the continuing high demand for liquor licenses illustrates the popular appeal of drinkselling. Such employment allowed the poor some measure of independence and the ability not only to maintain social ties but to provide a setting for gatherings in their neighborhoods. Between 1702 and 1737, 1,034 people filed 1,671 petitions for approval to sell drink. Between 1702 and 1732 a total of 598 people held licenses to sell drink in a town whose population reached a

---

was honored in 1741. Here gentleman traveler Alexander Hamilton presented letters of introduction to Boston gentry. But Wethered sank into impossibly deep debt, owing hundreds of pounds to upwards of 60 people. He owed for rent, for hundreds of gallons of wine, for 424 gallons of rum, and even small amounts to carters of goods. At his death in 1759 only four shillings and four pence could be paid on each pound of debt. Although extravagance and mismanagement contributed to this crash, the fact that selectmen approved so many other taverns on King Street made competition keen and profit margins slim for even gentlemen's houses. Suffolk County Probate Records, Record Books, LIV, 447–452, N.S., XXXVI, 101, 105, 107, 110–111, LVIII, 220–221; *Records of Boston Selectmen, 1736 to 1742*, 308, 370; Carl Bridenbaugh, ed., *Gentleman's Progress: The Itinerarium of Dr. Alexander Hamilton, 1744* (Chapel Hill, N.C., 1948), 107–108, 133–134; John A. Schutz, *William Shirley: King's Governor of Massachusetts* (Chapel Hill, N.C., 1961), 45.

77. Gary B. Nash, "The Failure of Female Factory Labor in Colonial Boston," *Labor History*, XX (1979), 165–188.

peak of approximately 16,925 in 1738.[78] Although few could make much money in this overcrowded trade, hundreds still applied to each decade.

I V

Coinciding with efforts to put the poor to work during this span, critics periodically called for the imposition of more stringent licensing policies, similar to those in force in the 1680s and from 1700 to 1719. In 1750 a writer to the *Boston Weekly News-Letter* chastised those licensing officials who permitted "swarms of rum-sellers (whether licensed or not, I cannot tell) in every remote corner and by-alley in the town." Licenses should not be granted, he declared, "to procure a living for people however poor and honest." There was "no need," he continued, "of a dramshop or a tavern almost within a stone's throw."[79]

Another critic writing to the *Boston Gazette* the same year agreed. Of public houses, there "are not less than ONE HUNDRED AND FIFTY-SEVEN" in the town. "If we add to these the numbers that sell without license, it is to be feared that an eighth part of our houses are either dramshops or taverns." This man had a servant who had been "ruined by one of the rum-sellers setting up" near his house. It seemed, he continued, that rum had become so pervasive that it had become a "necessity of nature" for the "youngest apprentice" to have his "large draught." Madam "the washer-woman" must also have her "drop of comfort" at least once a day to get through her work. How, he lamented, did the consumption of rum come to be a "necessity"? Do "we labor harder" than our ancestors that we need these liquors? Could the founding fathers see this "degeneracy" and hear that "necessity which is pleaded for the use of these spirituous liquors, would they not even repent that they had planted this land!" This critic concluded that masters must stop distributing rum to their workmen and that justices must act to reduce the number of public houses.[80] Significantly, he had little to say about the genteel patrons of taverns like the Crown Coffee House. His complaints focused on consumption by the lower ranks.

Under pressure from criticisms like these and from a petition drawn up by indignant inhabitants, in the 1750s the selectmen again took under

78. Compiled from *Records of Boston Selectmen, 1701 to 1715* and *1716 to 1736*; and Court of General Sessions, Suffolk, Record Books, 1702–1732.

79. *Boston Weekly News-Letter*, July 12, 1750, no. 2513.

80. *Boston Gazette*, July 17, 1750, no. 1582.

consideration the reduction of the incidence of public houses in the town. In 1752 there existed 162 licensed houses (36 taverns and 126 retailers) in Boston, or 1 for every 97 inhabitants. This was approximately the same incidence as in 1737, when the number of public houses reached their peak of 177, before Boston's population dropped. A committee appointed by the selectmen recommended that the number of houses be cut in half to 80, or 1 house for about every 200 inhabitants. This must be done, they advised, because these houses "threatened the utter destruction of the morals of this people." The committee noted that licenseholders are "constantly dying" and, if licensing authorities did not replace the deceased, then the number could be reduced by attrition.[81]

The selectmen did make an effort in the next few years to adhere to the spirit of this report. By 1758 they had reduced the number of public houses by 27, to 135. In 1759 the selectmen voted to cut the number again; the following year they resolved "to take every method in their power" to achieve this end, principally by not granting new licenses when license-holders moved or died. But the pressure from poor petitioners on the selectmen remained acute.[82] Licenseholders were "constantly dying," as the licensing system had become an informal means of relieving the elderly and infirm to keep them off poor relief. When they died, some of their neighbors in similar circumstances sought to take their place.

In their licensing decisions selectmen remained concerned over the growing expenditure for relief of the poor. Between the 1740s and 1750s the average annual expense for poor relief increased from £866 to £1,204. In the 1760s it would leap to £1,909.[83] In this crunch of conflicting imperatives, the selectmen retreated from making further cuts in the number of public houses. In 1765 there existed 134 public houses, only 1 fewer than in 1758, serving a population of 15,520 plus transients: 1 for every 116 inhabitants, or 1 for every 22 adult white males. It is no wonder that drinksellers made surreptitious sales to slaves at the risk of losing their licenses. If one excludes retail houses ("dramshops"), there was still 1 tavern (where on-site drinking was legal) for every 79 adult males. One in every 13 houses in Boston was licensed. The selectmen did not come close

81. Boston, Record Commissioners, *Boston Town Records, 1742 to 1757* (Boston, 1885), 219–220; population figure from Nash, *The Urban Crucible,* 402; Names of Persons Licensed in the County of Suffolk, 1737, Otis Papers, MHS.

82. List of Persons Licensed in the County of Suffolk, 1758, Otis Papers, MHS; Boston, Record Commissioners, *Boston Town Records, 1758 to 1769* (Boston, 1886), 20, 39.

83. Nash, *The Urban Crucible,* 402.

to meeting the goals of the 1752 committee or their own resolves of 1758 and 1759. Petitions from the poor during these years, supported by friends and neighbors, continued to conceive of the licensing system as a means to dispense charity.[84]

But with each passing decade, the social ties evoked in these petitions came under increasing strain. The high turnover in the drink trade reflected a broader climate of instability and decline in Boston's economy (as well as simple mortality). During the 1740s Boston lost approximately one thousand residents because of a prolonged recession in trade. Consequently, the number of public houses dropped from about 180 in 1740 to 162 in 1752, when the selectmen resolved to reduce their number still further. And in the 1750s, between one-half and two-thirds of the town's propertyowners tried to sell between two-thirds and three-quarters of the town's property.[85] Hundreds of debtors must have been forced to repay loans as either they or their creditors prepared to move. Creditors trying to sell property without success would be less charitable toward outstanding debtors. Negotiations in taverns over credit and debts might have reached a fever pitch at midcentury as recession deepened and so much real estate was dumped on the market. Residents moved out of Boston even as they contemplated the fate of those who had recently moved into the town. The town warned out twelve hundred newcomers between 1755 and 1759, rendering them ineligible for relief.[86] While taverns and retail dramshops remained a fixture on each street, alley, and wharf, the faces of their owners, keepers, and customers changed more frequently. Bostonians consumed high volumes of drink in settings more and more divorced from the

84. List of Licenses for Boston, June 14, 1765, Misc. Bd., MHS; Boston, Record Commissioners, *Selectmen's Minutes from 1765 through 1768* (Boston, 1889), 170; see, for example, petition of Rebecca Badger, July 20, 1768, etc., Misc. Bd., MHS.

85. In 1737 there existed 177 drinksellers in the town. By 1758 the number had dropped to 135, and to 134 in 1765. Names of Persons Licensed in the County of Suffolk, 1737, List of Persons Licensed in the County of Suffolk, 1758, Otis Papers; List of Licenseholders in Boston, June 14, 1765, all in MHS; G. B. Warden, "The Distribution of Property In Boston, 1692–1775," *Perspectives in American History*, X (1986), 88–89; Warden, "Inequality and Instability in Eighteenth-Century Boston: A Reappraisal," *Journal of Interdisciplinary History* (1975–1976), VI, 585–620. Warden emphasizes the chronic instability in individual life cycles rather than class conflict and finds no correlation between political issues and social stratification.

86. Allan Kulikoff, "The Progress of Inequality in Revolutionary Boston," *WMQ*, 3d Ser., XXVIII (1971), 400.

traditional networks of extended family and neighbors in stable, long-lived relationships of trust and cooperation.

Under these pressures, the popular culture of drink itself changed and assumed more insidious dangers for people caught up in unstable conditions. It is impossible to ascertain the incidence of alcoholism in colonial society. It is clear, however, that some individuals in colonial Massachusetts suffered from alcoholism and that many observers attributed self-destructive behavior to the habitual consumption of rum. Back in 1687, when rum was just becoming a common drink available to the mass of colonists, Increase Mather wrote, "It is an unhappy thing of later years, a kind of strong drink hath been common among us, which the poorer sort of people, both in town and country, can make themselves drunk with, at cheap and easy rates." The poor could purchase it "for a penny or two pence" and "make themselves drunk." Once "they are addicted to this vice," few "repent of it or turn from it." Mather repeatedly emphasized how difficult it was to stop this "addiction," that it was not just a sin that could be "repented" of in religious terms but also a habit that could rarely be "turned from" to regain control of oneself. "I will not say . . . there is no hope that ever a drunkard shall repent," but "how rarely have any of you known a man that has been addicted to this body-destroying and soul-murdering iniquity that has truly repented of it, or turned from it again!" Mather spoke of the habitual consumption of rum as something beyond sin, as something akin to an involuntary dependence beyond control. The same year, Sewall recorded in his diary the death of a man with the comment: "It's thought he killed himself with drink."[87]

Other ministers commented on the impact of rum in the same terms. Cotton Mather wrote in 1708 of the "inordinate cravings of too many of our poor people after" rum. In 1716 Benjamin Wadsworth thought it easy "to give instances of persons" brought to ruin by rum; yet "they have so craved rum, that they could not be without it" and "must have it" every "quarter of an hour (or very frequently)." Even in a small community like Natick in Middlesex County, the Reverend Stephen Badger could speak of many "instances" of addictive behavior "within the compass of our knowledge." He emphasized to his congregation in 1773 how "common" a thing it had become for persons "addicted" to excessive drinking, who had begun life with a considerable estate or at least a "capacity," to be reduced even-

87. Increase Mather, *A Sermon Occasioned by the Execution of a Man Found Guilty of Murder* . . . , 2d ed. (Boston, 1687), 25–26; M. Halsey Thomas, ed., *The Diary of Samuel Sewall, 1674–1729* (New York, 1973), I, 155.

tually to poverty and distress.[88] These observations cannot be dismissed as the querulous lamentations of clergymen jealous of the tavern's popularity. These ministers perceived in some rum drinkers a pathological pattern of behavior closely resembling modern diagnoses of alcoholism. In light of the liquor inventory of the elite Crown Coffee House, perhaps they dwelt too much on the behavior of the poor. But certainly rum had a greater impact on those without a social cushion, without stable family and neighborhood relationships. Moreover, rum was a luxury, much of it imported. Critics wished the poor to trade their meager resources for cider or beer instead, lower-priced beverages manufactured in farm households and not associated so often with addiction.

Clergymen were not the only observers who believed that rum had subverted the popular culture of drink. Some attributed addiction to the depression and anxiety caused by misfortune. A correspondent commented in the *Boston Gazette* in 1733 on the vice of drunkenness—which he believed gained "ground every hour, even among the fair sex"—that many "have recourse to it to drive away their cares, and drown their uneasy thoughts." But such a remedy is always "transitory," for no sooner are the effects of alcohol on the distraught diminished than "their troubles return upon them with a doubled violence." Unless "they live in a continual state of drunkenness," their uneasiness only deepens.[89] As the petitions and movements of drinksellers illustrate, many Bostonians were struggling with misfortune in the eighteenth century. The post-1719 licensing policy provided for numerous drinksellers to offer potent liquors at the lowest possible prices (because of competition) to customers as troubled by adverse circumstances as were poor drinksellers themselves. From this perspective the licensing policy that allowed rum sellers to proliferate had devastating consequences for an uncounted but surely significant number of Bostonians. The popular culture of drink, traditionally invoked to express fellowship and interdependence, now contributed to the self-destruction of some troubled individuals with only tenuous ties to the community.

Numerous cases of alcoholism there might have been, but no climate of crisis developed. Although alcoholism might have been as pervasive in the eighteenth century as it is today, it was far less dangerous to others in

---

88. Cotton Mather, *Sober Considerations, on a Growing Flood of Iniquity* . . . , (Boston, 1708), 2; Wadsworth, *An Essay to Do Good*, 8; Stephen Badger, *The Nature and Effects of Drunkenness* . . . (Boston, 1773), 12.

89. *Boston Gazette*, Aug. 27–Sept. 3, 1733.

this preindustrial society. Consumption remained so intricately bound up with networks of sociability, the negotiation of credit, and the course of labor itself that the more insidious impact on some individuals did not weaken the general appeal of drink and taverns. Bostonians clung to this vestige of a traditional society even as volatile market conditions made their hold on employment more precarious and undermined the sway of traditional values. People often left familiar environments and relationships because they must. Only 47 of 109 retailers in 1758 (or 43 percent) were still there in 1765.[90] The rest had died, moved, married, or taken up some other occupation. It may be that merchants and distillers developed an international trade in rum and other spirits at exactly the time when inhabitants of the Anglo-American world were ready to imbibe more potent liquors to calm the anxieties and soften in some way the impact of the vicissitudes of life in the more uncertain relationships structured by commerce. Rum became a more powerful tool for perpetuating at least the illusion of traditional social relationships in the face of conditions that seemed to undermine them. Colonists seemed ready to test the traditional uses of drink to their limits with more potent beverages before they would heed their preachers and alter their habits in order to cope with the emerging modern world of urbanization, capitalism, and geographic mobility.

This powerful attachment to popular traditions is nowhere better illustrated than in the accounts drawn up by the administrators of Elizabeth Hawksworth's estate in 1724. Officials, neighbors, and creditors had joined together to sustain her endeavors to support herself through the sale of drink. In the same spirit the community did so again upon the death of this poor yet well-known drinkseller. Although her estate could not come close to satisfying her creditors, the administrators allotted forty-five pounds for funeral and related expenses, including seven and a half gallons of wine for those neighbors who attended the funeral and gathered in her shop, another quart for the appraisers of the estate, and a memorial to be read at the funeral.[91] Though ministers might marshal many arguments against prevailing uses of drink, they faced a deep reservoir of commitment to its availability at all times, and particularly at ceremonial benchmarks like a funeral. Hawksworth owed money to twenty-three

90. See Table 3. The persistence rate from 1758 to 1765 was computed using lists of licenses for those years located at the MHS.

91. Estate of Elizabeth Hawksworth, Suffolk County Probate Records, Record Books, XXII, 704, XXIV, 6, 7, 8.

creditors, but the community must still use part of her remaining resources to provide alcohol at her funeral.

V

This attachment to tradition was equally present in farming communities in the countryside. In the rural interior, there occurred no sharp break in licensing policy like that discerned in Boston in 1719; but the number of public houses in country towns exceeded what the Assembly had tried to impose during the first two decades of the eighteenth century. The rapid increase and dispersal of population in the colony is reflected in the increasing number and density of taverns in the older counties on the seaboard, such as Middlesex, as well as in new counties, such as Worcester, organized in the eighteenth century. In 1701 there existed only 33 taverns and 5 retailers in Middlesex County. One-third of the towns had only 1 licensed house, and only Charlestown had 5 or more. Between 1720 and 1740 the number in the county more than doubled, from 50 to 119. Now eight of thirty-four towns had 5 or more public houses. By 1760 fourteen of thirty-six towns and districts had 5 or more, and by 1770 more than half of thirty-seven towns had 5 or more; four towns had more than 10 (see Table 3).

New generations of colonists from the counties established in the seventeenth century migrated into central Massachusetts after 1720, and thus Worcester County was organized in the 1730s. By 1740, seventeen towns and districts had been incorporated, and they contained fifty-three licensed houses. During the next three decades the number of houses more than doubled. The density of public houses began to approach that of Middlesex County. One-third of Worcester County towns had five or more. In 1765 (when population figures for all towns become available) both Worcester and Middlesex counties possessed one public house for every 200–250 inhabitants.[92]

Tavernkeepers in the countryside were a more stable group as a whole

92. Statistics compiled from Courts of General Sessions, Middlesex, Worcester, and Hampshire counties. Middlesex records are in Judicial Archives, ACM; the others are in their respective county archives.

Per Capita Density of Public Houses in 1765

	Local Range	County
Middlesex	Charlestown to Marlborough: 89–429	214
Worcester	Fitchburg to Grafton: 51–380	251

Table 3. *Drinksellers in Middlesex, Worcester, and Hampshire Counties,*
1688–1770

	1688	1720	1740	1750	1760	1770
Middlesex						
Tavernkeepers		41	80		107	135
Retailers	28	9	39		69	95
Worcester						
Tavernkeepers			62	76	116	145
Retailers			5	20	20	52
Hampshire[a]						
Tavernkeepers						
and retailers			38	59	118	162

[a]In Hampshire County, tavernkeepers also had licenses to retail in the first half of the
eighteenth century.

Sources: Statistics compiled from Courts of General Sessions, Middlesex, Worcester,
and Hampshire counties. Middlesex records are in Judicial Archives, ACM; the others are
in their respective county archives.

than their counterparts in Boston. Of forty-six Boston tavernkeepers in
1720 only eight, or 17 percent, were licensed a decade later. In Middlesex
County the persistence rate between 1740 and 1750 was 32 percent, and 44
percent the next decade.[93]

In the older counties the tavern landlord was still a familiar figure.
Instability and rapid turnover were not so rife as in Boston. Still, significant numbers of people chose to move from their place of birth in the
interior also. Central Massachusetts gave rise to many new houses as
population increased and dispersed in the middle decades. New companies
of drinking fellows were continually forming as migrants broke neighborhood and kinship ties of long standing.

In most country towns there existed no clearly defined hierarchy of
public houses through the 1750s and beyond. Of thirty tavernkeepers in
twenty-three Middlesex and Worcester County towns between 1738 and

93. Compiled from Court of General Sessions, Suffolk, Record Books, 1719–1725,
1725–1732, and Court of General Sessions, Middlesex, Record Books, 1723–1735, 1735–
1748, 1748–1761. The license rosters are reported annually in these records.

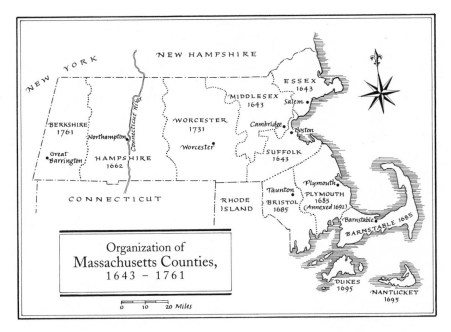

Map 1. Organization of Massachusetts Counties, 1643–1761. *Drawn by Richard Stinely*

1792, most were substantial yeomen or artisans or better. As in Boston, the patrons of country towns could expect to rest in chairs except for those crowded occasions like court days: in ten Middlesex taverns (for which there are data), the number of chairs ranged from sixteen to forty-four. Travelers could also expect to be provided with forks in most taverns by the mid-eighteenth century. Ephraim Jones of Concord had five dozen in 1767. But travelers might well be forced to share beds: Caleb Bloggett had only four in 1744, and no Middlesex tavernkeeper had more than eight. Nor was tea or coffee available in every tavern. John Adams remarked in his diary in 1759 on a landlady's airs about her use of tea to a group of Braintree militia officers. He deemed it imprudent of her to extol this ritual before "shoestring fellows that never use tea." Actions to exclude any but the indigent were unwelcome in the public rooms of country houses. Visitors became part of the household of the tavernkeeper, and local patrons expected them to become involved in the conversation of the house. They could hardly do otherwise in Jonathan How's tavern in 1738. In his East Room he had one long table, another smaller table, and twelve chairs.[94]

94. Butterfield *et al.*, eds., *Diary and Autobiography of Adams*, I, 114. Middlesex inventories: Jonathan How, Marlborough (1738); John Eveleth, Sudbury (1743); Capt. Caleb Blog-

Such inclusive arrangements continued to facilitate the ready interrogation of travelers by local patrons seeking news.

As in Boston, the number of public houses in country towns remained controversial despite the lapse of the Assembly's interference with licensing. In Haverhill, the town meeting decided to reduce the number from six to two in 1728. Forty-five residents of Cambridge signed a petition asking justices to reduce the number from eight to three in 1735. They had seriously considered the "distressing circumstances of our town, and apprehending the same to be very much owing to too great a number of taverns, pray that your honors would license no more than three persons to be innholders, one in the body and one in each wing of the town." Groton selectmen tendered their "judgments against so many innholders and retailers in the town" in 1749. There existed a "much larger number than is necessary, and when it so happens it must of necessity be very hurtful to any town which is the case with us." Concord selectmen moved against a tavernkeeper in 1742 because they feared that "such a multiplicity of taverns at such time when they were in hopes and expectation of a considerable reformation will be of very ill consequence and have a tendency to ensnare the youth and other unguarded persons in the town."[95]

gett, Woburn (1744); Capt. Jonathan Bowers, Billerica (1744); Capt. Nathan Bloggett, Woburn (1747); Jeremiah Abbot, Billerica (1748); Capt. John Fowle, Woburn (1744); Henry Pratt, Newton (1750); Samuel Hathorn, Wilmington (1752); Jerahmael Bowers, Chelmsford (1752); John Bradshaw, Medford (1754); Ebenezer Hubbard, Concord (1755); Jonathan Barron, Chelmsford (1756); Jonathan Raymond, Lexington (1760); Issac Baldwin, Sudbury (1760); Oliver Pratt, Newton (1763); John Parker, Chelmsford (1763); Henry Fletcher, Chelmsford (1764); Capt. Ephraim Jones, Concord (1767); Micajah Gleason, Framingham (1777). The Middlesex inventories are on microfilm at the Middlesex County Courthouse in Cambridge.

Worcester inventories: Ebenezer Merriam, Mendon (1754); Joshua Hutchins, Lunenburg (1763 will); William Richardson, Esq., Lancaster (1770); Josiah Converse, Esq., Brookfield (1771); Capt. Ezekiel Wood, Uxbridge (1772); Timothy Brigham, Esq., Southborough (1775); David Wilder, Lancaster (1776 will); Elijah Marcy, Sturbridge (1779); Israel Taylor, Esq., Harvard (1779); Henry Baldwin, Shrewsbury (1792). These estate papers are available in manuscript at probate division in Worcester County Courthouse. An alphabetized volume provides docket numbers.

95. George W. Chase, *History of Haverhill, Massachusetts . . . to 1860* (Haverhill, Mass., 1861), 283. Five men were licensed as tavernkeepers and one as a retailer in Haverhill in 1727. Court of General Sessions, Essex, Record Book, 1726–1744, July 11, 1727, 41–44; Cambridge Protest against Too Many Taverns, Court of General Sessions, Middlesex, File Papers, July 9, 1736, fol. 160a; Hezekiah Sawtell and Jonathan Holdin to Court of General

The religious revivals of the 1740s heightened concern over drinking habits. But, just as in Boston, the number of public houses considered necessary by Puritan standards continued to be at variance with the number actually sought and licensed.

Even in towns with only one or two taverns, the extent of patronage and volume of liquors consumed could arouse anxiety among some residents, as in tiny Hopkinton in 1738. The selectmen complained of "great numbers" of residents, young and old, flocking to the tavern on Sundays and indulging in "extravagance and excess." Some spent so much money there that they were forced to leave the care of their families to others. The selectmen told the justices, "It will be greatly for the interest both of religion and the commonwealth to have the tavern removed from being near the center" of the town. Otherwise, they feared, "tavern haunting will continue and be as a spreading leprosy that will in a very great degree infect the whole town."[96] Neither the local minister nor the selectmen had sufficient influence over townsmen to restrain their behavior, so they appealed to justices to change the location of the tavern to a point further from the church.

John Adams, a struggling young lawyer in the early 1760s, became obsessed with the number of taverns and retailers in Braintree and nearby towns. "Few things," he believed, "have deviated so far from the first design of their institution, are so fruitful of destructive evils, or so needful of a speedy regulation, as licensed houses." In this and later unpublished essays he proclaimed the necessity of returning to the licensing policies he believed were enforced in the seventeenth century: "The accommodation of strangers, and perhaps of town inhabitants on public occasions, are the only warrantable intentions of a tavern, and the supply of the neighborhood with necessary liquors, in small quantities (to be consumed at home) and at the cheapest rates, are the only excusable designs of a retailer." To this end, "it is necessary, that both should be selected from the most virtuous and wealthy people who will accept the trust." At the urging of Adams and others, the Braintree town meeting did vote to reduce the number of public houses from twelve to three. The town stated, "There is reason to apprehend that the present prevailing depravity of manners through the land in general and in the town in particular, and the shameful

---

Sessions, Middlesex, File Papers, July 6, 1749; Petition of selectmen of Concord to the Governor, Council, and Assembly, Nov. 18, 1742, Taverns, CXI, 114.

96. Selectmen of Hopkinton to Court of General Sessions, Middlesex, File Papers, July 3, 1738.

neglect of religious and civil duties . . . are in great measure owing to the unnecessary increase of licensed houses."[97]

Braintree minister Samuel Niles became so inspired by this vote that he sought to influence justices and selectmen in every county to take similar action, by publishing *A Pressing Memorial, Circularly Transmitted*, directed to all justices and selectmen. Here Niles argued that it was "the indispensable duty of all" in their respective capacities—heads of households as well as elected and appointed officials—to combat this "dangerous contagion." Rulers must act to "lessen the number of licensed houses" and grant licenses only to those who will "rule well their own houses, and such as frequent them." Niles also lamented the popularity of rum in the colony: "It comes rolling in, hogshead after hogshead!" He drew a contrast between prevailing consumption and the "abstinence of the fathers and first settlers of the town."[98] Like Adams, Niles regarded the seventeenth century as a kind of "golden age" of temperance that might yet be restored by a "contraction" in the number of public houses. In effect, he called for a reinvigoration of the legislative initiatives to reverse the increase of licensed houses that had taken place between 1681 and 1719.

Neither Niles's pamphlet nor the individual efforts of the towns effected the desired reforms. Although Suffolk County justices did act to reduce the number of licenses in the county after a tour of inspection, it is unlikely that their action had any long-term effects. Niles's entreaties had no discernible impact on Middlesex County. Between 1760 and 1765 the number of houses approved and licensed actually increased in twelve towns and decreased in only three. The rest of the thirty-seven kept the same number. Over the decade as a whole, from 1760 to 1770, the number of taverns and retailers in Middlesex County increased by 31 percent, by 28 percent in Worcester County, and by 37 percent in Hampshire County.[99] No "contraction" in the incidence of houses took place. Rather, it was a period of rapid expansion in public houses. As in the seventeenth century, taverns performed vital functions in community life in keeping with the traditional

97. Butterfield *et al.,* eds., *Diary and Autobiography of Adams,* I, 128–129.

98. Samuel Niles, *A Pressing Memorial, Circularly Transmitted, . . . to the Several Very Worthy Bodies of Justices, . . . in Their Respective Counties; and to the Select-Men in Every Town through the Province* [Boston, 1761], 1–4.

99. "Order, at Adjournment of a Court of General Sessions, Boston, July 19, 1762, for inspection of taverns in Suffolk County," Otis Papers, MHS. County growth in numbers tabulated from the Courts of General Sessions, Record Books, for Middlesex, Worcester, and Hampshire Counties. The latter two are located in respective county archives. For numbers, see above, n. 92.

ideal of collective cooperation and interdependence. Increasing numbers of people moved from town to town, but in newly established public houses they sought to perpetuate the face-to-face networks that embodied notions of community in its most immediate sense.

As in Boston, tavern companies in the countryside quickly incorporated rum into collective life. No amount of criticism abated the demand for rum, either West India or the New England variety. To be sure, cider remained the staple alcoholic drink. A majority of farm households continued to produce huge amounts of cider for home consumption and export to seaport towns. In Middlesex County, twelve towns with a total population of 14,028 produced 22,780 barrels of cider in 1771. But these same households wanted a retailer nearby with whom they could trade scarce currency or barter produce for rum. In Weston, sixty people petitioned in favor of Nathaniel Coolidge's application for a retail license in 1749, because they "found it a great difficulty last year for want of a retailer there not only for the conveniences of being accommodated on the Sabbath, but also that we may be supplied with rum and other things we have occasion for." Thirty-two neighbors of a Cambridge man petitioned in favor of his request for a license, and against the renewal of a Cambridge woman's license, because she "has been so extravagant in her demands in charging two or three shillings and sometimes more by the gallon for her rum than other retailers in the neighboring towns." A Medford distiller asked for a license to retail in 1744, because the carters bringing wood and other supplies to the distillery "utterly refuse to sell to your petitioner" unless they receive payment in rum. A Framingham tavernkeeper in the 1770s had 133 gallons of rum, 52 gallons of brandy, and 570 gallons of cider in stock.[100] Considering that this tavern was one of six public houses in a

100. Bettye Hobbs Pruitt, ed., *The Massachusetts Tax Valuation List of 1771* (Boston, 1978), 172, 190, 194, 208, 224, 228, 238, 250, 264, 280, 284, 288 (page numbers refer to the beginning of each town's tax list); Petition in support of Nathaniel Coolidge, July 11, 1749, Petition in support of William Whittemore, July 31, 1758, Petition of John Hall to Governor and Assembly, Court of General Sessions, Middlesex, File Papers, July 18, 1744; Inventory of Capt. Micajah Gleason, Middlesex Probate Records, docket no. 9213, box no. 1662, Middlesex Courthouse. The evidence on the volume of rum consumed in the country-side is ambiguous. On the one hand, most country tavern inventories assembled for this study do not include rum, or very much cider, for that matter. But petitions indicate a strong demand for rum. A notice in a newspaper in 1770 about a fire in a Chelmsford tavern stated that "a considerable quantity of brandy, rum and other spirituous liquors" was burned. It may be that the liquors of tavernkeepers near death in the country were usually sold before

town of 1,313 people, this inventory suggests a staggering rate of consumption. Samuel Freeman, a Sturbridge tavernkeeper, had almost 100 gallons of West India and New England rum in 1772 (besides seven empty rum barrels) and dozens of barrels for cider. A Worcester tavernkeeper had 68 gallons of West India, New England, and cherry-flavored rum along with 19 barrels of cider in 1776.[101] Although the country might have sent cider to Boston, Boston supplied rum and brandy to the interior. Country farmers were no longer self-sufficient in drink manufacture. They traded surplus produce for this foreign luxury.

Niles's circular pamphlet of 1761 had little effect not just because of popular demand for taverns and retailers selling rum. By midcentury selectmen in the more populous towns had also come under pressure to approve licenses to the poor. Indeed, to Adams it seemed that "poverty, and distressed circumstances, are become the strongest argument to procure an approbation." For these reasons "such multitudes have been lately licensed that none can afford" to accommodate any except "the trifling, nasty, vicious crew that most frequent them." Now "when the season of the year approaches, a swarm of candidates for approbation to keep taverns or dramshops" surrounds the selectmen for their favor, and some receive approval because of poverty. Adams might have exaggerated the extent to which the poor received licenses in country towns. Only 18 of the 232 licenses granted in Middlesex County in 1770 went to widows, 10 of them in the seaport of Charlestown.[102] Yet the fact that need had become a strong qualification for a license in Braintree is evidence that the compromises in Boston's licensing policy took hold also in communities of two thousand or more as the century progressed. As Massachusetts society became more mature, licensing officials succumbed to the traditional practice of distributing licenses to the poor characteristic of England.

After 1719 in Boston and by midcentury in most of the colony's towns, the selectmen and county justices assembled in sessions no longer exerted

_____
the license was lost and, hence, missing from many inventories. *Massachusetts Spy*, Nov. 26–29, 1770, no. 47.

101. Freeman's inventory is in Worcester County Probate Records, docket no. 22407, Worcester County Courthouse; Brown, docket no. 8195. The popular demand for rum is reflected in the acute resentment felt by New England soldiers during the Seven Years' War when they were denied their daily ration of rum. See Fred Anderson, *A People's Army: Massachusetts Soldiers and Society in the Seven Years' War* (Chapel Hill, N.C., 1984), 129, 182–183.

102. Butterfield *et al.*, eds., *Diary and Autobiography of Adams*, I, 205; Court of General Sessions, Middlesex, Record Book, 1761–1771, Sept. 4, 1770, 516–518.

themselves to restrict consumption and patronage in accordance with the policies enunciated by the clergy and the Assembly since 1681. Indeed, to the extent that they granted licenses to provide employment to the poor, they encouraged rather than discouraged intemperance, since the poor sought "to sell what drink they can." With this change in policy the Puritan mission to establish a society distinctively more pious, decidedly more temperate than what they had left behind in England foundered. To be sure, Boston never succumbed to a craze for gin as depicted in Hogarth's famous London prints.[103] And poverty never became even near as rife in any Massachusetts town as in London and the larger cities of eighteenth-century England. Still, the introduction of West India and New England rum on a mass scale in Massachusetts public houses made this province less a beacon to the Old World than a variant of its mores and customs in respect to drink. The renewed vitality of tavern life in the colony during the eighteenth century is thus an index of the transformation of the colony from a godly commonwealth, committed to the strict enforcement of temperance, to a provincial extension of English society. As in England, rulers tolerated drunkenness and tavern haunting out of necessity or indulgence.

The popular culture of drink of centuries' vintage did not simply triumph over the emerging modern imperative of temperance. The development of an international trade in rum and other distilled beverages changed the popular culture of drink. Households now purchased rather than manufactured a large proportion of their drink supply. The popularity of rum signals the growing impact of commerce on ordinary colonists. They must raise goods for trade and participate in market exchanges across the Atlantic in order to consume new luxuries like rum. But they consumed more of such potent liquors as population increase and the growth of commerce caused many to uproot themselves from familiar connections of neighbors and friends in order to pursue opportunities elsewhere. Thus, even as traditional drinking habits became more entrenched, they also became more dangerous for those anxiously breaking with tradition by seeking new connections or identities.[104] Some fell victim to misfortune, despair, and alcoholism. From this perspective there was

103. T. G. Coffey, "Beer Street: Gin Lane: Some Views of Eighteenth-Century Drinking," *Quarterly Journal of Studies on Alcohol*, XXVII (1966), 669–692; Clark, *The English Alehouse*, 238–242.

104. Douglas Lamar Jones, "The Strolling Poor: Transiency in Eighteenth-Century Massachusetts," *Journal of Social History*, [VIII, no. 3] (Spring 1975), 28–54. Gordon S. Wood discusses the "loosening bonds of society" caused by migration and commerce in *The Radicalism of the American Revolution* (New York, 1992), 127–130, 169–173.

greater reason than ever for the continuing warnings about drink. The social foundation for traditional drinking habits had weakened.

For now, rulers bowed to popular pressure. They had their own adjustments to make. For almost a century rulers in Massachusetts had stood over their constituents as paternal guardians of their public virtue. But that relationship was changing. It was not just that rulers no longer heeded clerical entreaties for new laws to restrict drinking. Increasingly, rulers and ruled no longer occupied the same public space. In Boston the elite, middling ranks, and the poor congregated in different taverns. In country towns the multiplication of public houses by midcentury also created social distance between geographically dispersed tavern companies. Thus in Boston and the countryside the relationship between rulers and ruled became more tenuous. In order to perpetuate control over the rank and file, rulers had to rely more and more on deference to the pomp and majesty of government, rather than on personal supervision. Yet by design and circumstance such ceremonial display had become less elaborate and awe-inspiring in New England than in England.[105] Tavern companies simultaneously became contexts out of which new webs of influence might develop, affecting established lines of authority.

Amid more distended patterns of local and neighborhood association, some aspirants to elective office perceived the advantage of engaging with the popular culture of drink rather than laboring to suppress it. The fear that Samuel Danforth expressed in 1710, that "none shall be improved in offices of trust but such as work at, favor, and countenance this vice," to some extent became a reality after 1719. Indeed, by the 1760s Adams had become convinced that the multiplication of taverns across the province in some cases represented a conscious "design" by some elected officials to gain popular support, gradually making Massachusetts offices and elections the "gratuity of tipplers, for drams" of drink "and slops!"[106]

---

105. Douglas Hay emphasizes the "majesty" and spectacle of the law at assize courts as a means of intimidating the masses. See his "Property, Authority, and the Criminal Law," in Hay *et al.*, eds., *Albion's Fatal Tree: Crime and Society in Eighteenth-Century England* (New York, 1975), 26–31.

106. Samuel Danforth, *The Woful Effects of Drunkenness* . . . (Boston, 1710), 25–26; L. H. Butterfield *et al.*, eds., *Diary and Autobiography of Adams*, I, 191.

Chapter 4

The Politics of Taverns

in Provincial Boston

The virtual collapse of drink regulation in the second decade of the eighteenth century was in part a consequence of the first stirrings of a more popular political culture in Boston. Instead of suppressing popular tavern assemblies, some elected leaders in Boston and the province began to incorporate the distribution of drink and the power to approve prospective licenseholders into strategies for the acquisition of political power. The decentralized structure of political power in Massachusetts had originally been cause for Puritan rulers to repress tavern gatherings, lest groups of intemperate drinkers influence the annual elections. Drink could not be allowed to corrupt the ritual renewal of trust in the "best men." But the installment of royal government caused some native leaders out of favor with this court to cast new eyes on the tavern as a vehicle to organize and focus popular sentiment. Resentment of the abridgment of the colony's autonomy by the imposition of royal governors became a catalyst for the formation of groups who dared to stand in opposition to the crown's appointees. And thus public rooms became a context for the airing of opposition sentiment.

For Samuel Sewall, these changes in the political configuration of Massachusetts were unsettling. From the founding of the colony forward, one measure of a ruler's fitness for office had been his personal restraint in the use of alcohol and his readiness to act to restrain consumption among lesser men. Many of the highest provincial officials had gone so far as to lead trains of lesser officials through the town to prevent disorders.[1]

As conflict between crown-appointed governors and native leaders became endemic after 1700, some members of the governing hierarchy began to divest themselves of the duty of strict regulation in order to court favor with the populace. Taverns became a public stage upon which voters and their friends and kinsmen openly expressed disdain for royal officials and those attached to them by interest. Pamphlets critical of the government began to be read in some King Street taverns. The crumbling of tavern and drink regulation thus represented more than the triumph of popular resistance and the demand by the poor for licenses. The virtual collapse of regulation was also a political decision. Political activism in taverns became a counterweight to interference by the crown in the colony's internal affairs. Puritan political principles had pitted the hierarchy of governing officials against a populace informally organized in taverns. Now resentment of the royal presence in Boston stimulated elected officials to seek cooperation with tavern constituencies. Public houses became settings for the emergence of a new "public sphere" separate from and sometimes critical of assemblies of the hierarchies of church and state.

I

The Massachusetts deputies to the House who drafted the drink laws had gradually constructed an elaborate system of controls involving an ever wider and deeper network of governing figures in the social hierarchy. Officials at all levels of government possessed varying responsibility for the approval and granting of licenses.[2] At every turn, in an ascending ladder of authority, patrons of taverns and purchasers of alcohol faced officials responsible by law for limiting their patronage and consumption.

The fact that the deputies to the Assembly (thirty-six from twenty-six towns in 1686) owed their positions to annual elections at town meetings by a relatively broad franchise did not deter them from taking more drastic steps to compel adherence to new and old drink laws. Judging from the

---

1. M. Halsey Thomas, ed., *The Diary of Samuel Sewall, 1674–1729* (New York, 1973), I, 252–253, 305–306, 425, 627, 978 (hereafter cited as *Diary*).

2. Nathaniel B. Shurtleff, ed., *Records of the Governor and Company of the Massachusetts Bay in New England, 1626–1686*, 5 vols. (Boston, 1853–1854), II, 171–173, IV, pt. 1, 59–60, IV, pt. 2, 463, V, 305; Massachusetts, *The Acts and Resolves, Public and Private, of the Province of the Massachusetts Bay . . .* , I (Boston, 1869), 329–330 (hereafter cited as *Acts and Resolves*).

tone of legislative preambles and orders, deputies considered their constituents wayward dependents in need of paternal guidance. They assumed that regulation would never become the subject of public debate in taverns or anywhere else, and never an election issue. Criticism of such laws by ordinary inhabitants constituted a breach of the respect owed to superiors. Habits of deference to distinguished, pious men—especially those elevated to the General Court or Assembly—remained so fundamental an attitude in the divinely ordained hierarchy of superiors and inferiors that the rulers who wielded law on this issue could do so without fear of incurring electoral disfavor. There was little regular communication between patrons of taverns from one town to the next and, hence, no connected constituency seeking modification of the laws. Thus when members of the Assembly required in 1681 that all applicants for licenses present proof of approval by their selectmen to county justices, they did so with the expectation that selectmen would also act without regard to popular sentiment. Selectmen must act to tighten scrutiny of those given license to sell drink, and thus govern collective drinking more closely. Within the electoral framework of Massachusetts' governing structure, a hierarchy of rulers elevated to office by vote of the people of each town must perpetually exert its influence against the popular proclivity of the people to patronize taverns.[3]

Nevertheless, the further down the social and governing hierarchy the Assembly reached in order to impose its will on public behavior, the more it risked provoking conflict between local rulers and the townsmen who voted them into office. Selectmen in particular had a pivotal role in this structure of enforcement when they became responsible for approving applicants in 1681. Under pressure from both above and below their place in the social and governing hierarchy, they wavered between repression and indulgence of intemperance. Selectmen continually juggled the Assembly's directives with popular demand for licenses and easy access to drink.[4]

The abolition of Massachusetts' self-governing charter and the inauguration of royal government by the crown in 1692 did not have any immediate impact on the erratic operation of the licensing system. Under the new charter the king now appointed the governor, and he selected the members of the Council from the deputies' list of nominees. Local selectmen, however, continued to approve all applications for and renewals of licenses. The

3. This is apparent especially in the list of "provoking evils" enumerated by the General Court in November 1675. Edmund S. Morgan, ed., *Puritan Political Ideas, 1558–1794* (New York, 1965), 226–233; *Acts and Resolves*, I, 190; Shurtleff, ed., *Records*, V, 305.

4. The role of selectmen in licensing is discussed in more detail in Chapter 2, above.

justices who actually granted the licenses now received their appointments from the royal governor, but this change had no immediate effect on the identities and numbers of those licensed.[5]

The royal presence in Boston, however, did indirectly undermine Puritan policies in respect to drink regulation, especially after Joseph Dudley became governor in 1702. Many royal officials, their visitors, and their political allies in Boston held no personal commitment to Puritan codes of morality. They looked to London for models of genteel deportment and did not consider sobriety essential in rulers. Sewall's pattern of tavern and drink usage—and his aversion to such customs as health drinking and English observations of anniversary days—were no longer emulated by those at the pinnacle of power in the royal colony. During the same years in which Sewall helped to patrol the streets of Boston assisting the hapless constables and tithingmen, he often became dismayed at the character of Town House gatherings presided over by Dudley. In 1703 Sewall protested the governor's plans to illuminate the Town House for the Queen's Birthday because it would profane the Sabbath. In 1704, the celebration of Coronation Day "gives offense to many," for it seemed to be "down Sabbath, up St. George." When many of the councillors went "to the Council chamber and there drink healths on account of it's being the Queen's Birthday," Sewall stayed at home "and went and heard Mr. Willard's catechizing lecture." He stayed away from the Town House in 1708 for the same reason. The Council treated the governor at the Green Dragon Tavern in 1710 and then in the Council chamber, but Sewall grew "wary and uneasy" and even slipped away without drinking.[6] Boston and colony leaders had, of course, always gathered in taverns on formal and informal occasions; but now such gatherings began to exceed the old boundaries of acceptable use of drink, especially when they included the heathenish custom of drinking healths.

Sewall and fellow justice Edward Bromfield even provoked Dudley's wrath when they dispersed and prosecuted the drinkers gathered in the Wallis tavern in 1714 to celebrate the Queen's Birthday. Sewall imprisoned John Netmaker, secretary to visiting General Francis Nicholson, after he refused to pay a fine for drinking and for "vilifying" the laws of the province, particularly the Act for the Better Observation and Keeping of the Lord's Day. This law imposed a fine of five shillings on persons remain-

5. The second charter's impact on Massachusetts is described in Richard L. Bushman, *King and People in Provincial Massachusetts* (Chapel Hill, N.C., 1985), 26, 102–103.

6. *Diary*, I, 481, 502, 518, 588, II, 632.

ing in a public house "drinking, or idly spending their time on Saturday night, after the sun is set, or on the Lord's Day, or the evening following." Upon learning of the imprisonment, Governor Dudley called a special meeting of the Council at which General Nicholson demanded "justice against Mr. Sewall and Bromfield for sending my secretary to prison without acquainting me with it!" Nicholson even went downstairs and "walked the Exchange, where he was so furiously loud, that the noise was plainly heard in the Council chamber." Dudley vehemently argued to the Council in favor of Netmaker's release, and the Council finally agreed to it. Although William Wallis, the proprietor of the tavern where the drinking celebration had taken place, eventually lost his license because of the incident, the secretary to Nicholson escaped punishment through the governor's intervention.[7] The days when members of the colony's government could expect swift admonition for violations of Puritan strictures on the conduct of godly rulers had passed.

Royal officials also contributed to the conscious emulation of London tastes, fashions, and standards by some tavernkeepers and their patrons. One expression of the more cosmopolitan yearnings of Boston's wealthiest residents is the establishment of coffeehouses modeled after those of London. The first coffeehouse was licensed in 1678, just before the Assembly's drastic reduction of public houses. Such taverns did not become distinctively exclusive and specialized in clientele, however, until the eighteenth century. Certainly by 1714 Boston possessed such an establishment in the Crown Coffee House, operated by Thomas Selby.[8]

Boston ministers persisted in trying to persuade royal officials and those who would ape their demeanor to set an example for the populace at large. In his 1708 attack on the "invasion" of rum into the colony, Cotton Mather asked all men of "better quality" to abstain from use of it and to "cast contempt on it." If gentlemen spurned rum, Mather declared, the

7. *Diary*, II, 741–745. Wallis was denied renewal of his license by the selectmen on July 26, 1714: "The reasons given by the selectmen of their objections against the renewal of Robert Rudgate and John Wallis's license, the said Rudgate's being gone, and the said Wallis his not keeping good rule and order, and not being suitably provided as the law directs." Boston, Record Commissioners, *Records of Boston Selectmen, 1701 to 1715*, Report of the Record Commissioners of the City of Boston (Boston, 1884), 213–214.

8. *Records of Boston Selectmen, 1701 to 1715*, 2, 100, 139–141, 213. Printer and political polemicist Benjamin Harris came to Boston in 1685 and established the London Coffee House as well as a short-lived newspaper, but he returned to London in 1695. Charles E. Clark, "The Newspapers of Provincial America," American Antiquarian Society, *Proceedings*, C (1990), 370.

people might follow their example. He reminded nervous rulers that, since "our people have been censured as being too much of a leveling disposition," such abstention might encourage "every man" to be "equal to the best, on the level with the highest." But the inventory of Selby's select Crown Coffee House indicates that fashionable gentlemen ignored such entreaties. Selby sold more distilled alcohol in the 1710s than any other tavernkeeper in Boston.[9]

Yet while royal officials might personally flout these prohibitions in Council chambers and the rooms of the Crown Coffee House, they supported strict regulation of tavern assemblies among the populace at large in the interests of public order. The governor and his closest associates no doubt listened approvingly to a sermon delivered by Ebenezer Pemberton on election day in 1710, a year when the Assembly took new action against the number of public houses. Pemberton decreed the "divinity" of government, going so far as to liken leaders to "gods" among men. To be sure, Pemberton warned Dudley and the rulers in Council and Assembly that "gods must not give loose to their lusts" and gratify "criminal appetites" such as drunkenness, wantonness, and love of luxury. Rulers must avoid "the least appearance" of such behavior as they simultaneously exerted their powers to "free the land" of sins, and especially the sin of intemperance. But the major aim of this sermon was to argue a divine injunction to the people to stand in awe of their rulers. For "if rulers are gods, then their character demands submission and obedience." They must not be "reviled, blasphemed, arraigned, and condemned by every haughty, insolent, and discontented spirit." Indeed, all "murmurings, discontents, evil surmisings, and jealousies, all seeds of faction and sedition must be suppressed with the greatest care among a people."[10] Thus did Pemberton sanction the continuing close control by authorities, though they now were royal instead of Puritan, of conduct and speech. With this sermon Pemberton established himself as one of the premier spokesmen for the emerging "court party" in Massachusetts politics, individuals closely tied to the royal governor.

Pemberton particularly condemned those men who would prompt and lead such "murmurings" of "discontent" so that they might be "popular."

9. Cotton Mather, *Sober Considerations, on a Gathering Flood of Iniquity* . . . (Boston, 1708), 18; Inventory of Thomas Selby, Suffolk County Probate Records, Record Book, XXV, 530–535, Judicial Archives, ACM. For a full discussion of Selby's tavern, see Chapter 2, above.

10. Ebenezer Pemberton, *The Divine Original and Dignity of Government Asserted* . . . (Boston, 1710), 7, 13–14, 54, 76, 82, 85, 98–100.

Such men, he argued, "pretend to see evil designs at the bottom of public administrations that their blind neighbors are not aware of." They would seek to "deny government" of its "just honors." Elections could be corrupted by such men: "Such, as have too much command of the public voice, will have this man preferred because he is of the Right Party, as they call it," and "will espouse this or the other interest, and oppose some others in place."[11] Pemberton admonished leaders to preserve the election as a device whereby the people renewed their trust in and obedience to a distinct set of rulers elevated above them and shining with the "beams of divinity." He warned against the emergence of leaders who cultivated popular support and thus acted to obscure the distinctions of station that distinguished leaders and people.

Royal officials had good reason to support the general intent of Pemberton's admonitions to rulers and ruled. Before and after 1710, members of the governor's inner circle directly and indirectly confronted examples of levelism in Boston society. These incidents could not but inspire anxiety about the character of tavern gatherings in the town, for they suggested that "murmurings" against royal government had become common even in houses catering to artisans and seamen. By 1710 Governor Joseph Dudley had become the target of breaches of deferential posture and speech. It was not just Dudley's personal arrogance that made him a reviled figure but also his past association with the hated Andros regime, a government that had suspended town meetings, ruled without an Assembly, and even placed the titles of colonists' property in danger. Moreover, Dudley continued to use his office to advance his personal interests. Even the Mathers—concerned as they were with upholding the prerogatives and discretionary powers of clergy and secular rulers—eventually accused him of "bribery" and "treachery" in print.[12] Of all Massachusetts governors in the eighteenth century, he came closest to personifying the stereotypical royal appointee—the avaricious, unprincipled placeman intent on exploiting his office for personal gain.

11. *Ibid.*, 76, 82.

12. *The Deplorable State of New-England, by Reason of a Covetous and Treacherous Governour* (London, 1708), reprinted in Boston in 1720. The authorship of this pamphlet is uncertain, but Cotton Mather either helped to write it or sponsored its printing. See Richard L. Bushman, "Corruption and Power in Provincial America," in *The Development of a Revolutionary Mentality* (Washington, D.C., 1972), 63–89. In my estimation, Bushman underestimates the extent of actual versus suspected corruption in the Dudley regime, and the popular participation in and knowledge of written and oral attacks on the Dudley administration.

Plate 5. Joseph Dudley. *Courtesy, Massachusetts Historical Society*

A number of incidents that came before the Suffolk County Sessions and Superior courts reveal not just "murmurings" of discontent with Dudley but open contempt and alienation. In 1702 Seth Gulliver and an unknown group of men were accused of destroying a symbol of royal authority—the royal pennant flying atop a ship of war at the North End of the town. Allegedly, the group assaulted the master and officers of the ship with clubs in order to seize the pennant. Presumably there existed eyewitnesses to identify Gulliver, but a jury of Bostonians found the defendant not guilty. The same month John Boult, a merchant, was indicted for making, spreading, or "publishing" a libel or false report concerning the governor. The next year another was brought before the court on the same charge. And in the following year rumors that Dudley was involved in a traitorous relationship with the French swept through the town. Suffolk justices presided over the presentment of a blacksmith for spreading the report that Dudley and Lord Cornbury (the governor of New York) had conspired with the French in shady dealings. The blacksmith "had heard or was told" (perhaps in a tavern) that Cornbury corresponded with the French while refusing to support joint efforts with Connecticut and Massachusetts forces. As in the case of Gulliver, a jury found the blacksmith not guilty.[13]

In the winter of 1705, Governor Dudley, riding with a party in his coach through Roxbury, became so enraged by the refusal of two men driving carts on the same road to move more completely and quickly out of his way that he drew his sword. John Winchester (who would become Brookline's first representative to the Assembly) broke the sword after he was struck with it, and he and Thomas Trowbridge of Newton were eventually arrested. Their testimony at Superior Court conflicted with Dudley's. Winchester said he tried to mediate the dispute "with my hat under my arm" before defending himself, but admitted to saying to Dudley's face that his furious epithets "don't become a Christian." Governor Dudley declared under oath that Winchester went so far as to assert, "I am as good flesh and blood as you; I will not give way; you may go out of the way." Not once did the two men, Dudley continued, "pull off their hats." Ultimately the judges placed more faith in the farmers' version by releasing them on bond.[14] Contradictory accounts of the altercation notwithstanding, the incident reflects Dudley's heightened sensitivity to any slight to his person and office because of the propensity of colonists to walk and talk more boldly in the early eighteenth century.

Just a year previous, resentment against crown officials found expression in the aggressive complaints of a woman against the Castle Island commander. Sarah Pitts, the wife of a laborer turned soldier, allegedly declared in the presence of several soldiers at the fort that a Boston man had told her that the men were "fools" to allow themselves to be treated so badly by the officers. The lieutenant governor, she continued, and the

13. Court of General Sessions, Suffolk, Record Book, 1702–1712, Judicial Archives, ACM, 9, 10, 18, 35–36. The charge against Boult was dropped because no one appeared to prosecute. The second accused merchant was found guilty.

14. *Diary*, I, 532–536.

commander of the Castle possessed a quarter's pay that rightfully belonged to the soldiers. She had been told and now repeated that the men should "rise all as one rather than be served so or words to the like effect." Pitts was prosecuted for stirring up sedition among the soldiers. She placed herself "on the country" (to present one's cause formally before the country as represented by a jury), however, and was acquitted by the jury.[15]

Still another incident, in 1713, two years after crowd actions to prevent exportation of grain, raised the specter of militia forces rebelling against royal government. Samuel Reeves, a "cooper or laborer," delivered an impassioned speech against General Francis Nicholson, the same Nicholson who walked the Exchange berating Sewall for jailing his secretary. On Boston Common, perhaps at a militia training, Reeves "damned" Nicholson, saying, "Let him come as soon as he will," for "we are ready for him." Someone else in the group mentioned that Governor Dudley planned to have the militia honor and welcome the visiting general. Reeves responded, "Damn the Governor, let him raise the militia and wipe his tail when he had done, for [when] we are raised, we can do what we please." He added, "If he had the said governor a mile or two off by himself, he'd as soon beat him as any man in the town." This was seditious speech indeed, proposing the unthinkable action of a laborer's actually laying hands on his majesty's royal governor. Of all those prosecuted for inflammatory words and actions since 1702, Reeves was only one of two to be convicted. But he received only light punishment for these extreme words, namely to sit on a high stool for an hour near the Town House with a sign describing his crime hung around his neck.[16]

The fact that the individuals who heard these words first- or secondhand chose to report them to authorities reveals the extent to which these speeches violated controls on conversation. Ordinary inhabitants must exercise restraint in conversation about the public affairs of the colony and particularly the conduct of their superiors, lest these words be considered inflammatory. The words uttered by this cooper-turned-laborer and a soldier's wife constituted a shocking breach of deferential behavior in a society in which individuals commonly and routinely demonstrated their loyalties to superiors and obligations to inferiors by careful words, gestures, and postures. Individuals daring to criticize or malign royal governors or lesser officials in effect challenged their auditors either to accept and agree with their sentiments or to act to restrain or report

15. Court of General Sessions, Suffolk, Record Book, 1702–1712, 100.

16. *Ibid.*, 1712–1719, 30.

them. Since most individuals received information and opinions by word-of-mouth networks employed constantly to transmit news and rumors, such speeches were acts to "publish" accusations against high officials.

Although these "mutinous" words found their way to the ears of his majesty's justices of the court of general sessions—and they might have represented only a fraction of the "vile" words used to attack Dudley—juries acquitted most of the defendants in these cases. The reasons for the acquittals are not certain, but jurors might have exercised their power to express their opinion of the truth of the charges and rumors surrounding Dudley and his administration. They in effect sanctioned the open criticism by common men and women of the royal government during Dudley's tenure. Moreover, the trial of these cases, several of which might have been heard in taverns, publicized the failure of the prosecutions. Instead of inhibiting such criticism, they might have emboldened groups of drinkers in taverns.

Given these incidents and their judicial outcome, it is no wonder that members of the governor's administration supported the Assembly's efforts to reduce the number of taverns in the town and so exercise a greater control over gatherings to drink and converse. The governor's son, Paul Dudley, the attorney general for the province and a justice of sessions, met with other officials in 1707 and agreed on the necessity of paying visits to the families of the town. Paul Dudley even led one of the eight teams of officials organized at this meeting. He did so again in 1709 and 1710. Whether he patrolled at night as did Sewall is not clear, but it is likely he did, since so many prominent men participated in these new efforts to prevent disorders. In 1714 he criticized the "extravagance" of the "ordinary sort," above all in their "excessive consumption of wine and rum."[17] Visits to the lower ranks during the day reminded members of households in the growing town of the proper regard and subservience owed their governors, especially those connected to the crown by patronage. The open and shocking disdain for Governor Dudley that had surfaced in this series of incidents might be partially offset by obligatory deferential speech and posture during these meetings in Boston households.

Yet the pressure from custom, law, and visitations to contain outbursts of criticism of prominent royal officeholders and their appointees began to

17. *Records of Boston Selectmen, 1701 to 1715*, 62, 88, 104; Paul Dudley, *Objections to the Bank of Credit Lately Projected at Boston* (Boston, 1714), in Andrew M. Davis, ed., *Colonial Currency Reprints*, I, Prince Society, XXXII (Boston, 1910), 255; T. H. Breen, *The Character of the Good Ruler: A Study of Puritan Political Ideas in New England, 1630–1730* (New York, 1974), 216.

weaken of its own accord as members of the Assembly themselves became more alienated from the governor in particular and the new royal charter in general. The unity of the Massachusetts hierarchy of government began to crack under these strains. The new charter had been divisive from the moment it took effect in 1692. After the revolt removing Andros, the House had appointed agents to negotiate a new charter with the crown. Elisha Cooke, Sr.—physician, lawyer, and councillor—had unsuccessfully lobbied for the renewal of the 1629 charter or some close facsimile. Thus when the first royal governor, Sir William Phips, arrived in 1692, Cooke and his associates found themselves out of favor with the inner circle of advisers and councillors to the new governor. Partisan feeling dividing court and popular factions in the government increased after Dudley assumed the governorship in 1702. Dudley removed the elder Cooke from the bench of the Superior Court and ejected his son, Elisha Cooke, Jr., from his position as clerk of the court. For the next twelve years Cooke Senior was elected regularly by the House to the governor's Council, but Dudley just as regularly vetoed the election. During these years the governor and the Assembly maneuvered against each other in a struggle to define the respective powers and prerogatives of the elected House versus the appointed executive. When Samuel Shute replaced Dudley as governor in 1717, the House tried to place the popular Cooke Junior in the Council. But Shute, on the advice of Paul Dudley, rejected Cooke from the Council.[18]

Sewall observed this deepening alienation of the popular Cookes from the royal government with dismay. In 1719 he recorded in his diary a conversation that probably also circulated throughout Boston. Cooke and four other officials—perhaps meeting together in order to ease the tension in the wake of Cooke's ejection from the Council—drank four bowls of punch at Cooke's rooms. "At last," Sewall wrote, "Mr. Cooke looked Mr. Auchmuty in the face and asked him if he were the man that caused him to be put out of the Council." Auchmuty answered: "No! I could not do it, but I endeavored it." Cooke angrily replied, "The governor is not so great a blockhead [as] to hearken to you." Report of Cooke's words caused Shute to declare before the House that "Cooke was such an enemy to his master the king and to him his lieutenant that he expected he should be removed from his clerk's place" in the House.[19]

Completely locked out of sources of royal patronage and prestige, Cooke began to look elsewhere for means to acquire and exercise influence in the

18. G. B. Warden, *Boston, 1689–1776* (Boston, 1970), 42, 60–64, 91–92; Bushman, *King and People*, 111–132; *Diary*, I, 310n.

19. *Diary*, II, 915–917.

colony's affairs. He already possessed extensive influence throughout Boston streets and wharves by virtue of his mercantile interests. Together with other merchants he had financed the construction of Long Wharf in 1711, the wharf that jutted out from the bottom of King Street into Boston Harbor for seven hundred yards providing docking space for large vessels. At this center of Boston's drinking culture, the town had rewarded him with a grant of property rights to buildings on the wharf for forty years. At his death in 1737 he owned nine houses—four of them definitely located on King Street—and two shops, nine warehouses, three ropewalks, various other lots of land in the town, and one thousand acres in Maine. His estate was valued at sixty-three thousand pounds, making him one of the richest men in the province. Many men looked to Cooke as their master directly or indirectly, and his extensive interests placed him in personal contact with merchants, shopkeepers, artisans, and laborers throughout the town. Moreover, Cooke was one master who did not hesitate to distribute drink to his employees and dependents in partial payment for their services. He himself possessed the reputation of a heavy drinker. Half of the expenses of the Lincolnshire Associates (a land company in which he held an interest) were for entertainments at Boston taverns. He also owned the Goat Tavern on King Street and rented it to a series of tavernkeepers.[20] Retailers might have rented parts of several of his buildings on the street and wharf. With these resources and connections, Cooke moved to control the outcome of Boston town meeting elections through a secret organization that later came to be known as the Boston Caucus.

II

Evidence about the Boston Caucus is sparse, so sparse that some historians doubt its existence and influence. There are no extant contemporary references to the Caucus before the 1740s, owing perhaps to its secret

20. For a short biography of Cooke, see John Langdon Sibley, *Biographical Sketches of Graduates of Harvard University* . . . (Boston, 1873–1885), I, 520–525. Warden, *Boston, 1689–1776*, 67–68; Inventory of Elisha Cooke, Jr., Suffolk County Probate Records, Record Book, XXXIV, 241–242; G. B. Warden, "The Caucus and Democracy in Colonial Boston," *New England Quarterly*, XLIII (1970), 29. William Knock was approved for a license "in Dr. Cooke's rents in King Street," July 6, 1719 (*Records of Boston Selectmen, 1701 to 1715*, 55); Edward Lutwyche was approved to "remove his license of tavernkeeper from his house in Linn St. to a house belonging to Elisha Cooke, Esq. in King Street" in December 1729 (Boston, Record Commissioners, *Records of Boston Selectmen, 1716 to 1736* [Boston, 1885], 192).

origins and operation. Loyalist Peter Oliver, the last royal chief justice of Massachusetts, said that the Caucus spent enormous amounts of money on liquor in the 1720s to win elections, in his manuscript on the origins of the Revolution written between 1777 and 1781. Historian William Gordon wrote that the Caucus originated in the 1720s, in his history of the United States published in 1788. In this century it has been persuasively argued that in or about 1719 Cooke and his political allies formed this secret organization in order to prepare a slate of candidates to be elected at the annual town meeting. In the 1690s only about 15 percent of the town's approximately one thousand taxpayers owned sufficient property to be able to vote. But the number of actual voters rose from 150 in 1692 to about 350 in 1698. Between 1698 and 1717 the average number of voters was about 225. But in 1719 a total of 454 Bostonians voted in the elections for selectmen, a sharp increase that suggests that someone acted to mobilize every eligible voter, and perhaps some ineligible, to turn out. Voter interest might also have increased in response to conflict between governor and Assembly. At this election five of seven places on the board of selectmen went to new men, including Cooke and several other men who appear to have been close associates. Several months later Cooke and two of the other new selectmen were elected as Boston's representatives to the House. Rarely had Bostonians elected the same men to these two offices at the same time. Moreover, except for two years when he visited England, Cooke continued to be reelected until his death in 1737. From 1719 forward there existed a remarkable continuity in the elected leadership of the town, including that vital office of tax collector, who possessed the power to issue abatements. Thus it is highly probable that Cooke did indeed actively solicit votes from Boston residents and distribute the huge amounts of alcohol—perhaps nine thousand pounds sterling worth—that Oliver claimed he did.[21]

There is strong circumstantial evidence to link Cooke to the change in licensing policy in 1719. He and his associates assumed control over the board of selectmen in March, before the annual licensing sessions in July, in precisely the same year when approvals of applicants for licenses by the selectmen increased sharply. Apparently a haunter of taverns himself, he and his associates most likely perceived how a change in licensing policy could help them to win popular support and consolidate control over

21. A discussion of references to the Caucus is included in Warden, "The Caucus and Democracy in Colonial Boston," *NEQ*, XLIII (1970), 19–44; Gary B. Nash, *The Urban Crucible: Social Change, Political Consciousness, and the Origins of the American Revolution* (Cambridge, Mass., 1979), 87–88.

Boston's electoral politics. Cooke and his allies broke with the Assembly's policies of the last twenty years in order to become the political patrons of the dozens of new tavernkeepers and retailers they approved for licenses on every street and alley in town.

Another consideration of the statistics tells the story. During the five years previous to 1719, the selectmen had approved only 87 (28 percent) of the 313 petitions for licenses; in the next five years the new board of selectmen dominated by Cooke approved 245 (80 percent) of 305 petitions. The justices blocked most of these approved applicants when they came before them. Still, Cooke and his associates approved so many petitions that the number of people actually licensed rose sharply, from 74 to 88 in 1719 and to 134 by 1722, an 81 percent increase in four years before the number began to level off.[22] Indeed, Cooke and other selectmen flooded the market for drink in Boston. Given the increasing numbers of widows and disabled men asking for licenses, the tight licensing policy in force from 1700 to 1718 would likely have been relaxed in any case. But the timing of the change in policy and the drastic extent of the change belong to Cooke. At a time of increasing political tension over the policies of royal officeholders, Cooke effected a sudden expansion of the number of places of public gathering presided over by men and women of low rank.

The words that John Adams used to describe the rise of a town representative in Braintree in the 1760s also seem apt for Cooke and his associates in 1719. Adams believed that this new breed of elected officials in the colony first set out to enlarge their "interest" and reputation by making it a point to become "well acquainted with the real and personal estates" of the townspeople and therefore "so very fit for select men." They might face "opposition from the most virtuous and independent part of the town," but after they win election "their reputation increases very fast." Such a figure becomes "to those not already grappled to his interest by fear or affection, very assiduous and obliging." And "when the season of the year approaches, a swarm of candidates for approbation to keep taverns or dramshops surround him for his favor." "For one he will use his utmost interest; for another, he really thinks there is occasion for a public house where he lives; for a third his circumstances are so needy he really thinks he ought to be assisted; for a fourth he is so unable to work, that he must be assisted; and to a fifth, he likes it very well, for he thinks the more there are the better, the more obliging they will be and the cheaper they will sell." Taverns are therefore "placed in every corner of the town," where men

22. Compiled from *Records of Boston Selectmen, 1701 to 1715*, and *1716 to 1736*; and Court of General Sessions, Suffolk, Record Books, 1712–1719, 1719–1725.

"grow attached to the tavernkeeper who is attached to his patron both by gratitude and expectation." And the "hero" of this drama is extolled as one of "the most useful men in town, as a very understanding . . . man, and is at the next May meeting set up for a candidate as representative." He wins. Then, by "extending and fortifying the parts of the same system, he increases his interest."[23]

The abrupt shift in licensing policy in 1719 by the new selectmen strongly suggests that Cooke and his allies set out to build such a system to combat the influence exercised by the governor and his appointees. By use of his power of approval over prospective tavernkeepers and retailers in conjunction with his existing commercial and landlord connections throughout the town, Cooke could and did build a stable political base from which to increase his influence in both provincial and town politics. This new board of selectmen abandoned even the pretense of enforcing the Assembly's policies and laws on the use of drink and taverns. Even those applicants approved by the selectmen but refused by the justices would regard Cooke as their friend and patron in the increasingly unstable society of Boston.

Although many of the poor who received licenses as a result of this change could not vote, their supporters and relations might have been eligible. Moreover, it was not just the right to vote that made the distribution of licenses and drink to Bostonians a politic move. By multiplying licenses Cooke made drink cheaper in taverns and retail dramshops and increased the propensity of drinkers to drink his health and advertise his role as patron and benefactor. And since extralegal crowd actions had already become an important part of the politics in Boston—against grain exporters and royal officials—even nonvoters could be useful to Cooke.[24]

It is shortly after this dramatic increase in public houses that John Yeamans, an apparent associate of Governor Shute, uttered "many threatening speeches" against Cooke in Hall's King Street tavern and finally struck him. The response of mariner Christopher Taylor (mentioned earlier) suggests the loyalty and support that Cooke had come to inspire among patrons of Boston taverns. Hearing the news, Taylor began walking to King Street in an "insolent, daring, and menacing manner." When he met Thomas Smith, a pewterer, on King Street, he asked him, in a "seditious" manner, "Do you applaud the thing, do you justify the action of

23. L. H. Butterfield *et al.*, eds., *Diary and Autobiography of John Adams* (New York, 1964), I, 128–129, 190–192, 204–205, 214.

24. G. B. Warden makes this point in "The Caucus and Democracy in Colonial Boston," *NEQ*, XLIII (1970), 30–31.

Mr. Yeamans beating or striking Mr. Cooke?" Then he declared to Smith, "They have begun with us, they have taken us by the beard, they are come to club law, knock them down is the word."[25] Taylor believed Yeamans's action reflected the governor's ambition to quell any opposition to him and his policies. The blow to Cooke simplified growing animosity between court and popular parties in the provincial government into a symbolic physical act that ordinary Bostonians could readily understand. Political controversies had been reduced to a physical exchange, the language of the streets.

Almost by stage design, Governor Shute happened to be riding up King Street in his coach while Taylor aired his views to Smith. Taylor turned to the coach and said, "By God I will face you," and "without any motion of respect boldly faced him in his coach." Presumably everyone else customarily bowed to the governor when he passed. After this daring display of contempt for the governor, Taylor later approached merchant Jacob Wendell, asking him whom he supported and telling him, "I have been by the Town House . . . and if I had seen or met Yeamans . . . or the governor I would have pulled them by the beard." But Taylor was not finished. He went on "to say and publish" to Jeremiah Allen that he, Taylor, "was for the old Charter [the 1629 charter revoked in 1684] and would lose ten lives if he had it in that account." He also warned Allen that his "House"—perhaps a reference to the Assembly or Allen's mercantile house—stood in danger from the governor, but that Taylor would "defend" it if he was able. Finally, he told Allen that he had "faced the governor."[26] Taylor did indeed "publish" his feelings and views on the conflict between Cooke and Shute, and on the busiest tavern-lined street in the town.

Taylor's conduct was a serious breach of the manners and speech expected of ordinary colonists in any social context, let alone that of King Street, a center for the exchange of news and rumors. When he was brought before Suffolk justices, eyewitnesses and the clerk of the court noted the manner and posture of the accused, how he had walked down the street in an "insolent" and "menacing" manner. The fact that he had

25. Gentlemen usually avoided any public show of disagreement before social inferiors so as not to encourage partisan expression among the lower ranks. This is exactly the impact that the altercation at the Hall tavern had on Taylor and probably others. See Richard D. Brown, *Knowledge Is Power: The Diffusion of Information in Early America, 1700–1865* (New York, 1989), 25; Court of General Sessions, Suffolk, Record Book, 1719–1725, Apr. 4, 1721, 76, 80–81.

26. Court of General Sessions, Suffolk, Record Book, 1719–1725, Apr. 4, 1721, 76, 80–81.

"faced" the governor without any bow or motion of respect was as much a crime as what he had said. Taylor himself boasted of this daring act later. Moreover, he had conjured up the shocking image of a mariner actually laying hands on his "excellency" the governor and "pulling him by the beard," completely reversing the body language expected between superiors and inferiors.

What Taylor said and did reveals just how much popularity Cooke enjoyed in the streets of the town. Taylor became so provoked that someone had laid hands on Coòke that he would go so far as walk to King Street in order to utter threats against the governor. The relaxation of the strict licensing policy two years earlier had helped Cooke to ingratiate himself with Bostonians. He had acted to satisfy popular demand for more public houses at a time when ordinary inhabitants as well as leaders of the House had become so angered by crown policies that they cast aside traditional restraints on the criticism of rulers. The greater and cheaper flow of drink facilitated the spread of these sentiments.

To be sure, the customary restraints on speech and posture in taverns or anywhere else did not entirely dissolve. At least three of the men whom Taylor accosted were sufficiently shocked by his words to provide detailed testimony to the justices as to their "seditious" nature. Despite this testimony, however, Taylor was acquitted of "raising seditions, tumults, and disquietudes." He paid a small fine for a lesser charge of "breach of peace." Presumably, Taylor was highly combative and volatile. The next year he was brought before the justices again for beating a Portsmouth mariner in no less prominent a place than the Town House, the seat of provincial authority. But together with other incidents, Taylor's actions were symptomatic of the more unguarded and emotional character of political expression in street and tavern by the 1720s. Taylor possessed friends of material substance who came to his aid at both court appearances. A Boston joiner and a Dorchester husbandman paid the one-hundred-pound bond for his release after the King Street fracas. For the second offense a wine cooper and Richard Hall, the baker-tavernkeeper near the Town House, pledged securities.[27]

From Governor Shute's perspective the number of Taylors in the town was legion. He wrote to the Board of Trade in 1721 that "the common people of this province are so perverse, that when I remove any person from the Council, for not behaving himself with duty towards H.M. or his orders, or for treating me H.M. governor ill, that he becomes their favorite,

27. *Ibid.,* July 30, 1722, 150–151.

and is chose a representative, where he acts as much in his power, the same part he did when in Council."[28] The people of Boston had made Cooke their "favorite." His reversal of the licensing policy not only helped him to establish ties of patronage and clientage throughout the town; it also sanctioned the development of more unguarded political expression within the increasing number of taverns and dramshops.

The weakening of restraints on oral commentary in taverns paralleled the loosening of the customary censorship of print. Up through 1713 most of the publications printed in Massachusetts besides statutes were sermons or otherwise religious. Sewall never distributed a political tract while traveling throughout the colony. Authorities considered print to be an extension of the oral authority of the best men bred and educated to govern and preach.[29] But after Sewall's resignation as manager of the government press, no one was appointed to replace him. Censorship almost collapsed during Dudley's administration because the governor made so many enemies that they began to resort to print to air their disagreements with his policies and even attack his character. The development of factional conflict over currency issues in the 1710s stirred a number of merchants to publish criticisms of government policy. Shute attempted to reestablish censorship between 1716 and 1723, going so far as to have merchant John Colman prosecuted for a pamphlet he wrote and published in 1720 because it contained many "passages reflecting upon the acts and laws of the Province . . . and has a tendency to disturb the administration of the government as well as the public peace." The government, however, dropped this suit without explanation. The House would not cooperate with Shute's efforts to reimpose censorship. It chided Shute for permitting "libels" against the House and acted to preserve the power to publish criticisms of the governor's policies. The appearance of James Franklin's *New-England Courant* in 1721—which openly ridiculed the clergy and particularly the Mathers—only lent further legitimacy to the criticism of rulers. The Assembly did act to restrain the *Courant*, but censorship as a comprehensive government policy virtually ceased. The principle of freedom of the press did not clearly emerge, but the use of the press for the

28. Shute to the Council of Trade and Plantations, June 1, 1720, in W. Noel Sainsbury *et al.*, eds., *Calendar of State Papers*, Colonial Series, *America and West Indies* (London, 1860–), XXXII, 45; Breen, *The Character of the Good Ruler*, 223n.

29. Michael Warner, *The Letters of the Republic: Publication and the Public Sphere in Eighteenth-Century America* (Cambridge, Mass., 1990), 19–23, 35.

public good, in keeping with a republican sense of public virtue, was fast becoming accepted.[30]

Cooke contributed to this dynamic by publishing a pamphlet in 1720, one year after the Caucus came to power and the number of public houses climbed dramatically. Governor Shute had just refused to accept Cooke's latest electoral triumph, the House's choice of him to be speaker. In his *Just and Seasonable Vindication* Cooke revealed a political philosophy directly at odds with that of court spokesman Ebenezer Pemberton. Here he argued that submission to the governor's decision to veto the choice of speaker would allow him to set a dangerous precedent. "Few men," he stated, "see the danger of little changes in fundamentals," and "every design therefore of alteration ought to be warily observed." Cooke put himself forward as one such close and critical observer, watching and guarding in the "interest of the people." Instead of revering leaders as gods and suppressing any "murmuring" against them, Cooke declared that the people should "inform themselves of their just rights." From a due sense of the "inestimable value" of these rights, they might be "encouraged to assert them" in the face of attempts to alter and reduce them. Cooke conceived of an activist role in public affairs for free white males. He spoke of his popularity as a kind of gift bestowed upon him from the people. Their "good opinion and kindness for me is a favor accompanied with all the obliging circumstances imaginable" and is a sign of "their approving my former service."[31] This kind of relationship between leaders and people stood in sharp contrast to the exalted position that Pemberton would have rulers occupy. Cooke sought favor in voters' eyes by presenting himself as a guardian of the public interest against the predatory private interest of rulers.

Pamphlets such as Cooke's contributed to the gradual change in the conception and organization of the public sphere in Boston. The public of the traditional order had always been embodied in the face-to-face relations of superiors and inferiors in gatherings reflecting and demonstrating hierarchy, such as church meetings and processions. In contrast, Cooke and other pamphleteers created an abstract conception of the public separate from the social and political hierarchy. Readers of pamphlets could

30. *The Deplorable State of New-England*; Nash, *The Urban Crucible*, 85–86; Court of General Sessions, Suffolk, Record Book, 1719–1725, May 2, 1720, 25, 29; Clyde Augustus Duniway, *The Development of Freedom of the Press in Massachusetts* (Cambridge, Mass., 1906), chap. 6; Leonard W. Levy, *Emergence of a Free Press* (New York, 1985), 29–33; Warner, *Letters of the Republic*, 29–43, 61–65.

31. Elisha Cooke, *Mr. Cooke's Just and Seasonable Vindication* . . . (Boston, 1720), 13–14, 18–19.

now impersonally identify themselves as being part of a public of provincewide proportions who together should ultimately play a supervisory role in the conduct of public affairs. Authors justified, and eluded prosecution for, such printed appeals to the public in the 1710s by writing anonymously, adopting pseudonyms, or claiming that they had no personal interest in the outcome of the issues they discussed. They defined a public sphere that legitimized printed criticisms of authority by ascribing pernicious private interests to figures of authority that anonymous writers could deny.[32]

This public represented in print could never be physically assembled; it transcended the local official gatherings at which considerations of status and rank ordinarily structured and inhibited discourse.[33] Yet informal tavern gatherings came closest to incarnating representative versions of this public, because rank was often slighted or submerged in such gatherings or absent altogether. Thus the expansion of printed political discourse and the emergence of a critical reading public paradoxically rendered the oral culture of taverns ever more important.

Thomas Selby, proprietor of the Crown Coffee House, provided a context for the physical display of a new public sphere. He owned sixteen pamphlets at his death in 1725, some of which probably considered the currency issue. As Selby's personal accounts illustrate, his coffeehouse was a center for the conduct of commerce.[34] His genteel patrons were engaged in similar transactions and probably purchased pamphlets in numbers comparable to Selby. The private purchaser and reader of pamphlets and newspapers could more fully realize his new identity as a member of the novel critical public through oral discourse with other members about the content of print. Thus the frequent patronage of taverns and the new critical discourse of pamphlets helped to legitimize each other.

32. Jürgen Habermas, *The Structural Transformation of the Public Sphere: An Inquiry into a Category of Bourgeois Society*, trans. Thomas Burger (Cambridge, Mass., 1989), 27–56; Warner, *Letters of the Republic*, 39–46.

33. Habermas draws a strong linkage between the emergence of a public sphere in England in the early 18th century and discussion in taverns and especially coffeehouses: "The periodical articles were not only made the object of discussion by the public of the coffee houses but were viewed as integral parts of this discussion. . . . When the *Spectator* separated from the *Guardian* the letters to the editor were provided with a special institution: in the west side of Button's Coffee House a lion's head was attached through whose jaws the reader threw his letter" (*The Structural Transformation*, 42).

34. Inventory of Thomas Selby, Suffolk County Probate Records, Record Books, XXV, 530–535, N.S., XIV, 72–76.

The coalescence of a critical reading public distinct from the social and political hierarchy gradually enveloped more men than the genteel patrons of coffeehouses catering to the elite. James Pitson clearly made his modest King Street tavern into a place where inhabitants of lesser rank, such as artisans and tradesmen, could obtain pamphlets or hear them read. Pitson's middling rank is revealed not only by his estate but by the fact that he once was elected constable. He declined to serve, excusing himself by stating that he already served the public by keeping tavern. This service included the provision of printed discourse to customers. Licensed between 1717 and 1737, Pitson had thirty-one pamphlets and eighty-eight books on the shelf in his barroom (a partially enclosed space in the public room), all readily available to customers, both familiars and strangers. Indeed, Pitson visually advertised his library by exhibiting it to public view and might have pressed pamphlets into customers' hands as had happened to one Bostonian "on the Exchange" under the Town House.[35] He might also have operated an early form of the lending library.

For those men of middling or low rank who did not ordinarily purchase printed discourse, it became still more important to patronize a tavern like Pitson's often because of the new access they enjoyed there to an expanding volume of news and opinion hitherto limited to a narrow elite. Now any reader could claim membership in the public represented in print by reading it not only himself but also aloud to the illiterate, making the latter members of the public also. Other tavernkeepers such as John Marston, who took over the Golden Ball off King Street in 1752, also owned extensive personal libraries that might have been available to patrons. Indeed, thirty of forty-four enumerated inventories of tavernkeepers and retailers contained "books," a "number of books," or "libraries"—an indication that the proprietor was at least literate.[36] Thus taverns helped to shape the dynamics of the expansion of print culture by not only embodying the genteel public whom the authors of most pamphlets and newspaper essays addressed but in some cases by helping to expand the public to include lesser men whom authors never intended or wished to address.

35. Inventory of James Pitson, *ibid.*, XXV, 534–535, XXXIV, 360–364; Petition of Pitson, Court of General Sessions, Suffolk, Record Book, 1719–1725, Apr. 15, 1720, 18; Warner, *Letters of the Republic*, 45.

36. Petition of John Marston to Governor, Council, and Assembly, Dec. 26, 1752, Taverns, 1643–1774, CXI, 255, ACM; Inventory of Marston, Suffolk County Probate Records, Record Books, LXXXV, 592. This information was gathered from 44 inventories (or wills) in Suffolk County Probate Records, Record Books.

If the tavern helped to shape the critical public invented by pamphleteers, tavern assemblies were in turn subtly altered by the printed discourse that enlarged the volume and quality of information transmitted through them. Customarily, it was not necessary to remain sober for men merely renewing ties with those members of a neighborhood with whom they most closely identified, or just transmitting news of illness, birth, death, or other items of local interest. And even if they attended a tavern to conduct business, once it was concluded the necessity of keeping one's wits clear waned, and the impulse to drink to mutual trust increased. To read a pamphlet from Pitson's shelf, however, and weigh it against other information heard or read, required a more cautious use of alcohol. The translation of print into public opinion through oratory and debate interrupted drinking, paced it, and probably stretched consumption out over longer periods. Men becoming engaged in the expanding print culture and beginning to identify with a wider public that transcended local face-to-face relations might even alter their drinking habits in keeping with the new responsibility of this public to inspect the ruling hierarchy. Certainly publishers of newspapers, as immersed in the print culture as ministers but with different emphases, readily included secular diatribes written by readers against intemperance and tavern haunting.[37] This may explain the growing popularity of coffee and chocolate as reflected in Selby's dedication of one elaborately decorated room to coffee consumption.

But it is clear that the expanding circulation and discussion of print in the eighteenth century did not decrease the volume of alcohol consumed in Boston. Selby's inventory of alcohol, as opposed to coffee, is evidence that even genteel coffeehouses sold far more rum and wine than coffee. Printers and publishers of the new criticism, like ministers before them, could not escape the fact that their publications still only supplemented a primarily oral culture; further, that tavern fellowship provided the most natural context for the coalescence of the new public represented in their publications. If it was now not only permissible but necessary to place high officials under scrutiny, and sometimes condemn them in vituperative terms, informal occasions of meeting unstructured by hierarchy and fostering free and open exchange became still more attractive. Collective

37. For example, see letters in *Boston Weekly News-Letter,* July 12, 1750, no. 2513, and *Boston Gazette,* July 17, 1750, no. 1582. For the emphasis that newspaper publishers placed on the maintenance of social order, see Clark, "The Newspapers of Provincial America," AAS, *Proceedings,* C (1990), 385–386.

drinking of alcohol facilitated this novel and heady form of empowerment by weakening traditional inhibitions of speech and posture.[38]

The impact of print on Boston taverns as a whole was uneven. Although most surviving inventories of Boston licenseholders include books, such a survey is skewed toward those possessing extensive property requiring probate. As a group, licenseholders included more of the poor of the town after 1719. As the licensing system became more geared to popular demand, it is probable that a large proportion of licenseholders—even those located on King Street—did not ordinarily acquire printed matter or make it available to customers. Sarah Wormall, Sarah Battersby, and Sarah Beane, all tavernkeepers on King Street after 1720, could not afford such purchases even if they were literate.[39]

But this absence of reading matter does not mean that the end of censor-

38. Jürgen Habermas limits his examination of the structural transformation of the public sphere to the way in which the "bourgeoisie" in England and on the Continent used print to redefine their political identity (*The Structural Transformation*). Although this social stratum is ill defined, he implies that only segments of the middle and upper ranks in English society developed a modern sense of citizenship in the 18th century. Certainly the periodicals he refers to such as the *Guardian* had very limited circulation even among the elite, and he mentions only elite coffeehouses as forums for the consumption and debate of such publications. Using Habermas as a model, Michael Warner also infers from his examination of the style and content of republican literature that only discrete segments of Massachusetts society interacted with this literature to divorce themselves from traditional social and political relationships (*Letters of the Republic*). In the case of Boston, I see a much more dynamic process of interaction between modern printed discourse and traditional oral patterns of association that involved a wider spectrum of people. The Boston leaders most involved in the invention of the public not only chose but needed to appropriate the traditional oral culture of taverns in order to promote a modern concept of citizenship. True, they ideally wished to contain the public sphere mainly to the middle- and upper-rank readers on whom Warner focuses, but they ultimately paved the way for the integration of print-inspired concepts of republican citizenship with the habitual collective drinking in taverns that many republican writers condemned. My understanding of the interaction between print and oral culture is more akin to that outlined by Charles E. Clark in "The Newspapers of Provincial America," AAS, *Proceedings*, C, (October 1990), 367–383. He states that newspapers still served as "extensions and reinforcers of the oral culture rather than substitutes for it" and that they "narrowed the cultural gap between the learned and the merely literate and the information gap between the privileged and the merely competent" (384, 387). It is probable that more people read newspapers in taverns than subscribed to them, and still more heard them read there.

39. Wormall died barely solvent (Suffolk County Probate Records, XXII, 528); Beane's inventory just barely covered her debts (LXXVI, 53, LXXXVI, 399–402).

ship, the growing number of booksellers, and the publication of four newspapers in the town by the 1760s did not have an effect on the mass of tavern patrons in Boston over the course of the colonial period. From the 1710s forward and especially by midcentury, much of the pamphlet literature published in Boston focused on the suspected machinations of royal governors and their political dependents, grist for excited accusations. As native leaders began to perceive their chartered government as a miniature version of the British constitution with its balanced division of powers between king, the House of Lords, and the House of Commons, they frequently communicated the fear that alien royal governors appointed by the king's ministry might enlarge their power and personal estates at the expense of chartered rights. The Massachusetts Assembly began to conceive of itself as the advocate of colonial interests in the face of ambitious, corrupt men appointed by the crown. Belief in manipulation and deceit at the highest levels of colony government, communicated to the reading public through pamphlets and newspapers at such taverns as Pitson's and Marston's, also probably reached a nonreading public avidly interested in exposure of the great. Such news empowered individuals of humble status to assert themselves verbally to men of similar or lesser rank, to rebuke or challenge the mighty in absentia but before one's fellows.[40]

This effrontery is evident in Taylor's behavior. When he "menacingly" sauntered up King Street, he accosted almost every man he met in order to assert his faith in the "old Charter" and his belief that the blow against Cooke symbolized a broader political agenda. Certainly the accusations of bribery and treachery that punctuated the administration of Joseph Dudley between 1702 and 1715 excited conversation among coopers and blacksmiths. As the intentions of royal appointees came into question again and again from one administration to the next in the eighteenth century, taverns became more central to the political culture because of

40. It is important to emphasize that the development and expansion of a critical reading public was very gradual. Pamphlets and newspapers continued to be written in a style easily accessible only to the gentry. Indeed, they were often written in the form of letters between gentlemen. Lesser ranks might need a more literate mediator like Pitson to wade through the high style of printed discourse. Their access was indirect. Moreover, it was mainly men that collected in taverns. Women's access to printed political discourse was still more indirect. Widow Frances Wardell hosted the courts in her tavern, defended her license against termination, but died illiterate and unable to read pamphlets. The reading public of pamphlets consisted mainly of free white propertied males, which is why a critical printed discourse was allowed to develop at all. Warner makes this point in *Letters of the Republic*, 48.

their role in the reception, dissemination, and sometimes embellishment of news and rumors.[41]

III

It is unlikely that Cooke circulated among taverns catering to the lower ranks to court popularity personally, as evident in the limits to the disorder that he would tolerate in such taverns even among his own tenants. When tavernkeeper Olive Smallpeice moved from the North End to King Street, she rented part of one of the King Street houses owned by Elisha Cooke himself. But two years later Cooke and the other selectmen refused to renew her husband's license because of disorders in their tavern. No doubt Olive and her husband besought their landlord-selectman to reconsider. But Cooke and his fellow selectmen remained unmoved and denied another petition from the couple for a retail license the next year, perhaps because their house had been so unruly as to offend even the Caucus.[42]

Nor did the solicitation of electoral support by Cooke and other Caucus leaders through the distribution of drink and licenses inaugurate a democratic political culture in Boston. Voter participation in town meeting elections declined after 1719 by roughly 50 percent. An elite group of leaders continued to govern the town. Moreover, in the 1740s the town meeting elected Thomas Hutchinson and Andrew Oliver to the Assembly—men who scorned the distribution of drink for votes. The Caucus might have lost influence after Cooke's death in 1737.[43] And the turnover

41. Several early examples of inflammatory attacks on royal officials are the pamphlets condemning Dudley; see *The Deplorable State of New-England;* and Philopolites, *A Memorial of the Present Deplorable State of New-England, with the Many Disadvantages It Lyes under by the Male-Administration of Their Present Governour, Joseph Dudley* . . . (Boston, 1707). These pamphlets have echoes in the incidents brought before the Suffolk sessions. They also reflect early examples of the adoption of Whig opposition ideology as a language used to inspect and criticize royal authority. See Bernard Bailyn, *The Ideological Origins of the American Revolution* (Cambridge, Mass., 1967); Paul S. Boyer, "Borrowed Rhetoric: The Massachusetts Excise Controversy of 1754," *WMQ,* 3d Ser., XXI (1964), 328–351.

42. *Records of Boston Selectmen, 1716 to 1736,* 71, 87, 99, 104, 128, 140; Inventory of John Smallpeice, Suffolk County Probate Records, Record Book, XXII, 199–201, N.S., X, 116.

43. Nash, *The Urban Crucible,* 88; Warden, *Boston, 1689–1776,* chap. 6. Gary Nash has argued that crowd actions to prevent exportation of grain, against a central market, and to prevent impressment gangs from seizing sailors all constituted expressions of "alternative ideologies" held by the unlettered, inarticulate lower classes of Boston. I do not find a consistent ideological point of view in these incidents. On some issues provoking crowd

in Boston licenseholders became so high that they could hardly be influential as a group. Most remained preoccupied with the struggle to acquire credit and remain solvent.

The selectmen who succeeded Cooke and his associates in the 1740s and 1750s were not always comfortable with his legacy. The revival of efforts to employ the poor in workhouses and manufactories after 1740 is evidence of official dismay over the popular resort to taverns. In the company of justices and constable the selectmen continued to walk the town to inspect households and prevent disorders. Under pressure from irate critics, the selectmen even agreed in 1752 to reduce the number of public houses, cutting it by twenty-seven by 1758. But the manufactories failed, and the ratio of public houses to inhabitants remained high in 1765.[44] Selectmen sought some measure of control over public houses, but not so much as to alienate the lower orders or stimulate greater numbers of unlicensed sales and gatherings. They balanced regulation and rhetoric extolling order and discipline (as opposed to idleness and dissipation) with appeasement of the demand for easy access to drink. And through appeasement selectmen could stand like Cooke as patrons of grateful client licenseholders struggling to stay off poor relief.

The sometimes uneasy relationship of elected officials to the dozens of lower-class public houses they approved is reflected in the dynamics and aftermath of the anti-impressment riot of 1747. There is no evidence revealing the role of taverns, but seamen instigated the riot to avoid capture by impressment gangs of the Royal Navy, who might have swept town wharves as well as merchant ships in the harbor. These confrontations quickly became a mass uprising involving the town as a whole pressing for release of those held by the navy. Members of the town and provincial government exhibited sympathy with the rioters as officials tried to negotiate between the demands of Commodore Charles Knowles and of angry, aroused Bostonians. But, after the riots, they joined Gover-

actions, crowds possessed the support of Boston society as a whole, especially if the targets were crown officials. For the extrainstitutional role of crowds in Massachusetts' political culture, see Pauline Maier, *From Resistance to Revolution: Colonial Radicals and the Development of American Opposition to Britain, 1765–1776* (New York, 1974), chap. 1.

44. Boston, Record Commissioners, *Boston Town Records, 1742 to 1757* (Boston, 1883), 219–220; List of Persons Licensed in the County of Suffolk, 1758, MHS; List of Persons Licensed in Boston, June 14, 1765, Papers of James Otis, Sr., MHS; Boston, Record Commissioners, *Selectmen's Minutes from 1764 through 1768* (Boston, 1889), 33, 36, 63, 133–134, 170; see petitions for licenses from poor, Misc. Bd., MHS. For ratios of inhabitants to public houses in the 1750s and 1760s, see above, Chapter 3.

nor William Shirley in blaming the uprising on seamen, servants, blacks, and "other persons of mean and vile condition." They sought to minimize this challenge to their authority as they took steps to reassert it.[45] Under certain circumstances elected officials could unite with the lower orders, especially in opposition to as unpopular a manifestation of imperial authority as impressment; but they remained wary of mass participation in the political culture in situations over which they held little control. Officials exhibited a similar ambivalence over the approval of the dozens of public houses presided over and patronized by the poor. Selectmen both condemned and sanctioned, feared and exploited, and sought to control but ultimately acceded to a separate subculture of collective drinking among the poor. They shifted their stances and positions as economic circumstances, attacks on intemperance, and political events dictated from the 1740s through the early 1760s.

Back in 1681 deputies to the Assembly had brought selectmen to participate in the granting of licenses, in the expectation that they would act to limit licenses to those pious and sober individuals who would govern their houses in accordance with Puritan social ideals. Selectmen must act as did Samuel Sewall—punishing, patrolling, and exhorting against intemperance. But in 1719 Cooke and his allies abandoned even the pretense of conforming to the "character of the good ruler." The distribution of drink became a means of influencing the operation of Boston's government. The apprehension that Samuel Danforth had expressed in 1710 had become a reality. The "drinking party" had become so "potent" that those who "work at, favor, and countenance this vice" are "improved in offices of trust."[46] However ambivalent selectmen sometimes felt about the dozens of humble establishments they approved for licensing, they had distanced themselves from the duty to suppress intemperance and disorder. Although the influence of the Caucus would ebb and flow in the eighteenth century, it remained a force in Boston politics. John Adams became aware of its power in 1763. At meetings of the Caucus, he noted, members "choose a moderator, who puts questions to the vote regularly, and selectmen, assessors, collectors, wardens, fire wards, and representatives are

45. John Lax and William Pencak, "The Knowles Riot and the Crisis of the 1740's in Massachusetts," *Perspectives in American History*, X (1976), 163–216. Lax and Pencak also show that Samuel Adams drew a more radical lesson from the riot, justifying it as a defense of natural rights. He would form a more tolerant attitude toward popular participation in politics, but still sought to manage it closely.

46. Samuel Danforth, *The Woful Effects of Drunkenness* . . . (Boston, 1710), 25–26.

regularly chosen before they are chosen in the town."[47] Such a careful system of management no doubt included considerations of the use of patronage in approving licenses.

When one considers the period between 1670 and 1720 as a whole, it is possible to place the rise of Elisha Cooke in perspective. By the late 1670s the number and character of tavern assemblies in Boston had become symbolic of growing levels of dissonance in the society as a whole. The multiplication of public houses represented one of the more visible centrifugal forces tugging and pulling at the unity and coherence of Boston society. Parallel to a rising tide of intemperance and disorder were the devastating war with the Indians in the 1670s, the loss of the self-governing charter and the imposition of the Andros regime in the 1680s, and the permanent modification of Puritan control in the 1690s by the new charter. The Puritan polity constructed in the 1630s suffered from multiple cracks and fissures in the last quarter of the seventeenth century.

The clergy readily interpreted the multiple crises that the colony faced as the consequence of God's wrath against a sinful people. They asked the government to take action, and leaders responded with steps to reassert their hegemony and demonstrate their character as good rulers. The drastic reduction in licenses in 1681 and the limitation of licenses pressed by the Assembly from 1698 through 1719 curtailed the number of houses where men might drink, assemble, and converse. At the same time, visits and patrols led by prominent members of the colony government made the hierarchy more visible amid the confusion of the growing, sprawling urban society.

But these efforts to restore order proved ineffectual. The failure of the 1712 prohibition of the sale of rum in taverns only exposed more clearly the weakness of regulations in general. Meanwhile, growing numbers of poor inhabitants in Boston pleaded before selectmen for licenses. Against clerical appeals to licensing authorities to reduce the number of public houses in the name of piety and order, the poor protested that it was God's will that they become drinksellers, that "providence" had cast them into this employment.[48]

Amid these conflicting interpretations of God's will, some men began to chafe at the restraints of a political culture in which the clergy defined the meaning of events. The harsh Calvinist God of retribution receded from the front stage of politics when Elisha Cooke not only lifted the restrictions on licenses but also flooded the town with drink. It is not just that

47. Butterfield *et al.*, eds., *Diary and Autobiography of Adams*, I, 238.
48. Petition of Thomas Jones, 1685, Taverns, CXI, 52–53.

Cooke revived the tradition of distributing drink and, now, licenses as a measure of a ruler's benevolence in contradiction to Puritan teachings. This charismatic, outspoken, and very successful public figure ushered in a politics that emphasized human agency rather than God's will and providence. Many considered the new charter imposing royal government on the colony as less a punishment from an angry God than a mercenary, calculating, deceitful maneuver by ambitious crown officials.[49] Cooke used taverns to help construct a new political culture that justified organized resistance to further innovations that threatened chartered liberties.

It is no coincidence that Puritan standards of drink and tavern regulation virtually collapsed in Boston at the same time as pamphlets critical of governing authorities, particularly royal officials, began to be published. Up through the 1710s print had been a weapon of the Puritan hierarchy against the popular culture of tavern assemblies. Now increasing criticism by the provincial elite of royal policies in the name of the public (thus inventing a public) made taverns an important part of the emerging public sphere that qualified submission to the hierarchy. Members of the upper ranks most immersed in the expanding culture of print were developing a more private, individual, modern sense of citizenship in the polities of town, province, and empire. But those associated with Cooke were ready, beginning in 1719, to relax the unpopular restrictions on traditional drinking habits in order to consolidate control over the public they claimed to represent. In so doing, members of the upper ranks multiplied the number of legitimate houses where those of middling and low status could gather to converse free of surveillance. Rather than being suppressed as a threat to the hierarchal order of a religious commonwealth, tavern assemblies had become a vital and necessary vantage point from which to inspect the hierarchy, in effect an emerging egalitarian alternative to hierarchy itself as the patrons of taverns of middle and even mean rank became involved in the discussion of public affairs. True, the actions of Cooke and

49. Gordon S. Wood explores the shift in conceptions of causality in his "Conspiracy and the Paranoid Style: Causality and Deceit in the Eighteenth Century," *WMQ*, 3d Ser., XXXIX (1982), 401–441. Providential explanations, of course, did not disappear. Fred Anderson has shown that New England soldiers interpreted the outcome of military engagements in the Seven Years' War as determined by God's will. Providential thinking was not so much replaced as undermined by competing frameworks of explanation emphasizing human endeavor over the course of the 18th century. It could be merged with or tacked on to causation explained by conspiracy. *A People's Army: Massachusetts Soldiers and Society in the Seven Years' War* (Chapel Hill, N.C., 1984), 209–217.

his successors show that they wished to control and contain this emerging public sphere more than expand and empower it. Members of the upper and middle ranks possessed mixed feelings in particular about the numerous houses kept by the poor for the poor. But to some extent they had to placate as much as contain the public they helped to invent, and accede to relaxations of controls over speech in all tavern companies as they themselves set unprecedented examples of bold oral and printed challenges to royal authority.

This change was very gradual. Nominally the principle and practice of hierarchy were reinforced on most public occasions. Indeed, to some extent Cooke merely replaced one system of control choked by contradictions with another that was more flexible and tolerant. Liquor licenses became part of a system of patronage. Annual renewals of licenses still required words and gestures of deference. There is truly an undertone of subservience in the excited, rash rush of mariner Christopher Taylor to defend and idealize this wealthy magnate who owned property all over Boston. Insofar as the loyalties of Bostonians of modest rank were engaged through gifts of drink, licenses, or analogous offerings, deference continued to inform social and political relations. As the eighteenth century progressed, advocates of republican concepts of private and public virtue on both sides of the Atlantic would more pointedly associate the thirst of voters with political slavery, with unthinking, dull-witted susceptibility to cheap forms of bribery.[50]

Yet in public houses the consumption of drink could also relax inhibitions and open up dialogue and debate among free white males without endangering in any immediate sense their authority over women and slaves, ordinarily not present in taverns. In the flexible space of public rooms an emerging critical public could hear and see itself. Cooke perceived the linkage; he effected a synthesis of traditional drinking habits and political innovation and helped to set in motion a different course of evolution in Boston society. Instruction in the new politics of constitutional liberties could proceed at a measured pace, in a social and political fabric woven of traditional and modern elements, without serious social disruption.

Thus the period between 1681, when the nervous Assembly drastically curtailed the number of public houses, and 1719, when the number suddenly mushroomed, was a period of transition in the public life of Boston. Members of the native ruling elite lost control over the colony's govern-

50. *New-London Gazette*, May 6, 1768, no. 234; *Connecticut Courant* (Hartford), Feb. 26, 1770, no. 270.

ment and a considerable measure of control over popular behavior. Led by Cooke, however, they regained some degree of control on new terms. Bostonians received the number of public houses they demanded, together with qualified encouragement to participate in local and provincial politics more vocally and assertively. Amid these shifts in policy and behavior, the clergy of Boston lost influence. Their churches could receive only a decreasing proportion of residents while the number of public houses expanded to accommodate everyone. The populace and native leaders alike largely ignored the continuing pleas by the clergy for fresh initiatives against intemperance and related behavior together with apocalyptic warnings of God's vengeance against a sinful people. Collective drinking at taverns had become part of the political culture, not the object of repression by it.

Chapter 5

The Politics of Taverns
in the Countryside

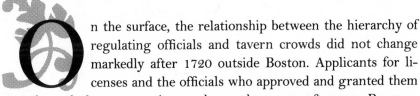n the surface, the relationship between the hierarchy of regulating officials and tavern crowds did not change markedly after 1720 outside Boston. Applicants for licenses and the officials who approved and granted them went through the same motions and procedures year after year. Prospective drinksellers and those seeking renewal came before selectmen at their annual licensing meeting. The selectmen decided whether to approve them by written recommendation to the county justices at their upcoming annual licensing session. Justices retained the right to refuse a license to any applicant and voted over individuals about whom there was any dispute. Applicants who wished to acquire a license at any other time must still first petition provincial authorities for their approval before going to the justices. Permission to sell drink continued to be a privilege granted to humble petitioners by an ascending hierarchy of elected and appointed officials—town selectmen, county justices, and provincial rulers.

Beneath the surface of these annual judgments, however, changes were occurring. The rapid multiplication of public houses within towns after 1720 contributed to the rise of neighborhood interest groups. Tavern companies became suspicious of any concentration of power in men with whom they did not have personal contact. In some towns selectmen became representatives of distinct tavern constituencies. And justices of the peace who also held seats in the Assembly became sensitive to local opinion in taverns because they faced annual election in their respective towns. The crumbling authority of both appointed and elected officials over the character of tavern gatherings became more apparent with each passing decade. Taverns were becoming forums for the participation of ordinary colonists in local and sometimes even provincial politics. Indeed, by mid-century the Assembly, which had once sought to curtail the role of taverns in public life between 1681 and 1719, now counted a significant number of tavernkeepers among its ever expanding ranks: so much so that John Adams trembled to think in 1760 that "these houses are become in many places the nurseries of our legislators."[1]

I

In towns across the Massachusetts countryside, local selectmen and tavern patrons were far less caught up than was Boston in the events and tensions of the Dudley and Shute administrations. However unpopular the introduction of royal government had been with all inhabitants, it seldom touched the lives of farmers directly. There is no evidence outside Suffolk of the outbursts of antipathy toward Dudley that aired in Boston streets. Rumors of Dudley's "schemes" and "treachery" no doubt gradually filtered from one town to the next when visitors to Boston returned. But, as in the past, the attention of the majority of tavern patrons ordinarily focused on local affairs.[2]

Together with their patrons, most country tavernkeepers were caught up in the annual cycle of clearing, plowing, planting, and harvesting. The accounts kept by Seth Bloggett, son of a Woburn tavernkeeper, for work done for his father in 1744 and 1745 illustrate how infrequently farmers could leave their towns during peak labor intervals. Bloggett's account begins in the spring of 1744, after a long winter that limited outdoor work. In March, when the ground was just beginning to thaw, Bloggett spent three days clearing ground, moving stones, and carting dung. Work intensified in April. He labored twenty-three and one-half days in the fields; on only one day did he leave Woburn to make a trip to Boston to purchase

1. L. H. Butterfield *et al.*, eds., *Diary and Autobiography of John Adams* (New York, 1964), I, 129.

2. Richard D. Brown describes the relative access of different farmers in rural areas to news and information, mainly by oral transmission. *Knowledge Is Power: The Diffusion of Information in Early America, 1700–1865* (New York, 1989), chap. 6.

goods. In May he was also busy furrowing, harrowing, planting, and carting dung for twenty-three days. One day he drove cattle to an unidentified destination. Bloggett also spent the months of June, July, and August mainly on the farm except to cart a load of wood to Medford.[3] The farmers of Woburn labored at the same tasks, and they converged on the elder Bloggett's tavern or closer establishments when they left their farms at all. They of course heard of the world of provincial politics—and the world beyond—but it remained a distant world.

Tied to the hard labor routine of farming, and indoor tasks during winter when weather hampered travel, farmers found it important to have a tavern close at hand for relaxation and a source of news. Groups of colonists in each town had long made the license limits imposed by the Assembly ineffectual by their insistent petitions for more houses. After 1720 these petitions more strikingly reflect the rapid increase and dispersal of population over a wider land area. In 1738, fifty-four people who lived in the eastern part of Sudbury petitioned in favor of Zachariah Heard for a tavern license because he lived "very near the center or middle" of the eastern part of the town, where a tavern was needed for "public days and other occasions." Although there existed five other public houses in the town by this date, these fifty-four future patrons felt a definite need for a house in their immediate neighborhood. Such local associations of drinkers sometimes straddled town boundaries. In 1749 eleven people from the "northerly part of the Holliston" and the "easterly part of Hopkinton" joined with nineteen residents of Sherborn to support the licensing of a tavern in the southeasterly part of Sherborn.[4] Two to three dozen families within several miles' radius created a need for another tavern.

Petitions to the justices of county sessions also reveal the active role that patrons now determined to play in the approval and renewal of licenses. When the justices and perhaps the selectmen refused to renew their approval of Ephraim Jones's Concord tavern in 1749, forty-three Concord residents signed a petition in support of renewal and delivered it to the justices. The petitioners insisted that they needed Jones's tavern for town and parish meetings, on training days, and "in the winter season." They not only made known their disagreement with the decision about Jones's license but declared their wish that the selectmen meet in Jones's

3. Estate of Caleb Bloggett, 1745, Middlesex County Probate Records, docket no. 1953, microfilm box no. 1581, Middlesex County Courthouse.

4. Petition of the inhabitants of the easterly part of Sudbury in support of Zachariah Heard, July 7, 1738, Petition of the inhabitants of Hopkinton, Holliston, and Sherborn, July 1749, Court of General Sessions, Middlesex, File Papers, Judicial Archives, ACM.

tavern. Jones eventually received renewal of his license. A similar impasse developed in Topsfield. When some of the town's residents attempted to relocate the sole tavern in the town in 1751, tavernkeeper Dan Clark recruited both selectmen and patrons to keep his license. Clark had been involved in some dispute, and his enemies complained to the Essex County justices that Clark kept a disorderly tavern and that the selectmen did not approve of it. On the basis of this report the justices refused to renew the license. Clark, however, persuaded at least some of the selectmen to plead in his behalf, saying that the loss of Clark's license "has thrown the town into difficult circumstances having no tavern in the same to negotiate public affairs." Significantly, Clark did not rely on the selectmen alone. He also persuaded seventy other residents to petition independently in his favor.[5] The justices relented and granted the license. When disagreements over the location and number of taverns in a town arose, patrons and voters readily became involved through independent petitions, thereby refusing to defer to the selectmen's discretion alone.

The multiplication of public houses within a town created neighborhood centers of socializing and communication, new settings for the airing of public affairs. The number of public houses doubled in Middlesex County between 1730 and 1770 from 106 to 231 and increased at an even faster rate in Worcester and Hampshire counties. By 1770 the proportion of towns with five or more taverns and retailers rose to more than 50 percent in these counties. At intervals in the cycle of agricultural labor, when farmers had the most time to assemble in the nearest public house, taverns became settings for the discussion of neighborhood interests and concerns. Access to a tavern helped to create sentiment for readier access to other institutions. Conflicts over the location of meetinghouses, schools, and roads became common as public houses multiplied and subcommunities were created.[6] Moreover, these more numerous companies of drinkers

5. Petition of the inhabitants of the town of Concord, and sundry of the neighboring towns, August 1749, Petition of the Selectmen of Topsfield, Oct. 1, 1751, Petition of Dan Clark, Nov. 20, 1752, Court of General Sessions, Middlesex, File Papers; Declaration in favor of Mr. Daniel Clark, July 13, 1752, Taverns, 1643-1774, CXI, 218, 223, 239–242, ACM.

6. An early instance of this phenomenon is the separation of Needham from Dedham in 1711. Benjamin Mills, tavernkeeper, is the first person who signed the petition to the Assembly asking for incorporation as a separate town. Mills's tavern served 39 other men and their families. More than half of these 40 petitioners shared nine surnames. Mills became one of the first selectmen. These 40 men had obviously nurtured a separate commu-

became less and less subject to the personal purview of selectmen and other town officers. The gatherings that the Assembly had once sought to suppress by giving selectmen a role in licensing now were poised to influence the makeup of the boards of selectmen themselves.

The tavern's increasing importance as a center for the coalescence of interest groups is reflected in licensing disputes. The annual meetings of selectmen to review and recommend licenses sometimes resulted in mutual accusations of party spirit among selectmen, licenseholders, and townspeople. Although Hopkinton had only one tavern and one retailer in 1738, the location of the tavern had become a thorn in the side of several selectmen. They decided to replace John Quarles with John Brewer, complaining to the justices that the former was "unfit" to be a tavernkeeper because of the "great numbers both of young and old people that flock to the tavern on the Lord's Day at all seasons of the year." But eight residents countered this complaint with the claim that the selectmen's words masked political considerations. If the justices would investigate the matter further, they would find a "spirit of opposition more than for reformation."[7] These and other residents in separate petitions to the justices dared to malign the integrity of their local selectmen before the justices of the county.

Licenseholders impugned the motives of several of the Wilmington selectmen in a similar fashion in 1750 when they attempted to prevent all three of the licenseholders in the town from renewing their licenses. Of Giles Alexander they charged that he sold liquors by the dram in his house contrary to his license. Two of the selectmen also wrote that there had been so many complaints against Benjamin Hardin that they could not approve him either. But both Alexander and Hardin went over the selectmen's heads and appealed to the justices successfully. Hardin was no doubt

---

nity ethos through meetings at the tavern in the fall and winter. One of the reasons for wishing to separate was distance: "The distance of our living from, and the difficulty of the way to, our church and school in Dedham, are such, that at some seasons of the year, by reason of the water being very high, we can neither attend church meetings, town meetings, nor school meetings; and so lose all our privileges at once." Stephen Palmer, *A Sermon, Delivered in Needham, November 16, 1811, or the Termination of a Century, since Incorporation of the Town* (Dedham, Mass., 1811), appendix, 42–43; numbers of public houses tabulated from Court of General Sessions, Suffolk, Record Books, Judicial Archives, ACM. Worcester and Hampshire records are located in the county courthouses.

7. Selectmen of Hopkinton to Justices on Licensing, July 3, 1738, Jacob Gibbs to Justices in support of Quarles, July 10, 1738, Petition against the decision of the selectmen not to approbate Quarles, July 10, 1738, Testimony of Peter How in support of Quarles, July 10, 1738, Court of General Sessions, Middlesex, File Papers.

helped by the fact that he was a selectman himself. By persuading the justices to override the objections of selectmen, the licenseholders successfully competed with them for influence. The third licenseholder, Samuel Hathorn, had not been approved by the selectmen for two years running but had still persuaded the justices to continue his license. The impact of divisive politics on licensing in the town is apparent in the third refusal by five selectmen to approve him for renewal. The five stated together unconvincingly that the "reason why he was not approbated the last two years was not out of any . . . party spirit but because of disorders in his conduct."[8] In their notes to the justices concerning the three applicants, the selectmen could not all agree who should be approved or rejected. John Beard had joined two other selectmen in a note against the license of selectman Benjamin Hardin, but then crossed his name out. The three licenseholders might have appealed to patrons in their efforts to win licenses despite the objections of two or more selectmen. Licensing had become politicized at the local level as selectmen divided over who should be approved and licenseholders challenged the decisions of selectmen by appealing to justices themselves.

Groton tavernkeepers also defied the town's selectmen—or became selectmen themselves. In 1733 a group of Groton residents persuaded the Middlesex justices to license John Bulkly instead of James Parker, claiming that the selectmen wanted only one tavern in the town. When the selectmen discovered this maneuver, they wrote to the justices that the group's claim was untrue and that Bulkly "cannot accommodate the town in their public affairs." An undetermined portion of the town's residents obviously wanted the site of informal and formal gatherings of townsmen to be in Bulkly's rather than Parker's house. And they eventually succeeded, for by 1740 Bulkly was the sole tavernkeeper in the town. But not for long. By 1743 two tavernkeepers hosted residents and also held the elected offices of selectman and militia captain. During the winter months, inhabitants gathered in two different taverns, presumably some distance from each other, and received drink, credit, and news from a selectman who also represented their interests in town affairs at the annual town meeting in the spring. Three years later the board of selectmen was made up almost entirely of tavernkeepers or former tavernkeepers. In 1748, however, a new board made a bold move to reduce the number of public houses in the town from seven to three, ostensibly in the name of reformation. Bulkly lost his license, but the selectmen failed to displace former selectman and

8. Notes by Wilmington selectmen to Justices, Court of General Sessions, Middlesex, File Papers, July 9, 1750.

licenseholder James Lawrence. Moreover, by 1755—at the latest—the number had been restored to the prereform level.[9] The selectmen's formal role in the regulation of the number and character of taverns became compromised when population sprawled, subcommunities formed, and the tavern emerged as an instrument for the cultivation of electoral support. When licensed selectmen drank with their customers, the distance between ruler and ruled narrowed, and lines of authority—who governed whom—became confused.

The increasing density of public houses within towns also had an impact on townwide support for the church and ministers. In the Worcester County town of Brookfield, for example, sectional conflict came to a head in the 1750s. George Harrington, one of eight tavernkeepers in the town, led a movement of friends, relations, and neighbors in the eastern part of the town to attach themselves and their land to the western parish of Leicester, which itself was set off as the new district of Spencer in 1753. Harrington and his supporters claimed that they lived several miles closer to the Spencer meetinghouse than to Brookfield's. Even the division of Brookfield into separate precincts did not daunt him and his supporters in pursuing this reorganization of community life.[10] It is probable that the sentiment for separation as well as the emergence of Harrington as leader was nurtured at regular gatherings at Harrington's tavern. Such gatherings made other town institutions and inhabitants seem too remote.

The district of Natick in Middlesex County also became divided into factions in the 1740s in a prolonged dispute over the location of the meetinghouse as colonists moved into what had once been a Christian Indian town. Tavernkeeper and militia captain David Morse led the southern faction in opposition to the central Natick group. In 1748, represen-

9. Selectmen of Groton to Justices, Aug. 9, 1733, fol. 128a, Approbation certificate, July 1744, Objection of selectmen to Benjamin Chase, May 19, 1747, Hezekiah Sawtell and Jonathan Holdin to Justices, Oct. 14, 1748, Groton selectmen to Justices, July 6, 1749, Approbation certificate, Aug. 26, 1755, Court of General Sessions, Middlesex, File Papers. See also the identities of those licensed for relevant years in Court of General Sessions, Middlesex, Record Books. A similar situation existed in Leicester in Worcester County in the 1740s. Thomas Richardson complained to the Assembly that his townsman Jonathan Sargent "who succeeded your pet[itione]r as tavernkeeper, was chosen a selectman last year, and he with two more of the selectmen (by his secret persuasion) did not see cause to continue your pet[itione]r's license to be an innholder." Petition of Thomas Richardson, November 1740, Taverns, CXI.

10. Louis E. Roy, *History of East Brookfield, Massachusetts, 1686–1970* (Worcester, Mass., 1970), 101–111.

tatives of the central Natick group lost their places in the district government and accused the Morse tavern group of allowing unqualified residents to vote. Upon appeal, the Assembly declared the results of the election invalid, but the controversy between the two groups continued to fester into the 1750s when Morse's son acquired his father's license and also was elected as district selectman. In 1753, when the Morse group hired Stephen Badger to minister over the disputed church, animosities still ran rife. Badger observed, "Those people [in central Natick] who now appear against and declare their nonconcurrence and dissatisfaction with the present situation of the meetinghouse will, in a short time, commence my personal enemies, as they have already manifested to my face, their disaffection and disregard to me as a minister in Natick, and by their insinuations have threatened to destroy my peace." Though Badger possessed the support of the Morse faction, the character of tavern gatherings in Natick proved a constant source of dismay to him. He would later address the tavernkeepers in the town directly in a sermon on intemperance, observing to them, "There is scarce any one person in common life, if any at all, that has so great an influence either to being serviceable, or hurtful to society and individuals, as your employment of tavernkeeping gives occasion for you to be."[11] The prominence of tavernkeepers in district disputes over the meetinghouse suggests that the balance of influence of ministers versus tavernkeepers shifted as sectional sentiment developed.

Disputes over the location of taverns and meetinghouses lend credence to John Adams's conviction that tavernkeepers had become very influential in local affairs in the eighteenth century. Sitting in a tavern in the evening in Suffolk County towns, he wrote, "You will find the house full of people, drinking drams, phlip, toddy" as well as "carousing" and "swearing." And "especially," one will find them "plotting with the landlord to get him, at the next town meeting and election, either for selectman or representative." For Adams this was the major cause of the collapse of regulation in country towns. These "artful men" gained "a little sway among the

11. Michael J. Crawford, "Indians, Yankees, and the Meetinghouse Dispute of Natick, Massachusetts, 1743–1800," *New England Historical and Genealogical Register*, CXXXII (1978), 278–292. In 1745 David Morse was the sole tavernkeeper; his relation Peletiah Morse kept tavern in 1755; William Morse in 1765; and Peletiah Morse in 1771. In the 1740s Ebenezer Felch led the central Natick faction. By the 1760s a "John Felch" had been licensed. Court of General Sessions, Middlesex, Record Books, 1735–1748, 400–403, 1748–1761, 370, 1761–1771, 254–257, Judicial Archives, ACM; Stephen Badger, *The Nature and Effects of Drunkenness . . .* (Boston, 1774), 35.

rabble of a town" and then multiplied taverns in the town in order to secure "the votes of taverner and retailer and of all." The consequence was lax regulation and the corruption of town politics. The "arts of gain" had become necessary in local politics; one must "mix with the crowd in a tavern, in the meetinghouse or the training field, and grow popular by . . . agreeable assistance in the tittle tattle of the hour."[12] Indeed, Adams implies that men distinguished by wealth, piety, family, and education could no longer depend on these traditional qualifications to win office. It had become necessary to reach out to voters in gestures that often included drink.

Adams's gloomy assessment, however, might have been motivated by his own initial lack of success in Braintree politics and his jealous observance of the rise of Ebenezer Thayer. He might have exaggerated the tavern's importance. Certainly, exhaustive studies of the men elected to local and provincial offices in the eighteenth century indicate that church membership, wealth, family connections, and education continued to characterize those elevated to positions of authority at annual town meetings. Only in the smaller towns of fewer than one thousand inhabitants or those recently established on the frontier of settlement did men of little means or distinction get elected in large numbers. In port and county towns, intermarried families of long standing well known at the county and provincial levels of government often dominated local government as well.[13]

Nevertheless, these families might have found it increasingly necessary to cultivate the support of local tavernkeepers or even get licenses themselves. Tavernkeepers who were elected by their town meetings to high office became very active in government over the course of the eighteenth century. Of the 34 tavernkeepers licensed in 1740 in twelve Middlesex County towns, 9 (26 percent) were elected selectmen or representatives between 1735 and 1745. Of 46 licensed in these same towns in 1755, 16 (35 percent) were selectmen, moderators, or representatives. The proportion active in office dropped in 1760, but it shot up again in the 1770s. By

12. Butterfield *et al.*, eds., *Diary and Autobiography of Adams*, I, 211, 224, 96, 128–129.

13. Edward M. Cook, Jr., *The Fathers of the Towns: Leadership and Community Structure in Eighteenth-Century New England* (Baltimore, 1976). I agree with Cook's conclusions but also assert the development of changes in the relationship between rulers and ruled over the course of the 18th century. These changes are evident in the decline of regulation of taverns and their complementary emergence as popular forums in local and provincial life. A significant number of tavernkeepers were elected to office, even in populous towns, and this is an important variable to take into account in making any assessment of the character of politics in the 18th century.

1776, 32 of 71 tavernkeepers (45 percent) in fifteen towns (adding Shirley, Townsend, and Weston) were elected to their highest town offices. These towns cannot be categorized as frontier or backwater. Although the shire town of Concord had no tavernkeepers active in town offices in the 1770s, 3 of 7 were active in Cambridge, 5 of 7 in Sudbury, and 3 of 4 in Marlborough, all substantial towns founded in the seventeenth century and with more than fifteen hundred inhabitants by 1776. Thus almost 2 of 4 tavernkeepers in these fifteen towns were town leaders in the 1770s. Retailers were also active, but at a lesser rate. When their numbers are added, a total of 39 of 119 licenseholders in this sample, or 1 in 3, presided over their town's affairs as well as their public houses in the 1770s.[14]

It cannot be assumed (as Adams claimed) that regularly being a host to one's neighbors had become a primary means for the elevation of a man to office. Some other attribute might have been more important, such as kinship. But being a drinkseller, and thus extending credit and disseminating news to townsmen, clearly aided a man ambitious for office. As towns increasingly divided into parishes and precincts jealous of each other's prerogatives and influence in town affairs, it is likely that individuals identified their sense of community with local tavern companies more intensely. The election of a tavernkeeper to the board of selectmen in a town or of someone with close ties to a tavernkeeper ensured that a group or neighborhood had a direct representative of its interests in town affairs, one with whom they regularly communicated at informal gatherings. It is significant that, when the Braintree town meeting voted to reduce the

14. The identities of Middlesex licenseholders come from the Court of General Sessions, Middlesex, Record Books. The identities of town leaders can be found in the following volumes: Lemuel Shattuck, *A History of the Town of Concord* (Boston, 1835), 233–236; Samuel Sewall, *The History of Woburn* . . . (Boston, 1868), 578–585; Francis Jackson, *A History of the Early Settlement of Newton* . . . (Boston, 1854), 216–221; Lucius R. Paige, *History of Cambridge, Massachusetts, 1630–1877* . . . (Boston, 1877), 460–467; J. H. Temple, *History of Framingham, . . . 1640–1880* (Framingham, Mass., 1887), 419–422; Charles Hudson, *History of the Town of Marlborough, . . . 1657 to 1861* (Boston, 1862), 279–284; Henry A. Hazen, *History of Billerica* . . . (Boston, 1883), 304–307; Wilson Waters, *History of Chelmsford, Massachusetts* (Lowell, Mass., 1917), 758–761; Charles Hudson, *History of the Town of Lexington* . . . (Boston, 1913), 402–408; Henry Bond, *Genealogies of the Families and Descendants of the Early Settlers of Watertown* . . . (Boston, 1860), 1064–1067; Daniel S. Lamson, *History of the Town of Weston, Massachusetts, 1630–1890* (Boston, 1913), 206–207; D. Hamilton Hurd, *History of Middlesex County* . . . (Philadelphia, 1890), III, 307–310 (Tewksbury), I, 597–598 (Townsend); Seth Chandler, *History of the Town of Shirley* . . . (Shirley, Mass., 1883), 188–189. Sudbury selectmen identified through certificates of approbation, Court of General Sessions, Middlesex, File Papers.

number of public houses from twelve to three in 1761, it stipulated that there be one tavern in each precinct of the town. Moreover, the town decided to elect these men by a written vote, just as it elected its selectmen to represent individual precincts.[15] Thus while the town meeting acted to reduce the number of taverns, it also appropriated the power to approve them. Even this reform of local licensing procedures, which proved fleeting, reflected the political muscle of tavernkeepers and their patrons in the town. Voters recognized the informal influence of tavernkeepers by insisting that the town vote them into their status as licenseholders.

Like their counterparts in Boston, selectmen in the countryside generally became detached from the hierarchy of officials who enforced temperance through the strict regulation of taverns. First, the number of licenses they approved exceeded Puritan quotas set in the seventeenth century, quotas reasserted periodically as reference points for reform by ministers and critical observers like Adams. More significant, they were becoming dependent on constituencies informally organized in taverns, or at the very least must consider opinions formed in public rooms. When the Assembly had invested selectmen with the power to approve licenses in 1681, it had assumed that selectmen would always act to suppress tavern haunting and that tavernkeepers would never enter the ranks of selectmen to the extent that they did by the 1750s. When Sewall and other justices had led processions of selectmen and other officials through Boston streets, the Assembly assumed that these recommended visits and patrols would become the model for town officials throughout the colony. Now taverns had become part of local politics, not the object of suppression by it. Instead of acting to suppress taverns, elected selectmen and the lesser local officials either became resigned to or actively promoted the integration of traditional drinking habits into local political culture. Taverns had become part of an emerging political tradition in local government—direct communication and consultation between elected officials and their constituents facilitated by the distribution and consumption of drink.[16]

The leveling character of tavern crowds that rankled Adams is also reflected in the earlier observation of Scotch-born physician and gentle-

15. Samuel A. Bates, ed., *Records of the Town of Braintree* (Randolph, Mass., 1886), 378–379; Butterfield *et al.*, eds., *Diary and Autobiography of Adams*, I, 129–130.

16. For more light on how localized systems of "interest" based in taverns and the exchange of drink might have aroused antipathy among colonists to extralocal systems of "interest" among royal officials structured by ties of clientage to crown patrons overseas and crown appointees in the colony, see Richard L. Bushman, *King and People in Provincial Massachusetts* (Chapel Hill, N.C., 1985), introduction, 91–98.

man Alexander Hamilton. Hamilton toured the colonies from Maryland as far north as York, Maine, in 1744, and in town after town he was astonished and affronted by the absence of clearly defined systems of rank and subordination. It was most evident in the manners of the people. He was offended at the bold inquiries by patrons he met in taverns of his identity, origins, and destination despite his status as a gentleman apparent by his dress, speech, bearing, and manservant. Near Portsmouth, New Hampshire, he met a man who was "very inquisitive about where I was going, whence I came, and who I was." Hamilton noted this dialogue "as a specimen of many of the same tenor I had in my journey when I met with these inquisitive rustics." He became both amused and dismayed by the inflation of honors that seemed to pervade tavern companies and society more generally, by which every man could claim elevation through pretended knowledge or title. At the Ship Tavern in or near Salem he drank punch as before with "several colonels, for colonels, captains, and majors are so plenty here that they are to be met with in all companies." After many such gatherings and encounters he concluded that the "aggrandized upstarts in these infant countries of America" have "never had an opportunity to see, or if they had, the capacity to observe the different ranks of men in polite nations or to know what it is that really constitutes that difference of degrees."[17]

With some modifications, Puritan lawmakers had striven to preserve and perpetuate acknowledgments of rank and degree within the covenanted communities they founded in New England, and had succeeded in some measure for most of the seventeenth century. But the post-1720 expansion of public houses in port towns and countryside had attenuated personal ties between the established elite figures and the new groups of townspeople settling on the periphery of town lands. Authority became diffused, as structures of oral communication were altered and reconstituted. New taverns outside the orbit of established figures of high station became forums for new voices leading new interest groups.

II

Still, if the authority of selectmen over taverns was compromised after 1720, it was the justices of the peace in county courts of sessions who actually granted the licenses to individuals approved by selectmen. And the crown enhanced the prestige and influence of the justices in the eigh-

17. Carl Bridenbaugh, ed., *Gentleman's Progress: The Itinerarium of Dr. Alexander Hamilton, 1744* (Chapel Hill, N.C., 1948), xxiii, 121, 124, 186.

teenth century. Under the new charter, the royal governor appointed justices, and they served at his pleasure. Beginning with Sir William Phips, each new governor assiduously used this power of patronage to cultivate county elites loyal to the crown's lieutenants. As a result the number of justices more than quadrupled between 1703 and 1765, from 106 to 465. These men, with the title "Esquire," sometimes lived in a manner that diverged conspicuously from their fellow townsmen's and enjoyed an honorific distinction that directly linked them to his majesty through his appointee the royal governor.[18]

Colonists converging on county sessions as well as the inferior courts and the Superior Court were continually reminded of the king's investment of authority in these men, most pointedly when their commissions were read in court. In 1714 at Suffolk Court of Sessions, "George, by the Grace of God of Great Britain, France and Ireland, King, Defender of the Faith, etc.," announced through proxy to his "trusty and well beloved" justices: "We have assigned you and every one of you jointly and severally Our Justices to keep Our peace in Our County of Suffolk within Our said Province of the Massachusetts Bay in New England."[19] Thus the gestures, the words of submission and respect, that Sewall had customarily received when he presided over the courts in the late seventeenth century continued to inform the posture and address of inhabitants attending the courts, perhaps with elaboration as the stamp of royal authority became more pronounced. Indeed, as licensing disputes in Hopkinton, Wilmington, and Groton demonstrate, groups of townsmen who dared berate orally or in writing this or that selectman for his decision to favor this petitioner over another, humbly continued to defer their grievances to their "honors" the justices of the county sessions.

Yet this attitude of submission might have been very thin or completely feigned, existing only on the ceremonial surface of the pageant of the courts, a pageantry far less imposing than the spectacles of English sessions. The prestige that justices enjoyed as crown appointees cut both ways. Their ties to the royal governor also made them objects of suspicion by some colonists, especially if they also held or sought seats in the Assembly. Royal governors from Phips forward awarded a high number of appointments to the bench and other offices to members of the Assembly in an effort to increase their influence over the House. Voters regarded those

18. John M. Murrin, Review Essay, *History and Theory*, XI (1972), 257–270, esp. 261, 267–268.

19. Court of General Sessions, Suffolk, Record Book, 1702–1719, Feb. 18, 1714, 71.

representatives who received appointments from Phips with so much distrust that some were not reelected.

This distrust and suspicion waned considerably as the new crown charter won some measure of acceptance. The proportion of members of the Assembly who also held appointments from the governor doubled in the five years between 1711 and 1716, from 10 to 20 percent. And when Jonathan Belcher became governor in 1731, the number of representatives given appointments as justices multiplied dramatically. More than any previous governor, Belcher distributed appointments to members of the Assembly in order to create a "governor's party" in the Town House. By 1737, 45 percent of the members of the House held a seat on the bench, and more held appointments as military officers.[20]

Belcher's successors continued to exercise their power of patronage in efforts to win allies for royal government in the House. This royal cultivation of county elites, with the propensity of the towns to reelect them, is a significant development in Massachusetts government in the eighteenth century. Indeed, it has been argued that this trend constitutes an "Anglicization" of the formerly autonomous Puritan colony. Members of prominent families in the respective towns routinely received favors from the governors in search of cooperation in the House. In England the king used this distribution of patronage to discipline and control Parliament. Yet if county and colony government seemed ever more closely tied to crown patronage by the mid-eighteenth century, there remained an undercurrent of suspicion and distrust of justice-representatives, which could be inflamed under certain circumstances. As colonists began to view selectmen as spokesmen for certain interest groups in town politics, the office of representative to the House also began to be conceived in a more popular mold. Voters no longer regarded representatives as exalted rulers of special wisdom with wide discretionary powers, the "gods" that Ebenezer Pemberton would have them be in his election sermon of 1710.[21] Rather, they were men susceptible to the temptations of power, men who might be lured away from their duties to their constituents if they received appointments from the crown and so became the governor's men, tied to his interest.

Governor Belcher put his carefully constructed system of patronage to a test in the 1730s when he repeatedly asked members of the House, among other things, to enforce and strengthen the vice laws. In one of his first

20. Murrin, Review Essay, *History and Theory*, XI (1972), 261, 267–268.
21. *Ibid.*

speeches to the Assembly in 1730, Belcher called on representatives to pursue "a strict execution of all the laws now in force against immorality and impiety" and to consider the enactment of additional legislation. The same month, he issued a proclamation for the "encouragement of piety and virtue" and for "preventing and punishing vice." In "humble imitation of the royal example," Belcher asked persons of authority to set an example for the populace at large. He prohibited gaming in all public and private houses on the Sabbath. He also commanded judges, justices, sheriffs, constables, grand jurors, and all other officials to suppress public gaming at any time and take action against disorderly houses. Echoing earlier similar instruction, he demanded that officers of the government enforce laws enacted at the turn of the century against vice and pressure drinksellers to limit patronage to "those permitted by law." In December of the same year Belcher once again asked the Assembly to enact further legislation to discourage "vice and wickedness." Considering "the great consumption there is of strong liquors among the people of this province, more especially of rum," Belcher specifically asked for a heavier excise tax on distilled liquors in order to "check" this "vast consumption." Parliament had lately made such an imposition, Belcher declared, and Massachusetts should imitate its example.[22] To some extent Belcher's requests and declarations represented a rebuke to justices and lesser officials responsible for enforcement. Justices who sat in the House must not only enforce existing laws but make new ones.

The members of the House were slow to respond, and, when they did, their response fell short of Belcher's demands. A committee chaired by Elisha Cooke, Jr., did propose to raise the excise duty on rum from eight pennies to two shillings per gallon, but nothing came of it. And the House did think "it may have a very good tendency if it be recommended to the several officers" to pay greater attention to enforcement of the laws to restrict drinking. But this mild response was hardly the new legislation and rigor that Belcher requested. So again in 1736 he asked for a law "putting a stop to gaming and excessive drinking, which seems to threaten the ruin of this people now more than ever." Finally, in 1737, the Assembly voted to raise the excise on distilled liquors and wines from eight to twelve pennies per gallon. But Belcher remained dissatisfied. He proceeded to tell the House that "the best and kindest care" that they could take of their

22. Ebenezer Pemberton, *The Divine Original and Dignity of Government Asserted* . . . (Boston, 1710); *Boston Gazette*, Sept. 7–14, 1730, no. 561. Belcher also issued a proclamation for enforcement of the vice laws where English precedents were mentioned. *Boston Gazette*, Sept. 28–Oct. 5, 1730, no. 565, Dec. 14–21, 1730, no. 573.

"people" would be to bring forward a law against excessive drinking. In 1739 Belcher continued to address this issue in vain when he issued a proclamation for preventing disorders on the Sabbath, to be read from every pulpit.[23]

Belcher's repeated return to this issue reflects a genuine concern about the levels of consumption and the incidence of gaming in public houses. No doubt he need not move far from the Town House to observe drunkenness in the numerous taverns that lined King Street. But Belcher's entreaties to the House on this issue also determined to establish a public order that reinforced hierarchy. He asked for legislation that would compel justices, selectmen, and lesser officials to impose more restrictions on behavior in taverns. He asked representatives to assume the same paternalistic posture toward the people as Puritan legislators had assumed in the seventeenth century. Disciplinary action against tavern companies might unite governor and House in a public show of authority throughout the province. The sovereign whose name Belcher repeatedly invoked in his speeches to the House had drawn such a direct linkage between "licentiousness" and "contempt of magistracy" in his own speech to Parliament printed in the *Boston Gazette*. "The licentiousness of the present times," George II proclaimed, gives offense "to all honest and sober men." It is "absolutely necessary" to "restrain this excessive abuse by a due and vigorous execution of the laws," because "defiance of all authority, contempt of magistracy, and even resistance of the laws" had become "too general."[24] How much more important it was to restrain the behavior and oratory in Massachusetts taverns in a society in which distinctions of rank and degree, and the institutions buttressing them, were weak and absent.

Despite the high number of justices who sat in the House, who were responsible for monitoring public drinking, the members did not act to meet Belcher's demands. Their near indifference to Belcher's urgent pleas for reform may in part be explained by skepticism that new laws would have any greater impact than those already on the books. Yet when considering exchanges between the governor and the House as a whole, there seems to be more behind their lack of compliance. In these same speeches to the House, Belcher asked that the representatives grant him an annual salary in accordance with the king's wishes. The House wholeheartedly re-

23. *Boston Gazette*, Jan. 11–18, 1731, no. 577, Dec. 27–Jan. 3, 1732, no. 627, Nov. 22–29, 1736, no. 881, May 23–30, 1737, no. 907; Massachusetts, *The Acts and Resolves, Public and Private, of the Province of the Massachusetts Bay . . .* (Boston, 1869–1922), II, 639, 849, 1016 (hereafter cited as *Acts and Resolves*); *Boston Gazette*, Aug. 27–Sept. 3, 1739, no. 1023.

24. *Boston Gazette*, Aug. 22–29, 1737, no. 920.

sisted such a measure, because it sought to influence the governor through manipulation of his salary from session to session. Other points of conflict formed. Indeed, Belcher at one point compared the House to Cato, who, "rather than submit to a power he could no longer rationally resist," left a "lasting brand of infamy" by committing suicide. Despite the fact that many enjoyed the governor's patronage, members of the House generally resisted the governor's authority rather than took any steps that would reinforce it. Under Elisha Cooke's leadership, they were ready to execute such business "as we judged consistent with the safety of the people we represent."[25] The more closely the representatives defined themselves as agents of the people, as protectors of the people's liberties, the less inclined they became to activate the hierarchy of officials in a decisive campaign to stamp out "licentiousness."

The more delicate relations between justice-representatives and their constituents by the 1730s are also suggested by a pamphlet published in 1739 entitled *A Letter to the Freeholders and Other Inhabitants of the Massachusetts-Bay.* The letter format evoked the earlier style of pamphlets written as exchanges or dialogues between gentlemen. But it departed from this format in that it was addressed not only to freeholders, who could vote, but also to "other inhabitants." The author, who chose to remain anonymous out of fear or "disinterest," in effect asked that readers lend it out or have it read aloud in companies so as to reach a wide public.[26] He aimed to make the reading, critical public more inclusive so as to envelop those without property. This inclusive impulse might have been motivated not only by the author's message but also because Boston printers had refused to publish it for fear of losing Governor Belcher's patronage. The greater the threat of arbitrary royal power to the public, the more individuals must be reached. Published instead through a Newport printer, it attacked Belcher's assiduous efforts to control the House by the politic distribution of offices and honors to its members.

25. *Ibid.,* Sept. 7–14, 1730, no. 561, Dec. 27–Jan. 3, 1732, no. 627.

26. Pitson's effort to advertise the availability of pamphlets in his Boston tavern and the obvious effort by the author of this pamphlet to prompt public readings lead me to question the emphasis of Michael Warner on the "impersonality" of the norms of protorepublican print discourse and its differentiation "from personal modes of sociability." Pamphlets were used to assemble representational versions of this new "public" and invested oral exchange in taverns, the most egalitarian contexts for gatherings, with new importance. See Michael Warner, *The Letters of the Republic: Publication and the Public Sphere in Eighteenth-Century America* (Cambridge, Mass., 1990), 39, 48.

The author asked all "inhabitants" to inspect closely the actions and character of their elected representatives. After explaining the ideal balance of power between the different branches of the English constitution and the Massachusetts charter, the author warned that "an ambitious or designing governor" will attempt "to corrupt or awe your representatives." He will execute "wicked bargains" at the expense of voters and their posterity. Therefore, he urged voters to act "to preserve your constitution entire in all its parts without suffering any one part to prevail so far over the other" as to reduce the government to a "tyranny." Voters should be careful to choose representatives "whose interests are at present the same with your own, and likely to continue the same." They must be wary of men whose "circumstances, profession, offices," and even "manner of life" render them liable to be "engaged in a contrary interest."[27] Indeed, the pamphlet came close to urging voters to avoid electing genteel men of substance.

The pamphlet did more than counsel voters to be wary of justices when choosing representatives. It presented and defined the relationship between rulers and ruled in such a way as to enhance the participation of the former and restrict the autonomy and discretion of the latter. It was a relationship conceived as a dialogue or exchange. Elections were no longer ritual renewals of faith in the wisdom and piety of superior men. Before an election candidates "exert themselves . . . in favor of themselves and their brethren." Now it was not only the right and duty of electors to "know the opinions and intentions" of candidates but "to examine" their "conduct" and "survey their past behavior" in office. Representatives, particularly those who held appointments from the crown, must be judged even as they sat in judgment in courts and House. A voter must "awaken" his spirit, "exert" his reason, and "assert" his "freedom." In the face of justices and other officeholders who "offer" themselves for election, voters must "tell them plainly" that they could not be so credulous or naive as to send them to the House. Voters must "tell" candidates that they are "not quite so blind as not to see" that, when trade declines, the number of men seeking office multiplies to the advantage of "prerogative" and detriment of "liberty." Of course, in the courts litigants must "treat" justices "with all due deference and respect," but only if "they behave well."[28] This pamphlet posited a relationship of frank and equal exchange and equivalency between office-

27. *A Letter to the Freeholders and Other Inhabitants of the Massachusetts-Bay* . . . (Newport, R.I., 1739), 1–5.

28. *Ibid.,* 7–11.

holders and constituents in which the latter might even air their suspicions of a candidate's character and motives to his face. If voters must submit to the decisions of local justices in the courts, they also now received encouragement to question the fitness of justices to represent their "interests" in the House. The justices themselves must be judged. This pamphlet in effect posited the republican principle that the private interest of officeholders posed a constant threat to the public interest of citizens.

Despite the fact that this pamphlet was published in Newport, it was intended to and actually did circulate in Massachusetts towns. This is evident from a letter to the *Boston Gazette* in 1739 complaining that a pamphlet had been "industriously dispensed in town and country" in order to "strike the passions, and so promote jealousies, distrust, and confusion among unthinking people." This writer deemed it necessary to assure readers that he had never received "a bribe, or a post of any kind" from the crown. Then he went on to criticize the popular character of recent elections in many towns whereby the man who makes a "clamor about LIBERTY" is regarded as a "true patriot." Such candidates "attack characters of the highest station and influence the people by the meanest acts, and poorest scandal." It is "mad," this defender of deference continued, to "imagine a country grows great by opposing its governor," but this had become a "test of elections." This observer had witnessed the election of a "man without modesty, good sense, or any qualification" through "votes that an honest man would be ashamed" of winning. The upstart carried the day against "two gentlemen of unquestionable abilities" accused of nothing more than "being distinguished fit for the commissioners [justice] of the peace."[29] It is probable that the *Letter to Freeholders* only gave further voice in the 1730s to already festering suspicion of justices who held seats in the House.

Neither the author of the *Letter* nor the writer to the *Gazette* specifically mentioned the role of taverns and drink in elections. The author of the *Letter* could hardly go so far as to advocate that voters patronize taverns in order to become better informed. This would be too flagrant an affront to the spirit of the drink laws that officeholders were supposed to uphold. But tavern discussions were a natural vehicle for voters to establish a mutuality of interest with an officeholder or candidate. The frank and extended interchange of opinion advocated in the *Letter* could best be accomplished by officeholders in the familiar context of taverns where men regularly assembled. Thus an officeholder's support of the popular culture of drink

29. Postscript to *Boston Gazette*, Apr. 30, 1739, no. 1006.

was in effect becoming crucial to his standing among and access to the emerging critical public.

Some justice-representatives (and their rivals) might have refused to enact additional drink regulations, as Belcher pressed them to in the 1730s, because they saw in taverns a vehicle for allaying the suspicions that the *Letter* aired concerning the ties of patronage between governor and crown appointees. Indeed, some officeholders might have been forced to tolerate or even contribute to the behavior condemned by Belcher. The treating of voters by candidates for office could facilitate and symbolize the trust and familiar exchange now considered necessary between rulers and ruled. It is difficult to measure how important the practice of treating voters with liquor was in colonial Massachusetts. In England judicious bribes of liquor and money had become customary in parliamentary elections in the eighteenth century. Genteel candidates placed themselves temporarily on a level with election crowds as they wheedled and flattered voters. For a time in some localities the rigid social hierarchy relaxed. A reversal of roles took place as candidates prostrated themselves before voters. Certainly it was much more difficult to buy elections in New England because of the much greater size of the electorate and the secret ballot. Yet one observer of elections in Pennsylvania, New York, and Connecticut claimed that the secret ballot did nothing to inhibit such tactics in Connecticut elections. At election time, he observed, patrons ate and drank at taverns what they pleased and paid no reckoning because the expense had been "defrayed by the candidates." Friends of the candidates also used "threats and other compulsory methods to bring about the completion of their designs." But a Connecticut correspondent contradicted this report by retorting, "Bad as the people in this colony are, such a practice would be deemed infamous and dishonorable." Indeed, this respondent claimed, there was no "spot of earth in the British Empire in which elections are conducted with so much freedom and good order as in this colony."[30]

It is probable that treating did occur in Massachusetts and other New England colonies, but not with the regularity or to the extent practiced in England and the southern colonies. Certainly Elisha Cooke appears to have found it useful in Boston in 1719. And Adams attests to its existence in town elections in Suffolk County within modest limits. In the 1760s and

30. Edmund S. Morgan, *Inventing the People: The Rise of Popular Sovereignty in England and America* (New York, 1989), chap. 8. I believe that New England elections were less "sober" than Morgan has argued. *Connecticut Courant*, Feb. 26, 1770, no. 270, Mar. 5, 1770, no. 271.

1770s critics issued numerous pleas for the elimination of treating at militia musters and elections. And in 1768 the editor of the *New-London Gazette* thought it appropriate to publish an English attack on election bribery with drink:

> When liberty is put to sale,
> For wine, for money, or for ale,
> The sellers must be abject slaves,
> The buyers vile designing knaves.[31]

Given the long efforts to promote and enforce temperance in New England, even modest amounts of treating with liquor represent a profound change in the political culture.

Certainly some men elevated to provincial office in the 1730s and 1740s found it useful, perhaps necessary, to maintain the closest ties to the popular culture of drink in their respective towns. Adam Cushing, licensed as a tavernkeeper in Weymouth according to a 1737 roster, ascended to multiple high offices. Cushing graduated from Harvard and at one time stood as a candidate for the ministry. But he gave up the church to satisfy ambitions in secular affairs. His militia company elected him captain, after which he advanced to the rank of major, and was elected to the House year after year in the 1730s and 1740s. In 1745 he was appointed a justice. Cushing's education, speech, and bearing no doubt contributed to the high esteem in which he was held by his townsmen. He also possessed a few items that set him apart materially from many of his neighbors—a silver watch, a silver-hilted sword for musters, a desk for his judicial records and perhaps his two pounds worth of books. Moreover, two slaves assisted Cushing and his wife in tending their twenty acres, cattle, and horses. But Cushing also established a fraternal bond with his townsmen by opening his house to them every day. There were thirty chairs in the house for patrons coming to buy drink from him and hear of events in Boston.

To be sure, Cushing regularly sat in judgment of his neighbors and residents of nearby towns in his public rooms. And on muster days he was his townsmen's leader to be obeyed. But Cushing's authority was also tempered by conviviality and largess as he served drink to his neighbors day after day. There existed a degree of intimacy between this justice-representative and his constituents that softened distinctions of rank and hierarchy. Only six candlesticks illuminated his house, so that on long

31. Americanus to *New-London Gazette*, Jan. 20, 1769, no. 271; *New-London Gazette*, May 6, 1768, no. 234.

winter evenings Cushing presided over companies closely gathered near the hearth. Moreover, this public house was full of the tools and equipment needed to farm and tend animals such as the smith's tools that Cushing probably used himself. Cushing lived in a modest manner like most of his neighbors and could readily talk of the problems of farming with his customers.[32] When Cushing traveled to Boston to sit in the Town House, he truly represented his constituents as well as ruled over them because he was on such close terms with them. Cushing had given up authoritative preaching for egalitarian advances to win political favor in part through the distribution of drink.

Framingham inhabitants could also visit their local justice at almost any time. Joseph Buckminster, Jr., first became a selectman in 1732. Six years later his townsmen elevated him to the House. Some time before that he was appointed a justice. Significantly, he was not reelected to the House in the years 1740 through 1743, at a time of intense conflict between the House and Belcher when many justices lost their seats in the Assembly. He won election in 1744, but lost the next six elections to rivals. Moreover, as a militia officer he was convicted of padding militia lists for material gain. He lost his officer's pay. But he regained favor, for beginning in 1751 he won election continually to the House for the next nineteen years. He would also serve as selectman uninterruptedly from 1747 through 1770. Through all these years as a multiple officeholder, while mixing with the provincial elite in Boston, this justice-representative kept a tavern, from the early 1740s to 1773, which perhaps helped him to gain public esteem despite a checkered past. He was not the only Framingham tavernkeeper who mixed drink with politics. Five others were active in town politics between 1740 and 1776.[33]

Woburn was another Middlesex County town where a tavernkeeper ascended to a preeminent position as justice and representative. This was

32. Clifford K. Shipton, *Biographical Sketches of Those Who Attended Harvard College . . .* (Cambridge, Mass.; Boston, 1933–1975), Sibley's Harvard Graduates, VI, 43; The Names of Persons Licensed in the County of Suffolk, 1737, Papers of James Otis, Sr., MHS; Suffolk County Probate Records, Record Books, XLIX, 322, LXIII, 336, Judicial Archives, ACM. Records of Cushing's election to the House and of the justices discussed in the following paragraphs are contained in *Acts and Resolves*, XII–XVIII.

33. Temple, *History of Framingham*, 419–423; Shipton, *Biographical Sketches*, Sibley's Harvard Graduates, V, 510. Buckminster was licensed by 1745. Court of General Sessions, Middlesex, Record Book, 1735–1748, 400–403. His name appears at five-year intervals in Record Books, 1735–1748, 1748–1761, 1761–1771. Records of approbations by selectmen in the file papers indicate he continued to be licensed up to 1775.

no easy task, since the town was almost perpetually divided into disputing parties from the 1720s through the 1770s. Two tavernkeepers were elected to a three-man committee to address the Assembly in response to petitions from a sectional interest group in 1727. Later, financial support for the two ministers in the First Parish became a chronic problem, resulting in lawsuits. Amid these multiple conflicts James Fowle returned from Harvard in the early 1730s, where he had distinguished himself as a Scholar of the House and the winner of the Mills scholarship. Beginning in 1734 he taught school for eleven years. But he left teaching in 1745; the same year he acquired a license to keep tavern. This move might have been inspired by political ambitions, since his father, John Fowle, had kept tavern and served as a representative in the 1730s. Shortly after setting up as a tavernkeeper, James was elected town clerk, a position he would hold until his death in 1779. In 1752 he won his first election as selectman and would serve almost continously until 1775. Then in 1759 the town elevated him to the first of nine terms as representative. And in 1761 he won recognition from the crown and became a justice. He had become a distinguished gentleman, perhaps Woburn's first citizen. Yet, like Buckminster, he did not give up his tavern license in order to remove crowds of drinkers from his house and retreat into genteel privacy. He and his wife kept tavern for approximately thirty years.[34] This scholar might have preferred books to conversation with farmers, but the tavern appears to have been instrumental to his rise to power. He might not have distributed drink on election days, but the regular extension of credit would weave the same ties of obligation.

Moses Marcy was another tavernkeeper who rose to high office. His father had moved from Roxbury to Woodstock (now in Connecticut) and amassed a substantial estate worth more than twelve hundred pounds, but the estate was divided equally among eleven children. Marcy, however, made the most of his legacy by acquiring land in Oxford, opening a sawmill in 1732, and then a tavern in 1736. He continued to sell drink when the town of Sturbridge was carved out of Oxford, and was elected as Sturbridge's first representative in 1751, an office he would hold until the 1770s. Sometime in the 1750s, he gave up the license, perhaps after he

34. Sewall, *The History of Woburn*, 245–319, 583; Shipton, *Biographical Sketches*, Sibley's Harvard Graduates, IX, 39. Fowle was first licensed in 1745 (Court of General Sessions, Middlesex, Record Book, 1735–1748, 400–403). His name appears at five-year intervals in the record books for Middlesex Sessions. Approbation certificates indicate that he was licensed as late as 1774. Court of General Sessions, Middlesex, File Papers.

Plate 6. Moses Marcy Overmantel Panel. *Overmantel panel from the Moses Marcy House, built in mid-eighteenth century in Sturbridge (now Southbridge), Massachusetts—no longer standing. Oil on wood panel, third quarter of eighteenth century, artist unknown. Probably based on unidentified English engraving of prosperous individual with symbols of affluence. Courtesy, Old Sturbridge Village*

received appointment as a justice in 1754, but his son Elijah acquired a license at about this time. Marcy had consolidated a claim to gentility on the Massachusetts frontier in Worcester County, but his years as a host to his townsmen might have continued to frame his relations with them. This is suggested by the overmantel painting done by an itinerant artist above one of his fireplaces, probably after 1754. The figure at the center dressed in officer's clothes with outstretched glass may represent Colonel Marcy himself, even though several of the icons of gentility in the background, such as the gambrel-roofed house, do not match his material establishment. The proud Marcy might not have minded these fanciful embellishments added by the artist. Portrait or not, clues to Marcy's character and manner emerge in the emphasis on the act of drinking. Although by this time a judge and representative responsible for making and enforcing laws, including the drink laws, it is the wine glass that the figure clutches, not the ledgerbook. Such an emphasis was not in keeping with Puritan traditions or portraiture, nor was it characteristic of the more studied repose favored by the Boston gentry by midcentury. The figure is not private, but with outstretched glass before a full punch bowl appears to stand in a public setting. Thus this choice of emphasis might have been influenced by Justice Marcy's long term as a tavernkeeper and, perhaps, a continuing propensity to preside over gatherings at his son's tavern, still licensed in 1765. Marcy wanted a painting emblematic of his gentility, and all the appropriate symbols are in place, but the emphasis and crude execution almost convey a lack of it by standards of taste current in Boston, which Marcy visited every year after 1751.[35]

It is not known to what extent justices Cushing, Buckminster, Fowle, and Marcy enforced the drink laws. But the records of another justice in

---

35. Clarence Winthrop Bowen, *The History of Woodstock, Connecticut*, VII (Worcester, Mass., 1943), 346–347, 457; Charles Edney Marcy, "History and Genealogy of John Marcy, 1661–1724, Woodstock, Conn.," MS (1981), 29 (copy at Sturbridge Village Research Library; Court of General Sessions, Worcester County, Record Book, I, 1731–1737, 82–83, II, 1737–1757, 58–60, 273–275, III, 1758–1767, 105–108, Engineer's Office, Worcester County Courthouse, Worcester; *Acts and Resolves*, XV, 167, XIX, 6. My understanding of this painting has been refined by discussions with Donna Baron and Sarah LeCount, members of the research and curatorial staff at Old Sturbridge Village. They believe the painting is an adaptation from English prints circulating in the colonies, and have doubts that it is a portrait of Marcy because such attributes as the gambrel roof and ship do not accurately reflect Marcy's material possessions or career. Gordon S. Wood discusses the weakness of the colonial aristocracy, its lack of gentility and openness to entry, in *The Radicalism of the American Revolution* (New York, 1992), 112–121.

Watertown are suggestive. Nathaniel Harris was elected selectman frequently in the 1730s and 1740s and received appointment to the bench in 1734. In 1739 he obtained a license to retail alcohol. His record of cases he heard between 1734 and 1761 displays a tolerant attitude toward drinking. By himself, he could hear only cases involving debts or fines up to forty shillings, including the ten-shilling fine for drunkenness. Of the more than three hundred cases he heard between 1734 and 1761, only a few involved violation of the drink laws. Of course, this might suggest that drunkenness was a rare condition. But he heard cases involving residents of three towns—Watertown, Waltham, and Weston. At the time of his appointment to the bench in 1734 there were seven drinksellers in these towns. When he died in 1761, there were seventeen, serving a total population of about 2,500 in these three towns, or one for about every 150 inhabitants. It seems likely that residents of these towns acted to prevent instances of drunkenness from reaching Harris and that he just as obligingly did not seek to prosecute this crime vigorously. One critic in 1767 observed, "Drunkenness is decried from almost every pulpit; but what justice punishes drunkenness?" Moreover, the ambitious Harris felt the power of public opinion. He won election to the House three years running after his appointment to the bench, but he was suddenly replaced by a less distinguished man and was never elected again. In 1749 the selectmen went so far as to refuse to renew approval of Harris's license, for unspecified reasons.[36] Maintaining the approval of townsmen was a delicate business, even for a justice with a liquor license.

Colonel Ebenezer Nichols of Reading was another tavernkeeper who was elected to the House, followed by an appointment to the bench, but who continued to keep tavern in the 1760s. He was preceded by a tavernkeeper and a retailer who held appointments as justices. In Stoughton, tavernkeeper and militia captain John Shephard became a justice and representative. In Worcester County, Captain Josiah Converse was elected to

36. *Records of the Court of Nathaniel Harris, . . . Together with a paper by F. E. Crawford Read before the Historical Society of Watertown, November 14, 1893* [Watertown, Mass., 1938], 4, 7, 36, 48–49, 56, 61 (copy at MHS); Court of General Sessions, Middlesex, Record Books, 1735–1748, 28–30, 1748–1761, 604–607; *New-London Gazette*, Jan. 2, 1767, no. 164. When one considers the amount of alcohol consumed in neighboring Woburn at the ordination of a minister in 1729, it seems unlikely that inhabitants never drank to the point of inebriation. Four hundred celebrants at this ordination consumed over several days a total of 205 gallons of cider, 25 gallons of wine, 4 gallons of rum, and 2 gallons of brandy, together with lime juice for mixed drinks. And this was an occasion when drunkenness was probably discouraged. Sewall, *The History of Woburn*, 263.

the House in the 1740s and remained a tavernkeeper when he became a justice. Captain Israel Taylor of Harvard also kept tavern when he was elected representative, and became a justice. In Hampshire County, Major Benjamin Day of Springfield kept a tavern when he became another justice who sat in the House.[37]

Of course, the vast majority of justices did not have liquor licenses, nor had ever had one formerly. But justices found taverns to be a useful means of mediating authority with popularity. Those who did hold licenses were numerous enough to suggest that justices who also held seats in the House had to strike a delicate balance between their official responsibilities in regulating public houses and their new need to please and be accountable to their constituents. Justice-representatives generally came under suspicion of being drawn into the governor's orbit through "wicked bargains." Ready mixing with constituents at taverns, with treats of liquor to inspire trust, could help to alleviate these suspicions. Justices sat in judgment of their neighbors but in some cases were also judged annually by them on election day. They tempered their regulation of the drink trade with an awareness of these houses' increasing importance as forums for the formation and expression of public opinion. Some became so sensitive to currents of opinion flowing through taverns that they obtained licenses themselves and kept them despite the obvious conflict of interest and the forfeiture of genteel privacy. At every annual licensing session of the courts of general sessions in the counties examined here, justices granted and renewed licenses to a few of their own.

37. Nichols: Court of General Sessions, Middlesex, Record Books, 1748–1761, 111–116, 604–607, 1761–1771, 254–257, 516–518. Nichols was elected to the House in 1752, 1753, 1754, 1757, 1762, 1763, 1764, 1765, 1767 (*Acts and Resolves*). Shephard: he was licensed in 1737 (The Names of Persons Licensed in the County of Suffolk, 1737, MHS), was first elected to the House in 1742 (*Acts and Resolves*, XIII, 126). By 1747 he had become a justice (*Acts and Resolves*, XIV, 4). Converse: he was licensed in 1740 (Court of General Sessions, Worcester, Record Book, II, 1737–1757, 58–60); he was still licensed in 1750 (273–275). Converse was first elected to the House in 1742 (*Acts and Resolves*, XIII, 126). By 1745 he had become a justice as well as a representative (*Acts and Resolves*, XIII, 462). Taylor: he was licensed in 1760, 1765, and 1770 (Court of General Sessions, Worcester, Record Books, III, 1758–1767, 115–118, 485, IV, 1768–1780, 123–124). He was first elected a representative from Harvard in 1766 (*Acts and Resolves*, XVIII, 5); he had become a justice by 1770 (*Acts and Resolves*, XVIII, 466). Day: he was licensed in 1760 and 1770 (Court of General Sessions, Hampshire, Record Book, IX, 177–186, X, 154–162, Hampshire County Courthouse, Northampton). He was first elected in 1770 (*Acts and Resolves*, XVIII, 464–465) and became a justice the next year (528–529).

III

The sometimes precarious position in relation to tavern crowds of those justices who also held elective office became evident in the wake of the Land Bank crisis of 1740–1741. The Bank was a scheme launched by a private group of investors to ease the chronic shortage of currency in the province by issuing currency notes guaranteed by mortgages on land. The original investors had no trouble in recruiting popular support for the bank throughout the entire province, because the bank favored debtors over creditors. It allowed the former to pay the latter with currency notes expected to depreciate over time. The bank agitation possessed an egalitarian undertone in that the dispensation of currency notes guaranteed by land would allow increasing numbers of people to participate in the economy more independently. Farmers would no longer have to prostrate themselves before local moneyed men for credit or be in a state of dependency on them. Thus the idea of the bank quickly gained wide support. In the spring of 1740 the original petitioners for the incorporation of the bank came from 64 towns; by 1741, men from 123 towns—or five-sixths of the towns in the colony—had pledged their support and resources.[38]

The crown ordered Belcher to destroy the bank by bringing all his power and authority to bear against its supporters. Consequently, the governor instructed all officials holding appointments at the pleasure of the crown, including justices and militia officers, to swear opposition to the bank or face the loss of their commissions. Further, he tried to extend his influence deep into the wellsprings of public opinion—the taverns—by ordering justices to refuse to renew or grant licenses to any tavernkeeper who supported the bank or accepted its notes already in circulation. In December 1740 Belcher sent a circular letter to all justices in the colony, telling them that he expected them to use all of their power inside and outside the courts to prevent the passing of the bank notes: "And inasmuch as we are given to understand that in sundry parts of the province, divers taverners, retailers, and common victualers pass, receive, and give encour-

---

38. George Athan Billias, *The Massachusetts Land Bankers of 1740*, University of Maine Studies, 2d Ser., no. 74 (Orono, Maine, 1959), 29; Wood, *The Radicalism of the American Revolution*, 140–141. Wood argues that the Bank movement was attractive in that it would allow ordinary colonists to buy and sell on more impersonal terms, thus loosening the intricate ties of personal bonds binding communities together. Thus insofar as tavern companies agitated for the creation of the Bank, drinkers acted to renegotiate the terms of their relationships with each other, including the traditional social bonds sealed through drink. It would no longer be as necessary, for example, to visit taverns in order to "solemnize" the extension and reception of credit and the payment schedules.

agement to the said bills . . . we desire and expect in the granting of licenses you carefully consider of this affair and do not give out the licenses to such persons," as they "disrupt" government and "disturb peace and good order."[39] Belcher and the Council feared not just the acceptance and passing of the notes by tavernkeepers but the influence they could bring to bear on the elections to the House in the spring. He wished to produce a show of strength by the exertion of pressure on the hierarchy of officials who enjoyed appointments at his pleasure, and thus indirectly on every license-holder in the colony.

But the elections to the House in 1740–1741 not only produced a resounding majority of representatives in favor of the bank but also unseated justices who had acceded to the governor's orders. The proportion of representatives who also held appointments as justices fell from 45 percent in 1737 to 28 percent in 1741. Justices felt the power of an electorate sifting through news of the controversy. This new Assembly swiftly condemned the governor's instructions to justices concerning licenses. A House committee defiantly declared that the laws on the procedures required to obtain a license were clear and that the justices "are under the strongest obligations and ties of law and conscience to observe all the rules laid down in law respecting their offices generally." To the Assembly, Belcher's circular letter to the justices represented a sinister innovation, a "direct infraction" of the laws of the land. The letter had "a manifest tendency to intimidate the justices in the execution of their offices respecting licenses.[40] The House seized on the explicit outline of justices' duties in law as a bulwark against Belcher's pressure and so resisted the effort to make all tavernkeepers dependents of the crown through the justices.

Belcher carried out his purge of all sympathizers with the bank in appointive posts, but his orders awakened undercurrents of hostility toward royal authority instilled among colonists and their descendants by the Andros regime of the 1680s. The rumors and incidents that had made royal government an issue since its inception—rumors that had provoked coopers, laborers, and mariners to revile governors Dudley and Shute—could reach country towns more than a day's journey from Boston only gradually, and with less impact. Yet while country residents were preoccupied primarily with the politics of roads and fences, they might have held fundamental reservations about royal government that could be in-

39. Billias, *The Massachusetts Land Bankers*, 29; Circular Letter from Governor and Council to the Courts, Dec. 20, 1740, Pecuniary, CII, 107–108, ACM.

40. Murrin, Review Essay, *History and Theory*, XI (1972), 270; Massachusetts, *Journal of the House of Representatives*, XVIII (Boston, 1942), Apr. 8, 1741, 227–228.

flamed with sufficient provocation. Indeed, it has been argued that Massachusetts farmers harbored a deep reservoir of hostility from one generation to the next toward any royal appointee or subordinate whose actions bore even a slight resemblance to the policies inaugurated during the tenure of Governor Edmund Andros between 1686 and 1689. Under this Dominion of New England government, all titles to land had come under question at the same time as local and House authority had been severely curtailed. A writer to the *Boston Gazette* would articulate these inherited attitudes in 1774 when he warned Governor Thomas Gage that the inhabitants of Massachusetts had long memories. Royal officials were naive if they thought "that none of our landholders ever heard that when the Old Charter of this colony was said to be vacated in the reign of King James II the government here insisted upon every person's applying for new grants of their lands." Gage should realize, the writer warned, "that the people bear these things in their minds" when assessing crown policies.[41]

Such suspicion of arbitrary action by crown appointees was newly reinforced in the first decades of the eighteenth century as selectmen began to represent distinct sections and interests in their towns and as close communication between elected officials and their constituents through taverns became common. The more active that townsmen became in the government of their communities and the more critical their posture and speech in respect to local leaders, the more threatening a royal governor's efforts to control county government and the House appeared. A growing populist tradition in local government placed royal efforts to manipulate justices and representatives in stark and sinister relief. Voters mingled with selectmen at taverns and engaged in dialogues that established mutual interest. They would naturally become more critical of their representatives, lest they become tools of the crown against public interest. Voters beginning to exert critical judgment up through the governing hierarchy faced efforts by the governor to exert influence down through it.

It is just such a clash that Belcher provoked when he took steps to purge all bank sympathizers—even tavernkeepers—from appointive posts. Colonists retaliated not only by electing probank men to the Assembly but by

41. Replies of militia officers to the governor and Council are contained in Pecuniary, CII, 99, 131, 136; dismissals of probank officials are included in Minutes of Council, 1733–1753, LXXXII, 248, ACM; Richard L. Bushman, "Massachusetts Farmers and the Revolution," in Jack P. Greene, Richard L. Bushman, and Michael Kammen, *Society, Freedom, and Conscience: The American Revolution in Virginia, Massachusetts, and New York*, ed. Richard M. Jellison (New York, 1976), 77–124; address to his excellency Governor Gage, *Boston Gazette*, Aug. 1, 1774.

making plans for more direct action. Rumors of crowd actions circulated through the countryside in 1741, so much so that Belcher instructed justices in Suffolk County to gather evidence for possible prosecutions. Hints of the extensive alienation in country towns are evident in that testimony. Seth Cushing, a Hingham tavernkeeper, testified that on the Sabbath John Lewis came to his house and asked him whether he had heard anything about a proposed march to Boston. Lewis told Cushing "that he had heard several men whose names he cannot remember say in his house that they would come to Boston and if corn was there [there had been a bad harvest] and merchants would not let them have it [using Land Bank notes] they would throw them on the Dock." Robert Brown, a Plymouth merchant, received warning that his warehouse might not stand if he did not accept Land Bank notes as payment. On another occasion Brown met Justice Isaac Lothrop and a Mr. Johonnot at a Plymouth tavern "talking of what Mr. Johonnot had heard on the road concerning the rise of the land bankers." While they talked, Nathaniel Cobb of Plympton arrived and told them "there was three hundred men that had signed" to march against the government. Cobb had probably come from a tavern, since Brown testified that he had been "disguised with drink."[42] Rumors and plans traveled from tavern to tavern.

It is likely that some taverns served as sites for the discussion of the proposed march to Boston. Josiah Kenney told William Royal of Stoughton that he "had seen a paper that was carried about" for the purpose of publicizing the march; he also said that two men from Braintree had told him that "there was a paper put up [at] one of the meetinghouses in said town or at the public houses" relating to the rising. A justice interrogated Thomas Vincent in the Weymouth tavern of Adam Cushing, the justice-representative. He questioned Vincent whether people had gathered at his house who talked of raising a mob in support of the Land Bank, or of any other matter. Vincent replied that he knew nothing. When asked whether subversive letters had been written at his house, he answered that he knew that "there were letters written but he did not know about what nor whether they were sent though they talked of sending them." It is likely that Vincent kept a tavern, since he claimed to have knowledge of letters written by a group meeting at his house but that he did not participate in writing them. He might have been trying to save his license. Listening to this interrogation, Adam Cushing must have felt uncomfortable. As a

42. Billias, *The Massachusetts Land Bankers*, 34; Depositions of Robert Brown, Thomas Crosby, William Royal, Seth Cushing, Adam Cushing, Samuel Raws, Thomas Jocelyn, Pecuniary, CII, 155–168.

justice, he had been forced to swear opposition to the bank. But he represented a town so solidly behind the Land Bank that it had voted to pay taxes in bank notes. Cushing was reelected, but he no doubt had to placate voters with explanations at his tavern as he juggled pressures from above and below.[43]

Worcester County taverns also became contexts for the airing of pro-bank sentiment. Of the ten leading towns with the greatest number of bank subscribers, six were in this county. In Uxbridge, Samuel Read and Solomon Wood, both tavernkeepers, subscribed to the bank; Wood also represented the town in the Assembly. Tavernkeepers Gershom Rice and Thomas Stearns of Worcester both had interests pledged to the bank. Tavernkeepers in Lunenburg and Harvard also supported it publicly. The bank conflict also motivated more towns in this county to send representatives to the Assembly. In 1739–1740 the county towns had sent only six representatives when they could have sent twenty-one. In the May election of 1740, Worcester County increased its representation to twelve, seven of whom held liquor licenses or would hold them by 1745. At least four of these seven were strong supporters of the Bank.[44]

These men did not condone mob action. Indeed, they might have helped to defuse such proposed measures. The Assembly meeting in the Town House at Boston never lent support to the talk of crowd action against the royal government. Instead, it became sufficiently alarmed about the state of public order in 1741 to pass a law In Further Addition to the Several Acts for the Observation and Keeping of the Lord's Day. (The governor and the Council had earlier that year issued a proclamation "for promoting virtue.")[45]

Nevertheless, the Land Bank conflict is a measure of the increasing participation of informal tavern groups in politics in Massachusetts, most forcefully at the local level but also more noticeably at the provincial level as well. At the turn of the century the Assembly had been composed of

43. Pecuniary, CII, 163; Thomas Crosby testified that papers were posted at meeting-houses (162); George W. Chamberlain, *History of Weymouth, Massachusetts* (Boston, 1923), 560. For information on Cushing, see n. 32, above.

44. Billias, *The Massachusetts Land Bankers*, 21–31; *Acts and Resolves*, II, 668–669. The seven who held licenses or would have them by 1745 were Samuel Willard, Esq. (Lancaster), Edmund Morse (Mendon), Capt. Josiah Converse (Brookfield), Nahum Ward, Esq. (Shrewsbury), John Grant (Lunenburg), Solomon Wood, Jr. (Uxbridge), and Capt. John Hazeltine (Upton). Willard and Ward held retail licenses. The rest were tavernkeepers.

45. *Acts and Resolves*, II, 1071; Proclamation of Governor and Council, Minutes of Council, 1733–1753, LXXXII, 248, ACM.

deputies determined to place public houses under strict control by suppressing their number and limiting their use. But by 1740 this much larger body allowed public houses to multiply almost unchecked and indirectly countenanced the use of drink and taverns to sway public opinion on issues of provincial importance. Voters in some towns and their representatives were forced to consider and act on popular opinion formed in taverns. Members of the Assembly were no longer moved by the principles and priorities that had governed Sewall's attitude toward taverns. The role of taverns in the colony's political culture expanded beyond what Sewall could ever have imagined. The politic distribution of drink and licenses, which had helped to elevate Elisha Cooke, Jr., first to control of Boston's board of selectmen and then to leadership in the House until his death in 1737, now influenced elections in country towns as well. A measure of the popular insurgence that Belcher's orders provoked is the decision of the Privy Council to remove him from the governorship.[46] Notwithstanding his careful cultivation of the House through patronage, his position relative to the new makeup of the Assembly had become untenable.

Belcher's successors continued to use their powers of patronage to cultivate ties of dependence and support between governor and House. The emergence of influential families who exercised a dominant role in the county courts and held seats in the Assembly was a political trend of real significance. While the proportion of members of the House who also held appointments as justices fell from 45 to 28 percent as a result of the Land Bank conflict, it rose again to a high of 71 percent by 1763. Yet these webs of patronage only thinly masked a political culture veering in a more populist direction. *A Letter to the Freeholders and Other Inhabitants of This Province* in 1742 asked them, "Look about us, and inquire, if there have been any such among us, who have been influenced by posts of honor and profit, to vote, and act too much as men in power would have them." Another *Letter* in 1749 extolled the "august and awful influence and power of the people" as a weapon against crown authority and patronage.[47]

46. Billias, *The Massachusetts Land Bankers*, 37.

47. *A Letter to the Freeholders and Other Inhabitants of This Province* ... (Boston, 1742), 2–3; *A Letter to the Freeholders, and Qualified Voters* ... (Boston, 1749), 5, 7. Belcher's successor, Governor William Shirley, did establish better relations with the House in part through the distribution of new patronage and contracts made available by crown expenditures during the Seven Years' War. See John A. Schutz, *William Shirley: King's Governor of Massachusetts* (Chapel Hill, N.C., 1961); and John L. Brooke, *The Heart of the Commonwealth: Society and Political Culture in Worcester County, Massachusetts, 1713–1861* (New York, 1989), 106–117.

IV

The more direct influence that tavern patrons in some towns exerted on their representatives was apparent in the overall number of licenseholders they elevated to the House. Six of the representatives from twenty-three Middlesex towns in 1740 either had held licenses in the past or did so at the time of their election (see Table 4). The number fell in the 1740s and 1750s but rose to five of thirty-four in 1775. In Middlesex, Hampshire, and Worcester counties, seventeen of ninety-six representatives held licenses in 1775, or almost one in five. In Suffolk County (for which few licensing records have survived) at least seven towns sent tavernkeepers to the House between 1740 and 1770. Thus even justices without licenses who also received election to the House almost always served with a few licenseholders elected from towns in the same county, a reminder, if they needed any, of the new intimacy and dependence between elected officials and voters. Adams did not exaggerate when he wrote in the 1760s that taverns had become the "nurseries" of legislators.[48]

Like Adam Cushing and James Fowle, many of these licenseholders elected to the House were men of some distinction in their communities, evident by the fact that they received appointments as justices. In Middlesex County eleven of the total of twenty-nine licenseholders elected to the House between 1735 and 1776 (counting year to year, not just five-year intervals) also received commissions as justices. In Hampshire County, eleven of the twenty-nine elected also became justices. And of this eleven, eight held retail licenses, an indication that they were country merchants selling a variety of goods besides alcohol. Several were from prominent families in the Connecticut River valley. But in Worcester County, only nine of the thirty-five licenseholders elected to the House became justices; twenty-six of this thirty-five were tavernkeepers selling drink in their public rooms. Moreover, when one considers the three counties together, tavernkeepers were elected more frequently than retailers. All told, 61

Brooke shows that pluralistic older towns in the southern portion of Worcester County were most prone to support opposition to the governor.

48. The Suffolk County towns that sent tavernkeepers to the House included Dedham, Weymouth, Bellingham, Stoughton, Wrentham, Medfield, and Hingham. More towns in this county might have elected licenseholders, but only two lists of licenseholders for Suffolk County, for 1737 and 1758, have survived for the period between 1730 and 1780. Both are at MHS. Braintree elected Ebenezer Thayer, whom Adams accused of approving licenses to win votes. He was not a tavernkeeper, but apparently had close ties to them. Butterfield *et al.*, eds., *Diary and Autobiography of Adams*, I, 129.

Table 4. *Representatives Holding Licenses within Five Years of Election, 1740–1775*

	Licenseholding Representatives / All Representatives			
Year	Middlesex	Hampshire	Worcester	Overall
1740	6/23	0/9	7/12	13/44 (30%)
1745	5/22	1/8	2/6	8/36 (22%)
1750	4/22	2/8	1/7	7/37 (19%)
1755	2/19	1/7	4/14	7/40 (18%)
1760	4/20	4/9	2/15	10/44 (23%)
1765	4/23	3/8	3/16	10/47 (21%)
1770	1/21	4/9	3/19	8/49 (16%)
1775	5/34	5/25	7/37	17/96 (18%)

Sources: Licenseholders in Record Books, Courts of General Sessions, Judicial Archives, ACM, and Worcester County Courthouse; representatives in Massachusetts, *The Acts and Resolves, Public and Private, of the Province of the Massachusetts Bay* (Boston, 1869–1922).

percent (fifty-seven of ninety-three) of the licenseholders who journeyed to Boston to sit in the House were tavernkeepers, not country merchants.[49]

What is most significant, however, is, not the proportion of representatives who held licenses, but the fact that tavernkeepers and retailers won election to the House at all. In the late seventeenth century, when the Assembly had repeatedly sought to activate all law enforcement officials to suppress tavern patronage, the governing assumption had been that tavernkeepers were not prominent rulers in local governments; certainly no one conceived that they would ever ascend to the ranks of county and provincial rulers. Sewall had opposed the appointment of a new justice in Newbury in 1721 in part because the man had recently kept a tavern and "sold rum." Sewall implied that being a drinkseller in the past disqualified him for the duties of a justice, one of which was to govern the drink trade. Granting an appointment to a drinkseller or former drinkseller, Sewall argued in Council, "will not be for the honor of the person"—meaning he

49. See Appendix for lists of all representatives counted from year to year who held licenses. In both Table 5 and the Appendix they are listed as licenseholders if they acquired a license five years previous to or after the year elected. Totals from the Appendix are used in this paragraph.

could not assume the proper judicial bearing—nor would it contribute to the honor of the "governor and Council, nor for the welfare of the country."[50] It was perhaps the first such instance when a tavernkeeper, even a former one, had come under consideration for an important appointive post.

Why Massachusetts—which more than any other colony was committed to the strict control of drink—never enacted legislation to prevent drinksellers from holding elective or appointive offices is not clear. In 1678 the legislators of Maryland passed a law that prohibited tavernkeepers from holding office as delegates (representatives), justices, attorneys, deputy commissioners, clerks, sheriffs, deputy sheriffs, jurors, or any other public office. But in Massachusetts the entrance of tavernkeepers to all levels of government after 1740 became common. Despite the weight of Puritan antipathy toward collective drinking, tavernkeepers came to possess an informal authority within this predominantly oral communication system that they began to translate into formal authority in the eighteenth century. The divergence from English as well as Puritan political assumptions and expectations is reflected in the contempt expressed by the English general and Massachusetts governor Thomas Gage for the members of the colony's judicial system. He was shocked and dismayed that his officers might be cashiered by just two colony justices in the 1770s, "the best of them a keeper of a paltry tavern."[51]

This divergence from English norms and expectations also received comment from William Douglas in his history of the colonies, published in Boston in 1749. Douglas referred to tavernkeepers while comparing the membership of the Massachusetts House with that of Parliament. He believed that representatives in both bodies should consist of gentlemen of "reading, observation" and those "conversant with the affairs of policy and commerce." Such men are better qualified "than a retailer of rum and small beer called a tavernkeeper, in a poor obscure country town, remote from all business," whom Douglas considered to be all too common among the

50. *Diary*, II, 978.

51. Kym S. Rice, *Early American Taverns: For the Entertainment of Friends and Strangers* (Chicago, 1983), 64; Thomas Gage to Lord Hillsborough, Oct. 31, 1768, Colonial Office documents, V, 86, Public Record Office, London, quoted in Hiller B. Zobel, *The Boston Massacre* (New York, 1970), 101. Zobel believes that Gage might have been exaggerating when he complained during the furor occasioned by the quartering of troops in Boston that in "this country, where every man studies law, and interprets the law as suits his purposes," an "officer of rank and long service may be cashiered, by the management of two justices of the peace, the best of them a keeper of a paltry tavern."

ranks of Massachusetts representatives. Douglas recommended that the law requiring local residence for representatives be repealed or qualified so as to restrict House seats to men of substance.[52] But voters had come to regard direct representation as a right, and personal instruction of their representatives to be necessary in some cases. Thus the House could never entertain the changes Douglas recommended even if some of the more genteel members were dismayed by the rum sellers among them. Even in this comment Douglas underestimated the influence of tavernkeepers, for they won election in substantial towns like Weymouth and Woburn close to Boston. But these rum sellers also possessed Harvard degrees, a measure of the confusion and loose boundaries of the colony's social and political leadership, the seemingly impossible necessity of being both popular and genteel.[53]

The social distinctions between leaders and constituents that prevailed in England had become blurred in Massachusetts. Drinksellers had entered the ranks of the justices and representatives, the two senior officials charged with regulating the drink trade. The growing weakness of regulation was not just a consequence of the continuing vitality of tavern life or the universal demand for rum but of the weakening of the practice and principle of deference in the changing political culture of Massachusetts. Elected officials had become more dependent on, in Adams's words, the "crowd in the tavern," and these crowds had in turn become suspicious of any discretionary authority concentrated in persons with whom they had little personal contact. Upper-class candidates for Parliament in England might have distributed more liquor at elections than their Massachusetts counterparts and temporarily prostrated themselves before the limited number of voters. But many Massachusetts representatives sat drinking with their supporters all year long when not in Boston or conversed with them over counters in shops. With so many licenseholders sitting in the

52. William Douglass, *A Summary, Historical and Political, of the First Planting, Progressive Improvements, and Present State of the British Settlements in North America,* I (Boston, 1749), 507.

53. Both crown officers and colonial gentry complained continually about the parvenu upstarts elevated to high office in the colonies. Gordon Wood believes that to some extent the Revolution was fought over this issue of who in America were the proper social leaders "who ought naturally to accede to positions of public authority." The fact that tavernkeepers acquired high offices is a measure of the inability of the colonial gentry to conform to classical conceptions of disinterested, educated leadership. Massachusetts had shed much of its Puritan political culture, but it did not conform to the republican model either. See Wood, *The Radicalism of the American Revolution,* 87, 120–121.

Town House in Boston, it is difficult to speak of the anglicization of the colony's political culture in the eighteenth century. Some new alchemy of political traditions and innovations had emerged. When members of the Massachusetts Assembly daringly compared their House to the House of Commons, they placed significant numbers of tavernkeepers on a plane with members of Parliament.

No one but the most resolute drinker and scoffer at the pious was completely comfortable with these developments. The politics of taverns flew in the face of every cherished ideal, every definition of virtue, every traditional point of reference that colonists possessed. For the clergy, these developments were the most visible manifestation of the colony's precipitous slide into corruption and apostasy. Jonathan Edwards despaired over the "licentiousness" that prevailed among the youth of the town of Northampton and the "spirit of contention" that divided the town into parties "prepared to oppose one another in all public affairs." Initially the religious revivals of the 1730s encouraged Edwards to believe that the church might eclipse the tavern's popularity, for the people caught up in the excitement seemed to put aside their differences, and the taverns stood "empty." In Northampton the "place of resort was now altered; it was no longer the tavern, but the minister's house that was thronged far more than ever the tavern had been."[54] Guilt over tavern haunting might have made many susceptible to evangelical appeals.

Once the revival fervor ebbed, however, taverns once again became crowded. In Northampton the number increased from three to four between 1730 and 1740. By 1760 the town had eight public houses, and ten years later a total of twelve, or one for every 107 people, according to the 1765 census. The revivals did nothing to slow or reverse the rapid multiplication of taverns and retailers in the decades after 1740 in the counties of Hampshire, Middlesex, and Worcester. Moreover, the revivals encouraged many laymen to speak with a new authority on religious doctrine and issues; some went so far as to challenge the preaching style and worthiness of ordained ministers. Taverns provided a forum for discussion and argument outside the purview of ministers. In a Connecticut tavern Dr. Alexander Hamilton contemptuously observed a "rabble of clowns" disputing upon "points of divinity so learnedly as if they had been professed theolo-

54. Jonathan Edwards, *Edwards on Revivals: Containing A Faithful Narrative of the Surprising Work of God in the Conversion of Many Hundred Souls . . .*, edited by [Isaac] Watts and [John] Guyse (New York, 1832), 30–34, 49, 355; see also Richard L. Bushman, ed., *The Great Awakening: Documents on the Revival of Religion, 1740–1745* (New York, 1970), chap. 4.

gians." Hamilton thought it strange to see these attitudes prevail "even among the lower class of people here."[55] Instead of eclipsing the tavern's popularity, the revivals seemed only to accelerate the diffusion of authority to speak and argue on subjects previously the prerogative of the clergy and the secular elite. This diffusion of speaking authority had already occurred in tavern companies across the province. After the revivals it exploded with new force and passion.

The clergy still pleaded for the better enforcement of laws controlling behavior and for new, more restrictive laws. In a 1747 election sermon to the provincial government, Charles Chauncy admonished rulers to "take an effectual care to enforce a proper regard" for these laws lest "the best laws, together with the authority that enacted them . . . be held in contempt." Chauncy acknowledged that laws had been repeatedly passed to suppress excessive drinking, but "multitudes" still were guilty of this "fault." Indeed, "hard drinking" had "become common all over the land." The money expended to consume the "astonishing" quantities of strong drink in the province "would suffice to answer the whole charge both of church and state." If "something further is not done by the government," he continued, then it might "prove the destruction of the country." Specifically, Chauncy asked rulers to do something about "the needless multiplication of taverns" and retailers. In general it seemed to him that "all ranks" had run into "excesses," spending their money on "that which is needless and extravagant."[56]

As in similar complaints made in the 1720s when inflation had devalued the currency paid ministers, Chauncy's observations on the amount of money expended on strong drink were all the more distressing and ominous to clergymen because of the declining amount of support many of them received from their congregations. Those who had made contracts for salaries ten or more years previous were paid in bills of credit that had lost half or more of their value. In this same election sermon Chauncy declared that there was not "an order of men" more "injured and oppressed in regard to their just dues." Their pitiful compensation had caused many to be "diverted from their studies, discouraged in their work, and too

55. Harry S. Stout, *The New England Soul: Preaching and Religious Culture in Colonial New England* (New York, 1986), 197–202, 207–211; Court of General Sessions, Hampshire, Record Books, II, 95, III, 600–604, Vd, 97–102, VI, 177–186, X, 154–162; Bridenbaugh, ed., *The Itinerarium of Hamilton*, 162–163.

56. Charles Chauncy, *Civil Magistrates Must Be Just, Ruling in the Fear of God* (originally published in Boston, 1747), reprinted in Ellis Sandoz, ed., *Political Sermons of the American Founding Era, 1730–1805* (Indianapolis, Ind., 1991), 151, 163, 172–173.

frequently treated with contempt." If they asked for "justice" from their congregations, it caused "uneasiness among their people"; if they pressed the issue, it caused "contention and strife" until there was "such a general alienation of affection" that it put "an entire end to their usefulness." Chauncy went on to "beseech" the provincial authorities listening to him to "make some special provision for [the clergy's] relief." He asked that they "put it out of the power of the people to turn off their ministers with anything short of the true value" of the salaries "settled" on them at the time of installment. Just several years after the peak of the revivals, Chauncy observed, "Religion is not in such a flourishing state, at this day, but that it needs the countenance of your example, and interposition of your authority, to keep it from insult and contempt."[57] The financial position of many ministers had become so dire that Chauncy asked the government to interfere with the time-honored autonomy of local churches.

Governor William Shirley did sympathize with the clergy's plight. He had heard "so much of the difficulties which many of the ministers . . . are brought under, through the great depreciation of bills of credit, by which their salaries are paid, and the little care taken by their people to make them proper allowances for it." Indeed, it seemed "probable many of them will soon be necessitated to quit the ministry and betake themselves to secular employments for a livelihood." But he sidestepped the issue by asking the House to take it up. The deputies did vote to recommend "strongly" to the towns that they make "honorable provision" for ministerial support. Furthermore, they required every precinct clerk in the province to file a copy of the contracts drawn up with ministers for their support at the time of settlement with the secretary of the province.[58] But, as in 1725, these were recommendations rather than intervention: the House tried to shame the towns into providing adequate support for their ministers.

That these recommendations might have been ignored by many congregations is suggested by a letter written by a minister to the *Boston Gazette* ten months later. He presented computations comparing the stipend he had received from his parish thirty years before to the expenses of living in 1747. Carefully noting every item of weekly expense, he stated

57. *Ibid.*, 159–161, 172. For a different evaluation of the position of the clergy at midcentury that deemphasizes the importance of the salary issue, see Patricia U. Bonomi, *Under the Cope of Heaven: Religion, Society, and Politics in Colonial America* (New York, 1986), 70–72.

58. *Acts and Resolves*, XIII, Feb. 3, 1747, 561. The House had made similar recommendations in 1725. See Sandoz, *Political Sermons*, 160–161.

that the price of goods for weekly sustenance for a family of eight had been two pounds and four shillings thirty years earlier. Now the same bare existence cost more than eleven pounds because of inflation. This cleric made a point of noting that his 1747 budget did not include the luxuries of coffee, tea, wine, spirits, chocolate, or even cider, only home-brewed beer. He concluded, "Government must come to [the] relief of ministers." Another correspondent writing in sympathy declared that they could not persuade the "major part" of congregations "to open their eyes, nor so much as seriously consider the matter."[59]

Many ministers had sunk into virtual poverty and were in danger of losing their status as gentlemen by the necessity of taking up manual labor on the lands allotted them. In contrast, the popular support of numerous taverns selling beverages and mixed drinks that the above cleric could not afford seemed a telling comment on the state, direction, and priorities of Massachusetts society. It was not just that men were purchasing luxuries like rum while balking at providing adequate support for their ministers. As the position of clergymen declined, numerous tavernkeepers acquired positions of influence in local and even provincial politics. Taverns had become places where men assertively and vocally redefined their relationships with each other and with figures of authority, including representatives to the House, in ways that departed from religious teachings.[60] Thus it is not surprising that the House decided on only recommendations to the towns rather than the direct intervention called for. They knew that more drastic measures would be construed as arbitrary and threatening to local autonomy and might endanger the positions of representatives themselves. If they did anything more on the issue at all, it was probably to plead for local clergy privately among their constituents, engaging in the sort of dialogue that was transforming relations between rulers and ruled by midcentury.

Ministers were not the only critics who believed that the social and political fabric of society was being corrupted by drink. Letters and pieces periodically published in Boston newspapers considered the issue. Some pointed to the demand for rum and other imported beverages as symptom-

59. *Boston Gazette,* Dec. 8, 1747, no. 1342, Dec. 22, 1747, no. 1344.

60. Generally the clergy put forth models of relations between rulers and ruled at odds with trends in Massachusetts politics. For the character of election sermons in the middle decades, see Richard D. Brown, *Revolutionary Politics in Massachusetts: The Boston Committee of Correspondence and the Towns, 1772–1774* (Cambridge, Mass., 1970), 9–14. They did, however, uphold the Whig ideal of a "balanced" constitution.

atic of a broader malaise afflicting the colonies, robbing them of the youthful vigor, industry, and self-sufficiency that made nations great. Philopatriae lamented the passing of the virtuous simplicity of Massachusetts society by the introduction of a variety of luxuries that he believed enfeebled and distracted the minds of colonists. Massachusetts was no longer a robust and youthful society. To this observer the colony exhibited signs of a corrupt old age like that of European societies and would undoubtedly meet the same fate as great nations and empires of the past. Vice had become so "rampant" that it might have already brought New England past its "meridian," with "the most dreadful and lasting ill consequences." It was nowhere more apparent than at "our tables" where "foreign liquors" must be served while "good beer and cider" are considered "rude and beggarly." Taverns had become "nurseries of vice and debauchery" frequented by idle people. Gentlemen should set an example and avoid expenses at taverns so they might be "better able to contribute to the relief of their unhappy country." Imported luxuries like rum had captured the soul of the colony. Is it not "high time," this critic concluded, "for the guardians of the people to interpose?"[61]

Adams echoed this refrain on taverns in 1760 in his diary. "It would be well worth the attention of our legislature to confine the number of and retrieve the character of licensed houses," lest ungoverned tavern companies "should arise at length to a degree of strength, that even the legislature will not be able to control."[62] The authority of government officers over drinking companies across the province had become so weak as to suggest that they did not regulate tavern assemblies so much as derive their power and office from them.

Such pleas and warnings formed a wellspring of dismay over the habits and manners of the populace of Massachusetts. But this criticism did not move members of the Assembly to act. They had shed their roles as guardians of the people's morality to become their agents. They were not prepared to intervene as in 1681–1719. For the most part, they remained preoccupied with "corruption" of the body politic from above, not below—from the actions and policies of royal governors, not the politic distribu-

---

61. *Boston Gazette*, Nov. 17, 1747, no. 1339, Jan. 19, 1748, no. 1445. Amicus Patriae accepted the fact that the "cream and marrow of our country is carried into the West Indies to purchase rum" and slaves. But he proposed that heavy excises be laid on the sales of each to create a gold and silver fund that could be used to back paper money. In effect he proposed a strengthening of the only effective deterrent to drinking—excise taxes—in order to harness "vice" for the benefit of society. *Boston Gazette*, Sept. 10–17, 1739, no. 1025.

62. Butterfield *et al.*, eds., *Diary and Autobiography of Adams*, I, 128–129, 190–192.

tion of drink and licenses. The location and exercise of power, that is, the distribution of patronage by alien governors appointed by the crown, consumed the interests of the Assembly. The array of powers given to royal governors—to veto legislation, dismiss the Assembly, and appoint members of the judiciary—became constant sparks to conflict. Belcher and his successors could never wholly pacify the expanding number of representatives with the patronage available to distribute, and so the offices he did control became all the more controversial. Many politicians increasingly felt alienated from royal authority and identified with the people now invoked often in print as the ultimate source of all governing authority.[63] On the eve of his removal in 1741, Belcher complained to future governor Thomas Hutchinson that the "common people here are taught by their advisers to believe they are pretty much out of reach of the government at home; nay, our Assembly are sometimes made to think by their leaders that they are as big as the Parliament of Great Britain."[64]

For members of the Assembly standing in opposition to the royal governors' powers, it was a natural step to inform at least some of their constituents of the danger posed by royal officials. And, given their popularity, taverns became natural vehicles for instruction of the people in opposition politics. Such had been the tactics of Elisha Cooke, Jr., in 1719 when he reversed the restrictive licensing policy and provided Bostonians with new places to assemble, with fewer restrictions on their conversation.

As the eighteenth century progressed, such employment of taverns received some partial, indirect justification from imported English political thought that emphasized the free flow of critical discourse on public affairs. The Whig opposition essayists, or the Commonwealthmen, received an especially wide reading in Massachusetts and other colonies. These Independent Whigs showed a perpetual concern with the discus-

63. For the invention of the concept of the "people" and its application in the colonies, see Edmund S. Morgan, *Inventing the People: The Rise of Popular Sovereignty in England and America* (New York, 1989), chaps. 3, 6. Morgan notes that members of the elite still used the concept cautiously at midcentury "lest they invite a wider participation than they bargained for" (147).

64. Jonathan Belcher to Thomas Hutchinson, May 11, 1741, *The Belcher Papers*, VII (MHS, *Collections*, LVII [Boston, 1894]), 388; Bernard Bailyn, *The Origins of American Politics* (New York, 1968), 82, 114–116, 154–155; Bushman, *King and People*, chap. 3. This does not mean that Massachusetts always teetered on the brink of rebellion. Richard Brown shows how such conflict could be contained within a relatively stable political system (*Revolutionary Politics in Massachusetts*, chap. 1).

sion of everything political. They claimed the "right of examining all public measures and, if they deserve it, of censuring them." They "never saw much power possessed without some abuse" and took it upon themselves "to watch those that have it" and "to acquit or expose them according as they apply it to the good of their country." These critics dwelt on a common theme—the fragility of English liberties as guaranteed by the precedents and traditions of the English constitution in the face of plots and conspiracies by the king's ministers and their dependents to control Parliament. Whig opposition writers feared the domination of the Commons by the king's ministers through the judicious distribution of bribes, pensions, and offices. Colonial leaders readily borrowed such rhetoric and adapted it to express their own grievances against royal authority in its guise in Massachusetts. The anonymous author of the 1739 *Letter to the Freeholders and Other Inhabitants* introduced this pamphlet by saying he "made use of some help from *Cato's Letters*," a series of Whig essays by John Trenchard and Thomas Gordon.[65] This pamphleteer without name or rank addressed every man and intended that possessors of the *Letter* inform the barely literate or illiterate by reading it aloud.

Through Whig essayists and by direct reading of history and the classical authors celebrated by the Enlightenment, colonists were also influenced by classical ideas emphasizing a critical public engaged in regular discussion and debate. The Roman Republic received particular attention as an era when men raised their voices in critical inspection without fear. The author of the 1749 *Letter to the Freeholders, and Qualified Voters* wrote that "Tacitus tells us" that during the republic men wrote and spoke with "boldness." But, after the empire replaced the republic, men became terrified by "august power" and dared "not open their mouths, but to flatter."[66] Open abuse of those justices and other appointees who gave even the appearance of "sycophantic" submission to royal governors to gain preferment received new justification.

The gradual but growing penetration of opposition ideology thus contributed to the further integration of taverns and politics in the face of the legacy of Puritan restriction, because taverns were the most ready and

65. Caroline Robbins, *The Eighteenth-Century Commonwealthman: Studies in the Transmission, Development, and Circumstance of English Liberal Thought from the Restoration of Charles II until the War with the Thirteen Colonies* (Cambridge, Mass., 1959), 120; Bernard Bailyn, *The Ideological Origins of the American Revolution* (Cambridge, Mass., 1967); *A Letter to the Freeholders and Other Inhabitants of the Massachusetts Bay*, 1.

66. Bailyn, *The Ideological Origins*, 22–26; Robbins, *The Eighteenth-Century Commonwealthman*, 106–107, 124–125; *Boston Gazette*, Oct. 18–25, 1736, no. 876.

conducive contexts for the abandonment of deferential, flattering speech and posture. Certainly some of the taverns close to the Town House on King Street became centers for instruction in Whig opposition politics for representatives coming to Boston from the countryside. James Pitson might have been inspired by one of the thirty-one pamphlets he owned to make them so accessible in his tavern. John Marston might have done the same with his "sundry pamphlets." Occasionally taverns in the vicinity of the Town House hosted sales of books. In 1726 a sale of seven to eight hundred books was held at the Royal Exchange Tavern, including history, law, physic, voyages, travels, poetry, and plays. Also included were volumes of the English periodicals the *Spectator* and the *Guardian.* The proprietor of the Sun Tavern held a similar sale in 1731 of a "valuable collection of modern books of the most celebrated authors."[67] Thus in the immediate vicinity of the Town House, representatives from country towns had a world of information available for sale or to borrow.

Books constantly circulated through networks of acquaintances, judging from the notices placed in the newspapers asking for their return. One owner offered a ten-shilling reward for the return of his first volume of the *Spectator* in 1729. Another offered a fifteen-shilling reward for the fifth volume of the *Spectator.* There existed so much demand for this English periodical that printer Richard Fry proposed in 1732 to print volumes by subscription. Clarendon's history of the English Civil War was also a popular item at loan; in 1732 Charles Apthorp published notices to recover his second and third volumes. Another asked for the return of his first volume. The heirs of Samuel Appleton asked that all of his books on loan be returned. Even Governor Belcher put a notice in the newspaper asking gentlemen to leave their names with him if they had borrowed books.[68] Tavernkeepers like Pitson and Marston, at the center of this vast exchange on King Street, were in a position to provide political tracts to a wider array of people.

Of greater regular impact than books on the conversation of country representatives gathering in the Town House and in King Street taverns were the newspapers published in Boston beginning in 1704. Printers of the four newspapers by 1760 continued to address the well educated, as evident by their newspapers' style and content. Yet there existed sufficient

67. Inventory of James Pitson, Suffolk County Probate Records, Record Books, XXXIV, 360–364, John Marston, LXXXVI, 12 (the contents of Marston's library are discussed in Chapter 6, below); *Boston Gazette*, Jan. 30–Feb. 6, 1727, no. 375, Mar. 3–10, 1731, no. 485.

68. *Boston Gazette*, Sept. 22–29, no. 514, Dec. 22–29, 1729, no. 527, May 3–10, 1731, no. 593, June 5, 1732, no. 648, Oct. 3–10, 1737, no. 926, Apr. 9–16, 1739, no. 1004.

demand for these newspapers to prompt proprietors of some public houses to keep them on hand for customers' perusal. When Mrs. Read opened a Chocolate House on King Street on the north side of the Town House, she informed customers that "they may read the news" in her rooms. When Daniel Jones opened a tavern on Newbury Street a quarter of a mile south of the Town House, he advertised that the house would be "supplied with the newspapers." Discussion as well as reading was customary. Dr. Alexander Hamilton encountered a group reading and discussing the news at a tavern near Portsmouth, New Hampshire: "I returned to my lodging at eight o'clock, and the post being arrived, I found a numerous company at Slater's reading the news." Their "chit-chat and noise kept me awake three hours after I went to bed."[69] Nonsubscribers, even the illiterate, could hear the news read and interpreted at taverns.

While representatives of country towns meeting in Boston received direct exposure to literature that helped them to define their postures toward the king's government in Massachusetts, it is difficult to assess the extent to which pamphlets, books, and newspapers circulated in the countryside among ordinary farmers. Doubtless the representatives who held licenses could inform their customers directly about opposition politics when they returned home. Captain Josiah Converse, a representative and justice who also kept a tavern in Brookfield, might also have loaned the "history books and pamphlets" that he owned to customers. Indeed, the entrance of so many tavernkeepers into politics probably facilitated greater diffusion of Whig opposition sentiments from members of governing bodies to ordinary men than in England, where these writings remained of marginal importance.

Country tavernkeepers commonly owned books. Of twenty-six tavernkeepers and retailers from Middlesex County and sixteen from Worcester County between 1738 and 1791, almost all were not just literate but also owned "books," according to their inventories. Moreover, appraisers distinguished between books and "old" books, a distinction suggesting a consciousness about new, current literature. In Middlesex County, four inventories included mention of "pamphlets," an indication that the owners tried to keep informed about current political issues. Thomas Symmes, a Charlestown retailer, owned forty bound books and nine pamphlets at his death in 1754. John Hunt, a Watertown retailer and justice, owned the most extensive library of the Middlesex group, including eight dozen "old books," sixty-seven quarto volumes, and thirteen folio volumes. Four of the

69. *Ibid.*, Sept. 6–13, 1731, no. 611, *Massachusetts Gazette Extraordinary*, Jan. 4, 1778 (supplement to regular edition); Bridenbaugh, ed., *Itinerarium of Hamilton*, 125.

sixteen licenseholders in the Worcester County group owned pamphlets; one had thirteen. Samuel Freeman, a Sturbridge tavernkeeper, owned a "right in a library" in 1772 as well as Bibles and "sundry other books." Samuel Andrews, a Worcester tavernkeeper in the 1760s, had a "library" in his barroom in 1791 like Pitson in Boston.[70]

The vast majority of tavernkeepers and retailers across the Massachusetts countryside probably possessed only a few books. Nevertheless, the fact that they appear in almost every inventory in this sample is evidence that licenseholders were prepared to make use of print if the occasion—political or otherwise—warranted. In a Somers, Connecticut, tavern Adams spied two books, located, like Pitson's books and pamphlets, "within the bar in Kibby's barroom," and asked for their titles. Kibby replied, "Every Man his own Lawyer, and Gilbert's Law of Evidence." Later, Adams "asked some questions of the people there, and they told me that Kibby was a sort of lawyer among them—that he pleaded some of their law cases before justices." Even two books could make a man more expert on some subjects than others were and help the advancement of a man who kept a public house. No doubt Kibby aired his opinion of justices to his customers. At the very next town Adams met a tavernkeeper who also represented the town at the Connecticut Assembly. And in a Sudbury tavern he found a tavernkeeper sufficiently well read to discuss "Captain Carver's Journal of his travels in the wilderness, among the savages in search of the South Seas."[71]

As in Boston, it is probable that many country tavernkeepers subscribed to Boston newspapers in order to enhance their house's importance as a center of communication. It took more than three hours for the company at Slater's tavern near Portsmouth to discuss all the news, to Hamilton's dismay.[72] Of course, private subscribers sometimes presided over readings of newspapers. A letter written to the *Boston Evening-Post* in 1760 might have described a private (as opposed to tavern) group who regularly gathered to hear the news read:

> As I live some distance from Boston, and am a customer to your weekly paper, my friends and neighbors generally meet at my house on Tuesday evenings, to hear your paper read, and talk about news, etc. We were

70. The inventories and wills of licenseholders in Middlesex County are on microfilm at the Middlesex County Courthouse in East Cambridge.

The Worcester County estate papers are located in the Probate Office of the Worcester County Courthouse.

71. Butterfield *et al.*, eds., *Diary and Autobiography of Adams*, II, 27, 33.

72. Bridenbaugh, ed., *Itinerarium of Hamilton*, 125.

all exceedingly pleased with what you published last October, about the raising of wheat, and the use and advantage of marl; the whole company agreed that the farmers in this country don't understand husbandry like the farmers in old England; and that our farmers are in the condition of the Ethiopians in the Acts, having no man to guide them.[73]

Newspapers were delivered via taverns; thus public houses were probably the most important gathering places to hear the news read and interpreted. Indeed, the limited circulation of newspapers in the eighteenth century might have increased the attraction of taverns as a source of extra-local news because of the tavernkeeper's or a regular patron's subscription.

As the reading public consumed printed appeals communicating fears about the intentions of royal governors, taverns became a means to diffuse this information orally to a wider public. In respect to the thorny subject of drink and tavern regulation, the priorities of elected representatives shifted from the strict and close regulation of the popular culture of drink to the exploitation of it to guard against greater dangers. Tavern patrons across the province caught up in the local tensions of sectional town politics, jealous of the rise of one interest over another, suspicious of justice-representatives falling under the control of the governor, could readily seize on simplified versions of opposition ideology to explain and justify their more ready engagement in the new political culture emerging in the colony. Whig opposition ideology could also provide a sense of unity for colonists as a whole in relation to the royal establishment even as their local communities fragmented into the interest groups of parish and neighborhood.

At the turn of the century Sewall, once the manager of the censored press, had assiduously distributed sermons and religious tracts to ministers and officials throughout the province to enhance the knowledge and authority of the hierarchy of church and state. The overwhelmingly religious content of this printed matter supported the simultaneous attack on taverns and intemperance by the state. But the shift to more secular political news, as evident in the pamphlets and books owned by some tavernkeepers and retailers, complemented the attraction of gatherings in public houses. While ministers preached sermons in the meetinghouse or published them for private reading, pamphlets and newspapers could be more suitably read and discussed in the tavern. At the same time, the introduction of printed political appeals altered the popular culture of drink in taverns, infusing local companies with new ideological agendas of

---

73. *Boston-Evening Post,* Mar. 3, 1760, no. 1279.

extralocal import. Readers and listeners became part of an abstract public that transcended face-to-face relationships and thus qualified their narrow identification with the local men with whom they drank.[74]

It was not the intermittent conflict between royal governors and the House over constitutional right and prerogative, nor the adaptation and diffusion of Whig opposition ideology in Massachusetts, that caused the virtual collapse of the system of controls over the drink trade instituted in the seventeenth century. Long before the installation of royal government, the efforts by Puritan rulers to enforce temperate use had been frustrated by the tavern's importance in communication and the formation of social bonds within communities. But constitutional conflict within Massachusetts government, together with the ideology that expressed and defined it, did help to render the system of tavern and drink regulation constructed by Sewall and his contemporaries even more of a shell, bereft of the substance of Puritan social and political ideals. Native colonial leaders did not openly appeal to the electorate often in this society nominally committed to elite governance; but when they did make such appeals, as during the Land Bank crisis, the importance of taverns as mediums of communication between elected officials and their constituents was amplified. The distribution of drink at elections as well as the election of tavernkeepers themselves strengthened the interest of representatives with their constit-

74. The secular quality of much of the printed matter most in demand in the 18th century is reflected in the libraries of John Marston and Timothy Bigelow, in the notices for the recall of books and periodicals at loan, and in the number of libraries containing pamphlets. Lucian W. Pye and associate contributors examine the transition between oral, traditional systems of communication and modern, print-based systems in Pye, ed., *Communications and Political Development* (Princeton, N.J., 1963). Pye defines "traditional" and "modern" systems of communication and the "transitional" systems, which characterize societies at crucial junctures in modernization. He believes that a key aspect of modernization in a transitional system is the integration of print (modern technology) with the local, face-to-face systems in community life: "Most of the problems of political development can be thought of in terms of the ways in which such fragmented communication systems can become more effectively integrated into a national system while still preserving the integrity of the informal patterns of human association" (26–27). Taverns had become a vital part of this process in 18th-century Massachusetts through the interaction of increasing numbers of tavernkeepers with the urban-based print media in Boston, the seat of provincial government. Taverns continued to be traditional, local, face-to-face seats of human association, but also served as points of reception for the transmission of a modern political ideology. See also Richard D. Brown, *Modernization: The Transformation of American Life, 1600–1865* (New York, 1976), chap. 3.

uents and simultaneously placed the private and secret agreements of those in the interest of appointed crown officials in a more sinister light.

At the same time, the authority of the regulators of taverns at every level in the ascending hierarchy of the province—selectmen, justices, and representatives—became compromised as tavern companies asserted themselves or became parts of local systems of patronage. Distinctions between rulers and ruled became blurred as tavernkeepers became officers of government and voters sat with them in their public rooms. Massachusetts colonists still scrambled for place and preferment and to distinguish themselves as genteel, but so many men of questionable quality succeeded that these distinctions and offices inspired less awe. If the genteel stooped to get licenses and unlettered tavernkeepers aspired to be genteel, who could maintain the traditional social distinctions supposed to distinguish the rulers from the ruled? The hierarchy of regulation as well as the force of the principle of hierarchy itself weakened. This was cause for much complaint in the rhetoric of "decline" and "declension" but no new initiatives by the Assembly against the popular culture of drink. Public houses multiplied faster than ever.

Amid these developments Adams tried to take comfort in his diary by declaring that "the English constitution is founded . . . on the knowledge and good sense of the people." A colonist "who can read, will find in his Bible, in the common sermon books that common people have by them, and even in the almanacs and newspapers, rules and observations that will enlarge his range of thought, and enable him the better to judge who has and who has not that integrity of heart, and that compass of understanding, which form the statesman."[75] Here Adams expressed the conviction that the expansion of print over the course of the eighteenth century had enlarged understanding and augmented public virtue.

Yet, as other passages in Adams's diary suggest, this perception of the political culture was wishful thinking. During the eighteenth century, consultations in the egalitarian temper of taverns had also become central to the electoral process. In Boston, opposition leader Elisha Cooke, Jr., had found it necessary to sanction the dramatic expansion of public houses and thus enhance the capacity of drinkers of low rank to support his sentiments by emulating his bold posture and speech themselves. The hierarchy of regulation as well as the force of the principle of hierarchy itself had weakened. The increasing number of country tavernkeepers who journeyed to King Street to take their seats in the House along with Cooke and

75. Butterfield *et al.*, eds., *Diary and Autobiography of Adams*, I, 220.

his successors only served to soften distinctions of rank further. These representatives might more comfortably drink at a tavern like Pitson's than at the elegant Crown Coffee House and personify leveling impulses to Bostonians already so inclined.

As Adams himself lamented, the multiplication of public houses in country towns after 1720 and the development of sectional and other interest groups invested new importance in the election of selectmen with whom voters regularly conversed in taverns. The pamphlets published by mid-century in the form of "letters" to "freeholders" and "other inhabitants" justified the redefinition of the relationship between voters and their representatives to the House in the same mold. The authors of these "letters" remained anonymous, claiming no social rank, and thus emphasized the need to address men of all ranks to inspect the conduct of elected officials with care, particularly if they also held office from the crown.

Thus while the proportion of men claiming the right to participate vocally in both local and provincial affairs was increasing, the pamphlet literature justifying that right to a wide public impressed on men not what they did know about public affairs—but what they did not know, what they were prevented from knowing, and the evils that they might all too readily suspect as a result. The men gathering in taverns across the province, becoming exposed in various degrees to the opposition ideology borrowed from English Whig essayists, in fact acquired new status as members of a critical public, but simultaneously received warnings of how little they knew of actual or potential corruption among rulers. Growing awareness of the uneven exercise of literacy and consumption of print only stimulated wide fears of the danger of conspiracy. Pamphlets addressed to all inhabitants, which seemed to demand public readings to the barely literate in taverns, brought into question the legitimacy of print traditionally addressed to a narrow reading public, not to mention that mass of private communications between crown officers and those in their patronage.

Any act or policy by the crown or its agents that enhanced the power of royal officials and their appointees at the expense of elected officials could only provoke immediate speculation as to hidden meanings, designs, and agendas. The Sugar and Stamp acts, passed in quick succession by Parliament in 1764 and 1765, became such catalysts. The first raised the price of molasses (and therefore New England rum as well) by providing for tighter enforcement against smugglers and for the systematic collection of duties; the second levied a tax on most printed documents, including liquor licenses and newspapers. Moreover, the passage and proposed enforcement of these new measures contained the alarming portent of a whole new set of offices and officials over whom the House had no control. This was something to which tavernkeepers were particularly sensitive, owing to the unpopular set of commissioners, deputy commissioners, and collectors of the excise tax who assessed and collected what every licenseholder owed to his majesty's government when excise taxes were levied.[76] As a consequence, tavern patrons received new written and oral injunctions to take an active role in the defense of chartered liberties, and new reason to flock to taverns to stay informed.

But the mobilization of a public informally organized in taverns contained its own alarming portent for men like Adams. The extent of tavern patronage and consumption of rum among the lower ranks already signified a dangerous loss of order and discipline in society to the genteel leaders who still dominated provincial affairs. Further empowerment of lesser men through acts of resistance might elevate more unfit men to positions of authority, or even result in the loss of all order.

76. For the various excise officials, see *Acts and Resolves*, III, 784–788. Paul S. Boyer describes the pamphlet war that ensued over the passage of a more comprehensive excise tax in 1754 in "Borrowed Rhetoric: The Massachusetts Excise Controversy of 1754," *WMQ*, 3d Ser., XXI (1964), 328–351. There are numerous examples of prosecutions by excise officers of licenseholders accused of understating their sales, or simply delinquent in payment of the tax. On Apr. 8, 1746, a collector of the Excise, Edward Sheaffe, prosecuted tavernkeepers in Watertown, Westford, Wilmington, Malden, and Cambridge for refusing to give an account in writing of their sales (Court of General Sessions, Middlesex, Record Book, 1735–1748, 429). On May 21, 1751, he prosecuted 10 other licenseholders in nine towns (Record Book, 1748–1761, 157).

Chapter 6

The Public Order of Revolution

Slowly, unevenly, but relentlessly a new political culture had emerged in colonial Massachusetts. The concept and practice of hierarchy had been strained, altered, and finally eroded by the restiveness, by the ready assertion of ordinary men shedding traditional constraints on their political behavior. They were most ready to do so in companies at taverns, whose number and use had long thwarted the full realization of the Puritan commonwealth. Informal meetings in public rooms had contributed to the expansion of men's capacity to criticize, berate, and even move to foil those leaders to whom deference in posture and speech was customarily due. In socially stratified Boston, men of middling and low rank did not ordinarily drink and mix with those of exalted status. But this separation only rendered the exalted easier targets for raillery and abuse. In country taverns, criticism of town leaders who lived in a different precinct, patronizing a different tavern, could also find ready expression and sometimes elevate the most glib and vocal critic to the status of a leader himself. In the face of such competition, more genteel leaders must follow suit. To the dismay of ambitious Harvard graduate John Adams, the "arts of gain" had become necessary. One must "mix with the crowd in a tavern, in the meetinghouse or the training field" to grow popular and become a figure of respect.[1]

1. L. H. Butterfield *et al.*, eds., *Diary and Autobiography of John Adams* (New York, 1964), I, 96.

This emerging political culture disturbed many. These developments flew in the face of everything that colonists had traditionally been taught to revere and preserve. Consensus, harmony, and deference had all weakened or dissolved into sometimes jarring conflict at both the local and provincial levels among groups competing to promote their interests. The more engaged and active ordinary colonists became in this vocal and combative conflict, the more prominent did taverns become as centers for the definition and prosecution of various interests. The institution nominally under the strict control of officials in local, county, and provincial government now began to influence the makeup and character of government at all levels. It was bad enough that political discourse should sometimes be charged with extreme words and excited accusations; but to have the political process so enmeshed with the distribution and consumption of drink represented a steep slide away from Puritan political values and philosophy. Where would it all end but in disaster?

Alternative conceptions of the political order had begun to gain influence. The maxims of Whig opposition ideology circulating among Massachusetts leaders after 1720 partially, indirectly justified this nascent political culture. These critics condemned the unceasing efforts by crown ministers to dominate Parliament by the shrewd and politic distribution of pensions, offices, and other forms of bribery to members. Native colonial leaders readily borrowed this rhetoric and applied it to their conflicts with royal governors. The people must be warned to resist the malevolent designs of ambitious men that might endanger their chartered liberties and interests. Such warnings implied that men must be vigilant, watchful, and active in protecting their interests—a justification for behavior that had become common amid the expanding and multiplying towns of eighteenth-century Massachusetts.

But other dimensions of Whig ideology and republican thought were as hostile to taverns as Puritan principles had ever been. Whig essayists also emphasized in their meditations on the English constitutional monarchy that the intemperance and sloth associated with taverns weakened the people's capacity to detect and defend themselves against incipient tyrants. English and colonial observers looked to the great republics of antiquity for solutions to present controversies over the English constitution. History said to them that ancient republics and nations had foundered in the past owing to the decline of virtue among their citizens. A principle cause of decline was the people's embrace of luxuries, which corrupted the simple manners and physical fortitude of a free people. Rum was such a luxury, rendering a people dull-witted and susceptible to bribery and exploitation. The circulation of such histories also invested new importance in the private act of reading as opposed to collective drinking. Republican precepts thus justified fresh criticisms of the popular culture of drink.

Massachusetts leaders grappled with these conflicting impulses as they confronted the threat that parliamentary legislation seemed to pose after 1764. For some, this threat must be met with not only resistance but also reformation. Only through a restoration of public virtue could Massachusetts colonists hope to triumph over the evils posed by the Sugar Act, the Stamp Act, and succeeding measures. Resolutions against the use of rum and public houses proliferated even among ordinary colonists in the 1760s. Reform became more imperative as popular participation in resistance and alienation from the monarchy increased. Yet for the mass of male colonists, it was in taverns that they followed and acted on the unfolding drama of the crisis with England. It was in taverns that men carried their examination of crown officials and policies to new levels of critical inspection and celebrated the creation of the Republic. Indeed, their activism went beyond what many Revolutionary leaders could accept by the 1780s. This would not be the classical republic of virtue that many state and national leaders hoped to create. Members of vocal, distrustful, and suspicious tavern companies would defer to no aristocracy, not even a natural one of merit.

I

From the beginning of the crisis in relations between England and her colonies, the virtue of leaders and people on both sides of the Atlantic was at issue. Instructive to Whig critics and their colonial leaders in their assessment of the state of the English constitution and society were the histories of and commentaries on the ancient republics, particularly the Roman Republic. Essayists and historians were drawn to critical classical writers such as Cicero, Tacitus, and Seneca, who juxtaposed the disorder and corruption under the empire to an imagined earlier era of rustic republican simplicity and virtue. Ancient history and texts contributed to the belief that all nations underwent a certain cycle of birth, youth, maturity, and decay. In the last stages of a nation's life it was believed that the people became enamored of luxuries of dress, domestic life, and table, which gradually weakened their devotion to the common welfare of the nation. Only through periodic renewals of private and public virtue—pledges to temperance, frugality, industry, and simplicity—could a nation's constitution, spirit, and health be preserved. A people sunk into vice and love of luxury and pleasure were too weak and distracted to resist the intrigues and maneuvers of an arbitrary prince and his ministers. Such appeared to be the condition of English society at midcentury to a significant group of English and colonial pamphleteers and newspaper essayists.[2]

In contrast to England, it was generally believed that the colonists remained capable of resisting incipient tyrants, because the colonies still possessed that rustic simplicity and virtue that Englishmen had lost. The colonies, many educated observers felt, were at a relatively young stage of development in comparison to the old, decrepit, corrupted mother country. Most white Americans owned property and were to a great extent self-sufficient. The sturdy, rustic yeoman was thought to be the backbone of an industrious, liberty-loving nation.[3]

Still, critics in Massachusetts and the wider colonial world had doubts about the character and virtue of colonists as the eighteenth century progressed. Reform and regeneration remained imperative, lest the colonies come to resemble the decayed, overripe society of England.[4] And nowhere was reform considered so necessary as in the colony that had been founded as a self-conscious alternative to English corruption in the seventeenth century. Boston society had become stratified; a majority of Bostonians owned no real property. In the older towns of the countryside the rising generation faced diminished prospects by the 1760s of owning their own farms. Simultaneously, public houses multiplied, some to support and accommodate the poor in these ports and towns. The consumption of rum appeared to rise to new levels, as Massachusetts society became more crowded and prospects for inhabitants narrowed. It seemed that, as Massachusetts society became more mature, it also became more intemperate and irreligious. English and Continental diatribes against luxury and dissipation in Boston newspapers addressed the visible em-

2. Caroline Robbins, *The Eighteenth-Century Commonwealthman: Studies in the Transmission, Development, and Circumstance of English Liberal Thought from the Restoration of Charles II until the War with the Thirteen Colonies* (Cambridge, Mass., 1959), 44–45, 106–107, 309–310; Bernard Bailyn, *The Ideological Origins of the American Revolution* (Cambridge, Mass., 1967), 23–26; H. Trevor Colbourn, *The Lamp of Experience: Whig History and the Intellectual Origins of the American Revolution* (Chapel Hill, N.C., 1965), 3–39; Drew R. McCoy, *The Elusive Republic: Political Economy in Jeffersonian America* (Chapel Hill, N.C., 1980), chap. 1, 50–61.

3. McCoy, *The Elusive Republic*, 63–75.

4. *Ibid.*, 70–75, 113–119. Criticism of refinement and luxury increased after 1765 because Whig essayists often identified the love of luxury as motivation for the actions of friends and allies of imperial government. Patriots evoked rustic simplicity as an alternative to the attraction of the elegant and "courtly." Richard L. Bushman, *The Refinement of America: Persons, Houses, Cities* (New York, 1992), 191, 193–195, 203.

brace of imported goods by colonists.[5] The legacy of clerical dismay over the use of drink and taverns from the seventeenth century received new injections of life from more secular arguments against creeping luxury, corruption, and decay in the eighteenth.

The passage by Parliament of the Sugar and Stamp acts in quick succession in 1764 and 1765 brought these concerns into sharper focus. The acts inflamed existing resentment by colonial assemblies of the restrictions on their autonomy and simultaneously seemed to pose a test of the civic virtue of colonists as a whole. The common belief that the revenues from these acts would support a host of new offices, filled by sycophantic parasites of the English court, touched chords of anxiety not just on constitutional grounds but in regard to public virtue. Would the colonists acquiesce to a new invasion of idle, penniless pensioners intent on milking the colonists of the fruits of their own industry? Amid this rising level of concern with the virtue of rulers and ruled, taverns and drink in Massachusetts quickly became the target of new criticism. The manners and spirit of Massachusetts inhabitants came under fresh scrutiny as ordinary colonists began to play a more active role in provincial politics in the 1760s.

Nathaniel Ames, an author of yearly almanacs and a Dedham tavern-keeper, spoke directly to these concerns in his almanac for 1767 in the wake of the Stamp Act protests. He congratulated his readers on their successful resistance to the act but also pressed them to reform their habits. He encouraged farmers to break free from their suffocating localism by reading history. Farmers should enrich their minds "at the intervals of cultivating your fields" and should pay particular attention to subjects like Roman history. Through such histories, Massachusetts inhabitants would "learn how gradually a rough and ignorant people, by cultivating the study of useful arts and manufactures, did emerge from obscurity to a state of grandeur and affluence." By analogy, this was also the story of the development of the colonies from rough backwater societies to centers of prosperity and cultivation. But the fate of the Romans, Ames warned, might also befall Massachusetts and her sister colonies if they did not learn the lessons of the history. The Romans had lost their "virtue." They became "indolent and luxurious, and therefore vicious and ignorant, which made them a prey

5. Kenneth A. Lockridge, "Land, Population, and the Evolution of New England Society, 1630–1790: And an Afterthought," in Stanley N. Katz, ed., *Colonial America: Essays in Politics and Social Development* (Boston, 1971), 446–491; Robert A. Gross, *The Minutemen and Their World* (New York, 1976), 77–79, 105–107; "The Prevalence of Luxury with a Burgo-master's Excellent Admonitions against It," *Boston Gazette*, Jan. 19, 1748, no. 1445.

to tyranny." Symptomatic of luxury and indolence was the enormous expense for distilled liquors. By implication this author-tavernkeeper strongly urged his countrymen to forsake habitual collective drinking for the study of texts that would justify their full and active participation in affairs of state. A great revolution had taken place, he wrote, when Britons had stopped praying in Latin "like a parcel of parrots" and learned to "keep Bibles in a language they understood." So should Americans continue to break free of ignorance, the "foundation of tyranny." They should despise "foreign luxury" and banish "from among us immorality and idleness."[6] If they failed to, they might meet the same fate as the Romans.

Such sentiments were enunciated so often during the early years of the resistance that they not only invested new faith in the "Puritan Ethic" but expanded and elaborated that ethic to include the lessons and morals drawn from the new focus on ancient history.[7] One of the most comprehensive early expositions on American virtue was that of Americanus in the *New-London Gazette* in 1769. In a series of essays on the long-term causes of the controversy with England, this writer pointed to the rising level of commercial trade in the colonies as a symptom of a society becoming more prone to the temptations of luxury. Farmers carried their "useful" commodities to the merchants who exchanged them for some "imported bauble scarce worth possessing." Thus the rising demand for extravagant dress and other luxuries had led the English and Europeans to conclude that the colonists were wealthy—that new revenues might be extracted from them. The rising taste for luxury had thereby contributed to the enactment of the controversial duties.[8]

What was more, the taste for one luxury in particular weakened the capacity of the colonists to defend themselves against unconstitutional

6. Nathaniel Ames, *An Astronomical Diary; or, Almanack for the Year of Our Lord Christ 1767* (Boston, 1766), 1–3. This tavernkeeper did not attack the use of rum directly, but for the month of May he offered the following verses: "The fatal effects of Luxury are these: / We drink our poison, and we eat disease; / Not so, O Temperance! when ruled by thee; / The brute's obedient, and the man is free."

7. The classic examination of this strain of Revolutionary thought is Edmund S. Morgan, "The Puritan Ethic and the American Revolution," *WMQ*, 3d Ser., XXIV (1967), 3–43. The clergy reiterated the need for reformation, sometimes blaming the colonists for bringing the imperial crisis upon themselves as punishment. See Harry S. Stout, *The New England Soul: Preaching and Religious Culture in Colonial New England* (New York, 1986), 285–287, 379n.

8. Americanus to *New-London Gazette* (Connecticut), Jan. 20, 1769, no. 271.

innovations. Significantly, Americanus reserved his sharpest words for the diet and drink of colonists. The wealthy had forsaken the "frugal diet of our ancestors," the "homely entertainment of our fathers fifty years ago," for innovations such as "the equipage of the tea table" and its unhealthy accompaniment. Still more serious as an "instrument in effecting our present calamities" was the universal demand for spirituous liquors:

> Our corn, our cattle and horses, the fat of our land have been exported for rum and wines, those promoters of vice, sickness, and want. This folly has become so prevalent, that it is now an established custom among our day laborers, that their employers afford not less than a half pint of the choice West India spirits for one day's consumption. For the truth of which I appeal to the times of our fathers, who were as virtuous, healthy, robust, and diligent as the laborers of our day. Idleness, the parent of every vice, has been introduced by the fatal and pernicious use of foreign spirits, which this people have run into. Not one extravagance, among the numerous follies we have been guilty of, has been more destructive to our interests than tavern haunting, and gratifying our appetites with intoxicating liquors. It has more impoverished this land than all our expense in supporting religion and government among us.[9]

For Americanus the demand for and use of imported liquors at taverns represented the most serious internal threat to the immediate future of the colonies at this time of constitutional controversy. He looked back to the Puritan past for the virtue that must be recaptured, but he also borrowed from republican theory to assess the impact of luxury on a free nation. Temperance had never been more important.

It was not just the exchange of New England produce and livestock for rum that Americanus condemned. The subsequent use of these spirits to influence elections also drew his censure. While Adams had singled out selectmen and representatives as most ready to manipulate voters through the distribution of drink, Americanus focused on militia officers as the worst promoters of this vice. According to his observations, it had become necessary to distribute one hundred pounds worth of food and drink to obtain the necessary support to win a captain's commission. Prospective captains recommended themselves to their soldiers, not by their martial skills, but by their generosity at local taverns where training bands mustered. For Connecticut, he estimated that "the entertainments of the cap-

9. *Ibid.*

tain and inferior officers . . . cost this colony not less than 7 or 8,000 pounds annually" and subverted the goals of martial exercise. Training days had become "frolics" that ended with drunkenness. The government, he continued, should act to prevent this expense for spirits and to forbid "every species of bribery."[10] He considered this subversion of militia training by the distribution of drink to be one step away from the subversion of government through drink. In both cases the ability of colonists to perceive, judge, and act on matters of civic importance became dulled and weakened. The traditional practices associated with the exchange of drink that had persisted in Massachusetts despite the Puritan assault on them now became the focus of republican censure. Public life must be more firmly purged of traditional drinking habits in keeping with ideas of virtue extracted from ancient history.

To be sure, Americanus had no doubts of the primary precipitant of the present controversy engulfing the colonies. The "English government is glutted with ministerial dependents, pensioners, and placemen." America had become their last resource; here the crown ministers hoped to "satiate a large number of their greedy minions, who have rendered themselves obnoxious at home." But Americanus, in expanding on Whig opposition arguments, also deemed the "causes of our misery, as they spring from among ourselves," to be no less important.[11] Implicitly, he linked the colonists' support of a large number of drinksellers and their imported rum and wines with the crown ministry's effort to use new colonial revenues to support a large number of parasitical office seekers. Both represented species of corruption that threatened the social and political fabric of the colonies. The subversion of rationality and reason by strong drink became symbolic of the tyranny that the ambitious "few" might come to hold over the "many," rendering them servile and dependent. Only through a reformation of broadly based social "vices," Americanus claimed, could colonists hope to oppose effectively that which threatened them from abroad. Only then, also, could new levels of participation in provincial and imperial politics by common men be justified. If the people entered into political life more actively and assertively (as had happened by this date), then they must demonstrate the necessary religious and civic virtue at the same time. They must demonstrate superiority to the ministerial placemen they sought to uproot and expel, to the parasites they agitated to prevent from descending on the colonies in even greater numbers. Implicitly, Amer-

10. *Ibid.*

11. *Ibid.*

icanus judged the capacity of colonists to become free citizens of a republican nation and found them wanting. Their judgment was clouded by drink.

The nonimportation movement, organized to resist the Townshend Duties enacted in 1767, also addressed the need for internal reform. Colonists must not only sacrifice imported luxuries. They were also encouraged to promote and start manufactures that cultivated the virtue of industry instead of the sin of idleness, productivity instead of tavern haunting. A writer to the *Boston Gazette* in 1767 calling himself Robinson Crusoe was very specific in his recommendations to the "Junto" of resistance leaders in Boston. He proposed that the Junto write to the selectmen of every town in the colony asking them to promote the cultivation of wool and flax instead of provisions so as to encourage the manufacturers of linen. This had been tried before in Boston as an antidote to idleness and unemployment. Now it was recommended that selectmen should give premiums to those who manufactured the best piece of linen or woolen and to those who invented the best machine of any kind. Manufacturers should now have not only a legitimate place but a high moral purpose in Massachusetts society. Significantly, Crusoe also asked that cider and small beer be promoted to replace rum. Even as early as 1767 Crusoe anticipated the establishment of a "Republic." He believed that the republic could not but benefit from a greater excise on spirits. Perhaps a heavy excise would reduce or even eliminate the one hundred to two hundred barrels of rum that he estimated many towns consumed in one year.[12]

It was not just newspaper essayists who criticized colonial drinking habits as needing immediate reform in the 1760s. In the wake of the novel levels of resistance to the Stamp Act and Townshend Duties by common men, local governments resolved to cultivate the virtue deemed necessary for patriots. In 1767 the Boston Town Meeting passed resolutions to promote "industry, frugality," and the renuncication of "superfluities." The Town Meeting specified rum as one of the unnecessary luxuries and even instructed Boston representatives to take action in the House to discourage the use of rum: "We cannot conclude this head, without observing to you, that the excessive use and consumption of spirituous liquors requires your particular care to discountenance," as "it is destructive to the morals as well as the health and substance of the people." Rum tended "to erase from the mind the sentiments of virtue and a disposition to industry." These resolutions became models for country towns. Groton selectmen agreed that "idleness and the excessive use of foreign superfluities" are the

12. Robinson Crusoe to *Boston Evening-Post,* Dec. 14, 1767, no. 1674.

"chief cause of the present distressed state of the province." Towns in Connecticut published resolves against the use of rum in general, and the distribution of liquor at militia musters and to laborers in particular.[13] In a burst of idealism, governments previously impervious to reform on this issue showed a disposition to move on it.

Boston selectmen also moved in 1767 to take action against gaming and other disorders reputedly rife in licensed and unlicensed houses. They published a call in newspapers to all "gentlemen and well-disposed persons" to inform against the proprietors of houses that permitted gaming. Selectmen also wanted more information about retailers of spirits who violated the terms of their licenses, probably the long-ignored prohibition against consumption on the premises. Two years later the selectmen appointed a committee to "consider the steps proper to be taken to check the progress of vice and immoralities, and promote a reformation of manners." The committee reported a great increase in idleness, drunkenness, profane cursing and swearing, and Sabbath breaking. Bostonians might indeed have become less guarded in their speech as crown officials came under open and excited contempt and criticism. The committee recommended the timeworn solution of making greater efforts to enforce existing laws and providing employment for the poor. Another committee appointed in 1770 to consider how to prevent unlicensed strangers from selling rum as well as break up "bad houses" tried to put teeth in its recommendations by proposing to restore the practice of electing tithingmen. Twelve were actually elected.[14] Thus a revival of efforts to reform manners accompanied the increasing conflict with the crown ministry. It was as if open distrust and defiance of crown authority rendered it more essential to shore up "legitimate" and "moral" authority, lest authority in general weaken. Native colonial leaders did not welcome independent agitation by tavern companies of the lower ranks.

The distribution of drink to influence elections also was censured by local governments. In 1766 the Worcester Town Meeting instructed the town's representatives to use their "utmost endeavor that a law be made to prevent bribery and corruption in the several towns in this province in the

13. S. C. to *Boston Evening-Post*, Dec. 28, 1767, no. 168, and Instructions to Boston Representatives; Caleb Butler, *History of the Town of Groton* . . . (Boston, 1848), 115–116; *Connecticut Gazette* (New London), Mar. 18, 1768, no. 227, Apr. 1, 1768, no. 229.

14. Boston, Record Commissioners, *Selectmen's Minutes from 1764 through 1768*, Report of the Record Commissioners of the City of Boston (Boston, 1889), 262; *Boston Town Records, 1758 to 1769* (Boston, 1886), 274; *Boston Town Records, 1770 through 1777* (Boston, 1887), 19.

choice of representatives." The House passed no law in the 1760s against bribery with drink in civil elections, but it did later move to outlaw "treating" in militia elections, because "bribery and corruption" had destroyed "many great and opulent nations" and "every species thereof should be discountenanced by a virtuous and patriotic people." By this law, officers could be court-martialed and removed if they provided liquor or food on any muster day, not just election days.[15] By these proposals and laws, Massachusetts towns took steps to purge the popular culture of drink from the political culture of the province. Self-control and discipline were deemed imperative as extralegal protest widened to include volatile crowds of ordinary men. Intemperance symbolized subversion from outside and inside Massachusetts society.

This subversion of virtue by drink received new emphasis after troops arrived in Boston in 1768, requested by Governor Francis Bernard to protect customs officials from intimidation and harassment. The presence of the troops became an inflammatory issue not just because of the ministry's decision to use a standing army to enforce order in Boston but also because of the troops' behavior in the town, particularly their use of drink and taverns. Boston leaders became so incensed by their presence that they published a *Journal of the Times* to record their impact. The *Journal*'s authors frequently dwelled on the "drunkenness, debaucheries, and other extravagances which prevail by means of the troops being quartered in the midst of a town, where distilled spirits are so cheap and plenty." Hardly a day passed without a report of new incidents. "Violences must be expected from soldiers, who have a raging appetite for spirits, and whose barracks are encircled with distilling houses and dramshops." The subculture of the soldiers in Boston became symbolic of the degeneracy of the government that requested and sent them and a mirror image of what the elite feared in crowd behavior. Bostonians must steel themselves to resist its influence and invest discipline in their individual and collective acts of resistance.[16]

15. William Lincoln, *History of Worcester* . . . (Worcester, Mass., 1837), 67; Massachusetts, *The Acts and Resolves, Public and Private, of the Province of the Massachusetts Bay* . . . (Boston, 1869–1922), V, 451 (hereafter cited as *Acts and Resolves*).

16. Oliver Morton Dickerson, ed., *Boston under Military Rule, 1768–1769, as Revealed in a Journal of the Times* (Westport, Conn., 1971), xi–xii, 28, 39, 89. Alfred F. Young believes that the arrival and behavior of the troops had a greater impact on shoemaker George Hewes than the Stamp Act. See his "George Robert Twelves Hewes (1742–1840): A Boston Shoemaker and the Memory of the American Revolution," *WMQ*, 3d Ser., XXXVIII (1981), 597.

Plate 7. Landing of British Troops at Long Wharf to March up King Street. *Detail from* A View of Part of the Town of Boston in New England and British Ships of War Landing Their Troops, 1768. *Engraving by Paul Revere. Courtesy, Massachusetts Historical Society*

The press vilified Governor Bernard not just for the corruption of Boston society by the troops. According to the *Journal,* he appointed new justices, responsible for maintaining order, without any regard to their moral character. Justices, the *Journal* observed, must be "of a spirit which will lead them to act up to the true character of *reforming* magistrates." In the past, the *Journal* claimed (falsely), magistrates had always "nobly exerted themselves for the suppression of drunkenness." Now, Governor Bernard was appointing justices with other ends in view. The governor had added men to the bench uninterested in reformation, intent only on strengthening his government. Thus did the governor undermine the reformation so needed in Massachusetts, in order to brace up his own government. The lately appointed justices constituted a network of dependents of the governor not unlike the placemen and pensioners who, Whig leaders warned, would descend on the colonies if the people did not resist unconstitutional taxes vigorously:

> It is a serious truth, that if the magistrates are vicious and immoral, the people will soon be so; and if in those appointments, so little regard is paid even to political characters, so that t[raitor]s and r[ogue]s, may be entrusted with the execution of laws, provided they will act in subserviency to the views of a selfish, arbitrary G[overno]r, the rights as well as the morals of such a people must be in the most deplorable situation.[17]

Now, the *Journal* implied, it was not the people who subverted the enforcement of drink and tavern regulations; it was the governor and his expanding army of idle, mercenary placemen who did. A people resolving to be virtuous, contending with the dissipation of an army of occupation, confronted a governor who undermined virtue among the people. The *Journal* portrayed the royal government in Massachusetts as a fountain of vice.

I I

In newspaper, in pamphlet, and by local resolution, commentators and leaders in the 1760s had professed a need and desire for reformation in respect to taverns and drink, especially rum. Only with reformation, these spokesmen claimed, could colonists successfully resist efforts to abridge their autonomy through measures like the Stamp Act. The insidious designs attributed by British ministers and their agents in America must be answered with the united resistance of a virtuous people. Virtue was indispensable to political participation. Drink could dull the colonists to appeals for vigilance and render them unruly when mobilized.

The need for reformation had been a continual refrain since the late seventeenth century. And the reform of drinking habits did have real, actual roots in Puritan New England. The first generation of colonists had voluntarily abandoned the traditional religious holidays, celebrated with drink, in favor of congregations devoted to hearing the Word interpreted by learned ministers. Real, tangible changes in patterns of drinking had occurred. Yet ordinary male colonists had continued to drink collectively

17. Dickerson, ed., *Boston under Military Rule*, 88.

in taverns, as necessary for defining and maintaining a local collective mentality. There were limits to the reform of drinking habits, beyond which the mass of colonists refused to move. Colonists invoked traditional values when they pressed licensing authorities to grant them licenses because of need. Drink continued to lubricate the mesh of human relationships throughout the social hierarchy. Massachusetts remained a society organized in tavern companies as well as congregations.

On this foundation a contrary development enhanced the importance of collective drinking in taverns. Puritan rulers sought to regulate taverns closely not just to reform behavior but also to preserve hierarchy. Pious rulers like Sewall acted to prevent collective drinking from undermining a hierarchal society of ranks and degrees. But when Massachusetts became a royal colony, this hierarchy bifurcated into elected representatives and appointed crown officers. Suspicion and criticism of royal officials had become rife, sanctioned even by native leaders of high status. Tavern assemblies were drawn into this opposition; the regulation of taverns had virtually collapsed at the same time as colonial leaders were challenging the power and policies of royal governors. In country towns as well as Boston, taverns had become settings for the renegotiation and transmutation of political values and assumptions. The principle and practice of hierarchy gradually weakened. While the church had purged itself of the popular culture of drink, taverns had become centers for the flowering and propagation of a new, secular, protorepublican political culture.

Thus when figures like Americanus appealed for reform of the popular culture of drink, their entreaties flew in the face of the actualities of political transformation. Theoretically the "Republic" must be purged of habitual collective drinking, especially of rum, in public houses. But, actually, taverns were where republican concepts gripped men's imaginations and unleashed new levels of participation. Here the novel but appealing republican ideal of an alert, active citizenry might be acted out in a setting that was also traditional and familiar. Here men interacted with each other on a common level, citizens all. Collective drinking at taverns could not be purged from the new political order that colonists were groping to establish, for such gatherings were important seedbeds of the new order. But if they were seedbeds of the new order, they also represented a potential loss of all order: tavern assemblies might act without restraint and go beyond the goals of native leaders. Much of the overriding concern with the maintenance of order in resistance stems from the anxiety over indiscriminate gatherings at public houses where local gentry possessed little influence.

This professed desire and necessity for reformation, which permeates the rhetoric of resistance in the 1760s and 1770s, must be measured against the actual need to use taverns and drink as mediums for the mobilization of colonists to repudiate crown policies and eventually monarchy itself. For on closer examination taverns were central to the formation of public opinion. It was difficult to impose restraints on collective drinking and related speech and amusement in taverns when they had simultaneously become points for the distribution of appeals for resistance and contexts for ordinary men to assert themselves more aggressively in speech and posture on issues of imperial scope. The Revolution sparked a more complete integration of the popular culture of tavern assemblies into provincial and imperial politics, not a repudiation of it. Leaders anxiously groped for a balance between the exigencies of mobilization and the ideal of reform—and often sacrificed the latter.[18]

Just as in the 1710s, reformers encountered limits to proposed changes in tavern and drink use. While the Boston Town meeting might have instructed its representatives to advocate that the House discourage the consumption of rum in 1767, selectmen simultaneously approved an expansion in the number of houses selling it. In 1765, 1 in every 13 houses sold alcohol, and there was 1 tavern for every 79 adult males. The arrival of troops in 1768 increased the demand for alcohol, and selectmen approved an increase in the number of public houses despite fierce criticism of the troops' behavior and resolves to break up "bad houses." Whereas only 23 new houses received approval in 1764–1765, selectmen approved 62 new drinksellers in 1768 and 1769. Petitions for licenses soared. In the countryside, the number of houses continued to climb steeply. Middlesex County witnessed an increase in public houses from 195 to 231, or 18 percent, in the five years between 1765 and 1770.[19] Sentiment for reforma-

18. Some individual clergymen also played a decisive role in mobilization, but the clergy as a whole often followed rather than instigated popular acts of protest. Moreover, they tried to present the affirmation of civil liberties as an instrument for the revival of piety and the reformation of vice. Yet the use of taverns and drink to organize and incite resistance suggests popular indifference or ambivalence to calls for reformation. For the content of clerical sermons in this era, see Harry S. Stout, *The New England Soul*, 262, 264–268, 271–275, 287–289. Richard D. Brown argues that clergymen were far more concerned with "spiritual" than "political" salvation. Few achieved the status of dominant patriarchs in their communities during these years. See *Knowledge Is Power: The Diffusion of Information in Early America, 1700–1865* (New York, 1989), 74–77.

19. Boston, Record Commissioners, *Selectmen's Minutes from 1764 through 1768*, 84, 86, 170, 184, 221, 222, 238, 251, 264, 270, 271, 282, 289, 304; *Selectmen's Minutes from 1769*

tion stopped short of action by either local or provincial authorities against the incidence of houses selling drink. Licensing officials acceded to popular demand as they sought to engage popular support.

Drinksellers, and particularly distillers and merchants in drink, also were active in leading the resistance from the outset. Overall, at least 26 of the 355 Sons of Liberty identified in 1769 had retail or tavernkeeping licenses in 1765 or acquired them in the next few years. Of the 89 men licensed in Boston in 1765, 20 can definitely be identified as Sons. Thus about 1 in 5 male drinksellers helped to form the leadership of the resistance in its early stages. Other drinksellers might have been warm supporters. Of the 26 Sons who held licenses, 19 were retailers, and at least some of this 19 sold in considerable volume. Of the 28 distillers and wine merchants in town, 12 attended a Sons of Liberty celebration in 1769, another 5 were supporters of resistance, and only 7 chose to remain loyal. The rest remained neutral or died before a choice had to be made. Seven of the distillers who were Sons held retail licenses.[20]

---

through April, 1775 (Boston, 1893), 29; Court of General Sessions, Middlesex, Record Book, 1761–1771, 254–257, 516–518, Judicial Archives, ACM.

License Approvals and Disapprovals in Boston

	1764	1765	1766	1767	1768	1769
Approved	10	13	11	27ᵃ	30	32
Disapproved			35	28ᵇ	26	31

ᵃPlus 4 later approved. ᵇMinus 4 later approved.

20. The Sons of Liberty who held tavern licenses were Capt. John Marston, Joseph Moreton, Joseph Jackson, Joshua Brackett, John May, Ezekiel Cheever (distiller who becomes a tavernkeeper in 1769), and Stephen Greenleaf. Sons who held retail licenses were John Avery, Esq. (also a distiller), Thomas Chase (distiller), Caleb Davis, John Hancock, Esq., Henry Hill, John Hill, Esq., Daniel Henshaw, Zachariah Johonnot, Esq. (distiller), Andrew Johonnot (distiller), John Ingersol, Ephraim May, Isaac Pierce (distiller), James Richardson, Ebenezer Seaver, John Waldo, Enoch Brown, Thomas Knox, John Scollay, Esq., James Thompson. An Alphabetical List of the Sons of Liberty Who Dined at Liberty Tree, Dorchester, Aug. 14, 1765, MHS; List of Innholders and Retailers of Strong Drink, Boston, June 14, 1765, MHS. Son John Greaton had been a tavernkeeper in Roxbury (Names of Persons Licensed in the County of Suffolk, 1758, MHS). Andrew Johonnot is identified as a distiller in *Selectmen's Minutes from 1764 through 1768*, 265; John Scollay, 192; Ezekiel Cheever, Jr., 305. Cheever is approved to be a tavernkeeper in 1769 at his distilling house near Rainsford Square in *Selectmen's Minutes from 1769 through April, 1775*, 29; James Thompson, 27. Johnson Jackson, a distiller, was probably brother to Joseph Jackson, tavernkeeper and Son of Liberty, because Johnson left clothes to "brother Joseph Jackson" in his will (Suffolk County Probate Records, LXXV, 211, Inventory, LXXIV, 147, LXXV,

Some of these distillers manufactured and sold spirits in substantial quantities. Zachariah Johonnot owned two distilleries worth twenty-four hundred pounds. His relation Francis Johonnot had 4,113 gallons of molasses in stock in 1775, together with 1,316 gallons of New England and West India rum. Johnson Jackson, brother to tavernkeeper and Son Joseph Jackson, had 916 gallons of New England and West India rum in his distillery in 1774. Merchant, retailer, and Son Enoch Brown had 2,000 gallons of Malaga, Tenerife, claret, and Fayall wines as well as 102 gallons of brandy in 1784. A select group of Sons, including several artisans, made Thomas Chase's distillery their meeting place in 1776. John Avery, another distiller, was present at a meeting when they planned the celebration of the repeal of the Stamp Act.[21]

These tavernkeepers, retailers, and distillers developed close ties with civil and militia officers through meetings of the Sons. The five Boston selectmen were also Sons. Of the 355 Sons who assembled in 1769, 28 were also active or retired captains in the militia. These officers had become notorious for their "entertainments" of the rank and file with drink. Thus it is not surprising that selectmen took no action against the rum trade or the incidence of houses between 1765 and 1776.[22] Selectmen and drinksellers worked together in the organization of protest. The manufacturers and importers of the most controversial commodity in the province and the colonial world stood at the very helm of the resistance movement.

Captain John Marston, the tavernkeeper and wine merchant who kept the Golden Ball Tavern on Merchants Row off King Street in the 1760s until he took over the Bunch of Grapes on King Street in 1775, also became a Son of Liberty. He kept a well-appointed tavern. Indeed, he possessed many of the "luxuries" that critics condemned as the ruin of the simple and virtuous manners of the people. Marston could serve tea and coffee using not only chinaware but a silver teapot, a tea urn, and thirty-four silver

---

222, Judicial Archives, ACM). The 28 distillers and wine merchants are identified in John W. Tyler, *Smugglers and Patriots: Boston Merchants and the Advent of the American Revolution* (Boston, 1986), 258–277.

21. Inventory of Zachariah Johonnot, Suffolk County Probate Records, LXXXIII, 482–486; Francis Johonnot, LXXIV, 415–420; Enoch Brown, LXXXVI, 475. The meeting at Chase's distillery is mentioned in Butterfield *et al.*, eds., *Diary and Autobiography of Adams*, I, 294.

22. The six Boston selectmen in 1769 were Joshua Henshaw, Joseph Jackson, John Hancock, Samuel Pemberton, Henderson Inches, and Jonathan Mason. Two named Joseph Jackson are on the 1769 list of Sons—one of them was a tavernkeeper and might also have been the selectman. The militia captains are identified on the 1769 list.

spoons. He accommodated large numbers of patrons to drink and dine, owning forty-eight wine glasses, forty-eight plates and pewterware, and no fewer than 288 knives and forks of bone and ivory handles. Fourteen paintings and prints adorned his walls. Newspapers and documents could be read at night with the aid of eighteen candlesticks, four sconces, and a lamp. Many of the Sons could meet comfortably at the tavern, since there were eighty-four chairs and seven benches. When he died in the 1780s he had only 20 gallons of rum and brandy on hand besides a pipe (92 gallons) of Madeira. But at an earlier date he had transferred 450 gallons of rum to his son. Fellow Sons also operated taverns on School Street on the Common, at Haymarket bordering the North End, at Rainsford Square near Boston Neck, and in the South End. Of the nineteen Sons who sold by retail (themselves or through hired help), the locations of four can be ascertained—on Boston Neck, off King Street on Cornhill, in the South End, and near the Fortification at the entrance to the town.[23] Sons sold drink, extended credit, and conversed with patrons in all parts of the town.

Marston's collection of books for his library suggests that he had a keen interest in history; he owned an unidentified eleven-volume history of England, a history of New England (probably by Hutchinson), and books on Oliver Cromwell and the Russian czars. He had also digested Addison and Steele's *Spectator;* his library included eight volumes of it. Marston also admired Jonathan Swift's essays, having an eight-volume edition that included "The Public Spirit of the Whigs." He had lately acquired the important Whig publications that London opposition leader John Wilkes published in the 1760s, the two-volume *North Briton.* These volumes championed liberty and reform in the face of English "corruption" and "oppression." Wilkes was a colonial hero. Marston also owned a four-volume work noted simply as "Whig," Defoe's *Robinson Crusoe,* the letters of *Theron and Aspasia* (an inquiry into the laws of nature), and Milton's *Paradise Lost.* Seventeen other books, including a two-volume *Geographical Grammar,* rounded out his library. Besides these books, Marston also purchased "sundry pamphlets," undoubtedly leading works of resistance writ-

23. Inventory of John Marston, Suffolk County Probate Records, Record Book, LXXXVI, 12, identified as innholder in his will, LXXXV, 592, died insolvent in 1786, XCIII, 42. Bracket was located on School St. (*Selectmen's Minutes from 1764 through 1768,* 304); Greenleaf near Haymarket (304); Morton in the South End (58); retailer Brown on Boston Neck (221); Knox on Cornhill (265); Davis near Fortification (258); Johonnot at Long Lane (*Selectmen's Minutes from 1769 through 1775,* 29).

ers.[24] This tavernkeeper at the heart of the town's public concourse had the appropriate reading background to lead and participate in discussions of the growing estrangement of the colonies in his public rooms from a Whig historical perspective.

Marston's fellow Son Zachariah Johonnot, a distiller who also sold his rum by retail, owned an even more extensive eighty-three volume library, including two volumes of the Whig history of England by Paul de Rapin-Thoyras and a historical dictionary. Another Son and merchant retailer Enoch Brown owned six volumes of Roman history and a two-volume history of the Netherlands by Gravesend, all reference books for the rise and fall of republics. Brown also owned a *Book of Constitutions*, two volumes on Cromwell, the earl of Clarendon's *History of England*, another four-volume history of England, and Buchanan's *History*, probably his *History of Scotland*. Clement Collins, a merchant retailer who was not listed as a Son in 1769, owned a ninety-six volume library and "pamphlets."[25]

The libraries of these drinksellers active in the resistance suggest that Whig opposition ideology framed their response to crown policies in the 1760s. They did not own the full panoply of Whig histories and commentaries, but they owned enough to underscore the importance of this historical perspective in shaping political thought. They possessed books that emphasized the fragility of republics in the past and the analogous dangers confronting the delicate balance of England's constitutional monarchy in the present. These books offered a framework within which these Sons could assess the threat to the chartered governments of the colonies by the Stamp Act and the troops. Of course, drinksellers like Marston, and particularly distillers like Johonnot, were directly affected by the new duties and restrictions of the Sugar Act. Economic interests were also at stake. The Sugar Act stiffened the earlier, unenforced regulations of the Molasses Act (1733) and tightened customs regulations long evaded by various means. And the Stamp Act would have made the newspapers provided by tavernkeepers more expensive. Still, it was the implications of these acts that excited the fears and passions of these Sons. The readings by these drinksellers in the history of ancient and modern republics and in Whig histories such as Rapin's history of England could shape their conceptual-

24. Inventory of John Marston, Suffolk County Probate Records, Record Book, LXXXVI, 12.

25. Inventory of Zachariah Johonnot, Suffolk County Probate Records, Record Book, LXXXIII, 482–486; Enoch Brown, LXXXVI, 473–475; Clement Collins, LXXXVI, 273–275. Zachariah's relation Peter Johonnot, also a distiller, did become a loyalist (Tyler, *Smugglers and Patriots*, appendix, 258–277).

ization of the Sugar and Stamp acts as initiatives by the crown in violation of the ancient liberties guaranteed by the British constitution. They were an opening wedge, a dangerous precedent, in a world where liberty was under constant assault from power.

The emphasis on private and public virtue in these Whig writings and histories, however, would also seem to create a dilemma for drinksellers active in the resistance, and particularly distillers like the Johonnots with their thousands of gallons of molasses and hundreds of gallons of New England and West India rum. Whig opposition writers in England expressed deep alarm over the invasion of luxury and the epidemic of vice among the gentry and the populace at large. In the 1760s the emulative criticism in the colonies of rum and the behavior and values associated with it directly and indirectly targeted distillers and merchants in drink as well as tavernkeepers and retailers as agents contributing to the corruption of New England society. The logic of Whig thought called for agitation against the rum trade, an expansion of the resolves of the 1760s. Distillers like the Johonnots, who had made their fortunes in the drink trade, would expectedly be put on the defensive as the discourse on relative virtue mounted amid increasing political participation by common men.

But this discourse against rum and taverns did not increase in the 1760s, or it remained so abstracted in resolutions against idleness and in support of industry that it did not pose a direct challenge to prominent members of the drink trade, some of them active as Sons. Ultimately, the Sons of Liberty as a whole, the men closest to the popular manifestations of resistance, chose to ignore, deflect, or deemphasize the criticism of luxury insofar as it affected the trade in rum and wine, the luxuries in most universal demand. Although rum had been the focus of social criticism since the late seventeenth century by Puritans, and with added meaning after 1765 by Republicans, it was tea that became the popular symbol of virtuous sacrifice during the mounting resistance in the late 1760s and early 1770s. Of course, the imposition of duties on tea in 1767 and the Tea Act of 1773 invested this beverage with a constitutional significance. But the Sugar Act had also made rum and molasses commodities of controversy in imperial affairs. It was the contrasting rate of and context for the consumption of rum versus tea that contributed to the mass enthusiasm for repudiation of the latter and the muffled criticism of the former.

The Sons' tendency to deflate and deemphasize republican criticism of rum in Massachusetts society is evident in the decision of fifteen Associates, ten of whom can definitely be identified as Sons, to commission jointly an elaborate, expensive silver punch bowl in 1768 from Paul Revere. One

Plate 8. Sons of Liberty Silver Punch Bowl. *Made by Paul Revere, 1768. Courtesy, Museum of Fine Arts, Boston*

of the Associates was John Marston, at whose tavern the bowl was probably used most often. In its inscriptions the bowl reflects the maturation of a public freely gathering in public houses to discuss matters of state. The Associates constructed no hierarchy among themselves, and each of their fifteen names was inscribed around the rim of the bowl. On one side of the bowl a decorative inscription honored key historical and contemporary texts that justified resistance—John Wilkes's pamphlet *North Briton No.*

Forty-Five, the Magna Charta, and the English Bill of Rights.[26] The Associates, coming together to drink and converse over this common bowl, identified themselves as members and descendants of the people, or public, named in these documents as possessors of rights inviolable by kings. Collective drinking in taverns had gradually become an important context for the coalescence of a critical public outside the institutions of state, so it was natural that these Associates should decide on a rum punch bowl as a material symbol of their free discourse over and examination of certain printed texts, ancient and modern. The bowl symbolized the relatively recent and gradual integration of printed discourse with the oral culture of tavern assemblies. Those fifteen wanted their membership in this novel new public immortalized.

As these genteel drinkers recognized, the collective drinking of rum had become so thoroughly enmeshed in the political discourse of men that it stood impervious to reform. Recruitment of ordinary colonists to participate in acts of resistance became an integral part of Whig tactics as early as 1765. Leaders cultivating contact with colonists at all levels of society risked alienation if they insisted on the sacrifice of rum in the name of civic virtue. Rum had been incorporated into traditional drinking; it was now a staple in the popular culture of drink. Tea, on the other hand, was a safe article to boycott and, eventually, to destroy, because this luxury was associated with elite equipage, special etiquette, and rituals orchestrated mainly by women. The latter had been particular targets of criticism for the promotion of this vice since midcentury. This "genteel custom impoverishes the country" because of the "vast sums of money" continually "sent abroad to support it," yet "fine ladies will hardly be persuaded to break this rule of politeness." Moreover, the growing demand for it among lesser women (which their husbands might not share) further clouded the distinctions of rank so many colonists craved so as to render such demarcations meaningless. Even "maids and washer-women follow this polite custom," making it "quite vulgar" as "every common jilt treats with tea."[27]

26. Kathryn C. Buhler, *American Silver, 1655–1825, in the Museum of Fine Arts* (Boston, 1972), II, 408–409.

27. Rodris Roth, "Tea Drinking in Eighteenth-Century America: Its Etiquette and Equipage," *Contributions from the Museum of History and Technology* (Washington D.C., 1969), 61–91; *Boston Gazette*, Nov. 17, 1747, no. 1339. A passage from Adams's diary in 1759 reveals the social distance that could separate habitual tea drinkers from drinkers in general: "She [a tavernkeeper] told the behavior of the people at the tavern they were at in the country about the tea, before all the Monatiquot officers, shoe string fellows that never

While repudiating the feminizing luxury of tea, men of all ranks could unite through collective drinking of rum at taverns that facilitated the airing of opposition discourse. Thus it was not just the fact that many prominent Sons were drinksellers and distillers that diminished the enthusiasm for the sacrifice of rum. It was a vital lubricant in establishing lines of communication and trust with the mass of white male colonists who composed the public.

In this endeavor the hierarchy among drinking establishments in Boston presented problems to Boston Sons seeking to mobilize tavern companies to orderly resistance. Literate, well-read tavernkeepers like Marston occupied the top rungs of this hierarchy (although he would eventually die insolvent). Marston could dispense books and pamphlets or arguments drawn from them to the literate gentry or tradesmen to whom he catered on Merchants Row and King Street. So also could Ezekial Cheever—Son, justice, and tavernkeeper in Rainsford Square near Boston Neck by 1769. Three other tavernkeepers who died in the 1760s owned libraries. But the licensing system continued to be used to extend relief to the poor, injured, and aged. The majority of licenseholders in Boston might not have participated in the culture of print often, some not at all. Frances Warden, a former housewright turned tavernkeeper, died in 1776 and left no printed material in his estate. Neither did tavernkeepers Captain Moses Bennett and William Campbell, who died in 1770 and 1773, respectively.[28] If these men were mobilized to participate in resistance, or celebrate it, it was not because of printed materials they had read personally, with the possible exception of newspapers. Presumably they and the more humble tavernkeepers and retailers beneath them served patrons with ties just as tenuous to the culture of print. Unlike Marston, they were not equipped to lead discussions of the historical and philosophical dimensions of the crisis in relations with England.

But such men and dozens like them presided over important public space, rituals of fellowship, and webs of connection. They and their customers must be reached. At the same time, it was imperative that these

---

use tea and would use it as [awkwardly?] as the landlady did. It was designed to divert and please, but it had a contrary effect. It made them all jealous and suspicious that they were remarked and laughed at as much as to the next company" (Butterfield *et al.*, eds., *Diary and Autobiography of Adams*, I, 114).

28. Inventory of George Tilley, Suffolk County Probate Records, Record Book, LIX, 330–333; Anthony Bracket, docket no. 13394; John Ridgeway, LX, 355; Frances Warden, docket no. 13864; Moses Bennett, docket no. 14793; William Campbell, LXXII, 539.

patrons of modest and mean houses be discouraged from taking unilateral action such as in August 1765, when a mob ransacked Lieutenant Governor Thomas Hutchinson's house. Thus the leaders of the Sons of Liberty consciously sought to dramatize and communicate the necessity of resistance, and of order in resistance, by means that could be understood and appreciated by the less literate patrons of King Street and neighborhood taverns. Yet, in doing so, the Sons further compromised the spirit of reformation that so many spokesmen like Americanus deemed so vital to the character and ultimate success of the movement. Now the Whig leaders cultivated evil customs, which Mather and other ministers had condemned in the early eighteenth century as a creeping corruption of civic life, in new forms in order to provide a street and tavern stage from which to influence public opinion and instill social unity throughout all the various layers of Boston society.

The repeal of the Stamp Act and its anniversary, for example, became an event celebrated with drink in the 1760s and 1770s. To complement fireworks, the decoration of the Liberty Tree with flags, and the construction of a pyramid on the Common with 280 lamps in 1766, Son and retailer John Hancock distributed at least one pipe of Madeira (92 gallons) to the populace in the streets.[29] Other retailers and distillers among the Sons probably made similar contributions; they had ample supplies of liquor upon which to draw. At such occasions, collective drinking in the streets by all ranks transcended the ordinary stratification of public houses on King and other streets. Sponsored by the wealthy, the Sons provided the context and the alcohol for hundreds of Bostonians to drink the health of leaders who had communicated such vital and revealing explanations to the people about recent acts of Parliament.

It seems a cutting irony that so many manufacturers and purveyors of strong drink on a large scale should also be prominent leaders of the resistance to British corruption, when strong drink and numerous taverns had for so long been criticized as subversive of Massachusetts society. But merchants in drink on a large scale had always ignored this discourse. They and their predecessors perceived the popular culture of drink as a base from which to construct a profitable, capitalist, international trade in distilled liquors. They had introduced rum into collective village drinking, transforming the popular culture of drink in sometimes insidious ways.

29. Caleb H. Snow, *A History of Boston, the Metropolis of Massachusetts, from Its Origin to the Present* . . . , 2d ed. (Boston, 1828), 263–264, 267; *Boston Evening-Post*, May 26, 1766, no. 1602.

Farmers across Massachusetts produced a surplus in part to purchase that most popular of luxuries—rum. These merchants and distillers supplied the multiplying drinksellers accused of helping to manage and influence elections. There was not much republican virtue in this commerce. Indeed, they were at the ultimate root of the need for internal reform at the outset of constitutional crisis.

Rather than stigmatize the movement they helped to lead as hypocritical or shallow, however, this irony catches the conflicting impulses and pressures in which colonists were caught up. These merchants in drink and their predecessors had also created market networks in a multitude of exchanges across the Atlantic trading world that permitted colonists to dispose of their produce. They had carved out a place for Massachusetts to occupy in the empire that allowed the colony to import manufactured goods. And they were quick to defend that place in the face of new imperial restrictions on colonial trade. Moreover, these merchants and manufacturers of rum were among those most ready to communicate the necessity of resistance to British policy on constitutional grounds to the populace at large and to invite them to greater participation in provincial politics. They sanctioned the flowering of the tavern-based political culture that had been developing in Massachusetts since 1720, even at the risk of weakening deference to the exalted positions they had come to occupy in Boston society. While critics like Americanus might identify and criticize cracks in their logic and contradictions in their strategies, these merchants in drink swept over them, caught up themselves in resistance to figures at the top of the governing hierarchy. Rather than becoming the objects of criticism for their contribution to the corruption of Massachusetts society, they made crown officers a focus of resentment, eventually hatred, among Bostonians at large by using taverns as a base from which to shape the issues unleashed by British policies and legislation.

Even John Adams—one of the most vehement critics of treating and bribery in the early 1760s—came to approve of the Sons' tactics. He recognized the importance and necessity of celebrations and ceremonies framed by a liberal distribution of drink. In 1769 he attended the annual anniversary of the resistance to the Stamp Act, which had led to the resignation of stamp agent Andrew Oliver. Adams ate a dinner on the grounds of a Dorchester Son's tavern with three hundred other Sons. At the dinner the group drank exactly forty-five toasts to various personages and things. They chose the number "forty-five" to honor the important pamphlet written by John Wilkes, the *North Briton No. Forty-Five*. After the toasts, the group indulged in mimicry and the singing of the Liberty Song. The entire group rode in processional display back across the neck to Boston.[30]

Like the meeting of the Associates, this was a gathering that cultivated links between the world of print and the oral culture of taverns. The toasting of a particular pamphlet helped to bridge the gap between the literate and the less literate, between the readers of pamphlets and those who learned of the meaning of events through taverns. Toasts to the pamphlet drew attention to its contents and message and stimulated efforts to communicate simplified versions of it. Such meetings forced leading Sons to articulate their fears about British policies in the most simple and direct terms. And what could be more simple and direct than a series of toasts that, when printed in the newspapers, could be reenacted in similar gatherings in taverns throughout the colony? Indeed, the dinner at Robinson's tavern could serve as a model for Sons in inland towns reading of it. Such gatherings also helped to invest royal officials with a greater aura of treachery, deceit, and secrecy. *They* remained outside these festive gatherings of leaders and people, *removed* from the people, and *dependent* on their patrons in England. Suspicions concerning the private correspondence of crown officers with English patrons were heightened. So Adams put aside his distaste for the mixture of drink and politics and concluded that James Otis and Samuel Adams "are politic in promoting these festivals, for they tinge the minds of the people, they impregnate them with sentiments of liberty" and "render the people fond of their leaders in the cause."[31]

Of course, such strategies continued to be condemned as unrepublican. A writer to the *New-London Gazette* in 1768 believed that more effort should be made to educate the people and less in offering toasts of liquor. Specifically, he advocated that John Dickinson's *Farmer's Letters* be printed in a "neat pocket volume" as a companion for "every British American" who dares to be "free." By forwarding such a project gentlemen would better serve their country "than is or can be done by toasting" Wilkes, Dickinson, or others. A later writer to a Boston paper, who had read of "loyal toasts" and "patriotic toasts," attacked this ritual as a heathen "devotion" that the founders of Massachusetts had repudiated. This writer cited a meeting of ministers presided over by Increase Mather eighty years before as proof that such behavior was unlawful for Christians.[32] Such

30. Butterfield *et al.*, eds., *Diary and Autobiography of Adams*, I, 341.

31. *Ibid.*

32. *New-London Gazette*, Aug. 5, 1768, no. 247; *Massachusetts Gazette; and the Boston Weekly News-Letter*, Sept. 2, 1773, no. 3090. The advocate for "pocket volumes" wanted the

criticisms, however, did not deter the Sons from using drink and taverns to organize and focus popular sentiment and to construct linkages between the world of print and the oral discourse of taverns. They acted in the tradition of Cooke, not Sewall.

To be sure, the Sons of Liberty always emphasized that such festivals and meetings had been conducted with the greatest "order" and decorum. The Sons were sensitive to criticism that they sanctioned expensive drinking events when so many called for reformation and sacrifice. They also feared popular protest that went beyond symbolic gestures like the burning of effigies. At a 1766 celebration of the Stamp Act resistance, the Sons took care to toast their "detestation of the villainous proceedings of the 26th of August last," the day when a mob destroyed Thomas Hutchinson's house. At the celebration of 1769, Adams claimed that he saw no one drunk or near it.[33] The Sons probably discouraged drunkenness, lest it give ammunition to critics. Still, the Sons broke with, instead of affirming, the ideals of the Puritan founders. They anticipated the democratic electoral tactics of the early nineteenth century rather than evoked Puritan virtues. The expansion of drinking holidays that the Sons organized represents yet another compromise of the standards of alcohol use articulated and codified into law by the first generations. Leaders such as Samuel Adams and the numerous drinksellers who surrounded him sought a delicate balance between the preeminent ideal of order in resistance on the one hand and the need to arouse and excite the populace on the other. And by their efforts they groped toward a fresh perception of the actual process of

---

act of citizenship to be closely linked to private readings of republican literature, which was in fact a principle of republican virtue. But the Sons consistently sought to synthesize the new importance of this discourse with formal and informal gatherings to drink, to assemble a symbolic public gathering outside institutions of government. For many colonists, participation in these assemblies was crucial to investing meaning to the public represented in print. See Michael Warner, *The Letters of the Republic: Publication and the Public Sphere in Eighteenth-Century America* (Cambridge, Mass., 1990), 39.

33. Pauline Maier, *From Resistance to Revolution: Colonial Radicals and the Development of American Opposition to Britain, 1765–1776* (New York, 1974), 63; Butterfield *et al.*, eds., *Diary and Autobiography of Adams*, I, 341. Restraint and order were not always in evidence. But I believe that the leaders of the resistance, and the rank and file of colonists active in crowd actions, acted far more in concert than not, in part because tavernkeepers and retailers helped to infuse a loose discipline into resistance by providing linkages of communication between leaders and followers. For a different emphasis, see Gary B. Nash, *The Urban Crucible: Social Change, Political Consciousness, and the Origins of the American Revolution* (Cambridge, Mass., 1979); Jesse Lemisch, "Jack Tar in the Streets: Merchant Seamen in the Politics of Revolutionary America," *WMQ*, 3d Ser., XXV (1968), 371–407.

political transformation in Massachusetts long under way, a process at odds with republican theory and models.

The reformation of manners and habits considered so vital by critics like Americanus also suffered because the very officials responsible for the enforcement of the drink laws, the justices of the peace, came under attack as a group early in the resistance. The fact that justices received their appointments from the royal governor at his pleasure had long made them objects of suspicion. Royal governors from Phips to Belcher to Bernard had always tried to use this power of patronage to create a loyal governor's party in the House, a ploy at odds with the nascent popular political culture developing in town politics. Now such tactics assumed a still more malevolent aura of manipulation and deceit in the wake of the Sugar and Stamp acts. Fresh efforts to manipulate the House membership through appointments to the bench began to be considered part of a program with the ultimate purpose of abridging colonial liberties.

Sentiment quickly developed after the Stamp Act to remove all justices from the House who did not demonstrate open support for the opposition. As early as 1766 the *Gazette* and the *Post* published a list of thirty-one representatives who held appointments as justices. A writer to the *Post* advised that their constituents scrutinize the conduct and views of these justices in and out of the House in order to determine whether "they have not been tools to a party, nor frightened nor wheedled into measures destructive of the civil constitution." If so, then "their names ought to be hung up, and exposed to contempt, not only in the most public places in their own towns, but also in every town in the province." Men that are "unshackled with posts and preferments" should be elected instead.[34] Although it is doubtful that such lists of suspected tools of the governor were posted in every town, it is probable that they were publicized in the taverns of towns at which county sessions were convened—the shire towns of Boston, Cambridge, Plymouth, Worcester, Taunton, Barnstable, Salem, and Northampton. The conduct of tavernkeepers coming to renew their licenses annually before the justices in these towns ordinarily was reviewed by his majesty's justices of the peace. Now tavernkeepers were urged, with their patrons, to monitor the conduct of justices closely, especially if they held seats in the House.

A Son of Liberty from Bristol County went to still greater lengths to fan suspicion of justices. Writing to the *Post* in 1766, he criticized the blending

34. *Boston Evening-Post,* Apr. 28, 1766, no. 1598.

of executive and legislative authority in one person (by electing justices to the House). He condemned them as "creatures and dupes of men in higher, or supreme authority." Such "rulers" are "safely secured in their places, and the ruled kept in awe by their understrappers." Justices and other appointed officials, he continued, are always in "dread of losing their commissions." A recent shower of appointments to the bench, by which "justices run down our streets as a stream," could only be a prelude to "a still more abundant effusion of their worships" together with new laws fixing their fees for their attendance at courts. The people should not stand in "awe" of these men. Nor should they be elected representatives. "It is to be hoped," this Son concluded, "that the towns in general will make choice of Sons of Liberty for their representatives," men who can "espouse the cause of liberty" without fear.[35]

Such sentiments proved persuasive in the towns. Despite the rash of new appointments made by Bernard to the bench, the proportion of members of the House who also held judicial appointments fell from 68 percent in 1765 to 40 percent in 1772, and to 30 percent in 1774.[36] The House was transformed from an Assembly dominated by men who held crown appointments to one controlled by Sons of Liberty or their sympathizers. The political authority of justices, who regulated the popular culture of drink, was weakened by the Sons of Liberty, who embraced the popular culture of drink. Whereas once men elected to the House had been charged with the responsibility of suppressing tavern assemblies, they now became dependent on currents of opinion forming in taverns. The entire hierarchy of officials, elected and appointed, came under scrutiny as to their devotion to the will and interests of the people.

As Governor Bernard and those linked to him through patronage came under closer inspection and sometimes excited attack in the press during the late 1760s, their stature as men of authority, men who customarily received postures and words of esteem and deference, diminished. Justices were torn between their ties to the crown and the mounting pressures of popular sentiment. Lord Hillsborough repeatedly instructed Bernard to eliminate justices who did not punish mobs harassing those merchants

35. *Ibid.*, Apr. 21, 1766, no. 1597.

36. The percentage drop is taken from John M. Murrin, Review Essay, *History and Theory*, XI (1972), 270. The drop was not solely a consequence of justices' being voted out of office, since the number of representatives sent by the towns nearly tripled during this period, from 116 in 1763 to 303 in 1776 (*Acts and Resolves*, XVI, 378–379, XIX, 418–419). In either case the justices of the county sessions felt the pressure of popular sentiment if they also held seats in the House. Of course, some were ardent Whigs from the start.

who violated the boycott of British goods adopted to resist the Townshend Duties. But Bernard did not dare to divest Whig justices of their commissions, or other justices intimidated by the mobs. Belcher had used such tactics in 1741 against the Land Bankers. Openly, Bernard ventured only to create new justices in the hope that they would remain more loyal to his person and dampen the excited opposition rhetoric of leading members of the Assembly. But this strategy only sparked more severe criticism of the governor and suspicion of the character of new justices.[37] Bostonians held crown officials, especially customs officers, in such odium that it became more and more difficult for officials and military men under Bernard's patronage and command to mix in public companies, especially those dominated by Sons of Liberty.

The British Coffee House at the end of King Street on Long Wharf, however, still welcomed crown officials—a house where they could feel at ease. Operated by Cord Cordis and his wife, Hannah, it was in some ways less ornate than the Crown Coffee House had been in the 1710s. No paintings or prints hung on the walls, and Cordis did not own even one silver punch bowl. Selby had owned eight. Cordis was less wealthy and had only one hundred gallons of rum in stock as opposed to Selby's 691 gallons, and two pipes of Madeira wine (184 gallons) as opposed to Selby's twelve pipes (1,100 gallons). Along with less volume, there was less variety. Two slaves helped to operate the tavern instead of Selby's four.[38]

Yet in other ways the British Coffee House eclipsed the Crown of the 1710s and reflects the expansion of the British establishment in Boston. There were eighty-six chairs and eight benches, far more than Selby had possessed. And Cordis could accommodate more overnight guests, with fifteen beds. Cordis could entertain large companies of officers and officials, having 338 plates on which to serve and 108 knives and forks. Selby had owned far fewer. Cordis could provide seventy-two drinkers with individual wine and beer glasses, as opposed to Selby's forty-two. It is also clear that Cordis could and did entertain far into the night, to large numbers of gentlemen in every room. He owned forty-seven candlesticks, twenty-four of them brass, and three lamps. Selby had owned fewer than half that number and only one lamp.[39] Almost everything was on a greater scale. This establishment could easily accommodate the influx of British officers who commanded the troops arriving in 1768. When assembled in

37. See Hiller B. Zobel, *The Boston Massacre* (New York, 1970), 85.

38. Inventory of Thomas Selby, Suffolk County Probate Records, Record Books, XXV, 530–535; Cord Cordis, LXXII, 137, docket no. 15192.

39. *Ibid.*, Cordis, LXXII, 137.

this beaming tavern at night, they must have seemed a formidable presence to Bostonians gathering in other public houses along King Street and environs.

But this Tory sanctuary in the heart of a town increasingly controlled by the Sons of Liberty was not immune to the violent feeling developing against crown officials. Emotions reached a higher pitch after the Sons obtained copies of letters written by Governor Bernard to the secretary of state together with the correspondence of several customs commissioners who frequented the Coffee House. In his letters, Bernard had urged that the governor's Council be changed from a board elected by the Assembly to one appointed by the crown and that the loyalty of crown officeholders in America be reviewed. This was alarming enough, new evidence of a conspiracy to reduce chartered liberties. But it was the letters of customs commissioners John Robinson and Henry Hulton that enraged leading radical James Otis the most, because he felt that they represented him as "disaffected to his majesty" rather than to his majesty's ministers. Consequently, the high-strung Otis marched down King Street on September 5, 1769, to the Coffee House to demand satisfaction from the customs commissioners. He quickly became involved in a brawl in the tavern, with onlookers and men from the street rushing to aid both sides. The treatment of Otis outraged the Sons. It was difficult to prosecute Robinson, the official who had hit Otis, but a civilian who had helped Robinson and who had remained hidden in the tavern for a day was routed out. A crowd of two thousand seized him and brought him to Faneuil Hall to stand before two Whig justices. A third justice loyal to the king's government tried to intervene but was hissed and eventually divested of his wig.[40] Anyone, even a justice of the peace, who dared to thwart the Sons of Liberty opened himself up to abuse by the crowds that sometimes went further than the leading Sons wished.

As the 1760s drew to a close, the authority of crown appointees had begun to ebb away. The courts still convened, cases were still heard, and the justices still exercised their authority to license houses for the sale of drink. But the judicial hierarchy that regulated public life proved helpless in the face of crowd actions against importers and customs commissioners. Even sanctuaries of crown officials like the British Coffee House near the seat of crown government could be overwhelmed by crowds forming in King Street. The Sons virtually controlled public space.

In this tense and troubled environment, former lieutenant governor and

40. Zobel, *The Boston Massacre*, 145–151: Bernard Bailyn, *The Ordeal of Thomas Hutchinson* (Cambridge, Mass., 1974), 130–132.

native merchant Thomas Hutchinson replaced the hapless Bernard as royal governor. Like Bernard, Hutchinson failed to mobilize justices to bring this new, extra-institutional public under control. In early 1770 he issued a declaration urging members of the Council and justices to terminate the extralegal meetings, christened as the "Body" of the people, convened to discuss the presence of the troops in the town. But the justices took no action. Meanwhile, the "Body" composed resolutions of its own. At the conclusion of one of its meetings it recommended that those resolutions be posted up "over the chimney piece of every public house, and on every other proper place, in every town," not only in Massachusetts but in all the colonies.[41] Boston's Whig leadership promoted the identification of tavern companies across the province with the "body" of the people physically realized in Boston meetings. This formal effort to post exhortations in taverns reflects the informal use of taverns by Sons to influence public opinion.

In a less challenging move to restore "public order," Hutchinson issued a proclamation for the encouragement of piety and virtue in 1771, a conventional expression of royal authority often exercised by royal governors. Once again, all judges, sheriffs, justices, and other officers, in descending rank, received orders to prosecute excessive drinking, blasphemy, profanation of the Lord's Day—and gaming and disorderly houses in particular. Yet in the early 1770s this exhortation to impose greater discipline over public life had an even more hollow ring than previous ones issued by a series of royal governors. If anything, controls over public houses, never very effective, were becoming more relaxed. The times were not propitious for reformation, no matter who urged it. A Natick minister struggling to combat the influence of local tavernkeepers, reiterating Puritan strictures against drunkenness, even went so far as to condemn from the pulpit those "Sons of Licentiousness" who "are known to be inclined to excess and would use their endeavors to intoxicate others."[42] Taverns had become centers for extralegal agitation, in some cases against the very hierarchy that Hutchinson pressed to shut down "disorderly" houses.

Hutchinson and other anxious observers had hoped that passions would cool after the repeal of the Townshend Duties (except on tea). A writer to the *Massachusetts Gazette* claimed to have met a farmer in 1770 at a country tavern who was convinced that such a change in sentiment had occurred,

41. Zobel, *The Boston Massacre*, 170–171.
42. *Massachusetts Gazette; and the Boston Weekly News-Letter*, Mar. 28, 1771, no. 3521; Stephen Badger, *The Nature and Effects of Drunkenness* ... (Boston, 1774), 24, 25, 26, 36, 39.

that "matters had been carried too far." The farmer claimed that the people in general were ashamed that they had so readily "lent an ear" to the Boston newspapers that "come among us." They were disillusioned with the "detraction, slander, and calumny" against "persons of the first character in the province."[43] This correspondent also claimed to have heard similar sentiments in other places along the road he traveled. Doubtless there were people in the countryside who remained skeptical in the early 1770s of the speculations about the ultimate intentions of crown ministers and their agents in Boston. True, these accusations had been given the sanction of print, but farmers in the interior routinely heard reports that often proved exaggerated or untrue.

Yet this writer might also have been indulging in wishful thinking or a propaganda ploy. Most writers to the *Massachusetts Gazette*, whose editor claimed to present both sides, were convinced that a swelling tide of Whig sentiment was overwhelming the countryside. The repeal of the Townshend Duties could not stop it. The manner of persuasion and argument in public and private companies frightened these observers. Orators promoted Whig viewpoints with such a passionate conviction that men were intimidated into conforming with radical sentiments. "Those who call themselves patriots," one writer complained, go into a "violent passion" if they encounter opposition. They think it "sufficient" if they "splutter out the words tyrannical, venal, corrupt, prostituted ministerial hirelings."[44] Such complaints testify to the success of Whig leaders in borrowing and elaborating a vocabulary of resistance that could be readily grasped and expressed by ordinary men in taverns and private companies. Animosity was personalized in the figures of current crown officials, and abstract constitutional grievances were given meaning by their actions.

Alarmed correspondents to the *Gazette* also complained of a change in the "nature and manners" of the "mass of the people." Common men asserted themselves more emphatically and did not hesitate to criticize figures in harsh terms. "Every obscure and unprincipled incendiary," another writer exclaimed, "stands forth daringly to commit every outrage against the character and persons of those who stand in the way of their detestable machinations." Anyone who speaks of "moderate measures" is immediately accused of being a "Tory" and an "enemy to his country."[45] Orators who would have been prosecuted in the 1720s for their words now

43. *Massachusetts Gazette; and the Boston Weekly News-Letter*, Dec. 5, 1771, no. 3457.

44. *Ibid.*, Feb. 20, 1772, no. 3468.

45. *Massachusetts Gazette Extraordinary* (supplement), Apr. 9, 1772.

not only shed all restraints in their assessment of their superiors but placed pressure on those hearing their words to agree.

Such excited sentiments circulating through taverns sometimes exploded into incidents unplanned by Whig leaders and over which they had no control. The bloody confrontation between a crowd on King Street and British soldiers guarding the Customs House in 1770—the Boston Massacre—is an example of a spontaneous outburst of festering antipathy between residents and the occupying army. But the Sons moved quickly to make the funeral of the victims into a disciplined display of unity among all ranks before the varied tavern companies that collected in different establishments along King Street. With the bells of the town's churches pealing, pallbearers carried two of the "victims who fell in the bloody massacre" from Faneuil Hall, "attended by a numerous train of persons of all ranks." Two others were borne from their families' houses to meet with the other hearses at the head of King Street, which the recorder of this event described as "the theater of that inhuman tragedy." This funeral was also "theater," artfully played on the busiest tavern-lined street in the town. There was no reason for the "immense concourse" of mourners to proceed down King Street other than to make a very public display of unity and order in resistance as well as of grief to the spectators on the street and in shop and tavern windows. "A long train of carriages belonging to the principle gentry of the town" followed the people of "all ranks" walking with the hearses.[46] Boston society put itself on display in a procession calculated to appeal to and include "all" those "ranks" and degrees of men who did not ordinarily drink and converse together in the stratified hierarchy of public houses in the town.

Whig leaders faithfully observed the anniversary of the massacre in the 1770s not only by an oration at the Old South Meeting House but by observances on King Street. In 1773 a "select number of the Friends of Constitutional Liberty" met "at Mrs. Clapham's in King Street" for a specific purpose. This might have been the same Mrs. Clapham who had once operated a public house in Merchants Row off King Street before her license was taken away for "misrule" in 1758.[47] If so, she was not only back in business but selected by Sons of Liberty for the display of several "transparent paintings" on her balcony. Lighted from behind by a lantern, they depicted the massacre and lessons drawn from it. Clapham's house

46. *Massachusetts Gazette; and the Boston Weekly News-Letter*, Mar. 15, 1770, no. 3467.

47. Boston, Record Commissioners, *Selectmen's Minutes from 1754 through 1763* (Boston, 1887), 93–95.

might have been chosen for this display not only because it was "near the spot" of the altercation but because she—like the widows Smallpeice, Wormall, Battersby, and others before her—catered to the lower ranks of Boston society. The "select number" of adherents of "constitutional liberty" could mix and converse, probably with the aid of drink, with the spectators of all ranks who gathered in the street and the house during the four to five hours that the luminous paintings were on display. By 1774 a new painting had been added to the annual display, depicting Governor Hutchinson and Justice Oliver betraying their country for bags of gold labeled fifteen hundred and four hundred pounds sterling, their salaries as crown officials.[48] Such calculated appeals to the less literate and illiterate in public houses and streets inevitably undercut parallel appeals for reformation of drink and taverns.

As Adams traveled on the Superior Court circuit to plead cases during these years, he witnessed how tavernkeepers influenced this change in the "nature and manners" of common men. On a journey from Boston to Falmouth, Maine, in 1770, Adams stopped overnight at a militia captain Jewett's tavern in Rowley. Jewett engaged Adams in conversation about the recent dismissal of the Assembly by the governor. Jewett vehemently told him that he would "rather the House should sit all year round (defying the governor), than give up an atom of right or privilege." The "governor can't frighten the people," Jewett stated.[49] Doubtless Jewett urged the same sentiments at militia musters when he both commanded and entertained the local company. Adams could only appreciate how closely country tavernkeepers followed events in provincial government by 1770.

At a tavern in Maine, Adams encountered a landlord who was a "staunch, zealous Son of Liberty," a "high Son." He eagerly informed Adams of the state of political resistance in the area. He named off the prominent men who had not taken up publicly (the only way that would satisfy) "the liberty side" and who presumably adhered to the "prerogative side." They were crown officials (probably justices) who were "afraid" for their "commissions." Rather than "hazard" the commissions, the tavernkeeper continued, "they would ruin the country." The landlord also told Adams that he had suffered "opposition" and "persecution" from these Tories because of his "zeal and firmness against their schemes." These officials had tried to "thwart, vex, and distress him," costing him at least one thousand pounds sterling. But "providence" had "favored him." He

48. *Massachusetts Gazette Extraordinary*, Mar. 11, 1773; *Boston Evening-Post*, Mar. 14, 1774, no. 2007.

49. Butterfield *et al.*, eds., *Diary and Autobiography of Adams*, I, 354.

also told Adams that he had his doubts about a Maine man recently elected and confirmed to the governor's Council. This gentleman "always runs away till he sees how a thing will go," and will probably "lean to the other side." The landlord wanted the issues settled on friendly terms "without bloodshed." Still, "he would venture his own life, and spend all he had in the world before he would give up." This tavernkeeper had already conceived of the possibility of war. In keeping with his views he served only to those men who supported the Sons, having inscribed on his signboard "Entertainment for the Sons of Liberty."[50] Thus did the Sons in taverns focus suspicion on local justices and others, following their every utterance and action for signs they had betrayed the people's "interest."

On another occasion Adams found this tavernkeeper celebrating the renewal of his license by treating his friends and patrons. Though he claimed they had given him trouble, local justices had not dared to deny this "high Son" a license, despite the tavern's notorious use as a center of resistance to the crown's authority. And thus, Adams wrote in his diary, does the "spirit of liberty" circulate "through every minute artery of the province."[51] But taverns were not "minute arteries" for ordinary farmers tied to their farms. They were their windows on the world, and the tavernkeeper a trusted informant on the looming crisis that had stretched the boundaries of their concern and urged on them a greater role in politics.

Taverns served not only as centers to pass judgment on local leaders but as places where abstract concepts and grievances could be translated into terms familiar and immediate to the lives and labor of ordinary colonists. In a Shrewsbury tavern Adams overheard a group of farmers discussing the latest events in Boston in 1774. Significantly, one expressed shock over the actions of Boston crowds, deeming them "distracted." But the others brought him around by drawing out implications of the Stamp Act and regulations of trade for the purpose of extracting revenue. One asked, "What would you say if a fellow should come to your house and tell you he was come to take a list of your cattle, that Parliament might tax you for them at so much a head?" This elevated violations of the English constitution into a scenario in the farmer's yard. Another said, "If Parliament can take away Mr. Hancock's wharf and Mr. Rowe's wharf, they can take away your barn and my house."[52] This comment implied that all

50. *Ibid.*, 355–356.

51. *Ibid.*

52. John Adams to Benjamin Rush, May 21, 1807, in Charles Francis Adams, ed., *The Works of John Adams, Second President of the United States*, IX (Boston, 1854), 597–598.

propertyowners, high and low, faced a common threat and that Parliament would expand its demands if not firmly opposed. Encouraged to do so, ordinary farmers unleashed their imaginations as to the ultimate, hidden meaning of recent crown acts. They conceived of imperial tax collectors in their yards.

Another farmer at the Shrewsbury tavern leapt to the conclusion: "We had better rebel now. . . . If we put it off . . . , they will get a strong party among us, and plague us a deal more than they can now."[53] Since the 1690s the royal governors had tried to create a governor's party in the House through the politic distribution of offices to members. This Shrewsbury farmer saw recent crown policies as an extension and elaboration of these long-resisted efforts. A discussion that had begun with comments about the "distracted" Bostonians had escalated into a call for rebellion and, implicitly, Independence. Thus did colonists who had long used taverns to identify and protect their own local interests gradually take steps to evaluate imperial policy.

The ultimate intentions of crown ministers and their dependents in the colonies provoked new speculation when the ministry announced in 1772 that henceforth the governor, chief justice, and four associate justices would receive their salaries from the crown instead of by grant from the Assembly. Samuel Adams believed that this "civil list" would be expanded shortly to undermine colonial autonomy. The list inspired the creation of the Boston Committee of Correspondence to communicate this new development to all the towns and elicit discussions and replies.[54]

At least 119 of the 260 towns and districts in the colony replied by early 1773 to the Boston Committee's summary of the history of the resistance capped by the news of the new civil list. The committee elicited more than just commentary on specific issues. From some towns came replies bristling with injunctions on the morality of present crown officials and of those expected in the future. In a reply written by tavernkeeper Obadiah Sawtell, a selectman and future representative, the district of Shirley commended Boston for its efforts to warn the towns about their enemies, enemies "who are endeavoring to rob us of the fruits of our honest industry, that they may riot in idleness and luxury themselves." Charlestown communicated its disgust at the idea of the colonists' money being used to maintain "in idleness and luxury an infamous set of spies, pimps, informers,

53. *Ibid.*

54. Richard D. Brown, *Revolutionary Politics in Massachusetts: The Boston Committee of Correspondence and the Towns, 1772–1774* (Cambridge, Mass., 1970), chaps. 3–4.

etc. with many of [whom] the sole qualification is a total unfitness for any honest calling."[55] The Boston Committee stirred afresh the issue of the morality of England's agents in America.

Inevitably, fresh assessment of the morality of crown officials and the viability of the English constitution revived talk of the need for reformation among the colonists themselves. Cambridge concluded its reply to Boston with the wish "that this land may be purged from those sins wich are a reproach to the people, and be exalted by righteousness, that God Almighty be our God as he was the God of our fathers, and that we may be possessed of the same principles of virtue, religion, and public spirit, which warmed and animated the hearts of our renowned ancestors." A year after the Boston Committee's initiative, the town of Chelmsford appointed a fifteen-man committee to "obtain the best information that may be had of idle, disorderly persons who waste their time and substance at public and private houses, in unlawful gaming" and "excessive drinking." The company of such persons should be "shunned" thereafter. Caught up in speculation about the designs and motives of crown officials, the town of Chelmsford attempted to reform its own.[56]

But it was not a revival of Puritan ethics that took place in the 1760s and 1770s, whatever the pronouncements and rhetoric of individuals and towns. Rather, it was an expansion of the kinds of conversation and activities that had been characteristic of taverns in the 1720s, when regulation of taverns had virtually collapsed. It was difficult to draw a line between tavern haunting and converging on taverns for necessary political organization and mobilization. As the imperial crisis deepened, taverns became a more important source of news and information.

55. *Ibid.*; Seth Chandler, *History of the Town of Shirley, Massachusetts* . . . (Shirley, Mass., 1883), 118; Richard Frothingham, Jr., *The History of Charlestown, Massachusetts* (Boston, 1845), 291–292. A writer to the *Boston Gazette* in 1774 reported on the state of knowledge by country people in a "distant colony," but also came close to describing the situation which the Boston Committee had helped to create: "What never happened before," he wrote, "has happened now because the COUNTRY PEOPLE have so exact a knowledge of fact and of the consequences attending a further surrender of the points in question, that they are, if possible more zealous than the citizens who lay in the direct line of information." "Extract of a Letter from One of the First and Best Men in a Distant Colony to His Friend in Boston," *Boston Gazette*, Aug. 15, 1774, no. 1009.

56. Lucius R. Paige, *History of Cambridge, Massachusetts 1630–1877* (Boston, 1877), 147; Wilkes Allen, *The History of Chelmsford, from Its Origin in 1653, to the Year 1820* (Haverhill, Mass., 1820), 62–63.

Besides centers for reading, listening to, and echoing Whig criticism and speculation, taverns became settings for physical acts and demonstrations of commitment to the cause of resistance. In 1770 a report about a man selling tea circulated through Danvers taverns and prompted local Sons to act. The Sons brought the tea seller to the Bell Tavern and pressured him to sign a confession and apology for his conduct. The Sons, presumably through connection with the town officials, also produced formal "votes of the town" against purchasing and vending tea for the tea seller to sign.[57] Thus did Sons dramatize and invigorate their convictions in public rooms.

The Boston Tea Party became a model for similar symbolic acts in the countryside in 1774. A "number of Indians" set out from Northborough in Worcester County to seize a bag of tea from a peddler who had been seen traveling to a Shrewsbury tavern. They caught up with him at the tavern, because the tea was burned in front of it. When another peddler brought a bag of tea into a Montague tavern in Berkshire County, local residents assembled at the tavern and prepared to tar and feather him, until he begged for mercy. When Sons discovered tea in Charlestown, they burned it in the training field in front of the Cape Breton Tavern.[58] Now the Sons even pressed against the prescribed limits to resistance activity—the sanctity of property. Such activities put teeth into oral resolutions and toasts committed in drinking companies. Aggressive physical acts infused oratory with added meaning.

By the mid-1770s prominent Tories observed the change in manners of the people in public and private companies with deepening alarm. It seemed that every "ordinary person" had turned "statesman." Even if he had "hardly wit enough to govern his own little family," he takes it upon himself "to settle the affairs of kingdoms" and "give this or the other prince advice how to govern his subjects." Such men "spend that time they should employ in their callings" in "running about after news." Tories were outraged by the deliberations taking place not only in committees and town meetings but in "tavern and temple associations." From these meetings men make "excursions to prey upon the lives and properties of their fellow subjects." Tories blamed the publications of "wretched scribblers," whose newspapers and pamphlets are "read in all companies" and

---

57. *Massachusetts Gazette,* July 5, 1770, no. 3482.

58. *Boston Gazette,* Feb. 14, 1774, no. 984, Mar. 7, 1774, no. 987; *Massachusetts Gazette,* Nov. 10, 1774, no. 3711.

"in everybody's hands," for this transformation in manners. The stream of accusations against royal officials had been rumors now regarded as fact. No "reputation" these "scribblers" ventured to "attack" remained uninjured.[59]

The mounting passion infusing local companies across the countryside gradually brought to fruition the popular political culture developing in towns since midcentury. Informal groups of voters began to take direct action against prominent men who had not openly subscribed to resistance or were suspected of opposing it. Such was the case in Weston in Middlesex County. For two decades Elisha Jones had dominated the town's government. Through his business activities in shopkeeping and moneylending, Jones held many of the 159 households in the town in a relationship of clientage through debt. By 1774 Jones had served eleven terms as representative of the town, also as selectman and treasurer previously, and became a justice in 1757. Jones had succeeded under royal patronage, and he tried to keep Weston loyal. On January 13, 1774, he presided over a town meeting where voters rejected a motion to elect a Committee of Correspondence to communicate with Boston. His views accorded with those of his cousin Isaac Jones, a tavernkeeper who had been elected a selectman in 1772 and a captain in the local militia company.[60]

Weston's other taverns, however, had become centers of agitation against the influential Jones family. Elisha Jones fitted exactly the character of the justice-representative who now appeared to be more a servant of the governor's interests and his nefarious designs than a protector of the people's constitutional liberties. In March 1774 a crowd of three hundred men ransacked Isaac Jones's tavern and seized some liquor. They became still more agitated when the more important Elisha Jones dared to recruit men in defense of the king's government in 1774. This proved too much for the town's voters. In September they replaced Elisha with a staunch Whig as representative. The same month, three hundred men converged on Elisha's house and "made his mightiness walk through their ranks with his hat off and express his sorrow for past offenses." They also forced Elisha to

59. *Massachusetts Gazette*, Jan. 27, 1774, no. 3669, Jan. 5, 1775, no. 3719, Feb. 16, 1775, no. 3725.

60. The story of Elisha and Isaac Jones is in Brenton H. Dickson and Homer C. Lucas, *One Town in the American Revolution: Weston, Massachusetts* (Weston, Mass., 1976), chaps. 6–10; see also Howard Gambrill, Jr., and Charles Hambrick-Stowe, *The Tavern and the Tory: The Story of the Golden Ball Tavern* (Cambridge, Mass., 1977).

promise that he would not repeat these offenses in the future. Eventually he fled to Boston.[61] It was deemed important by the farmers who unseated Jones to make him walk humbly among them, with his hat off, reversing the gestures of deference that had customarily been accorded him. Such a ceremony symbolized the transformation of the relationship between voters and elected representatives.

The momentum to challenge, unseat, and humiliate Jones had developed in Weston taverns kept by Sons of Liberty. Just how instrumental they had been in this endeavor is reflected in the election in late September of two tavernkeepers, Samuel Baldwin and Benjamin Peirce, to the three-man committee of correspondence. Peirce was a humble man to ascend to such a position. He was not well educated, possessing only "two old Bibles and other old books" at his death eight years later. The fact that he possessed a set of shoemaker's tools suggests that he made shoes during the winter months. The farmers who gathered in his public rooms to discuss the crisis in the town's affairs sat on thirty chairs grouped around four small tables and one long table. Only six candlesticks and an old lamp provided light at evening meetings. Documents and newspapers could not be read by everyone. Nevertheless, Peirce had acquired enough information about events in Boston and other towns to persuade his customers not only to reject Jones but to invest Peirce with the responsibility to correspond with other towns. In 1775 Peirce took it upon himself to write a letter to the Reverend Asa Dunbar, a minister from another town who was married to Jones's daughter. Peirce and his fellow Sons took exception to critical remarks made by Dunbar of the Sons in a Fast Day sermon.[62] Tavernkeepers Peirce and Baldwin rose in esteem and trust as Jones fell.

Like Weston, the county seat of Worcester had influential loyalists among its inhabitants. Indeed, since the 1740s the town had been dominated by men linked to royal government through judicial appointments. The leaders who organized to wrest control of town politics from this group were Joshua and Timothy Bigelow, a Land Banker and the son of a Land Banker. A blacksmith by trade, Timothy Bigelow acquired in 1767 a

61. Gambrill and Hambrick-Stowe, *The Tavern and the Tory*, 15–17; *Boston Gazette*, Sept. 12, 1774, no. 1013.

62. Daniel Lamson, *History of the Town of Weston, Massachusetts, 1630–1890* (Boston, 1913), 71–73, 189–190; Inventory of Benjamin Peirce, Middlesex County Probate Records, docket no. 17432 (Judicial Archives, ACM), microfilm box no. 1808, Middlesex County Courthouse.

license to keep tavern during court sessions. He did this probably because he decided that he wanted to play a larger role in town and county politics. By 1776 he kept tavern year-round.[63]

Like many of his fellow Sons in Boston, Bigelow had purchased history books and pamphlets. This blacksmith owned a broken set of the ten-volume ancient histories by Charles Rollin on the Egyptians, Carthaginians, Assyrians, Babylonians, Persians, Macedonians, and Greeks. He also owned a *Compendius History of the World, from the Creation to the Dissolution of the Roman Republic,* a reference work for the rise and decline of those fragile entities, republics. Another lesson in republican history was provided by a book on the history of the city and state of Genoa, undoubtedly instructive in the corruption of republics from without and within. For contemporary observations of the Roman Republic, he had a copy of *Seneca's Morals*, abstracts of the writings of Roman philosopher and observer Seneca. Further, Bigelow acquired the six volumes of *The British Plutarch,* a history of England from the accession of Henry VIII to the eighteenth century containing the biographies of eminent statesmen and divines. In his library there was still another book on the philosophy of history. Thus he possessed the capacity to make analogies between the course of ancient history, particularly republican history, and the rise and decline of England's constitutional monarchy. He could place the colonies' position in known historical time.

As far as religion is concerned, Bigelow appears to have leaned toward unorthodoxy. He owned the works of freethinker Peter Annet, including the essay "Judging for Ourselves; or, Free-Thinking the Great Duty of Religion." There were also several other psalm and sermon books, but this was a decidedly secular library overall. Bigelow even purchased Laurence Sterne's novel *A Sentimental Journey through France and Italy,* published in 1768. This was perhaps an apt choice for a freethinking politician who sold drink, because of its bodiless, plotless form seemingly structured only by a continuous flow of talk.[64] In a rural outpost of the Massachusetts

63. John L. Brooke, *The Heart of the Commonwealth: Society and Political Culture in Worcester County, Massachusetts, 1713–1861* (New York, 1989), 136, 143. Bigelow was licensed "during sessions of court" in May 1767 (Court of General Sessions, Worcester, Record Book, 1758–1767, 485, Worcester County Courthouse). He continued to keep tavern in court weeks through 1770 (Record Book, 1768–1780, 123). By 1776 he kept tavern all year round (Record Book, 1768–1780, 353–354).

64. The inventory and estate of Timothy Bigelow are located in the probate records at the Worcester County Courthouse, docket no. 5574. The administration of his estate was

hinterland, this blacksmith eagerly sought out knowledge of a wider world. His library suggests that he used print of a critical and historical nature to judge the institutions around him.

Like Marston in Boston, Bigelow quickly acquired the important pamphlets of the resistance, judging from the thirteen he owned at his death. Bigelow was not the only Worcester County tavernkeeper to own pamphlets. Of the inventories of thirteen other tavernkeepers in the county, almost all owned books, and three others owned pamphlets. And former tavernkeeper Elijah Marcy of Sturbridge had a collection of "paper books" as well as bound books in 1779. Captain Josiah Converse of Brookfield—tavernkeeper, justice, representative, and militia captain—owned "history books" as well as pamphlets.[65] All probably knew Bigelow, and some might have used his tavern during court weeks when they came to renew their licenses. Indeed, Bigelow might have been a central transmitter of republican thought, being eminently accessible to not only his fellow townsmen but county inhabitants as a whole. He stood at the center of a web of tavern connections by the 1770s.

In December 1773 Bigelow founded in Worcester with two others a semisecret organization called, significantly, the American Political Society. From its inception this organization anticipated movement toward independence. More immediately, the fifteen members conceived of the society as an instrument to combat the still influential Tory minority. The Society quickly took it upon itself to manage town government behind the scenes, voting on communications to be sent by the Committee of Correspondence, taking steps to arm all townsmen, and composing instructions for the town's delegate to the Provincial Congress of 1774. In effect the Society controlled town meetings in much the same manner as the Boston Caucus. Members took oaths to keep debates at their meetings secret for tactical reasons, but much of what was voted and discussed at Society meetings was made public, and the thirty-one original members expanded to seventy-eight during the next two years. The Society even took the inclusive step of drawing up a covenant to boycott British goods for adult women to sign.[66]

Significantly, the Society decided that its monthly and quarterly meet-

---

processed in 1790. Individuals whose estates required probate are listed alphabetically in volumes at the courthouse.

65. *Ibid.*; Inventory of Elijah Marcy, Worcester County Probate Records, docket no. 38672, Josiah Converse, docket no. 13218.

66. Records of American Political Society, 1773–1776 (typescript copies by Charles Estus), 4, 10, 15, 21–22, American Antiquarian Society.

ings would be held in the public houses of Worcester. Besides Bigelow, four other Worcester tavernkeepers became members, and more hosted meetings. Despite their wish to keep parts of their deliberations secret, the members obviously identified gatherings at taverns with their purpose— "to advise with each other on proper methods to be pursued by us . . . respecting our common rights and liberties."[67] Bigelow and company recognized that taverns had become more vital than ever before as forums for the debate of public affairs. They provided a context for the expansion of participation and prepared voters for key decisions at town meetings. The founders now acted to organize and focus these informal gatherings more systematically. Meetings of the Society held at the various public houses of the town also enabled nonmembers collecting at these taverns at other times more readily to identify their interests with the Society and accept its guidance. The Society was a more formal representation of the greater public of male tavern companies in the town.

Yet tavernkeeper Bigelow and other members of the Society remained sensitive to the concurrent calls for the reformation of vices, including intemperance and tavern haunting, considered antithetical to republican virtue and society. Meetings of the Society at taverns were long; members voted on a limit of four hours for monthly meetings, longer for quarterly ones. They could readily be accused of tavern haunting and consume so much liquor that their wits became dulled and their debates wayward. Thus at the second meeting of the Society they voted that expenses for drink be limited to an average of sixpence per man at monthly meetings and two shillings at quarterly ones. Some members, however, continued to drink too much, for in August 1774 they resolved that no members shall "call for or otherwise convey or caused to be conveyed into our said Society any spiritous liquor of any sort whatever."[68]

Either because of their readings in Whig history and literature owned by members like Bigelow or newspaper essays to the same point, members struggled to reconcile the precepts of republican virtue with the pragmatic politics of collective drinking. The town had formally called for a law against the use of drink to bribe voters in 1766. In the end, however, the insistence that the Society meet at a public house is an indication that leaders considered collective drinking at taverns, not as a fountain of vice,

---

67. *Ibid.*, 3. The four others were Samuel Woodburn, David Bigelow, Robert Smith, and Asa Ward. Records of American Political Society, 25; Records of Court of General Sessions, Worcester, Record Book, 1768–1780, 353–354.

68. Records of American Political Society, 6, 24.

but as a vital means of instruction, debate, and resolution for common men. Men with libraries were becoming more numerous, so numerous as to include blacksmiths like Bigelow. Yet they were not so many as to constitute a wide and deep reading public, and so Bigelow had taken the steps to acquire a license year-round to instruct and guide his clientele as well as expand his business. The Society paid lip service to some reform aspects of republican ideology but nevertheless vigorously pursued the arousal and organization of a republican citizenry in taverns with drink.

Tensions between the Society and the loyalist minority came to a head in 1774 when forty-three opponents of Bigelow and his associates met in Widow Stearns's King's Arms Tavern and signed a petition subsequently published in the *Massachusetts Gazette* repudiating the latest proceedings of the town. These influential petitioners condemned Bigelow and other Sons in terms that relegated them to the status of ignorant tavern incendiaries, calling them upstarts who neglected their own "proper business and occupation in which they ought to be employed for the support of their families." Instead, they spent their time "discoursing of matters they do not understand, raising and propagating falsehoods and calumnies of those men they look up to in envy, intending to reduce all things to a state of tumult, discord, and confusion." These Tory reactions to Worcester's new political configuration referred back to a political culture in which ordinary farmers and blacksmiths like Bigelow did not usually participate in the resolution of issues of provincial scope. But the members of the Society reading newspapers and pamphlets no longer deferred to these men. The town responded to the Tory petition by electing a committee to refute it and elected Bigelow as its delegate to the extralegal Provincial Congress in 1775.[69] Virtuous or not, Bigelow and his associates had grasped the essential role that taverns had played and would play in the transformation of the colony's political culture. Worcester's Tory minority, led by influential gentry, might use a tavern to organize their opposition to Bigelow, but their simultaneous wish to confine political discourse to a narrow elite prevented them from moving to exploit every Worcester tavern for rotating meetings as did Bigelow's American Political Society. Instead of trying to confine the public, the Society identified itself with the expanding informal public of taverns.

A similar process was under way in the taverns of Hardwick, also in Worcester County, where residents gradually, reluctantly moved to re-

69. Lincoln, *History of Worcester*, 80–82, 86. A neutral, or secret loyalist, William Jones, also kept a tavern (95–96).

pudiate the leadership of the town's most respected and prominent figure, Timothy Ruggles. A brigadier general in the Seven Years' War, Ruggles was also the foremost justice in Worcester County, a fifteen-year representative to the House, and the speaker of the House. Despite his opposition to the Sons of Liberty, Ruggles continued to be elected representative. But by 1770 the oral reports of events in other towns and presumably the newspapers began to undermine the enormous prestige Ruggles enjoyed. In 1771 and 1772 the town did not elect a representative at all. Doubts about Ruggles had gained currency, but the town could not yet bring itself to replace him with another man. Then, in 1773, the town elected Paul Mandell, a tavernkeeper, to represent it. The speaker of the House, once its most important member, had been replaced by a tavernkeeper and small-scale country merchant. Hardwick also proceeded to elect a fifteen-man Committee of Correspondence, which included five tavernkeepers.[70]

Tavernkeepers became so prominent in the politics of Hardwick perhaps because of the sea change in loyalties that the majority of inhabitants underwent. Townsmen had been accustomed to deferring to Ruggles in matters of provincial import, to receiving and supporting his interpretation of events. When this filter through which political information was processed came under doubt, tavernkeepers in contact with travelers, perhaps receiving newspapers to be shared, filled the growing vacuum of leadership. Their role as purveyors of news and hosts for collective drinking became more central after Ruggles fled the town and formed a loyalist association. He sent back the covenant of this association to recruit signatures in support.[71] Presumably, then, taverns became clearinghouses for townsmen to discover and identify those traitors still loyal to Ruggles and the king's government. The committee seized the covenant and sent it to the extralegal Provincial Congress, acknowledging its new loyalties and establishing new lines of communication with the outside world. Given the deep divisions, the wrenching change in loyalties, it is no wonder that

70. Lucius R. Paige, *History of Hardwick, Massachusetts* (Boston, 1883), 67–68, 70–75, 82–87. Thomas Robinson had been a retailer in the 1750s and was a tavernkeeper by 1760. By 1765 he kept tavern for the "fairs." Daniel Warner was first licensed between 1765 and 1770. Paul Mandell had been a retailer in the 1750s and was a tavernkeeper by 1767. See Court of General Sessions, Worcester, Record Books, 1737–1757, 273–275, 1757–1768, 105–108, 1768–1780, 123–124, 353–354. The licensing records for Capt. Constant Merrick (1765, 1776) and Jonathan Warner (1776) can be found on the same pages.

71. Paige, *History of Hardwick*, 82–87.

townsmen should elevate the local sources of news—the tavernkeepers—to leadership. As Ruggles's enormous prestige evaporated, taverns became magnets for inhabitants coming to the decision that they must overturn his leadership and seeking unity and consensus in that daring decision.

The bellicosity of tavern gatherings reading the Boston press resulted in the removal of numerous justices and prominent men from the House like Ruggles by the early 1770s. But up to 1773 personal confrontations and heated exchanges between ordinary colonists and high royal officials were few. True, stamp agent Andrew Oliver had been forced to resign under the Liberty Tree in Boston. The residences of customs officers had been defaced. But there had been few face-to-face breaches of the deferential posture and tone customarily demonstrated before royal officials. The most visible institution of royal authority, the courts of justice, continued to function despite the abuse articulated against many justices in nearby taverns.

The increasing intensity of oral and printed criticism, however, led some men to dare call for open violations of deference to judges. In September 1773 Aristophanes, a pseudonymous writer to the *Massachusetts Gazette*, declared that in an "Age of Liberty" everyone is invited "to publish his thoughts on matters of public importance." He thought that the time had come for elected grand jurors of the various counties to lecture and instruct the appointed judges of the Superior Court. He observed that "it is the practice at the opening of our courts" for the chief justice "to administer a charge to the grand jurors to see that the laws are duly observed." Now, Aristophanes proposed, "instead of a charge from the judges to the jury," the jurors should regularly give a "solemn charge" to the judges to "pay due attention to the public liberties." More radical still, this critic suggested that, if the judges should prove "unwilling to hear such a charge with proper meekness and submission," if they should "refuse to stand up" when lectured or "show any mark of sneer or contempt," then the elected representatives to the Assembly should enact a law to force the judges to pay respect to the jurors.[72] Here was a proposal to reconceive the ceremony of judicial sessions in a way that subverted the principle of hierarchy. The agitated sentiments of an ever widening critical public informally assembled in taverns should be brought into the courts in an effort to reverse the flow of authority and communication.

Royal governors, of course, had been attempting to strengthen the

72. *Massachusetts Gazette; and the Boston Weekly News-Letter,* Sept. 15, 1773, no. 3650.

downward flow of authority and communication through the judicial hierarchy. When General Thomas Gage arrived in May 1774 to replace the beleaguered Hutchinson, he did everything he could to shore up the king's authority, especially over the judicial system. He commanded all judges, justices, and other officials in descending order of authority to enforce the laws promoting religion and virtue. As in the past, this governor linked vice with sedition. He also asked all ministers to work to commence a reformation of manners. Gage sought a show of solidarity among officeholders and clergy to reinforce their rule over the populace. Of course, many ministers actively promoted Whig principles, but they also called for the reformation of vices like tavern haunting. And some justices actually did respond to Gage by publishing assurances to him that they would not only promote order but that they wished for a reconciliation with England. Essex County justices took this opportunity to bear "testimony against lawless riots which render the enjoyment of property and even life itself precarious." Justices from Plymouth and Bristol counties published similar addresses. But such assurances had a hollow ring. Already the grand jurors of Worcester County, including Timothy Bigelow, had met in Asa Ward's tavern in April 1774 and resolved not to be sworn into office if Peter Oliver presided as chief justice. Oliver was the only judge to refuse to renounce his crown salary, and the House had voted to impeach him in response.[73]

When news of the Coercive Acts, the punishment for the Boston Tea Party, reached the Massachusetts countryside in the summer of 1774, challenges to the authority of judges and justices and other crown officials became still more common. The Massachusetts Government Act decreed that henceforth members of the governor's Council would receive their appointments from the king without nomination from the House. Now also the attorney general, the lesser judges, sheriffs, and justices of the peace would be appointed and removed at the pleasure of the governor without the advice and consent of the Council. Further, juries would now be selected by sheriffs rather than elected or summoned by local constables.[74] Like the civil list of 1772, this act strengthened the king's authority over the judicial system at the expense of the electoral power of the people. It seemed to confirm the belief that had steadily gained currency since 1765, that there existed in Whitehall a conspiracy to curtail gradually the

73. *Ibid.*, June 30, 1774, no. 3691, July 14, 1774, no. 3693, July 28, 1774, no. 3695; *Boston Gazette*, Apr. 11, 1774, no. 992, May 9, 1774, no. 996.

74. Brown, *Revolutionary Politics in Massachusetts*, 190; Richard L. Bushman, *King and People in Provincial Massachusetts* (Chapel Hill, N.C., 1985), 186–189.

traditional liberties of the colonies while inflicting on them a host of new officials in need of patronage and employment. This was considered to be a forewarning of still more drastic measures.

In response the Sons of Liberty across the province decided to inhibit the judicial process and eventually close the courts down. Such actions, however, brought resistance to a more dangerous plane in regard to internal order. Could the crowds informally gathered in taverns be restrained even as the seats of law and order were disrupted? The closing of the courts and the humiliation of high officials might encourage independent and more physical forms of intimidation against the law enforcement hierarchy. The liberal use of drink and taverns to organize and articulate resistance might unleash something more radical than leaders wished when they turned the traditional hierarchy of the courts upside down. These worries are reflected in the careful way in which leaders executed actions to subvert the judicial process. Sons orchestrated events to invite maximum participation and access but also invested them with a deliberate ceremonial agenda to emphasize restraint and emulate the majesty of the courts themselves.

They commonly moved to reconstruct the ceremony of the courts. In September, twenty-two grand jurors from Boston and sixteen other Suffolk towns, including Paul Revere, met before the convening of the Superior Court in Boston to decide how to proceed. They drew up a list of reasons why they refused to serve as jurors to the court. This document, which they all signed, reiterated accusations by the House against Judge Peter Oliver for high crimes and misdemeanors, noting that he had not been acquitted of impeachment. (The House had voted to impeach Oliver, but Governor Hutchinson had blocked the proceedings.) The jurors also condemned Oliver and judges Foster Hutchinson and William Brown for taking oaths as councillors under the new act. Before a crowd in the courthouse to witness the event, the chairman of the jurors prepared to read their charges, in effect bringing what was read in taverns into the courts to be formally proclaimed. The jurors sought to reverse roles by having elected officeholders lecture and pass judgment on the highest judges of the courts. But the five judges quickly refused to hear the document read in open court, stating that they would read it themselves. Nervous, perhaps still a little in awe of these men face-to-face, the jurors complied and handed over the document for a private reading. But they then left the courthouse as a body and reassembled at the Exchange Tavern on King Street. Here in the public rooms of open debate they regained their original temper of defiance and challenge, for at the tavern they resolved to publish "to the world" their reasons for refusing to serve. They had not quite dared to read the document in court before the austere Oliver, but in the tavern they could more readily decide to publish it in the newspapers. Thus they fell back on the close integration of republican discourse and informal gatherings in taverns. It was this use of taverns to read and elaborate on radical criticism that had made face-to-face challenges to high officials conceivable.[75]

Whigs staged subsequent subversions of the Superior and lesser courts from the fall of 1774 to the spring of 1775 without being foiled. In Berkshire County a crowd of people filled the courthouse jam-tight to prevent the justices from walking to their seats. The action invited physical participation, empowered ordinary men to refuse gestures of deference, but did not jeopardize the physical safety of the justices or even invite verbal abuse. In Worcester County Bigelow and his associates pushed for more coercive actions but still carefully managed and staged their course. They forced newly appointed member of the Council and justice Timothy Morse, together with a group of critics of the Sons, to march through lines of assembled militia from nearby towns, stopping every few feet to read recantations and apologies. The next February thousands assembled once again in two long files through which the judicial hierarchy—justices, sheriff, and gentlemen of the bar—were compelled to walk while reading a disavowal of convening the courts under the Massachusetts Government Act. The Sons also forced them to hold their hats in their hands as they walked, reversing the customary gestures of deference to them expected of ordinary men. In Springfield the justices, sheriff, and lawyers also took their hats off to the crowd assembled to block them from entering the courthouse.[76]

75. *Boston Gazette*, Sept. 5, 1774, supplement to no. 1012. Even casual laborers were reading newspapers or hearing them read in the 1770s. In Keene, N.H., Abner Sanger did some work for a tavernkeeper but spent most of the morning reading his employer's newspapers in September 1776. With another employer he stayed until nightfall "to hear them read." In 1782 he engaged to do some work for a man, but instead proceeded to "spend all the while until night reading in his newspapers." See Brown, *Knowledge Is Power*, 147.

76. *Massachusetts Gazette; and the Boston Weekly News-Letter*, Sept. 1, 1774, no. 3701, Sept. 8, 1774, no. 3702, "Plain English" to Provincial Congress, Feb. 23, 1775, no. 3726; Oath of Elisha Jones, *Boston Gazette*, Sept. 12, 1774, no. 1013; Lincoln, *History of Worcester*, 86–87. In Concord 10 justices proposed to the crowd blocking the courthouse door that they be allowed to open the court provided they conduct no business. The "Body of the People" consulted on the matter, probably in the courthouse, but kept the justices waiting in a

Inviting men to come out of their taverns to disrupt the courts of law was an anxious undertaking, but staged ceremonies of resistance invested every participant with a role, if only as witnesses. Colonists were accustomed to tableaux and processions exhibiting traditional structures of authority. These events of 1774–1775 evoked the solemnity and order of these tableaux, but with the purpose of repudiating traditional authority instead of buttressing it. However solemn and restrained these actions, the Sons simultaneously had to satisfy the sentiments of the people they had aroused. Thus they deemed it important that the justices walk through the long files so that all of the men could hear the words of recantation and see the gestures of submission to the assembled people, just as the *Letter* of 1739 attacking justices in the House had been addressed to "all freeholders" and "other inhabitants." The public invoked in republican pamphlets could never be physically realized, but these assemblies in Worcester and other counties rendered powerful representative versions of it, expanding on the scale and egalitarian temper of tavern assemblies.[77] The public existing outside the hierarchy of government here confronted it to transform it, acting out the emerging principle that all officers—even judges—did not constitute a separate order of men and were ultimately subject to the people's will.

Along with descriptions of court closures, readers of newspapers in taverns pored over numerous accounts that reinforced identification with an active republican citizenry across the province in the fall and winter of 1774–1775. The forced recantations and apologies of officeholders to local crowds filled the pages. Those men who had signed addresses of respect and esteem to the departing Governor Hutchinson became particular targets for crowd action. The publication of edited versions of Hutchinson's letters to Thomas Whatley in 1773, followed by the interpretations by Whig commentators of the governor's tortured efforts to resolve the dilemma of the extent of parliamentary sovereignty, had seemed to offer proof to native leaders of his involvement in a plot to reduce colonial liberties.[78] It was as if the curtain had been lifted on a dark drama, provid-

---

nearby tavern until after dark before rejecting the proposal. By then it was too late to open the courts anyway. Gross, *The Minutemen and Their World*, 54.

77. For a detailed examination of the transformation of a poor, humble, and deferential shoemaker to a vocal, active citizen and member of the public, see Young, "George Robert Twelves Hewes," *WMQ*, 3d Ser., XXXVIII (1981), 561–623; Warner, *Letters of the Republic*, 102–103.

78. *Boston Gazette*, Sept. 5, 1774, no. 1012, Oct. 17, 1774, no. 1018, Oct. 31, 1774, no.

ing explanations for all the events of the past ten years. A writer to the *Boston Gazette* placed Hutchinson at the center of a network of secret confederates:

> We shall ever find the grand mover of their mischievous operations lurking in the dark;—for in all the more capital movements, the arch agent keeps himself as much as possible disguised, while, like the master of puppets, he holds the political wire, and directs all their motions— behind the curtain.[79]

Signees of the respectful addresses to Hutchinson provoked fury mainly because they called into question this public judgment of Hutchinson as a traitor. But these addresses also incensed colonists because they evoked the private interest and communications of royal governors with appointed officeholders, particularly with the justices who made up the bulk of signees. Publication of these recantations for colonists to read in taverns inspired visions of ceremonies at which justices symbolically severed these secret ties of patronage and communication and replaced them with public dialogues with groups of local citizens. Communication must be open, as in public readings in taverns, purged of the pursuit of private self-interest.

Secret ties of patronage and loyalty to the royal establishment, believed to be held among some colonists across the province, became a source of more anxiety in the spring of 1775, when rumors circulated through the countryside that General Gage planned exploratory forays into the interior to seize accumulated military stores and that spies had been sent out to reconnoiter major roads. Gage did indeed send out spies, since the report of two of them has survived as evidence. Among other things the report is valuable for its revelations about the tenor of tavern assemblies on the eve of Revolution.

Disguised as country surveyors looking for work, a Captain Brown and an Ensign Bernière set out for Worcester through Cambridge. They stopped at prominent Whig Jonathan Brewer's tavern in Waltham. Brewer was a member of the committee that drafted instructions to Waltham's delegates to the Provincial Congress of 1774. Another Waltham tavernkeeper, Samuel Livermore, esquire, was a member of the town's committee

---

1020, Jan. 2, 1775, no. 1029. In Concord Colonel Prescott was forced to apologize to irate townsmen for signing an address to Hutchinson. Gross, *The Minutemen and Their World*, 54–55; Bailyn, *The Ordeal of Thomas Hutchinson*, 223–252.

79. *Boston Gazette*, Jan. 3, 1774, no. 978.

of correspondence in 1773. At Brewer's, a slave recognized the spies as British officers but did not raise an alarm. After leaving Waltham, they traveled a distance with two men and a team, but suspected that the men had guessed their true identities and so left them by stopping at a Weston tavern. This stop might have been intentional, since the tavern was kept by loyalist Isaac Jones, still holding on to his property despite virtual ostracism in the town. When Jones told them they might have tea to drink, they knew they were safe.[80]

The two spies asked Jones to recommend taverns on the road to Worcester where they might be welcome or tolerated. Jones could tell them of only two—Buckminster's in Framingham and another Jones tavern in Worcester itself. They left Weston the next day without incident and lodged at Buckminster's. Joseph Buckminster was not a Tory. He had in fact been elected to Framingham's Committee of Correspondence in 1773. But he was also a justice and had served as the town's representative. Jones might have considered that Buckminster's duty to enforce law and order might bode well for the two if they encountered sharp questioning or were discovered. Buckminster's son, a Rutland minister with Tory leanings, had also been castigated in print by the Sons. But the two did not meet the father and were served by an uninquisitive woman.[81]

The next day they passed through Shrewsbury on their way to Worcester. It was perhaps fortunate for them that they did not stop at any of the six Shrewsbury taverns, for staunch and vigilant Whigs kept the taverns of Shrewsbury. Three tavernkeepers and one retailer in the town were elected to town offices in the 1760s and 1770s. Tavernkeeper and selectman Ezra Beaman was also a militia captain in 1776 and would become a major by 1779. Another tavernkeeper-selectman became a captain and eventually a major. Both of them also served on the town's Committee of Inspection along with another tavernkeeper and a retailer in 1774. Still

80. Captain Brown and Ensign D'Bernicre [*sic*], ["Narrative of Occurrences, 1775"], MHS, *Collections*, 2d Ser., IV (1816), 207.

81. *Ibid.* Buckminster's son had become controversial because of statements he had purportedly made in several companies. In 1768 he was asked through the press whether he had declared that the acts of Parliament "were just, and ought to be submitted to," because "it is necessary for all men, clergy as well as laity, to speak their sentiments, and declare themselves either for God or Belial." He was asked either to retract his statement or to explain his understanding of the British constitution. "Let us know on which side you appear; this is all we ask." Such printed inquiries put clergy and laity on a level. *Boston Gazette*, July 11, 1768, no. 693.

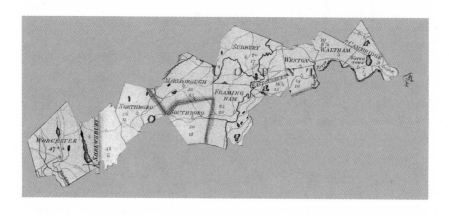

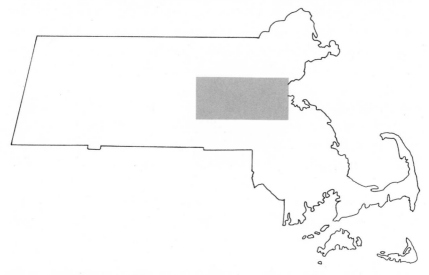

Map 2. Route of British Spies, 1775. *Details from Osgood Carleton,* Map of
Massachusetts Proper . . . *(Boston, 1802), courtesy, Massachusetts Historical Society.*
(Some names present here were different in 1775, and some boundaries vary
from 1775)

another tavernkeeper, Henry Baldwin, helped to keep his patrons abreast
of Whig arguments, owning "a number of pamphlets" besides books when
he died in 1790. It was in a Shrewsbury tavern that Adams had overheard
talk of the need for rebellion in 1774.[82] The town's blacksmith, Ross

82. Brown and D'Bernicre, ["Narrative"], MHS, *Collections,* 2d Ser., IV (1816), 208;
Andrew Ward, *History of the Town of Shrewsbury, Massachusetts, from Its Settlement in 1717 to
1829* (Boston, 1847), 38–39, 70–75; License records from the Court of General Sessions,
Worcester County, III, 105–108, IV, 123–129, 353–354; Henry Baldwin's inventory, at the

Wyman, had together with tavernkeeper Timothy Bigelow organized a convention of blacksmiths that met at Worcester the previous fall. Forty-three blacksmiths had resolved to refuse to do any work for officials and private persons connected to them who had "given sufficient proof of their enmity to the people and constitution of this country."[83] Thus the black-smiths inhibited these figures' movements.

In a similar spirit the people of Shrewsbury had gradually come to the conviction that they must remove one of their ministers, Ebenezer Morse, from his pulpit because of his loyalist sympathies. As early as 1770 his congregation had become affronted by his prayers for the "king, queen, and royal family, the lords spiritual and temporal." In 1771 a committee interrogated him and decided to dismiss him. In May 1775 the Committee of Correspondence disarmed Morse and forbade him from leaving his former parish on any occasion without a permit from the Committee.[84] The taverns of the town were alive with discussions that led to efforts to prevent open or secret Tories like Morse from communicating with Gage in the spring of 1775. Thus the spies might have encountered suspicion here.

After a day's journey of thirty miles, sketching roads as they traveled, the two spies reached William Jones's safe tavern in Worcester. Jones had made enough of a show of neutrality to be tolerated; he had even hosted some meetings of Bigelow's Society. But he had found it necessary to apologize in print for questioning too closely an express rider to Boston from the Committee of Correspondence of New York. Jones guessed the identity of his guests and offered them tea. Over a bottle of wine he told them that the "friends of government at Petersham were disarmed by the rebels, and that they threatened to do the same in Worcester in a very little time." The two spies did not linger in Worcester for more than a day. They set off for Framingham with some brandy, which allowed them to avoid going into taverns "where perhaps they might be too inquisitive." But someone had noticed them in Worcester. The two had not traveled four miles before they were overtaken by Timothy Bigelow himself—the leader of Worcester's resistance. Bigelow examined them "very attentively" and then rode swiftly to Marlborough, where he presumed they were headed.[85]

Probate Office at Worcester County Courthouse, docket no. 2822; Adams to Rush, May 21, 1807, in Charles Francis Adams, ed., *The Works of John Adams*, IX, 597–598.

83. Lincoln, *History of Worcester*, 92.

84. *Ibid.*, 92–93; Ward, *History of Shrewsbury*, 39, 202–203.

85. *Massachusetts Gazette; and the Boston Weekly News-Letter*, Jan. 12, 1775, no. 3720;

The two spies, however, took the Framingham road. They reached Buckminster's tavern without incident, but later experienced the uneasiness of witnessing a militia muster next to the tavern: "After they had done their exercise, one of their commanders spoke a very eloquent speech, recommending patience, coolness, and bravery." He told them "they would always conquer if they did not break" and quoted Caesar, Pompey, officers Putnam and Ward, and other famous officers. He also reminded them of Cape Breton and other battles that colonial troops had won or helped to win. Indeed, he observed, "the regulars must have been ruined but for them." The company then came into the tavern to drink, and the two spies presumably retreated hastily to a lodging chamber. Such musters were frequent in the winter and spring of 1775. Another traveler stopping at a tavern outside Boston witnessed a company listening to "dissertations on liberty." The tavernkeeper was captain of the company.[86] Musters at taverns in anticipation of movements by Gage had become opportunities for speeches to inspire and prepare men to take the final step of rebellion against the king's government.

Brown and Berniére reached Weston the next day and "received several hints" from Jones to return to Boston immediately. But the two risked a survey of the Sudbury road (the main road to Worcester). They did not stop at any of the six Sudbury taverns, a wise decision since Sudbury companies had become very agitated in the spring of 1775. The town had continued to reelect its longtime representative, Justice John Noyes, despite the fact that he was one of the thirty-one justice-representatives named in Boston newspapers in 1776 as royal officeholders deserving inspection. Sudbury, however, carefully instructed Noyes on how to vote on all imperial issues. Still, the suspicions surrounding justices became so virulent by 1773 that voters dropped Noyes as representative after a contentious series of votes and replaced him with a former selectman. The next year townsmen forced Sudbury's other local justice to apologize to a crowd for signing an address of esteem to Hutchinson and to answer publicly a rumor that he had helped to purchase equipment for British troops. He was also dropped as town clerk at the next election. That such agitated feelings were coming to a head in Sudbury taverns is evident by the fact that five of the six tavernkeepers in the town were elected select-

Brown and D'Bernicre, ["Narrative"], MHS, *Collections*, 2d Ser., IV (1816), 208–210. The horseman who overtook the spies is identified as Bigelow in Charles Hudson, *History of the Town of Marlborough* . . . (Boston, 1862), 157.

86. Brown and D'Bernicre, ["Narrative"], MHS, *Collections*, 2d Ser., IV (1816), 208–210; *Massachusetts Gazette; and the Boston Weekly News-Letter,* Jan. 5, 1775, no. 3719.

men between 1773 and 1776. Indeed, tavernkeepers dominated the board of selectmen. Three of them were also militia officers. Tavernkeeper Eze-kiel How—selectman, town moderator, member of the Committee of Cor-respondence, and militia colonel—had joined Bigelow's American Political Society the year previous and would become chairman of it in 1776.[87] As local justices were stripped of elective office, the town's tavernkeepers presided over ever more intense discussions of the crisis of affairs in general and the loyalties of fellow townsmen in particular. Leaders and constituents increasingly consulted as fellow drinkers.

The spies might have avoided the Sudbury companies, but in Marl-borough they faced an aroused citizenry. Timothy Bigelow had ridden there the night before to warn the town's leaders that two suspected spies were headed in that direction. And just outside the town, a horseman interrogated them as to their origins and business. When they entered the central village, "the people came out of their houses . . . to look at" them, even though it was snowing. Again they were questioned, and answered that they intended to visit Henry Barnes (a known loyalist). When they reached Barnes's house, he quickly told them that he "knew [their] situa-tion, that they were very well known . . . by the town's people" and that they would be "safe no where except in this house" because "the town was very violent." The spies had been expected at Colonel Abraham Williams's tavern the night before, "where there had gone a party of liberty people to meet" them. Meanwhile, as they talked to Barnes, "the people were gather-ing in little groups in every part of the town." Barnes told the two that they should expect "the worst treatment from them."[88]

A servant then informed Barnes that the liberty men "intended to attack" them. Thus after only twenty minutes at Barnes's house, the two left by another road and walked thirty-two miles to Jones's Weston tavern. They just barely escaped. Marlborough's Committee of Correspondence came to the house just after they left and "demanded" them. The Commit-

87. Brown and D'Bernicre, ["Narrative"], MHS, *Collections*, 2d Ser., IV (1816), 210; *Boston Evening-Post*, Apr. 28, 1766, no. 1598; Victor L. Neumeier, *The War Years in the Town of Sudbury, Massachusetts, 1765–1781* (Sudbury, Mass., 1975), 104–148; *Boston Gazette*, Sept. 5, 1774, no. 1012; Records of the American Political Society, roster (the five tavernkeepers active in town politics were Ezekiel How, Jonathan Rice, Jacob Reeves, Elisha Wheeler, and Elijah Bent); D. Hamilton Hurd, *History of Middlesex County . . .* (Philadelphia, 1890), II, 400, 402; Records of the Court of General Sessions, Middlesex, File Papers (approbation re-turns), 1776, Record Book, 1761–1771, 8–11.

88. Brown and D'Bernicre, ["Narrative"], MHS, *Collections*, 2d Ser., IV (1816), 210–213.

tee then searched the house from top to bottom and told Barnes that, if they had found the spies, they would have pulled the house down "about his ears." The Committee then sent horsemen after the spies, but Brown and Berniére somehow eluded them. The next morning Jones showed the two a road that allowed them to bypass Watertown, as they "did not choose to go through that town" or near Brewer's tavern. They reached Boston safely.[89]

Tavern companies had become political tinderboxes, ready to explode into action against real or suspected enemies to resistance and, eventually, the new Republic. Loyalists were in fact few in the countryside. Jones could recommend only two taverns on the road to Worcester where Gage's spies would be safe, and one was kept by a staunch Whig. But Tories such as Jones in Weston, Barnes in Marlborough, Ruggles in Hardwick, and the group in Worcester were numerous enough to excite passions among tavern companies groping toward a new political identity. The politicization of taverns had become not only complete but invested with high purpose—the discovery and intimidation of enemies to the right of common men to claim and protect certain liberties. On the eve of the creation of a Republic, a citizenry of men informally organized in taverns when not assembled in town meetings and militia companies had coalesced against the king's government. A citizenry converging on taverns to hear news related, read, or explained kept abreast of every new development in this crisis of authority.

From the vantage point of public houses, the social foundation and course of Revolution in Massachusetts takes on a new coloration. In a variety of ways scholars have drawn a number of connections between the rise of Puritanism in the seventeenth century and the American Revolution. Certainly Puritans established the electoral foundation of the colony's government, qualified only by the arrival of royal government in 1692, which was purged by the Revolution. And the antiauthoritarian strain of Puritan rhetoric that defined and condemned the corruption of the Stuart monarchy received fresh enunciation and assumed new dimensions in the guise of Whig opposition ideology in the eighteenth century. The Puritan ethic—the constellation of ideas sanctioning sustained methodical application to one's calling—received new emphasis as an inspiration for the sacrifice of imported luxuries and as a basis for attacking the character of crown officials already present and those hordes of pensioners expected to

89. *Ibid.*

descend in the future. Indeed, the language of republican virtue borrowed from classical and Renaissance writers recast and elaborated on Puritan virtues. Thus many scholars have come to consider the defense and renewal of ethics and ideas rooted in Puritanism to be a major dimension of the Revolution in not only New England but the colonies as a whole.[90]

But from the vantage point of taverns and the popular culture of drink, it was the subversion of Puritan ethics that laid the foundation in Massachusetts for the rise of a new political configuration eventually taking the form of a Republic. During the seventeenth century the uppermost tiers of the Puritan hierarchy had made a concerted effort to limit taverns to a marginal place in public life. But public rooms had gradually become the context for idle tavern crowds to exercise influence over selectmen and representatives, a context for the reception and articulation of a secular ideology that sanctioned the concept of a critical public. The entire hierarchy constructed in the seventeenth century to regulate public life swayed, shifted, and ultimately refashioned itself under pressure from the populace at large into a system that would have shocked Samuel Sewall as it deeply troubled John Adams.

Like Adams there were others who remained uncomfortable with this nascent political culture in the 1760s. Indeed, the voters of Braintree assembled in town meeting momentarily joined him in the conviction that the number of taverns must be drastically reduced from that approved by the selectmen. Other towns periodically made similar efforts. It was troubling to have leaders who seemed to encourage rather than discourage intemperance by lax policies, or even treating or bribery at elections. It was troubling to observe the widespread demand for rum amid social and economic developments that narrowed opportunities for an anxious rising generation. And ministers never allowed their congregations to forget how far they had deviated from the principles and standards of the founding generation of the colony. While this new political culture might have provided expression for a wider number of male colonists in local and provincial affairs, insofar as it was structured by taverns and drink it

90. The classic statement on the link between Puritanism and the Revolution is Morgan, "The Puritan Ethic and the American Revolution," *WMQ*, 3d Ser., XXIV (1967), 3–43. Bailyn acknowledges some Puritan origins to Revolutionary thought in *The Ideological Origins*, 32–33. See also Perry Miller, "From the Covenant to the Revival," in James Ward Smith and A. Leland Jamison, eds., *The Shaping of American Religion* (Princeton, N.J., 1961), 322–368. For still a different connection between religion and revolution, see Harry S. Stout, "Religion, Communications, and the Ideological Origins of the American Revolution," *WMQ*, 3d Ser., XXXIV (1977), 519–541.

represented an insidious corruption of civic life as judged from all the points of reference colonists possessed. It was no accident that a Natick minister chose to deliver and publish a temperance sermon in 1774 with a reference to the "Sons of Licentiousness."[91]

The strains, conflicts, and contradictions in this emerging political culture may help to explain the high level of excitement and passion generated by what was believed to be an unfolding English conspiracy. As Americanus suggested, British policies loomed as an additional source of malaise for a society and political culture already under internal censure because of the numerous ways in which it violated the Puritan legacy. The prevalence of taverns and intemperance symbolized a range of ways in which colonial society seemed to be spinning out of control, in directions that undermined the quality of bonds that ideally held members of society together. The general disgust with a corrupt and chaotic world that pervades colonial attacks on British policies and leaders might have answered a widespread need among colonists to clarify somehow their own values and stake a claim to high moral ground despite misgivings about their own behavior.[92]

At the popular level, mobilization for resistance against the moral as well as constitutional threat of British policies might have provided an avenue for the resolution of conflict between popular activism and sinful behavior. Male colonists congregated in taverns more than ever, indulged in collective drinking in heated discussions of events, and even launched political missions from public rooms, but their behavior now was justified by its high moral purpose and urgent necessity. Tavern haunting was temporarily transformed from a blight on the social and political landscape, from a symptom of decline and decay, to a vehicle for necessary political vigilance. Towns divided into tavern-based factions could now achieve that elusive unity on the broader, more transcendent terms of republican citizenship.

Yet, as the courts were closed and as royal authority crumbled, these vocal and volatile gatherings of men made the definition and maintenance of public order more problematic. The sometimes unruly nature of large

91. Badger, *The Nature and Effects of Drunkenness*, 24–26, 36–39.

92. Gordon S. Wood has suggested that anxiety over the use of drink and other forms of bribery by candidates to win elections in Virginia might account for the frenzied nature of some aspects of Revolutionary rhetoric there. See "Rhetoric and Reality in the American Revolution," *WMQ*, 3d Ser., XXIII (1966), 3–32. Wood expands his treatment of underlying social conditions in this "truncated" society in *The Radicalism of the American Revolution* (New York, 1992), 117–137.

assemblies of men in and out of taverns, particularly in connection to the organization of the militia and the first American army in Massachusetts, worried elite observers. A correspondent of Adams wrote to him in 1775 that "officers and privates are so far on a level, that the former do not receive the respect and obedience which is due to their station." In the spring of 1776 another correspondent wrote to Adams that the formal dissolution of royal government would result in the "greatest anarchy as it would leave the people for a time without government." The "solemnity of a senate has left us," he continued, "and such a leveling spirit prevails even in men called the first among the mighty, that I fear we shall finally be obliged to call in a military force to do that which civil government was originally designed for."[93] This critic believed that levelism might destroy all order.

Certainly tavern companies received enough provoking reports in the decade after 1765 to inspire deep distrust of government in general. Worries about the onset of anarchy in 1775 were not unfounded. The inhabitants of Massachusetts had been progressively bombarded with reports of a malevolent conspiracy hatched by British ministers in collusion with their appointees in the colonies. Colonists had gradually moved to exorcise the very foundation of law and order in the colony—the offices of justices of the peace—of loyalists. Even clergymen came under suspicion if they did not openly profess Whig sentiments. A resident of Concord wrote to the *Massachusetts Gazette* in 1773 asking for more information about a rumor circulating that ministers "are leaving their good old Whig principles" and "getting daily into the line of Tories."[94] By 1774–1775, when every citizen had become engaged in carrying and interpreting news and when secret cadres of Tories were thought to be forming in some towns, the situation had become ripe for violent crowd actions against suspected Tories and traitors. Boston had already witnessed such spontaneous outbursts against occupying troops.

Yet in the face of the seeming anarchy and levelism that some observers feared after 1774, there were strenuous efforts to maintain stability and discipline amid the reconstruction of the social and political order. In part this was a consequence of entreaties made by leaders for restraint from the very beginning of resistance in 1765. Order in resistance was a Whig

93. Jonathan Williams to John Adams, July 7, 1775, in Robert J. Taylor *et al.*, eds. *The Papers of John Adams*, III, IV (Cambridge, Mass., 1979), III, 66, James Sullivan to Adams, May 9, 1776, IV, 179.

94. *Massachusetts Gazette; and the Boston Weekly News-Letter*, Aug. 5, 1773, no. 3644.

principle.[95] But the effectiveness of these entreaties was enhanced by the fact that tavern companies had long played a role in the political culture of town and province. The election of so many tavernkeepers to local and provincial office since 1720 had woven linkages between formal institutions of government and informal assemblies of drinkers. A respect for procedure and order existed among many tavern companies, as evident in the meetings of the American Political Society, because these companies had been so successful in translating their discussions and resolutions into formal influence over local affairs. There existed channels of communication through which Whig leaders could present their alarming convictions to the populace at large but also mediate public response. By the same token, ordinary men possessed in taverns an outlet for the airing of their concerns that influenced elected leaders and an arena for self-assertion in speech and posture. The mobilization of tavern companies of middling and lesser rank had been a source of anxiety among leaders since the beginning of resistance. But the careful integration of ceremony and procedure in popular assemblies of protest mitigated these fears. Taverns became a medium by which a rising pitch of political tension could be released but be constructively engaged.

True, in the stratified society of Boston's King Street, members of the gentry, artisans, and laborers did not collect in the same public houses. Genteel Bostonians had set themselves apart in taste, style, and demeanor; they had withdrawn into select companies and clubs. But the tradition of the Boston Caucus—the effort to mobilize common men in terms they could understand and appreciate—continued to soften and qualify this stratification in public life. Whig leaders were quick to establish common ground with the populace in part through public observances. Son of Liberty captain John Marston avidly consumed the high culture of the Enlightenment but also sang songs, applauded mimicry, and drank numerous toasts at anniversary celebrations of resistance viewed by Bostonians of all ranks. Son of Liberty Enoch Brown also possessed a library full of formal histories. But when he wrote to the *Boston Gazette* in 1774, it was not to deliver a formal political treatise, but to describe in detail an altercation between him and a hostile British soldier buying rum in his shop, something with which a poor shoemaker like George Hewes (who had experienced similar encounters with soldiers) might identify when it was read to him. As issues crystallized and engaged popular interest, taverns became a crossroads where leaders and followers might unite, exchange

95. Maier, *From Resistance to Revolution*, 62–63.

mutual confidence, and translate apprehension and fear into studied, measured responses.[96]

Leaders fostered stability amid Revolution by the expansion of the number of elected offices and the inclusion of tavernkeepers among those elected to new committees and posts. As belief of a concerted effort to abridge colonial liberties became more common and intense in the 1770s, the fears of an aroused populace were partially redressed by the election of a wider range of leaders who engaged in regular communication with their constituents. In divided towns like Weston and Hardwick, the election of tavernkeepers to committees of correspondence provided for closer consultation between leaders and followers confronting the possibility of covert communication among resident Tories. When an extralegal county convention of town committees assembled in Middlesex County in 1774 to decide how to respond to the changes imposed by the Massachusetts Government Act, 17 of the 150 delegates held liquor licenses.[97] They could report immediately and directly to waiting constituents in the public houses over which they presided. What more reassuring way to confront a con-

96. Suffolk County Probate Records, LXXXVI, 473; *Boston Gazette*, Oct. 3, 1774, no. 1016; Young, "George Robert Twelves Hewes," *WMQ*, 3d Ser., XXXVIII (1981), 561–623. Robert Darnton describes a growing alienation between "patricians" and "plebeians" in 18th-century France. Because of differences in language, dress, eating habits, and amusements, there developed a wide cultural gap between common men and polite society. This gap might have figured importantly in the process and result of revolution in France. In Massachusetts an analogous if less yawning gap existed between the genteel and the lower ranks, but political traditions involving taverns had woven threads of contact and cooperation. In comparison, see Darnton, "A Bourgeois Puts His World in Order: The City as a Text," in Darnton, *The Great Cat Massacre and Other Episodes in French Cultural History* (New York, 1985), esp. 130–131.

97. "Meeting of Committees from Every Town and District in the Country of Middlesex Held at Concord in August, 1774," *Boston Gazette*, Sept. 12, 1774, no. 1013. The tavernkeepers were Obadiah Sawtell, Shirley; Capt. Ezekiel How, Sudbury; Capt. Josiah Bowers, Billerica; Solomon Pollard, Billerica; Benjamin Pierce, Weston; Josiah Smith, Weston; Abel Perry, Natick; Capt. Thomas Mellen, Hopkinton; David Bayley, Tewksbury; Ebenezer Stone, Ashby; Benjamin Jacquith, Wilmington; Oliver Prescott, Esq., Westford; Capt. John Webber, Bedford; Capt. Roger Dench, Waltham. The retailers were Capt. Samuel Whittemore, Cambridge; Loammi Baldwin, Woburn; Col. Samuel Thacher, Cambridge. Mellen, Dench, Bayley, Stone, and Jacquith did not have licenses in 1774, but certificates of return from the town selectmen for licenses in the files of the Middlesex County Court of Sessions indicate that they did have licenses by 1776. The others are listed in the Court of General Sessions, Middlesex, Record Books.

spiracy than to elevate men accustomed to hearing, interpreting, and dispensing news in their neighborhoods, men who already possessed informal status as sources of knowledge about the wider world?

Even in the tense months before Gage's anticipated foray into the countryside, there was a measured quality to the actions of tavern assemblies in close consultation with local leaders. When the inhabitants of Marlborough received a warning from tavernkeeper Timothy Bigelow that two of Gage's spies were headed for the town, it was not an indiscriminate mob of men that descended on Henry Barnes's house to ferret them out. The Committee of Correspondence of the town assembled to discover and question them. The night before, a "party of Liberty men" had waited for the spies to arrive at Williams's tavern. Yet even if they had trapped them there, they would no doubt have been restrained by the influence of Colonel Abraham Williams himself—former selectman, justice, militia officer, and tavernkeeper.[98]

Tavernkeepers also acted to increase the flow of information from the world of print to their customers, thus helping to integrate the resistance movement and temper its actions. In December 1774 tavernkeeper Timothy Bigelow invited Boston newspaper publisher Isaiah Thomas to set up his press in Worcester. Circulation of the *Massachusetts Spy* quickly increased after Thomas established himself there. By May 1775 Thomas had thirty-seven individuals in thirty-three Worcester County towns processing new subscriptions. Seven tavernkeepers and two retailers were among them. One was Paul Mandell, the Hardwick tavernkeeper and militia officer who replaced Timothy Ruggles, esquire, as the town's representative. Five of the licenseholders were militia officers. Another ten on the list

98. Brown and D'Bernicre, ["Narrative"], MHS, *Collections*, 2d Ser., IV (1816), 209, 211, 213. Williams was licensed (counting at five-year intervals) in 1750, 1755, 1760, 1765, 1770, but had given license up by 1776. He served as selectman in 1741–1743, 1746–1749, 1752, and 1754, after which he became a justice. In 1776 the town had five public houses. Three of them were kept by local leaders: Col. Cyprian Howe (elected a selectman in 1774 and 1778), Munnings Sawin (elected a selectman in 1768, 1772, and 1779–1783), and Joel Brigham (elected in 1763 and 1772). Benjamin Sawin, licensed in 1787, was one of the town's delegates to the Massachusetts convention to ratify the Constitution. Court of General Sessions, Middlesex, Record Books and Files; Charles Hudson, *History of the Town of Marlborough* . . . (Boston, 1862), 279–285. Committees of Correspondence with close ties to tavernkeepers could help to discipline the process of detecting loyalists (*Acts and Resolves*, V, 479–480). By this law Committees of Correspondence and Safety were instructed to acquire declarations of fidelity to the United States from every male over 16.

held rank of captain and above.[99] With so many licenseholders processing subscriptions, it is probable that most tavernkeepers in the county took the paper. To be sure, the paper inflamed the sensibilities of men hearing the news read. Still, order and restraint were an explicit or implicit message in the *Spy* and other Whig papers. No independent popular movement coalesced to challenge the leaders of the Revolution in Massachusetts, in part because those closest to the pulse of everyday life and oral structures of communication—tavernkeepers—already occupied positions of influence and leadership.

The number of licenseholders active in electoral politics increased as Massachusetts drew closer to open revolt. In 1765, 32 percent of tavernkeepers (nineteen of fifty-nine) in fifteen Middlesex County towns were active as officeholders at either town or colony level. By 1776 the proportion of active tavernkeepers had increased to 45 percent (thirty-two of seventy-one). There was also a change in the character of representation to the Assembly by the dawn of the Republic. In 1765 the ten tavernkeepers and retailers elected to the House from Middlesex, Worcester, and Hampshire counties almost all held appointments as justices of the peace. Ten years later the proportion of representatives who held licenses did not rise, but their actual number increased from ten to seventeen. Of this seventeen, only one was a justice. Whereas in 1765 justices had outnumbered licenseholders by thirty to ten (with significant overlap) in these three counties, by 1775 licenseholders outnumbered justices by seventeen to eleven.[100] It was the justices, with their ties of interest to royal patrons, who appeared to subvert Republican values to voters in many towns, not the publicans who drank with their public.

Militia officers, notorious for distributing drink to their companies at taverns, also became more active as elected representatives to the House.

99. Lincoln, *History of Worcester*, 242–243; list of men who processed subscriptions for the *Massachusetts Spy*, May 3, 1775, no. 219. The tavernkeepers were Capt. Stephen Maynard, Westborough; Capt. David Goodridge, Fitchburg; Col. Paul Mandell, Hardwick; Capt. Timothy Newell, Sturbridge; Abiel Sadler, Upton; Capt. James Woods, New Braintree; John Child, Holden. The retailers were Dr. John Taylor, Lunenburg; Simeon Dwight, Esq., Western.

100. These figures were reached by comparing rosters of licenseholders in 1765, 1770, and 1776 for Middlesex County, and those for 1765 and 1770 for Worcester and Hampshire counties, taken from the records of the Courts of General Sessions for these counties, with rosters of representatives listed in *Acts and Resolves* for the period between 1760 and 1780. Tavernkeepers and retailers are counted as active in electoral politics if they held office within five years before or after holding a license.

In 1765, 19 percent (9 of 47) of the delegates from these three counties held commissions, most of them as captains. By 1776 this proportion had increased to 31 percent (37 of 121). There was a significant overlap with licenseholders. Of the 37 officers, 8 also held licenses. Although it became unlawful in 1776 for officers to distribute liquor to their companies at any time, the Assembly never formally forbade the distribution of liquor on election day when civil officers were selected.[101]

The House as a whole recognized the formal and informal influence of tavernkeepers among their townsmen when the closure of the courts prevented the annual review and granting of licenses. The House did not wish to dispense with these proceedings, because it might send the wrong message in respect to public order. So it sanctioned the convening of special sessions staffed by Whig justices for the purpose. But it took special care to order selectmen, if they needed any urging, to recommend only those who are "firmly attached to the rights and interests of their country."[102] With so many tavernkeepers among their ranks, members of the House sought to ensure that all licenseholders so enmeshed with the formation and flow of public opinion be men devoted to the emerging Republic.

Yet this order by members of the Assembly instructing justices to approve only ardent republicans to be tavernkeepers evoked a hierarchical flow of authority which had all but collapsed, for in some cases justices and selectmen approved tavernkeepers who commanded far greater public influence, particularly those drinksellers who sat in the Assembly. The authority of justices over republican tavernkeepers had all but vanished, bringing into stark relief a citizenry informally organized in taverns.

A public composed of high numbers of habitual tavern patrons still posed fundamental contradictions to republican theory, principles, and ideals. In the exigencies of mobilization, under the pressure of events, these contradictions could be ignored and smoothed over. But as the colony organized for defense and as it became probable that a Republic would be created, literate patriots imbued with classical ideals renewed their criticism of popular behavior and the leaders who indulged it. A month before Independence was declared, a writer to the *Boston Gazette* related an experience he had while traveling through towns in Maine. He was "agreeably entertained" in many towns "by the company" he "fell into," presumably in taverns. And he was especially gratified by the company in one town in particular noted for its "spirited resolves." Here was "sweet enjoyment of a

101. *Acts and Resolves*, XVIII, 4–5, XIX, 418–420.

102. *Ibid.*, XIX, 142.

set of men who breathed nothing but liberty at any hazard of life and fortune." Their "common language was death rather than slavery." Indeed, he fancied himself "among the ancient Spartans whose prevailing passion was the love of their country." But these classical illusions were shattered when on election day this observer witnessed a majority vote for "a raw unexperienced man" for "a member of our Parliament." When asked why they made this choice, one replied that the winner was a relation of two principal electors and that he was "a tavernkeeper, and could treat well." How, this critic asked, could "these high pretenders to the love of liberty" make "such an improper choice, in such a critical time, such as America never saw before, or ever shall again"? This was the "face of party spirit," and such behavior "laid the foundation of the ruin of the Jewish state, and the same fate has followed every nation that has been infested with that disease." Voters must "promote the best men to the most important services."[103] This was the lesson of ancient republics, if they would survive. A sober, industrious citizenry must recognize and elevate a natural, disinterested aristocracy of merit among men.

Provincial leaders took action in the spirit of this criticism. In preparation for armed conflict, the Provincial Congress reorganized the militia in 1776. It outlawed the custom of treating because it "subverted" martial strength and "injured" a free people. Two years later, when the towns debated and voted on the state constitution of 1778, the lack of any provision outlawing bribery with drink proved of wide concern. Sutton, a Worcester County town, advised that a clause forbidding "the purchasing of seats in the Legislature" be included. No person should be allowed to vote for representatives without first taking oath that his choice was not made in the hope of receiving a "treat, loan, or gratuity, directly or indirectly." The town of Lexington also asked for a provision against "canvassing for elections, corrupt influence, and open bribery." The Essex County assessment of the constitution of 1778, representing the view of twelve towns, stated the need to ensure that elections be free. "Bribery, corruption, or undue influence" should not "stifle the free voice of the people, corrupt their morals, and introduce a supineness of temper" and "inattention to their liberties" that paves the road for "the approach of tyranny."[104] Republican citizens must spurn social ties based in drink and exercise their wits so as to be able to discern disinterested candidates on election day.

103. *Boston Gazette,* June 10, 1776, no. 1099.

104. *Acts and Resolves,* V, 451; Robert J. Taylor, ed., *Massachusetts, Colony to Commonwealth: Documents on the Formation of Its Constitution, 1775–1780* (Chapel Hill, N.C., 1961), 64, 67, 82.

Yet it must have made sense to the voters in that Maine town, as in so many other towns, to elevate one of their tavernkeepers, or a tavern orator, to "our Parliament" at the dawn of the Republic. A number of towns had been doing so since the 1720s, blurring the lines between the gentry and middling ranks even as so many sought to distinguish themselves as genteel. By the 1770s, however, the distinction of gentility had become a liability among officeholders if it was not combined with democratic manners most easily exercised in taverns. It was not just that tavernkeepers could "treat well" but that they were accessible fellows in regular communication with their constituents. And this had become still more important as the fear of a conspiracy to reduce the power of the voting public had eroded royal authority and led to the creation of the Republic. Over the past decade numerous officeholders of high social rank had been convicted in the public mind of avarice and self-interest through the printing or public reading of private communications. In 1769 copies of Governor Bernard's letters to the crown ministry surreptitiously obtained by Boston radicals had been publicly read into Boston town records at town meeting and analyzed at length for their many base insinuations and "virulent charges" against the town. Governor Hutchinson had become infamous after the publication of edited versions of his letters to Thomas Whately in the Boston press.[105] It was natural that the tavernkeepers who facilitated the diffusion of the printed and oral discourse that "exposed" these men to a wider public should be held in esteem and even thought suitable for "our Parliament."

Indeed, tavern companies reached the height of their influence among Protestant white males in Massachusetts in the 1770s. Despite the repeated efforts to suppress them by Puritan authorities in the colony's first century, traditions of collective drinking had persisted as an integral part of community life. And after 1720, taverns had become a context for men to cast off gradually the traditional restraints on their political behavior. In this most flexible and egalitarian of colonial institutions, inhibitions of speech and posture in reference to figures of authority had dissolved over the course of the eighteenth century. Tavernkeepers still waited attendance before the hierarchy of local and county leaders every year to renew their licenses, but taverns had simultaneously become the institutional base for the reception and dissemination of ideas that encouraged ordinary

---

105. Boston, Record Commissioners, *Boston Town Records, 1758 to 1769* (Boston, 1886), 303. The impact of the publication of Hutchinson's letters cannot be exaggerated, for they acted as a confirmation of rumors and suspicions circulating in taverns. See Bailyn, *The Ordeal of Thomas Hutchinson*, 91, 130–131, 223–228, 242–243.

men to seize a greater role in political life at the expense of those hierarchies. Colonial leaders borrowing Whig opposition ideology to resist exercises of authority by royal governors perceived to be unconstitutional justified their actions in the name of an abstract public that existed outside formal institutional assemblies. In public houses white men gathered to realize representative versions of this public, but simultaneously were made aware of how little they knew of the operation of the crown's government and of how much they had to fear as a consequence. After 1765, they gathered with new purpose and reinvented themselves as republican citizens in 1776. Thus taverns stood at the crossroads of tradition and modernity in the 1770s, at once fusing centuries-old English customs of local association with nascent democratic participation in affairs of state. That this should happen in the English colony most committed to the suppression of intemperance and tavern haunting in the name of order is testimony to the transforming nature of the American environment and the republican ideology borrowed to justify a new order.

Epilogue: After the Revolution

At the conclusion of the war, some republican leaders in Massachusetts and the nation as a whole began to quake at the aroused citizenry they had helped to create. This was not the classical republic originally envisioned by the national and state leaders who presided over its creation. The public virtue necessary to ensure a fragile republic's survival everywhere seemed absent. The vocal, assertive tavern assemblies of the 1770s became agents of disorder and disruption in the eyes of many political observers by the 1780s and posed a still more stark contradiction to republican ideals than they had in 1776.

Once again, proposals for a wholesale reduction in the number of public houses received airing. But no steps were taken, perhaps because leaders feared the popular reaction such a move might provoke. Leaders also condemned the proliferation of extralegal associations and conventions that sprang up to express popular sentiment. Even Samuel Adams, leader of the Sons of Liberty, became dismayed over the tenor of the oratory and organization when he wrote to John Adams in 1784. He believed that, when the focus of hostility had been the agents of crown authority, popular committees and county conventions had served an "excellent purpose." But now that all officeholders had become dependent on annual free elections, the country had become "safe without them." Indeed, such committees and conventions now were not only "useless but dangerous," according to Adams. Jonathan Jackson, a Newburyport merchant, wrote bluntly in 1788 that the people "are nearly as unfit to choose legislators or any of the more important public officers as they are in general to fill the offices themselves." In fact, the proportion of legislators of wealth and substance dropped from 50 percent in 1765 to 21 percent in 1785. The promotion of special interests by individual representatives seemed to accompany the democratization of the legislature. A Republic characterized by self-sacrifice and disinterest seemed more elusive than ever.[1] The elite of Boston and the countryside began to recoil from the popular character of politics.

The grass-roots uprising led by Daniel Shays in protest of debt actions by the courts in the western counties in 1786 shocked Massachusetts and national leaders. In the aftermath of the rebellion William Shepard wrote to Governor James Bowdoin that the legislature must "rivet" in the people's minds "a complete conviction of the force of government and the necessity of an entire submission to the laws." The tavernkeepers and retailers, Shepard observed, "have generally been very seditious." These houses "have been the common rendezvous for the councils and comfort of the people." Shepard recommended that rebellious licenseholders suffer a "total disqualification for a limited time or forever of enjoying those priv-

---

1. Resolve Directing the Committee to Revise the Laws, to Take into Consideration the Laws for the Due Observation of the Lord's Day, and to Prepare a Bill for Preventing Drunkenness and Other Atrocious Vices, in Massachusetts, *Acts and Resolves, Public and Private, of the Province of the Massachusetts Bay* (Boston, 1869–1922), 1780–1, 634–635. The resolve stated: "And inasmuch as drunkenness and the intemperate use of spirituous liquors enfeebles the bodies and enervates the minds of men—shortens life—lessens the quantity of labor in the Commonwealth—tends to promote every other vice—extinguishes the moral sense, and is in the most striking manner disgraceful to human nature: Therefore, Resolved, that the said committee prepare a bill, as soon as may be, for effectually preventing or punishing so atrocious a vice, and for lessening the number of, and better regulating taverns and other licensed houses within this commonwealth." A new law regulating the sale of drink was enacted in 1786, but it mainly reiterated past laws and only urged justices "not to license more persons than are necessary for the public good." It did provide that the names of common drunkards should be posted in taverns. Massachusetts, *Acts and Laws of the Commonwealth of Massachusetts*, 1786–7 (Boston, 1893), 206–214. Samuel Adams to John Adams, Apr. 16, 1784, Samuel Adams to Noah Webster, Apr. 30, 1784, in Harry Alonzo Cushing, ed., *The Writings of Samuel Adams* (New York, 1904–1908), IV, 296, 305–306; [Jonathan Jackson], *Thoughts upon the Political Situation of the United States . . .* (Worcester, Mass., 1788), 54–62, 76–79, 117–118; Gordon S. Wood, *The Creation of the American Republic, 1776–1787* (Chapel Hill, N.C., 1969), chaps. 8, 12, quotations on 327, 509–510; Jackson Turner Main, "Government by the People: The American Revolution and the Democratization of the Legislatures," in Jack P. Greene, ed., *The Reinterpretation of the American Revolution, 1763–1789* (New York, 1968), 335.

ileges" and that this proposal should "be the subject of serious discussion" in the legislature.[2]

The legislature did decide to act and stripped known Shaysites of their licenses. In 1787 the legislature enacted a new license law requiring selectmen to testify through their certificates of approbation that those recommended for licenses or renewal were "firmly attached to the Constitution and the laws of this Commonwealth." Further, every licenseholder must now take an oath before a justice or a clerk of the legislature that he "will bear true faith and allegiance to the Commonwealth of Massachusetts" and will "defend the Constitution and Government thereof against traitorous conspiracies and all hostile and violent attempts whatsoever."[3] In 1776, licenseholders had been required to swear loyalty to the new United States in a great groundswell of popular repudiation of royal government. Now Massachusetts leaders sought to curb the propensity of tavernkeepers to criticize and agitate against government.

Such controls, however, did not hinder the emergence of the public house as a political institution. The punitive measures enacted by the Assembly against the Shaysites created a backlash of feeling against the government. A majority of representatives were unseated in the next election together with Governor James Bowdoin. The new government quickly repealed the Disqualifying Act, and former Shaysites could now renew and get liquor licenses. The backlash extended into the election of delegates to the convention convened in 1788 to consider the new national Constitution. More towns than ever before elected delegates, some of them former insurgents. It required extraordinary efforts of persuasion and conciliatory proposals for amendments for the Federalists finally to carry the day and win ratification. Popular feeling over the exercise of political authority remained so impassioned that, when Massachusetts towns divided into Federalists and Democratic-Republicans in the 1790s, taverns became known by the political affiliation of their keepers.[4] Moreover, the

2. William Shepard to James Bowdoin, Westfield, Feb. 18, 1787, *The Bowdoin and Temple Letters*, pt. 2 (MHS, *Collections*, 7th Ser., VI [Boston, 1907]), 141–142; Wood, *Creation of the American Republic*, 374–376, 412–413.

3. Robert J. Taylor, *Western Massachusetts in the Revolution* (Providence, R.I., 1954), 164; *Acts and Laws of the Commonwealth of Massachusetts*, 1786–7, 206–208.

4. Taylor, *Western Massachusetts in the Revolution*, 165–167; Richard D. Brown, "Shays's Rebellion and the Ratification of the Federal Constitution," in Richard Beeman, Stephen Botein, and Edward C. Carter II, *Beyond Confederation: Origins of the Constitution and American National Identity* (Chapel Hill, N.C., 1987), 113–127; Charles Warren, *Jacobin and*

intensity of discussion in public rooms in the 1770s and 1780s, where men learned to "breathe nothing but liberty" and spoke a "common language" of "death rather than slavery," began to have an effect on the very language of politics.

William Manning kept tavern for his father in Billerica in the early 1770s and became "a constant reader of public newspapers." He wrote lengthy proposals in the 1780s and 1790s to put forth his perception of a fundamental division between the "few" men of wealth and leisure and the "many" who labored with their hands for sustenance. These manuscripts are studded with examples of earthy, epigrammatic phrases, quips, and barbs common to oral discourse among farmers. Manning's style reflects the kind of tavern oratory more men had come to expect from their leaders. He admired but also distrusted the eloquence traditionally striven for in political expression; he accused the "few" in past and present of seeking to monopolize the creation and diffusion of knowledge, of writing constitutions and laws in a style that inhibited popular understanding. This would become a common complaint among Antifederalists in general, that the Federalists deceived men through the manipulation of language.[5]

Thus not only the meaning but the expression of republican precepts would become more confused, a cacophony of voices, as more men laid claim to them and adapted them to reflect their circumstances and perspective.

For the gentry of Massachusetts imbued with classical ideals, the licentiousness of the many seemed to spiral out of control. The Revolution wrought no transformation in virtue in respect to drinking habits. The number of public houses continued to multiply according to population growth. In Middlesex County the number rose from 242 in 1776 to 289 in 1791. In the 1790s farmers on the New York and Pennsylvania frontiers began to inundate the eastern seaboard with cheap corn whiskey. The per

Junto; or, Early American Politics as Viewed in the Diary of Dr. Nathaniel Ames, 1758–1822 (Cambridge, Mass., 1931), 78–80.

5. Gordon S. Wood, *The Radicalism of the American Revolution* (New York, 1992), 271–273; Michael Merrill and Sean Wilentz, eds., *The Key of Liberty: The Life and Democratic Writings of William Manning, "A Laborer," 1747–1814* (Cambridge, Mass., 1993), 9, 16, 18, 54–56, 62. Merrill and Wilentz point out that Manning brought a skeptical mind to conventional republican theory. He admired Benjamin Lincoln's "Free Republican" essays concerning the reasons for the decline of ancient republics, but refused to accept Lincoln's argument (which echoed that of Whig historians) that the "licentiousness" of the "many" had destroyed free governments in the past. Rather, it was the artifice and cunning of the "few," coupled with the ignorance of the "many," that had undermined republics.

capita consumption of hard liquor in the new nation rose from 3.7 gallons in 1770 to 5 gallons by 1830. But governments did not act to repress consumption, because it was still entwined with political discourse. Not only had Americans refused to forswear rum, but they now supplemented it with whiskey. The popular behavior that had been condemned for centuries as a primary reason for the legitimacy of elite control and dominance of public affairs now became a vehicle for repudiation of elite governance, indeed of the concept of an elite altogether. The gentry had always been an elastic and ill-defined group in Massachusetts, as even tavernkeepers won some toehold in it. Now the gentry risked being branded with the new epithet "aristocrat" if they did not adopt democratic manners.[6] The Revolutionary generation had unleashed a level of participation in politics that it could not contain. In contradiction to every republican precept, intemperance and democracy seemed to proceed and deepen hand in hand after 1790.

Still, during the decades spanning the Revolution it is possible to glimpse how this redefinition of American life could gradually begin to weaken the hold that the popular culture of drink had on the new citizens of Massachusetts. Puritan leaders had never been able to surmount the importance of the tavern in communication within and between communities, in part because of the Puritan reverence for traditional ties of cooperation and dependence within communities. Despite formal efforts to suppress them, taverns remained instrumental as a setting for cultivating ties of interdependence. Moreover, Puritan devotion to the use of print for religious edification was qualified by equally intensive efforts to limit and control the use of the press. Thus taverns remained a vital part of a predominantly oral system of communication. During and after the Revolution, however, the use of the press and the diffusion of printed discourse expanded to unprecedented levels as the demand for information became more acute. In the short run this discourse only heightened the importance of tavern gatherings because of their role in the diffusion of the contents of printed discourse. Yet implicit in the calls for the printing of pocket volumes of John Dickinson's *Letters* for every American and in the increase in newspaper subscriptions in rural counties like Worcester was the fundamental belief that individual citizens of a Republic must consume and

6. W. J. Rorabaugh, *The Alcoholic Republic: An American Tradition* (New York, 1979), 6–12; Wood, *The Radicalism of the American Revolution,* 276; Court of General Sessions, Book of Licenses, 1791–1810, Judicial Archives, ACM.

weigh political information in a more private capacity.[7] The ideological foundation for a modern, more impersonal communication system that transcended oral networks like tavern companies had been laid.

The tavernkeeper's traditional role as a purveyor of news and information began to be eclipsed by the broader consumption of print. Tavernkeeper and almanac author Nathaniel Ames welcomed and encouraged this change. In 1776 he urged Massachusetts farmers to "study not only religion but politics and the nature of civil government." "[We must] become politicians every one of us" and "take upon us to examine every thing, and think for ourselves." The world of print more forcefully invaded and altered the oral culture of taverns during the Revolution and decades following. Now it was not just some men who should and would possess books and newspaper subscriptions. Republican ideology justified and recommended that all men should participate in the world of print.[8] The localism that helped to sustain the popular culture of drink began to recede.

7. Jürgen Habermas and Michael Warner both analyze the development of "reading as a new kind of institution" in the 18th century, which enabled individuals to conceive of themselves privately as members of a "public sphere" separate from the individuals who embodied institutions of state. But this "privatization" of reading, particularly the "letters" of the Republic, was balanced by the perceived need to disseminate a major message of republican literature—the "corruption" of government by "private" interest. Public readings and discussions of pamphlets in, first, genteel taverns and, later, those for common men provided a physical representation symbolic of the content of print. Only after the Revolution, when the volume and variety of print expanded, did reading become a more exclusively private institution. "Public" readings to the barely literate in taverns gradually became less important. See Habermas, *The Structural Transformation of the Public Sphere: An Inquiry into a Category of Bourgeois Society,* trans. Thomas Burger (Cambridge, Mass., 1989), 31–56; and Warner, *The Letters of the Republic: Publication and the Public Sphere in Eighteenth-Century America* (Cambridge, Mass., 1990), 39–43, 61.

8. Nathaniel Ames, *An Astronomical Diary; or, Almanack for the Year of Our Lord Christ 1767* (Boston, 1766), 1–2. Richard D. Brown discusses the multiplication of printing presses in "The Emergence of Urban Society in Rural Massachusetts, 1760–1820," *Journal of American History,* LXI (1974–1975), 29–51. In 1778 a rural farmer in Shirley decided to subscribe to Thomas's *Massachusetts Spy.* By the 1830s reformers promoted mass subscriptions to newspapers as a means for farmers to avoid wasting time at taverns in order to hear news by word of mouth. See Richard D. Brown, *Knowledge Is Power: The Diffusion of Information in Early America* (New York, 1989), 150–151, 159. William J. Gilmore traces the expansion of the use of print even among humble households in his *Reading Becomes a Necessity of Life: Material and Cultural Life in Rural New England, 1780–1835* (Knoxville, Tenn., 1989), 285–342, 346–352.

The Revolution not only stimulated an expansion in the use of print; it justified and inspired new forms of voluntarism that set people apart from indiscriminate neighborhood gatherings and companies. Puritan voluntarism in the seventeenth century—the withdrawal from churches considered corruptions of the primitive church, and the organization of gathered congregations—had placed tavern companies on the defensive, but never supplanted them, to the continuing frustration of the clergy. But Republican ideology and the experience of resistance and revolution inspired the creation of new voluntary organizations in the countryside as well as in Boston. Once almost the only voluntary organizations, by the 1790s churches constituted fewer than half of the 373 organizations being formed in Massachusetts as a whole. During this decade 73 educational (libraries, academies, debating, learned), 29 civic (fire, law enforcement, military, political), and 39 occupational (agricultural, professional, mechanic, merchant) societies were founded. A reorganization of community life that justified new departures from tradition was under way. William Manning proposed the creation of a national society for laboring men that would publish a monthly magazine to instruct and edify common men in neighborhood meetings.[9]

To be sure, many of these new organizations met in taverns as the clubs of the Boston gentry had in the late-colonial era. Still, their members qualified their identification with and participation in local drinking companies. And some of these societies conceived of themselves as distinct alternatives to the tavern crowd. The Concord Social Circle, first formed in the 1770s and reorganized in 1787, originated in one of the town's Revolutionary organizations, the Committee of Safety. The Circle convened in order to "strengthen the social affections, and disseminate useful communications among its members." It limited membership to twenty-five and met in a private home. Significantly, the Circle stipulated that refreshment be "moderate," although it did permit mixed drinks of rum as well as cider. In a retrospective of the organization written in 1828, minister Samuel Ripley stated that one of the underlying purposes of the Circle had been "to provide a substitute for the supposed needfulness of collecting at taverns to learn the news of the day, and thereby to prevent the practice of tavern haunting, and the temptation to needless expense and injurious drinking." The Circle was a vehicle for its members to acquire

9. Brown, "Emergence of Urban Society," *JAH*, LXI (1974–1975), 40–41; Merrill and Wilentz, eds., *The Key of Liberty*, 65.

and converse about news "in an easy and respectable manner."[10] In organizations like the Circle a middle class gradually began to distinguish itself from tavern crowds.

The expansion of commerce after 1790 also ate away at the old ties of interest and dependence forged in taverns. The creation of banks and the greater issuance of currency notes gradually rendered purchases of all kinds more impersonal, eliminating the necessity of bargaining over credit and payment schedules solemnized with drink. This change was liberating in the sense that it freed individuals from dense networks of obligation and dependence. But participation in this more commercial cash nexus also left men and women more alone and anxious in a more complicated world. Increasing rates of migration to western lands and northern New England set more individuals adrift among strangers.[11] The sinister effects of alcoholism described by ministers throughout the eighteenth century loomed a greater threat to citizens caught up in this more mobile, risky, and competitive society. There was more reason to guard against the seductively appealing but potentially addictive oblivion that strong drink could bring to men as they confronted the dizzying array of changes in post-Revolutionary America.

The Revolution also encouraged the creation of a manufacturing sector of the economy of Massachusetts as a means to break dependence on European products and simultaneously promote industrious work habits. Previous experiments in Boston had proved to be short-lived failures. But population growth and density in New England by the end of the century led some men to conclude that the time was ripe for developing manufactures to employ excess labor. Ames observed in 1766 that the country had become "too thick inhabited for all to get a living by the present methods of farming." The boycotts of English goods in the 1760s and 1770s stimulated calls for home manufactures of necessary products. When the crown closed the port of Boston in 1774, the town committees set up a number of projects to provide employment, including a brick factory, house and ship construction, a linen factory, and shoemaking. Work days continued to be punctuated by the consumption of alcohol. In Charlestown the committee in charge of employing the poor when the port closed made sure that laborers received, along with provisions, a "half pint of rum each day, and

10. *The Centennial of the Social Circle in Concord, March 21, 1882* (Cambridge, Mass., 1882), 60.

11. Wood, *The Radicalism of the American Revolution*, 127–141, 169–170, 173.

sugar in proportion."[12] But the leaders conceived the new enthusiasm for manufactures as an antidote for indolence and intemperance. It was also a spur to farmers to labor to produce a surplus to sell in order to purchase manufactured products (besides rum). As never before in Massachusetts, the development of manufactures became linked with the creation of a society marked by public virtue. And the gradual growth of manufactures in decades after the Revolution would create a body of employers with an investment in the temperate behavior of their employees.

Simultaneous with the enthusiasm for and actual growth of manufactures was the gradual withdrawal or ejectment of widows from the occupation of drinkselling in Boston. In the middle decades of the eighteenth century, widows had comprised approximately one-third of the license-holders in Boston and figured prominently in all the seaports as drink-sellers. In 1768, 11 of 25 new retailers were women. But this presence would diminish after the Revolution. By 1796 only 9 of 128 retailers in Boston were women. Of 56 tavernkeepers licensed in 1812, there were no women; of 273 retailers licensed, there were only 10 women.[13] Widows had always been unwelcome in the drink trade in Massachusetts; most of them received licenses only to avoid placing them on relief. Now that alternative forms of employment opened up and there existed less pressure to grant licenses to the poor and widowed, licensing authorities might have rejected petitions from widows in increasing numbers. In 1788, newspapers announced the manufacture of sailcloth and glass in Boston. Among other things, the press extolled these manufactures as providing employment "to a great number of persons, especially females, who now 'eat the bread of idleness' from the want of some calling whereby they may gain an honest livelihood." The same issue reported that a building would be erected for the employment of "loose and vagrant women." Proposals for charity schools for poor children and work programs for beggars also received airing. Women were forced to retreat from the limited presence in the public life of taverns that they had carved out for themselves in desperation. Institutional solutions were gaining ground. Ironically, the steep decline in the number of women licensed

12. Ames, *An Astronomical Diary*, 3; Robinson Crusoe to *Boston Evening Post*, Dec. 14, 1767, no. 1674; Richard D. Brown, *Revolutionary Politics in Massachusetts: The Boston Committee of Correspondence and the Towns, 1772–1774* (Cambridge, Mass., 1970), 221–222; Richard Frothingham, Jr., *The History of Charlestown, Massachusetts* (Boston, 1845), 311.

13. Court of General Sessions of the Peace, Suffolk, Record Book, 1796–1807, Oct. 3, 1796; Court of General Sessions, Suffolk, Innholders and Retailers, 1812–1822, Judicial Archives, ACM.

in Boston coincided with the first recorded licensing of a "black man," George Middleton, in the town.[14]

Licensing authorities could move to exclude women because widows had never been able to use their businesses to alter gender roles fundamentally. True, widows licensed in eighteenth-century Boston had presided over and regulated to some extent the behavior of mostly male companies. They had survived in a very competitive trade. But they remained exceptions to the rule, formally expelled from the trade as soon as they remarried. Generally, they had not been able to translate this presence in the drink trade into an effective means of augmenting the indirect political influence that women in general wielded as wives and economic partners. To be sure, this influence could be weighty and bold, as when Sarah Pitts repeated the charge to her soldier-husband and his fellows, that they were "fools" if they did not "rise all as one rather than be served so" by the Castle Island commander. But it remained indirect. Female licenseholders might host political meetings, as Widow Stearns did for the American Political Society in Worcester, but they normally could not participate in the decisions made at them. Drinkselling had been a vehicle for only a limited renegotiation of restrictive gender roles.[15] The trade became so crowded that women left it as readily as men, some to get married.

It was in churches as full communicating members that women possessed a voice (albeit a muted one). Indeed, over the colonial period women came to outnumber men in church membership as men became reluctant to take the steps necessary to become members.[16] But the influence of ministers declined as the eighteenth century progressed, except for the periods of revivals at midcentury. In some ways the center of political and institutional innovation shifted from the church to taverns because they were more flexible institutions. In public houses men could assert themselves more readily and more easily redefine their relationships with each other and authority figures, redrawing the very boundaries of community life.

14. Drew R. McCoy, *The Elusive Republic: Political Economy in Jeffersonian America* (Chapel Hill, N.C., 1980), 64, 77, 82, 116, 117; *Massachusetts Centinel*, Sept. 6, 1788, no. 50; Court of General Sessions, Suffolk, Record Book, 1796–1807, Oct. 3, 1796.

15. Court of General Sessions, Suffolk, Record Book, 1702–1712, 100; Linda K. Kerber, *Women of the Republic: Intellect and Ideology in Revolutionary America* (Chapel Hill, N.C., 1980), 154 (Kerber notes that Whig opposition ideology never addressed the status of women, 27–32); Records of the American Political Society, December 1774, Feb. 6, 1775, American Antiquarian Society, Worcester, Mass.

16. Laurel Thatcher Ulrich, *Good Wives: Image and Reality in the Lives of Women in Northern New England, 1650–1750* (New York, 1991), 215–217.

Moreover, they could do so while still maintaining dominance over women. Less often at taverns because of their myriad tasks in tending foodways and children, women took little part in the institutional innovation that evolved in taverns.

After the Revolution, however, women would gradually organize to reduce the gender gap that had developed in public life in the eighteenth century. The new importance invested in temperance by republican ideology helped to redefine women's roles. Women must now become the nurturers and instructors of virtuous republican citizens in the home, architects of a new domesticity. The construction and refinement of a private family life by women, in part through the purchase of material luxuries, placed new pressure on men to reduce expenditures on that preeminent luxury, strong drink.[17] This new sphere of dominance gradually invested some women with the authority to criticize and challenge the tavern haunting and drinking habits of men. After 1790 women formed voluntary societies which enhanced their ability to administer and promote domestic felicity in their own houses and the households of the poor. Organization to cultivate domesticity along republican guidelines eventually lent sanction for women to organize temperance societies to oppose the male-dominated public sphere of taverns. Not in taverns, but in agitation to get men out of them, women gradually enlarged their political influence and drew closer to men in public life, especially in meetings, parades, and ceremonies of the temperance movement.[18] Thus the eject-

17. Nancy F. Cott, *The Bonds of Womanhood: "Woman's Sphere" in New England, 1780– 1835* (New Haven, Conn., 1977); Ruth M. Bloch, "American Feminine Ideals in Transition: The Rise of the Moral Mother, 1785–1815," *Feminist Studies,* IV, no. 2 (June 1978), 100– 126; Kerber, *Women of the Republic,* 283–288; Richard L. Bushman, *The Refinement of America: Persons, Houses, Cities* (New York, 1992), 256–279.

18. This conclusion is drawn from a reading of temperance reports and literature at the Massachusetts Historical Society. In a tract published in Boston by the Charlestown Association for the Reformation of Morals in 1813, Jedidiah Morse addressed women with these words: "The female part of my audience will permit me, in one word, to say to them respectfully and affectionately, that I calculate with great pleasure, and with entire confidence in their prayers, and their influence, by all exertions suited to their sex and circumstances, to aid in effecting the objects of this Association. I refer it to your own good sense to devise the ways in which you can most effectually promote these great objects" (Charlestown Association for the Reformation of Morals, *A Tract, Containing, I. A Discourse Delivered at the Organization of the Association, by the Rev. Jedidiah Morse, D.D.* . . . [Boston, 1813], 20– 21). I do not mean to suggest that women led the antebellum temperance movement; membership in the above association was limited to men. But women formed part of the

ment of mostly poor women from the trade in the 1790s corresponded with the beginnings of a distinctive feminine voice raised in criticism of the popular culture of drink by mostly middle- and upper-class women.

If the Revolution did not witness the desired and expected reformation of drinking habits in the name of republican virtue and survival, it did initiate movements that would in time climax in a truly popular temperance crusade that challenged the very existence of taverns in community and neighborhood life. Everywhere, inhabitants of Massachusetts began to transcend the local, close-knit fellowship of public rooms to become consumers of print that informed them about a wider world.[19] Temperance received a boost when inhabitants became citizens of a Republic, less devoted to tradition and to the way things had always been done and ready to invent new, voluntary organizations intent on molding society anew. Life revolved less and less around the male representatives of thirty to fifty families who patronized the local taverns.

Temperance could be espoused with a new clarity. During the colonial era conflicting pressures in Puritan social and political ideals had made public houses a constant focus of criticism and anxiety among rulers, but they were still vital institutions for ordinary colonists. Over the long term the Revolution resolved these contradictions between the promotion of temperance on the one hand and the preservation of hierarchy, including censorship, on the other. Puritan social ideals respecting drink would be more fully realized by the abandonment of long-held principles respecting political life. By the 1830s a temperance movement based, not in law, not in the preservation of hierarchy, but in hundreds of voluntary societies and the mass distribution of printed appeals would eliminate drinksellers in many Massachusetts towns.[20]

---

lyceum and lecture audiences of the early 19th century and eventually formed women's temperance societies. After the Civil War, women expanded their role in the temperance movement and would dominate some campaigns for temperance. Barbara Leslie Epstein, *The Politics of Domesticity: Women, Evangelism, and Temperance in Nineteenth-Century America* (Middletown, Conn., 1981), 89–114; Ruth Bordin, *Women and Temperance: The Quest for Power and Liberty, 1873–1900* (Philadelphia, 1981), 52–94; Paul Goodman, *Towards a Christian Republic: Antimasonry and the Great Transition in New England, 1826–1836* (New York, 1988), 84–85, 95. Women criticized meetings of Masons as sessions for drinking.

19. Brown, "Emergence of Urban Society," *JAH*, LXI (1974–1975), 43–44.

20. By the 1830s, 217 of the state's towns reported a combined membership in 384 temperance societies of 105,463 people out of a total population of 456,007, or more than half of the adult population of these towns. Some counties no longer granted liquor licenses

The success of the temperance movement in the 1830s represented a profound shift in the politics and society of Massachusetts, but it was accompanied by the development of excited divisions over a wide array of new issues created by the growth of commerce and manufactures, not to mention the emerging national issue of the existence and expansion of slavery. And if temperance societies helped many individuals to cope with alcoholism and integrated them more completely into a reading public, the leaders of these societies and the movement as a whole often promoted temperance reform as a panacea for all of society's ills, and thus obscured the complexities of individual and social distress. Moreover, as most printed assessments of the origins of the problem of alcohol abuse in this period demonstrate, reform was accomplished without any real understanding of the history of alcohol use or the vital role that taverns had played in colonial Massachusetts, especially among the revered and eulogized Revolutionary generation. Thus Massachusetts inhabitants as a whole were unprepared for the cultural diversity introduced in the 1840s by the flood of Irish immigrants, a largely illiterate immigrant group even more ready to use taverns and drink to construct community life than the English colonists who preceded them.[21] It is a wonder that these immigrants' prompt claims to be part of the political public did not provoke still greater conflict than did arise.

---

at all. *Twenty-first Annual Report of the Massachusetts Temperance Society* (Boston, 1834), 15, 33.

21. The annual reports of the Massachusetts Temperance Society tend to idealize the colonial fathers as models of temperance. The course of the movement is treated in Robert L. Hampel, *Temperance and Prohibition in Massachusetts, 1813–1852* (Ann Arbor, Mich., 1982); Oscar Handlin, *Boston's Immigrants: A Study in Acculturation*, rev. ed. (New York, 1972), 121, 225–229. For the gradual abandonment of the saloon as the center of social and political life by 19th-century immigrant groups, see Madelon Powers, "Decay from Within: The Inevitable Doom of the American Saloon," in Susanna Barrows and Robin Room, eds., *Drinking: Behavior and Belief in Modern History* (Berkeley, Calif., 1991), 112–131.

Appendix: Licenseholders, 1735–1776

Middlesex County Representatives Who Hold Licenses

1. Capt. Samuel Hunt, Tav., Littleton
2. John Fowle, Tav., Woburn
3. Benjamin Willis, Ret., Medford
4. Joseph Buckminster, Esq., Tav., Framingham
5. Jonathan Barron, Tav., Chelmsford
6. John Jones, Esq., Ret., Hopkinton
7. Capt. Thomas Reed, Esq., Tav., Westford
8. Capt. John Stevens, Tav., Townshend
9. Joseph Livermore, Tav., Weston
10. William Lawrence, Esq., Ret., Groton
11. John Hunt, Esq., Ret., Watertown
12. Ephraim Jones, Ret., Concord
13. Daniel Proctor, Tav., Chelmsford
14. William Rice, Tav., Sudbury
15. Capt. Ebenezer Nichols, Esq., Tav., Reading
16. James Fowle, Esq., Tav., Woburn
17. Stephen Hall, Esq., Ret., Medford
18. Samuel Livermore, Esq., Tav., Waltham
19. Sampson Stoddard, Esq., Ret., Chelmsford
20. Benjamin Hall, Ret., Medford
21. Samuel Thatcher, Ret., Cambridge
22. Israel Hobart, Tav., Townshend
23. Deacon Amos Bradley, Tav., Dracut
24. James Tyng, Esq., Ret., Dunstable
25. David Cheever, Esq., Ret., Charlestown
26. Obadiah Sawtell, Tav., Shirley
27. Mark White, Tav., Acton
28. Capt. Nathaniel Adams, Tav., Charlestown
29. William Henry Prentice, Tav., Littleton

Note: 18 of 29 are tavernkeepers; 11 of 29 are or become justices.

Worcester County Representatives Who Hold Licenses

1. Col. Josiah Willard, Esq., Ret., Lunenburg
2. Capt. Daniel Levett, Tav., Mendon
3. Ebenezer Merriam, Tav., Mendon
4. Samuel Willard, Esq., Ret., Lancaster
5. Capt. Josiah Converse, Esq., Tav., Brookfield
6. Nahum Ward, Esq., Ret., Shrewsbury
7. John Grant, Tav., Lunenburg
8. Solomon Wood, Tav., Uxbridge
9. Capt. John Hazeltine, Tav., Upton
10. Capt. William Richardson, Tav., Lancaster
11. Moses Marcy, Esq., Tav., Sturbridge
12. Duncan Campbell, Esq., Ret., Oxford
13. John Haywood, Tav., Lunenburg
14. Jabez Upham, Ret., Brookfield
15. Capt. Joshua Hutchins, Tav., Lunenburg
16. Timothy Brigham, Esq., Tav., Southborough
17. David Wilder, Tav., Lancaster
18. Capt. Bezaleel Eager, Tav., Westborough
19. Capt. Ezra Taylor, Esq., Ret., Southborough
20. Capt. Israel Taylor, Tav., Harvard
21. Capt. Ezekiel Wood, Tav., Uxbridge
22. Capt. Stephen Maynard, Tav., Westborough
23. John Chandler, Jr., Esq., Ret., Petersham
24. Dr. John Taylor, Ret., Lunenburg
25. Joseph Read, Tav., Uxbridge
26. Simeon Dwight, Esq., Ret., Western
27. Paul Mandell, Tav., Hardwick
28. Abiel Sadler, Tav., Upton
29. Hezekiah Ward, Tav., Lancaster
30. Major James Wood, Tav., New Braintree
31. John Child, Tav., Holden
32. Major Caleb Hill, Tav., Douglas
33. Major Jacob Davis, Tav., Charlton
34. William Campbell, Ret., Oxford
35. Capt. Elisha Ward, Tav., Petersham

Note: 25 of 35 are tavernkeepers; 9 of 35 are or become justices.

Hampshire County Representatives Who Hold Licenses

1. Samuel Kent, Ret., Suffield (later attached to Connecticut)
2. Eleazer Porter, Esq., Ret., Hadley
3. Israel Williams, Esq., Ret., Hatfield
4. Nathaniel Kellogg, Tav., Hadley
5. Moses Marsh, Tav., Hadley
6. Joseph Barnard, Tav., Brimfield
7. Fellows Billing, Tav., Sunderland
8. Elijah Williams, Esq., Ret., Deerfield
9. Capt. Luke Bliss, Tav., Springfield
10. Oliver Partridge, Esq., Ret., Hatfield
11. John Ashley, Esq., Ret., Sheffield (later attached to Connecticut)
12. Josiah Dwight, Esq., Ret., Springfield
13. Eldad Taylor, Esq., Ret., Westfield
14. Timothy Danielson, Ret., Brimfield
15. Capt. John Moseley, Ret., Westfield
16. Major Benjamin Day, Esq., Tav., Springfield
17. John Ingersol, Tav., Westfield
18. David Field, Ret., Brimfield
19. James Bridgham, Esq., Ret., Brimfield
20. Major Benjamin Ely, Tav., West Springfield
21. Noah Goodman, Esq., Tav., South Hadley
22. Col. Samuel How, Tav., Belchertown
23. Deacon Nathaniel Leonard, Tav., Worthington
24. Capt. Joseph Lock, Tav., Shutesbury
25. Capt. Israel Hubbard, Tav., Sunderland
26. Jonathan White, Ret., West Springfield
27. Major John Chester Williams, Ret., Hadley
28. Thomas Ingersol, Esq., Tav., Westfield
29. Josiah Pierce, Ret., Hadley

Note: 14 of 29 are tavernkeepers; 11 of 29 are or become justices.

Total for three counties: 57 of 93 (61%) are tavernkeepers; 31 of 93 (33%) are or become justices

Bibliography

A number of the central sources for this study have been relocated. When I examined the record books for the Court of General Sessions of Middlesex County, the file papers for this court, and the probate records for Middlesex licenseholders, they were stored at the Middlesex County Courthouse in Cambridge. I read the volumes of Suffolk Sessions for the years 1702–1732 at the office of the Supreme Judicial Court in the Suffolk County Courthouse in Boston. Suffolk County Probate Records for the colonial period were also located at the courthouse. These above records and file papers are now part of the Judicial Archives at the Archives of the Commonwealth of Massachusetts (ACM) at Columbia Point in Boston. Middlesex probate records, however, may still be examined on microfilm at the courthouse. The record books of the court of general sessions for Worcester, Hampshire, and Plymouth counties are still at the respective courthouses of these counties. The record books for the Court of General Sessions of Essex County can be examined at the Peabody Essex Museum in Salem.

PRIMARY SOURCES

Manuscripts

American Antiquarian Society, Worcester

> Worcester, Mass., American Political Society Records, December 1773–June 1776 (typescript copies by Charles Estus).

Archives of the Commonwealth of Massachusetts (ACM), Columbia Point, Boston.

Massachusetts Archives Collection

> Judicial Records, 1683–1724, XL.
> Minutes of Council 1733–1753, LXXXII.
> Pecuniary Records, 1740–1752, CII.
> Taverns, 1643–1774, CXI.
> Towns, 1632–1693, CXII.

Judicial Archives

> Middlesex
>> Court of General Sessions of the Peace, Middlesex, Record Books, 1686–1771, Bound Volumes.
>> Court of General Sessions, Middlesex, 1735–1776, File Papers.

Court of General Sessions, Middlesex, Book of Licenses, 1791–1810.
Middlesex County Probate Records, Colonial, File Papers (also on
   microfilm at courthouse in Cambridge).

Suffolk

Court of General Sessions, Suffolk, Record Books, 1702–1732, 1796–1807.
Court of General Sessions, Suffolk, Innholders and Retailers, 1812–1822.
Suffolk County Probate Records, Colonial Period, Bound Volumes and File
   Papers.

County Court Records at County and Museum Archives

Court of General Sessions, Essex, Record Book, 1726–1744, Peabody Essex
   Museum, Salem.
Court of General Sessions of the Peace, Hampshire, Record Books, 1735–
   1771, Hampshire County Courthouse, Northampton, County
   Commissioner's Office.
Court of General Sessions, Plymouth, Record Book, 1686–1727, Plymouth
   County Courthouse, County Commissioner's Office.
Court of General Sessions of the Peace, Worcester, Record Books, 1731–1780,
   Worcester County Courthouse, Engineer's Office.
Worcester County Probate Records, Colonial Period, File Papers (Probate
   Office).

Massachusetts Historical Society, Boston

List of Sons of Liberty, 1769, Misc. Bd.
List of Licenseholders, 1765, Boston, Misc. Bd.
Miscellaneous petitions, Misc. Bd.
James Otis, Sr., Papers (List of Licenseholders in Suffolk County, 1737, 1758).
Prince Collection (Nathaniel Saltonstall correspondence, 1696).

Published Sources

Adams, John. *Diary and Autobiography of John Adams*. Edited by L. H. Butterfield
   et al. 4 vols. Cambridge, Mass., 1961.
——. *Papers of John Adams*. Edited by Robert J. Taylor *et al.* Vols. III–IV.
   Cambridge, Mass., 1979.
——. *The Works of John Adams, Second President of the United States*. Edited by
   Charles Francis Adams. 10 vols. Boston, 1851–1856.
Adams, Samuel. *The Writings of Samuel Adams*. Edited by Harry Alonzo Cushing.
   4 vols. New York, 1904–1908.
Ames, Nathaniel. *An Astronomical Diary; or, Almanack for the Year of Our Lord
   Christ 1767*. Boston, 1766.
*At a Court Held at Punch Hall, in the Colony of Bacchus: The Indictment and Tryal of
   Richard Rum, a Person of Noble Birth and Extraction Well Known Both to Rich and
   Poor throughout All America*. Boston, 1724.

Badger, Stephen. *The Nature and Effects of Drunkenness Considered.* . . . Boston, 1774.

——. *A Sermon Delivered in Needham, Nov. 16, 1811, Term of a Century since Incorporation of the Town.* Dedham, Mass., 1811.

Belcher, Jonathan. *The Belcher Papers.* 2 vols. MHS, *Collections*, 6th Ser., VI–VII. Boston, 1893–1894.

Boston. Reports of the Record Commissioners of the City of Boston.

——. *Boston Marriages, 1700 to 1751.* Boston, 1898.

——. *Boston Records from 1660 to 1701.* Boston, 1881.

——. *Boston Town Records from 1700 to 1728.* Boston, 1883.

——. *Boston Town Records, 1742 to 1757.* Boston, 1885.

——. *Boston Town Records from 1758 to 1769.* Boston, 1886.

——. *Boston Town Records, 1770 through 1777.* Boston, 1887.

——. *Records of Boston Selectmen, 1701 to 1715.* Boston, 1884.

——. *Records of Boston Selectmen, 1716 to 1736.* Boston, 1885.

——. *Records of Boston Selectmen, 1736 to 1742.* Boston, 1886.

——. *Selectmen's Minutes from 1764 through 1768.* Boston, 1889.

——. *Selectmen's Minutes from 1769 through April, 1775.* Boston, 1893.

Boston Evening-Post: and the General Advertiser.

Boston Gazette.

Boston News-Letter.

Bowdoin and Temple Letters, The. Pt 2. MHS, *Collections*, 7th Ser., VI. Boston, 1907.

Breck, Robert. *The Only Method to Promote the Happiness of a People and Their Posterity.* Boston, 1728.

Brown, Captain, and Ensign D'Bernicre. ["Narrative of Occurrences, 1775"]. MHS, *Collections*, 2d Ser., IV (1816), 207–213.

Bushman, Richard L., ed. *The Great Awakening: Documents on the Revival of Religion, 1740–1745.* New York, 1970.

Centennial of the Social Circle in Concord, March 21, 1882, The. Cambridge, Mass., 1882.

Channing, William Ellery. "Public Opinion and Temperance." In J. G. Adams and E. H. Chapin, eds., *The Fountain: A Temperance Gift.* Boston, 1847.

Charlestown Association for the Reformation of Morals. *A Tract, Containing, I. A Discourse Delivered at the Organization of the Association, by the Rev. Jedidiah Morse, D.D.* . . . Boston, 1813.

Chauncy, Charles. *Civil Magistrates Must Be Just, Ruling in the Fear of God.* Boston, 1747.

Colman, John. *The Distressed State of the Town of Boston.* . . . Boston, 1720.

Connecticut Courant (Hartford).

Cooke, Elisha. *Mr. Cooke's Just and Seasonable Vindication.* . . . Boston, 1720.

Danforth, Samuel. *Piety Encouraged.* . . . Boston, 1705.

——. *The Woful Effects of Drunkenness.* . . . Boston, 1710.

Deplorable State of New-England, by Reason of a Covetous and Treacherous Governour, The. London, 1708.

Dickerson, Oliver Morton, ed. *Boston under Military Rule, 1768–1769, as Revealed in a Journal of the Times.* 1936; Westport, Conn., 1971.

Douglass, William. *A Summary, Historical and Political, of the First Planting, Progressive Improvements, and Present State of the British Settlements in North America.* Vol. I. Boston, 1749.

Dudley, Paul. *Objections to the Bank of Credit Lately Projected at Boston.* Boston, 1714. In Andrew M. Davis, ed., *Colonial Currency Reprints,* I, Prince Society, XXXII, 239–262. Boston, 1910.

Edwards, Jonathan. *Edwards on Revivals: Containing a Faithful Narrative of the Surprising Work of God in the Conversion of Many Hundred Souls. . . .* Edited by [Isaac] Watts and [John] Guyse. New York, 1832.

Hamilton, Alexander. *Gentleman's Progress: The Itinerarium of Dr. Alexander Hamilton, 1744.* Edited by Carl Bridenbaugh. Chapel Hill, N.C., 1948.

Harris, Nathaniel. *Records of the Court of Nathaniel Harris, . . . Together with a Paper by F. E. Crawford Read before the Historical Society of Watertown, November 14, 1893.* [Watertown, Mass., 1938].

Herttell, Thomas. *An Expose of the Causes of Intemperate Drinking, and the Means by Which It May Be Obviated.* New York, 1820.

[Jackson, Jonathan]. *Thoughts upon the Political Situation of the United States. . . .* Worcester, Mass., 1788.

Letter to the Freeholders and Other Inhabitants of the Massachusetts-Bay . . . , A. [Newport, R.I.], 1739.

Letter to the Freeholders and Other Inhabitants of This Province . . . , A. Boston, 1742.

Letter to the Freeholders, and Qualified Voters . . . , A. Boston, 1749.

Massachusetts. *Acts and Laws of the Commonwealth of Massachusetts.* 13 vols. 1781–1805. Rpt. in 12 vols. Boston, 1890–1898.

———. *The Acts and Resolves, Public and Private, of the Province of the Massachusetts Bay.* 21 vols. Boston, 1869–1922.

Massachusetts Centinel (Boston).

Massachusetts Gazette; and the Boston Weekly News-Letter.

Massachusetts Society for the Suppression of Intemperance. *Report of the Board of Counsel to the Massachusetts Society for the Suppression of Intemperance, . . . June 2, 1820.* Boston, 1820.

Massachusetts Spy (Boston).

Mather, Cotton. *Fair Dealing between Debtor and Creditor. . . .* Boston, 1716.

[———]. *A Faithful Monitor, Offering, an Abstract of the Laws in the Province of the Massachusett-Bay. . . .* Boston, 1704.

———. *Optanda: Good Men Described. . . .* Boston, 1692.

[———]. *Proposals, for the Preservation of Religion in the Churches, by a Due Trial of Them That Stand Candidates of the Ministry.* [Boston, 1702].

[———]. *Sober Considerations, on a Growing Flood of Iniquity. . . .* Boston, 1708.

Mather, Cotton, Benjamin Wadsworth, and Benjamin Colman. *A Testimony against Evil Customs*. Boston, 1719.

Mather, Cotton, *et al. A Serious Address to Those Who Unnecessarily Frequent the Tavern, and Often Spend the Evening in Publick Houses. . . .* Boston, 1847.

[Mather, Increase]. *The Necessity of Reformation. . . .* Boston, 1679.

——. *A Sermon Occasioned by the Execution of a Man Found Guilty of Murder. . . ,* 2d ed. Boston, 1687.

——. *A Testimony against Several Prophane and Superstitious Customs. . . .* London, 1687.

——. *Wo to Drunkards. . . .* Cambridge, Mass., 1673.

Morgan, Edmund S., ed. *Puritan Political Ideas, 1558–1794.* New York, 1965.

Neumeier, Victor L., ed. *The War Years in the Town of Sudbury, Massachusetts, 1765–1781.* Sudbury, Mass., 1975.

New-London Gazette (Connecticut).

Niles, Samuel. *A Pressing Memorial, Circularly Transmitted, . . . to the Several Very Worthy Bodies of Justices, . . . in Their Respective Counties; and to the Select-men in Every Town through the Province.* [Boston, 1761].

Palmer, Stephen. *A Sermon, Delivered in Needham, November 16, 1811, on the Termination of a Century, since the Incorporation of the Town.* Dedham, Mass., 1811.

Pemberton, Ebenezer. *The Divine Original and Dignity of Government Asserted. . . .* Boston, 1710.

Philopolites. *A Memorial of the Present Deplorable State of New-England, with the Many Disadvantages It Lyes under, by the Male-Administration of Their Present Governour, Joseph Dudley. . . .* Boston, 1707.

Pruitt, Bettye Hobbs, ed. *The Massachusetts Tax Valuation List of 1771.* Boston, 1978.

Rawson, Grindal. *The Necessity of a Speedy and Thorough Reformation.* Boston, 1709.

Sandoz, Ellis, ed. *Political Sermons of the American Founding Era, 1730–1815.* Indianapolis, Ind., 1991.

Sewall, Samuel. *The Diary of Samuel Sewall, 1674–1729.* Edited by M. Halsey Thomas. 2 vols. New York, 1973.

Shakespeare, William. *The Life of King Henry the Fifth.* Edited by Alfred Harbage. New York, 1971.

——. *The Merry Wives of Windsor.* Edited by Louis B. Wright and Virginia A. Lamar. New York, 1964.

——. *The Second Part of King Henry the Fourth.* Edited by Allan G. Chester. New York, 1970.

Shurtleff, Nathaniel B., ed. *Records of the Governor and Company of the Massachusetts Bay in New England, 1628–1686.* 5 vols. Boston, 1853–1854.

Stoddard, Solomon. *An Answer to Some Cases of Conscience respecting the Country.* Boston, 1722.

——. *The Danger of Speedy Degeneracy.* . . . Boston, 1705.

Taylor, Robert J., ed. *Massachusetts, Colony to Commonwealth: Documents on the Formation of Its Constitution, 1775–1780.* Chapel Hill, N.C., 1961.

W., J. *A Letter from New-England concerning Their Customs, Manners, and Religion Written upon Occasion of a Report about a Quo Warranto Brought against That Government.* London, 1682.

Wadsworth, Benjamin. *An Essay to Do Good.* . . . Boston, 1710.

——. *Faithful Warnings against Bad-Company-Keeping.* Boston, 1722.

——. *Vicious Courses, Procuring Poverty Describ'd and Condemn'd.* . . . Boston, 1719.

Warning-Piece to All Drunkards and Health-Drinkers: Faithfully Collected from the Works of English and Foreign Learned Authors of Good Esteem, Mr. Samuel Ward and Mr. Samuel Clark, and Others, A. London, 1682.

Willard, Samuel. *The Character of a Good Ruler.* . . . Boston, 1694.

Williams, William. *A Plea for God, and an Appeal to the Consciences of a People Declining in Religion.* Boston, 1719.

SECONDARY WORKS

Adler, Marianna. "From Symbolic Exchange to Commodity Consumption: Anthropological Notes on Drinking as a Symbolic Practice." In Susanna Barrows and Robin Room, eds., *Drinking: Behavior and Belief in Modern History,* 376–398. Berkeley, Calif., 1991.

Allen, David Grayson. *In English Ways: The Movement of Societies and the Transferal of English Local Law and Custom to Massachusetts Bay in the Seventeenth Century.* Chapel Hill, N.C., 1981.

Allen, Wilkes. *The History of Chelmsford, from Its Origin in 1653, to the Year 1820.* . . . Haverhill, Mass., 1820.

Anderson, Fred. *A People's Army: Massachusetts Soldiers and Society in the Seven Years' War.* Chapel Hill, N.C., 1984.

Anderson, Virginia DeJohn. *New England's Generation: The Great Migration and the Formation of Society and Culture in the Seventeenth Century.* New York, 1991.

Bacon, Oliver N. *A History of Natick.* . . . Boston, 1856.

Bailyn, Bernard. *The Ideological Origins of the American Revolution.* Cambridge, Mass., 1967.

——. *The New England Merchants in the Seventeenth Century.* New York, 1964.

——. *The Ordeal of Thomas Hutchinson.* Cambridge, Mass., 1974.

——. *The Origins of American Politics.* New York, 1968.

Barrows, Susanna, and Robin Room, eds. *Drinking: Behavior and Belief in Modern History.* Berkeley, Calif., 1991.

Billias, George Athan. *The Massachusetts Land Bankers of 1740.* University of Maine Studies, 2d Ser., no. 74. Orono, Maine, 1959.

Bloch, Ruth. "American Feminine Ideals in Transition: The Rise of the Moral Mother, 1785–1815." *Feminist Studies,* IV, no. 2 (June 1978), 100–126.

Bond, Henry. *Genealogies of the Families and Descendants of the Early Settlers of Watertown.* . . . Boston, 1860.

Bonomi, Patricia U. *Under the Cope of Heaven: Religion, Society, and Politics in Colonial America.* New York, 1986.

Bordin, Ruth. *Women and Temperance: The Quest for Power and Liberty, 1873–1900.* Philadelphia, 1981.

Bowen, Clarence Winthrop. *The History of Woodstock, Connecticut.* Vol. VII. Worcester, Mass., 1943.

Boyer, Paul S. "Borrowed Rhetoric: The Massachusetts Excise Controversy of 1754." *WMQ*, 3d Ser., XXX (1964), 328–351.

Braudel, Fernand. *Capitalism and Material Life, 1400–1800.* Translated by Miriam Kochan. New York, 1967.

Breen, T. H. *The Character of the Good Ruler: A Study of Puritan Political Ideas in New England, 1630–1730.* New York, 1974.

Bridenbaugh, Carl. *Cities in the Wilderness: The First Century of Urban Life in America, 1625–1742.* New York, 1938.

Brooke, John L. *The Heart of the Commonwealth: Society and Political Culture in Worcester County, Massachusetts, 1713–1861.* New York, 1989.

Brown, B. Katherine. "The Controversy over the Franchise in Puritan Massachusetts, 1959 to 1974." *WMQ*, 3d Ser., XXXIII (1976), 212–241.

Brown, Richard D. "The Emergence of Urban Society in Rural Massachusetts, 1760–1820." *Journal of American History*, LXI (1974–1975), 29–51.

——. *Knowledge Is Power: The Diffusion of Information in Early America, 1700–1865.* New York, 1989.

——. *Modernization: The Transformation of American Life, 1600–1865.* New York, 1976.

——. *Revolutionary Politics in Massachusetts: The Boston Committee of Correspondence and the Towns, 1772–1774.* Cambridge, Mass., 1970.

——. "Shays's Rebellion and the Ratification of the Federal Constitution in Massachusetts." In Richard Beeman, Stephen Botein, and Edward C. Carter II, eds., *Beyond Confederation: Origins of the Constitution and American National Identity*, 113–127. Chapel Hill, N.C., 1987.

Buhler, Kathryn C. *American Silver, 1655–1825, in the Museum of Fine Arts.* 2 vols. Boston, 1972.

Bushman, Richard L. "American High-Style and Vernacular Cultures." In Jack P. Greene and J. R. Pole, eds., *Colonial British America: Essays in the New History of the Early Modern Era*, 345–383. Baltimore, 1984.

——. "Corruption and Power in Provincial America." In *The Development of a Revolutionary Mentality*, 63–92. Library of Congress Symposia on the American Revolution. Washington, D.C., 1972.

——. *King and People in Provincial Massachusetts.* Chapel Hill, N.C., 1985.

——. "Massachusetts Farmers and the Revolution." In Jack P. Greene, Richard L. Bushman, and Michael Kammen, *Society, Freedom, and Conscience: The*

American Revolution in Virginia, Massachusetts, and New York, ed. Richard M. Jellison, 77–124. New York, 1976.

——. *The Refinement of America: Persons, Houses, Cities.* New York, 1992.

Butler, Caleb. *History of the Town of Groton.* . . . Boston, 1848.

Cappon, Lester J., *et al.*, eds. *Atlas of Early American History: The Revolutionary Era, 1760–1790.* Princeton, N.J., 1976.

Chamberlain, George W. *History of Weymouth, Massachusetts.* Boston, 1923.

Chandler, Seth. *History of the Town of Shirley, Massachusetts.* . . . Shirley, Mass., 1883.

Chase, George W. *History of Haverhill, Massachusetts, . . . to 1860.* Haverhill, Mass., 1861.

Clark, Charles E. "The Newspapers of Provincial America." American Antiquarian Society, *Proceedings*, C (1990), 376–389.

Clark, Peter. "The Alehouse and the Alternative Society." In Donald Pennington and Keith Thomas, eds., *Puritans and Revolutionaries: Essays in Seventeenth-Century History Presented to Christopher Hill*, 47–72. Oxford, 1978.

——. *The English Alehouses: A Social History, 1200–1830.* New York, 1983.

——. "The Migrant in Kentish Towns, 1580–1640." In Peter Clark and Paul Slack, eds., *Crisis and Order in English Towns, 1500–1700: Essays in Urban History*, 117–163. London, 1972.

Coffey, T. G. "Beer Street: Gin Lane: Some Views of Eighteenth-Century Drinking." *Quarterly Journal of Studies on Alcohol*, XXVII (1966), 669–692.

Colbourn, H. Trevor. *The Lamp of Experience: Whig History and the Intellectual Origins of the American Revolution.* Chapel Hill, N.C., 1965.

Cook, Edward M., Jr. *The Fathers of the Towns: Leadership and Community Structure in Eighteenth-Century New England.* Baltimore, 1976.

Cott, Nancy F. *The Bonds of Womanhood: "Woman's Sphere" in New England, 1780–1835.* New Haven, Conn., 1977.

Crawford, Michael J. "Indians, Yankees, and the Meetinghouse Dispute of Natick, Massachusetts, 1743–1800." *New England Historical and Genealogical Register*, CXXXII (1978), 278–292.

Darnton, Robert. "A Bourgeois Puts His World in Order: The City as a Text." In Darnton, *The Great Cat Massacre and Other Episodes in French Cultural History*, 107–143. New York, 1985.

Demos, John. *A Little Commonwealth: Family Life in Plymouth Colony.* New York, 1970.

Dickson, Brenton H., and Homer C. Lucas. *One Town in the American Revolution: Weston, Massachusetts.* Weston, Mass., 1976.

Douglas, Mary, ed. *Constructive Drinking: Perspectives on Drink from Anthropology.* Cambridge, 1983.

Drake, Samuel Adams. *Old Boston Taverns and Tavern Clubs.* . . . Boston, 1917.

Duniway, Clyde Augustus. *The Development of Freedom of the Press in Massachusetts.* Cambridge, Mass., 1906.

Earle, Alice Morse. *Stage-Coach and Tavern Days.* New York, 1900.

Epstein, Barbara Leslie. *The Politics of Domesticity: Women, Evangelism, and Temperance in Nineteenth-Century America.* Middletown, Conn., 1981.

Felt, Joseph B. *Annals of Salem.* 2 vols. Salem, Mass., 1845–1849.

Field, Edward. *The Colonial Tavern. . . .* Providence, R.I., 1897.

Fischer, David Hackett. *Albion's Seed: Four British Folkways in America.* New York, 1989.

Flaherty, David H. "Law and the Enforcement of Morals in Early America." *Perspectives in American History,* V, 203–256. Cambridge, Mass., 1971.

———. *Privacy in Colonial New England.* Charlottesville, Va., 1972.

Foster, Stephen. *The Long Argument: English Puritanism and the Shaping of New England Culture, 1570–1700.* Chapel Hill, N.C., 1991.

Frothingham, Richard, Jr. *The History of Charlestown, Massachusetts.* Boston, 1845.

Gambrill, Howard, Jr., and Charles Hambrick-Stowe. *The Tavern and the Tory: The Story of the Golden Ball Tavern.* Cambridge, Mass., 1977.

Geertz, Clifford. "Thick Description: Toward an Interpretive Theory of Culture." In Geertz, *The Interpretation of Cultures,* 3–32. New York, 1973.

Gilmore, William J. *Reading Becomes a Necessity of Life: Material and Cultural Life in Rural New England, 1780–1835.* Knoxville, Tenn., 1989.

Goffman, Erving. *Behavior in Public Places: Notes on the Social Organization of Gatherings.* New York, 1963.

———. *Interaction Ritual: Essays in Face-to-Face Behavior.* Chicago, 1967.

———. *The Presentation of Self in Everyday Life.* New York, 1959.

Goodman, Paul. *Towards a Christian Republic: Antimasonry and the Great Transition in New England, 1826–1836.* New York, 1988.

Greven, Philip J., Jr. *Four Generations: Population, Land, and Family in Colonial Andover, Massachusetts.* Ithaca, N.Y., 1970.

Gross, Robert A. *The Minutemen and Their World.* New York, 1976.

Habermas, Jürgen. *The Structural Transformation of the Public Sphere: An Inquiry into a Category of Bourgeois Society.* Translated by Thomas Burger. Cambridge, Mass., 1989.

Hall, David D. *The Faithful Shepherd: A History of the New England Ministry in the Seventeenth Century.* Chapel Hill, N.C., 1972.

———. "Religion and Society: Problems and Reconsiderations." In Jack P. Greene and J. R. Pole, eds., *Colonial British America: Essays in the New History of the Early Modern Era,* 317–344. Baltimore, 1984.

———. "The World of Print and Collective Mentality in Seventeenth-Century New England." In John Higham and Paul K. Conkin, eds., *New Directions in American Intellectual History,* 166–180. Baltimore, 1979.

———. *Worlds of Wonder, Days of Judgment: Popular Religious Belief in Early New England.* Cambridge, Mass., 1990.

Hartog, Hendrik. "The Public Law of a County Court: Judicial Government in

Eighteenth Century Massachusetts." *American Journal of Legal History*, XX (1976), 282–291.

Haskins, George Lee. *Law and Authority in Early Massachusetts: A Study in Tradition and Design*. New York, 1960.

Hay, Douglas. "Poaching and the Game Laws on Cannock Chase." In Hay *et al.*, eds., *Albion's Fatal Tree: Crime and Society in Eighteenth-Century England*, 189–253. New York, 1975.

Hazen, Henry A. *History of Billerica*. . . . Boston, 1883.

Hill, Christopher. *Society and Puritanism in Pre-Revolutionary England*. London, 1964.

Hill, Thomas W. "Ethnohistory and Alcohol Studies." In Mark Galenter, ed., *Recent Developments in Alcoholism*, II, 313–337. New York, 1984.

Hodgman, Edwin R. *History of the Town of Westford*. . . . Lowell, Mass., 1883.

Hudson, Charles. *History of the Town of Lexington*. . . . Boston, 1913.

——. *History of the Town of Marlborough*. . . . Boston, 1862.

Hudson, Harris Gary. *A Study of Social Regulations in England under James I and Charles I: Drink and Tobacco*. Chicago, 1933.

Hurd, D. Hamilton. *History of Middlesex County*. . . . 3 vols. Philadelphia, 1890.

Isaac, Rhys. "Dramatizing the Ideology of Revolution: Popular Mobilization in Virginia, 1774 to 1776." *WMQ*, 3d Ser., XXXIII (1976), 357–385.

Jackson, Francis. *A History of the Early Settlement of Newton*. . . . Boston, 1854.

Jones, Douglas Lamar. "The Strolling Poor: Transiency in Eighteenth-Century Massachusetts." *Journal of Social History*, [VIII, no. 37] (Spring 1975), 28–54.

Judd, Sylvester. *History of Hadley*. . . . 1863; rpt. Somersworth, N.H., 1976.

Kerber, Linda K. *Women of the Republic: Intellect and Ideology in Revolutionary America*. Chapel Hill, N.C., 1980.

Konig, David Thomas. *Law and Society in Puritan Massachusetts: Essex County, 1629–1692*. Chapel Hill, N.C., 1979.

Kulikoff, Allan. "The Progress of Inequality in Revolutionary Boston." *WMQ*, 3d Ser., XXVIII (1971), 375–412.

Lamson, Daniel S. *History of the Town of Weston, Massachusetts, 1630–1890*. Boston, 1913.

Larkin, Jack. "From 'Country Mediocrity' to 'Rural Improvement': Transforming the Slovenly Countryside in Central Massachusetts, 1775–1840." Paper presented at Boston area Seminar in Early American History at the Massachusetts Historical Society, Apr. 18, 1991.

Laslett, Peter. *The World We Have Lost: England before the Industrial Age*. New York, 1973.

Lax, John, and William Pencak. "The Knowles Riot and the Crisis of the 1740's in Massachusetts." *Perspectives in American History*, X, 163–216. Cambridge, Mass., 1976.

Lemisch, Jesse. "Jack Tar in the Streets: Merchant Seamen in the Politics of Revolutionary America." *WMQ*, 3d Ser., XXV (1968), 371–407.

Levy, Leonard W. *Emergence of a Free Press.* New York, 1985.

Lincoln, William. *History of Worcester. . . .* Worcester, Mass., 1837.

Lockridge, Kenneth. "Land, Population, and the Evolution of New England Society, 1630–1790: And an Afterthought." In Stanley N. Katz, ed., *Colonial America: Essays in Politics and Social Development,* 466–491. Boston, 1971.

——. *A New England Town, the First Hundred Years: Dedham, Massachusetts, 1636–1736.* New York, 1970.

McCoy, Drew R. *The Elusive Republic: Political Economy in Jeffersonian America.* Chapel Hill, N.C., 1980.

McCusker, John J. "Distilling, the Rum Trade, and Early British America." Paper presented at Boston area Seminar in Early American History at Massachusetts Historical Society, Oct. 17, 1991.

Maier, Pauline. *From Resistance to Revolution: Colonial Radicals and the Development of American Opposition to Britain, 1765–1776.* New York, 1974.

Main, Gloria L., and Jackson T. Main. "Economic Growth and the Standard of Living in Southern New England, 1640–1774." *Journal of Economic History,* XLVIII (1988), 27–46.

Main, Jackson Turner. "Government by the People: The American Revolution and the Democratization of the Legislatures." In Jack P. Greene, ed., *The Reinterpretation of the American Revolution, 1763–1789,* 322–338. New York, 1968.

Merrill, Michael, and Sean Wilentz, eds. *The Key of Liberty: The Life and Democratic Writings of William Manning, "A Laborer," 1747–1814.* Cambridge, Mass., 1993.

Miller, Perry. "From the Covenant to the Revival." In James Ward Smith and A. Leland Jamison, eds., *The Shaping of American Religion,* 322–368. Princeton, N.J., 1961.

——. *The New England Mind: From Colony to Province.* Cambridge, Mass., 1953.

——. *The New England Mind: The Seventeenth Century.* Cambridge, Mass., 1954.

Morgan, Edmund S. *American Slavery, American Freedom: The Ordeal of Colonial Virginia.* New York, 1975.

——. *Inventing the People: The Rise of Popular Sovereignty in England and America.* New York, 1988.

——. *The Puritan Dilemma: The Story of John Winthrop.* Boston, 1958.

——. "The Puritan Ethic and the American Revolution." *WMQ,* 3d Ser., XXIV (1967), 3–43.

Murrin, John M. Review Essay. *History and Theory,* XI (1972), 257–270.

Nash, Gary B. "The Failure of Female Factory Labor in Colonial Boston." *Labor History,* XX (1979), 165–188.

——. *The Urban Crucible: Social Change, Political Consciousness, and the Origins of the American Revolution.* Cambridge, Mass., 1979.

Ong, Walter J. *The Presence of the Word: Some Prolegomena for Cultural and Religious History.* New Haven, Conn., 1967.

Paige, Lucius R. *History of Cambridge Massachusetts, 1630–1877....* Boston, 1877.

——. *History of Hardwick, Massachusetts.* Boston, 1883.

Patrick, Clarence H. *Alcohol, Culture, and Society.* Durham, N.C., 1952.

Pencak, William. *War, Politics, and Revolution in Provincial Massachusetts, 1630–1730.* Boston, 1981.

Phalen, Harold R. *History of the Town of Acton.* Cambridge, Mass., 1954.

Phythian-Adams, Charles. "Ceremony and Citizen: The Communal Year at Coventry, 1450–1550." In Peter Clark and Paul Slack, eds., *Crisis and Order in English Towns, 1500–1700: Essays in Urban History,* 57–85. London, 1972.

Piersen, William D. *Black Yankees: The Development of an Afro-American Subculture in Eighteenth-Century New England.* Amherst, Mass., 1988.

Pye, Lucian W., ed. *Communications and Political Development.* Princeton, N.J., 1963.

Rice, Kym S. *Early American Taverns: For the Entertainment of Friends and Strangers.* Chicago, 1983.

Richards, Audrey I. *Land, Labour, and Diet in Northern Rhodesia: An Economic Study of the Bemba Tribe.* London, 1939.

Robbins, Caroline. *The Eighteenth-Century Commonwealthman: Studies in the Transmission, Development, and Circumstance of English Liberal Thought from the Restoration of Charles II until the War with the Thirteen Colonies.* Cambridge, Mass., 1959.

Roeber, A. G. "Authority, Law, and Custom: The Ritual of Court Day in Tidewater Virginia, 1720 to 1750." *WMQ,* 3d Ser., XXXVII (1980), 29–52.

Rorabaugh, W. J. *The Alcoholic Republic: An American Tradition.* New York, 1979.

Roth, Rodris. "Tea Drinking in Eighteenth-Century America: Its Etiquette and Equipage." *Contributions from the Museum of History and Technology,* 69–91. Washington, D.C., 1969.

Roy, Louis E. *History of East Brookfield, Massachusetts, 1686–1970.* Worcester, Mass., 1970.

Royster, Charles. *A Revolutionary People at War: The Continental Army and American Character, 1775–1783.* Chapel Hill, N.C., 1979.

Rutman, Darrett B. *Winthrop's Boston: Portrait of a Puritan Town, 1630–1649.* Chapel Hill, N.C., 1965.

Salmon, Marylynn. *Women and the Law of Property in Early America.* Chapel Hill, N.C., 1986.

Schutz, John A. *William Shirley: King's Governor of Massachusetts.* Chapel Hill, N.C., 1961.

Sewall, Samuel. *The History of Woburn....* Boston, 1868.

Shammas, Carole. "The Domestic Environment in Early Modern England and America." *Journal of Social History,* XIV (1980–1981), 3–24.

Shattuck, Lemuel. *A History of the Town of Concord.* Boston, 1835.

Shipton, Clifford K. *Biographical Sketches of Those Who Attended Harvard*

College. . . . Vols. IV–XVII of Sibley's Harvard Graduates. Cambridge, Mass.; Boston, 1933–1975.

Sibley, John Langdon. *Biographical Sketches of Graduates of Harvard University.* . . . 3 vols. Cambridge, Mass., 1873–1885.

Snow, Caleb H. *A History of Boston, the Metropolis of Massachusetts, from Its Origin to the Present.* . . . 2d ed. Boston, 1928.

Stone, Lawrence. *The Causes of the English Revolution, 1529–1642.* New York, 1972.

Stout, Harry S. *The New England Soul: Preaching and Religious Culture in Colonial New England.* New York, 1986.

Sutherland, Stella H. *Population Distribution in Colonial America.* New York, 1936.

Taylor, Robert J. *Western Massachusetts in the Revolution.* Providence, R.I., 1954.

Temple, J. H. *History of Framingham, Massachusetts, . . . 1640–1888.* Framingham, Mass., 1887.

Tessler, Mark A., William M. O'Barr, and David H. Spain. *Tradition and Identity in Changing Africa.* New York, 1973.

Thomas, Keith. *Religion and the Decline of Magic.* New York, 1971.

——. "Work and Leisure in Pre-Industrial Society." *Past and Present,* no. 29 (December 1964), 50–66.

Thompson, E. P. "The Moral Economy of the English Crowd in the Eighteenth Century." *Past and Present,* no. 50 (February 1971), 76–136.

——. *Whigs and Hunters: The Origins of the Black Act.* New York, 1975.

Tyler, John W. *Smugglers and Patriots: Boston Merchants and the Advent of the American Revolution.* Boston, 1986.

Ulrich, Laurel Thatcher. *Good Wives: Image and Reality in the Lives of Women in Northern New England, 1650–1750.* New York, 1991.

Underdown, David. *Revel, Riot, and Rebellion: Popular Politics and Culture in England, 1603–1660.* New York, 1973.

Walzer, Michael. *The Revolution of the Saints: A Study in the Origins of Radical Politics.* New York, 1985.

Warden, G. B. *Boston, 1689–1776.* Boston, 1970.

——. "The Caucus and Democracy in Colonial Boston." *New England Quarterly,* XLIII (1970), 19–45.

——. "The Distribution of Property in Boston, 1692–1775." *Perspectives in American History,* X, 81–128. Cambridge, Mass., 1976.

——. "Inequality and Instability in Eighteenth-Century Boston: A Reappraisal." *Journal of Interdisciplinary History,* VI (1975–1976), 585–620.

Warner, Michael. *The Letters of the Republic: Publication and the Public Sphere in Eighteenth-Century America.* Cambridge, Mass., 1990.

Warren, Charles. *Jacobin and Junto: or, Early American Politics as Viewed in the Diary of Dr. Nathaniel Ames.* Cambridge, Mass., 1931.

Waters, Wilson. *History of Chelmsford, Massachusetts.* Lowell, Mass., 1917.

Webb, Sidney, and Beatrice Webb. *The History of Liquor Licensing: Principally from 1700 to 1830.* 1903; Hamden, Conn., 1963.

Whitehill, Walter Muir. *Boston: A Topographical History.* Cambridge, Mass., 1968.

Wood, Gordon. "Conspiracy and the Paranoid Style: Causality and Deceit in the Eighteenth Century." *WMQ,* 3d Ser., XXXIV (1982), 401–441.

——. *The Creation of the American Republic, 1776–1787.* Chapel Hill, N.C., 1969.

——. *The Radicalism of the American Revolution.* New York, 1992.

——. "Rhetoric and Reality in the American Revolution." *WMQ,* 3d Ser., XXIII (1966), 3–32.

Wrightson, Keith. *English Society, 1580–1680.* New Brunswick, N.J., 1982.

Young, Alfred F. "George Robert Twelves Hewes (1742–1840): A Boston Shoemaker and the Memory of the American Revolution." *WMQ,* 3d Ser., XXXVIII (1981), 561–623.

Zobel, Hiller B. *The Boston Massacre.* New York, 1970.

Zuckerman, Michael. "The Fabrication of Identity in Early America." *WMQ,* 3d Ser., XXXIV (1977), 183–214.

Index

Adams, John: on justices in drink trade, 97n; on number of public houses, 151, 230; on licensing of poor, 154; on use of drink and licenses in elections, 156, 171–172, 241, 299; on Boston Caucus, 184–185; in taverns, 235, 275–277; on Sons of Liberty, 265–266; letters to, on public order, 301

Adams, Samuel, 267, 277, 310

Alcohol: consumption of distilled, 1770–1830, 314. *See also* Brandy; Cider; Drink; Rum

Alcoholism, 144–146, 317

Alehouses; first licensing of, in England, 26; fear of disorder in, 27–28; as agent of corruption, 29; elimination of, in Massachusetts, 31; repression of, in England, 101–102

American Political Society (Worcester), 283–285, 297, 302

Ames, Nathaniel: on colonists' loss of virtue, 245–246; on reading and republican virtue, 315; on manufactures, 317

Andros, Gov. Edmund, 60, 218

Assembly (General Court) of Massachusetts, 14n; and orders on licensing, 58–59, 64–65; on clergymen's salaries, 84, 228–229; as balance to royal authority, 181; royal governors' efforts to control, 201–202, 216; as guardian of morality, 204–205, 230, 236; election of drinksellers to, 222–223, 305–306; elections to, 268–269;

democratization of, 311; license-holders in, 323–325

Associates (drinking company of Sons of Liberty), 260–262

Authority: uses of drink to establish, 7; men of, and intemperance, 11; of figures of high social rank, 17, 162–163, 167, 200–201; signified by dress, manner, and speech, 17; deference to figures of, 17–18; as reflected in furniture, 18; decline of clergymen's, 49–50, 84, 227–229; drinking and defiance of, 50–51, 53, 57–59, 68, 80; effort to strengthen, 69–70, 167; of poor drinksellers over customers, 103; of female drinksellers, 104, 109; of drink regulators, 124, 154–156, 202, 222–226; of gentlemen over slaves, servants, and Indians, 125; of women before men, 134–137; personal defiance of, 165; libels against, 165–166, 181; defiance of royal, 165–166, 172–173, 181; and emergence of critical public, 177, 179–180, 206–207; confusion of lines of, 195, 199–200; diffusion of, in speaking, 206–207, 226–227; fears concerning, after 1765, 250, 263–264, 289, 301; of judiciary, after 1765, 268–271; reversal of, in courts, 287–292; collapse of traditional, 306, 312–313. *See also* Hierarchy; Hierarchy of drink regulators; Public sphere

Badger, Rev. Stephen: on addiction to drink, 144–145; on influence of tavernkeepers, 196; on Sons of Liberty, 272

Battersby, Sarah (Boston drinkseller), 133, 180

Belcher, Gov. Andrew: and Assembly, 201–202, 231; and greater drink regulation, 203–205; against Land Bank, 216; and loan of books, 233

Bernard, Gov. Francis: and English troops, 251; and royal authority, 252–253, 269–270, 272, 308

Bigelow, Timothy (Worcester tavern-keeper), 281–282; library of, 282–283; as organizer of resistance, 288, 290–291, 295, 304

Black Act: and English public houses, 28

Blue Anchor Tavern (Boston), 102

Books: owned by drinksellers, 89–90, 119, 121, 177–178, 234–235, 258–259, 282–283

Boston, 1, 9–10, 13–15, 18, 20, 31–32, 35, 37, 39, 47–48, 50, 54–55, 57–59, 61, 64, 67–74, 77–78, 80, 83, 84, 87–95, 99–100, 102–148, 154–156, 158, 160–188, 199, 204, 219, 233–235, 241, 244, 249–253, 255–265, 268, 270–275, 277, 279, 287, 289–290, 302, 304, 316, 318–319

Boston Caucus: references to, 169–170; control of elections by, 170; and licensing policy, 170–171; decline of, 182–183; in resistance, 302

Boston Massacre, 274

Boston Tea Party: as model for towns, 279

Bowdoin, Gov. James, 311–312

Braintree, 151–152, 171–172, 197;

election of tavernkeepers in, 198–199, 299

Brandy, 93, 119–120, 153–154, 295

Breck, Rev. Robert: on election of drink regulators, 79–80

British Coffee House (Boston), 270–271

Brookfield, 195, 283

Brown, Captain: narrative of, 292–298

Buckminster, Joseph (Framingham tavernkeeper), 210–211, 293, 296

Bunch of Grapes Tavern (Boston), 102, 125, 132, 257–258

Cambridge, 14, 31, 150, 153, 198, 278

Cambridge Platform, 34

Charlestown, 14, 31, 58–59, 277, 279, 318–319, 320n

Chauncy, Rev. Charles: on drink laws, 227; on authority and compensation of clergymen, 227–228

Chelmsford, 278

Christmas, 32

Cider, 68, 73, 119–122, 153–154

Clapham, Mary (Boston drinkseller), 136–137

Clergymen: on intemperance, 8–9; loss of formal authority of, 34; book ownership of, 42–45; influence of, 49–50, 188; pleas of, for new regulations on drink and tavern use, 52, 54, 65, 68, 227; sermons and tracts of, against intemperance, 66, 74, 75–76, 79–80, 82–84; decline of salaries of, 84, 227–229; on intemperance and colony's setbacks, 185; on resistance and reformation after 1765, 255n, 293n, 295, 301. *See also individual clergymen*

Coercive Acts, 288

Coffee, 92, 121, 179

Coffeehouse: emergence of, in Boston, 161. *See also* British Coffee House; Crown Coffee House

Collective drinking: in England, 22–24; repression of, in Massachusetts, 32; new customs of, 82; perpetuation of, and Puritanism, 83; decline of symbolic significance of, 127, 139, 143–146; as part of political culture, 188. *See also* Drink; Traditional drinking habits

Colman, Rev. Benjamin: on new drinking customs, 82

Committees of Correspondence: in Boston, 277; in country towns, 277–278, 280–281, 286, 293, 297

Concord, 150, 198, 290n; Social Circle of, 316

Connecticut: drink and tavern use in, 187n, 235, 246–250

Converse, Capt. Josiah (Brookfield tavernkeeper), 283

Cooke, Elisha, Jr.: assault on, in tavern, 1, 172–174; conflict of, with royal government, 168, 176, 186, 203, 205; drinking habits of, 168–169; as owner of Boston taverns, 169, 182; and restrictive licensing policy, 170–171; and popular base of influence, 172; as inventor of a public interest, 176; and identification with lower ranks, 182; rise of, in perspective, 185–186; on human agency in politics, 186

Cooke, Elisha, Sr., 168

Copp, David (Boston tavernkeeper), 73; and Widow Patience, 131–132

Courts: meetings of, in taverns, 12, 14, 17, 21, 135; disruption and closure of, 287–292. *See also* Justices

Credit: negotiation of, by drinksellers, 111–114, 131–132; negotiation of, in taverns, 114, 143, 317

Crowd actions: against grain exportation in Boston, 72; against impressment, 183–184. *See also* Boston Tea Party

Crown Coffee House (Boston), 73–74, 77, 89–96, 119, 130, 132, 133, 161–162, 177. *See also* Selby, Thomas

Cushing, Adam (Weymouth tavernkeeper), 209–210, 219–220

Danforth, Rev. Samuel: on intemperance and political authority, 51, 156, 184

Danvers, 279

D'Berniére, Ensign: narrative of, 292–298

Deference: posture of, among lower ranks, 124, 167; breaches of posture of, 165, 172–174, 181. *See also* Courts; Speech

Dickinson, John: publications of, 266

Disorders: in Boston public houses, 108–109, 139; and tavern licensing, 123

Distillers: in Boston, 61; as Sons of Liberty, 256–258

Douglas, William: on drinksellers elected to Assembly, 224–225

Drink (alcoholic): in England, as symbol of reciprocity, 4, 6, 22–25; criticism of, in England, 6, 8, 27–31; persistent symbolic use of, 40, 43–44, 75–78, 114, 143, 247; and criticism of leaders, 51; expansion of trade in distilled, 61–62; excise taxes on, 62, 240; criticism of distilled, 96, 229–230, 242, 244; in elections, 158, 170–171, 187, 247–248; expansion of use of distilled, 227; change in use of, 253–254; republican censure of, 260–262; use of, to unite all ranks, 263–264. *See also* Alcoholism; Brandy; Cider;

Gloucester, 58
Golden Ball Tavern (Boston), 178, 257–258
Green Dragon Tavern (Boston), 16, 20, 67, 160
Groton, 150, 194

Hall, Richard (Boston tavernkeeper), 1, 172, 174
Hamilton, Dr. Alexander: on tavern companies, 200; on lack of hierarchy, 200; on revivals, 226–227; on reading of news in taverns, 234
Hampshire County: increase of public houses in, 192; election of drinksellers in, 222–224; representatives holding licenses in, 325
Hancock, John, 264
Hardwick, 285–287
Harris, Nathaniel (Watertown retailer): and drink crimes, 214
Hats: and deferential posture, 57, 165, 281, 290
Haverhill, 63, 150
Hawksworth, Elizabeth (Boston retailer), 99–100, 112, 139, 146–147
Health drinking: in England, 24–25, 27, 30; at issue in Massachusetts, 33, 40; prevalence of, 51, 57, 160; to Cooke, 172
Herttell, Thomas: on drink regulation before 1820, 4
Hierarchy: in taverns on court days, 12; displays of, in processions, 18, 70; relaxation of, in taverns, 48–49, 68; effort to strengthen, 52, 54–55, 157, 167, 185, 187, 204; violation of manners of, 57; as principle of government, 65–66, 68, 158–159; and temperance, 70, 79–80; submission to, 162; weakening of, 164–168, 181; and emergence of

public sphere, 176–177, 179–180, 185–186, 236–237; versus gatherings in public houses, 177, 186; lack of, in colonies, 200; effect of royal charter on, 200–201; attempted anglicization of, 202, 226; and pamphlet literature, 206–207; and election of drinksellers, 222–226; distinctions of, after 1765, 241–242, 263–264, 271, 287–292; collapse of, 312–314. *See also* Authority
Hierarchy of drink regulators: orders to, 59; elaboration of, 63–64, 158; weakening of, in Boston, 66, 79–80, 127, 154–155, 158, 170–172, 174; visits of, to Boston households, 69–70; and voters, 79–80; and renewal of regulation in Boston, 141–142; in country towns, 189; weakening of, in countryside, 193–199; efforts to strengthen, 203–204; entrance of drinksellers into, 193–199, 214–215, 222–226; and conflict with royal authority, 237–238; after 1765, 268–269, 272, 299, 306, 312. *See also* Justices; Selectmen; Tithingmen
Hingham, 58
Holliston, 191
Holmes, Francis (Boston tavernkeeper), 102, 125, 132
Holmes, Rebecca (Boston tavernkeeper), 134, 137
Hopkinton, 151, 191, 193
Hutchinson, Thomas, 182; as lieutenant governor and governor, 264, 267, 272, 275, 289, 291–292, 308

Indians: gatherings of, 125
Intemperance: Puritan definition of, 30; as provocation for God's punishment, 29–30, 75

on new drinking customs, 82; on addiction, 144; on Governor Dudley, 163n

Mather, Increase: on drink and tavern use, 3, 20, 50; on addiction, 144

Mears, Samuel (Boston tavernkeeper), 73; and Hannah, 119

Meetinghouse: contrast of, with tavern, 2, 21

Middlesex County, 147, 152–154; increase of public houses in, 192, 255, 313; election of drinksellers to office in, 197–198, 222–224; drinksellers owning books in, 234; licenseholding delegates from, 303; licenseholding representatives from, 323

Middleton, George (Boston drinkseller), 319

Militia: and taverns and drink at musters, 18, 38, 82, 248; distribution of drink by officers of, 247, 257, 307; before rebellion, 296; levelism of, after Independence, 301

Monk, George (Boston tavernkeeper), 14, 18, 58–59, 87, 89, 92, 102, 106–107

Montague, 279

Natick, 195–196, 272

Newbury, 58

Newspapers: in taverns, 234–236; circulation of, after 1765, 279–280, 290, 304–305, 313. See also Print

Nicholson, Gen. Francis, 160–161, 166

Niles, Rev. Samuel: on drink and taverns, 152

Northampton, 226

Northborough, 279

Oaths: made with drink, 24

Oliver, Andrew, 182, 265, 287

Oliver, Peter, 170, 275, 288–289

Otis, James, Sr., 271

Pamphlets: ownership and circulation of, 158, 177–179, 180n, 233–235, 258–259, 279–280, 283, 294; and Whig essayists, 232–233; and what public does not know, 239. See also Newspapers; Print; Public sphere

Pemberton, Rev. Ebenezer: on subjection to rulers, 65, 162–163; on degrees of men, 70

Pitson, James (Boston tavernkeeper): as cidermaker, 68; tavern of, 88; and Hannah, 119–121; and reading public, 178

Plymouth County: number of public houses in, 31–32

Political culture: change in, 181–188, 241–242; tavern's role in, 302, 308–309

Poor: in Boston drink trade, 99–100, 103–105, 108–115, 117–118, 123, 138–140, 145; as drinksellers in England, 101–102; and drink trade in Massachusetts, 102–103, 154, 185; and licenses as charity, 105–107, 112–113

Pots: of drink, 30; limits on consumption of, 39; sizes and numbers of, 39

Print: use of, against intemperance and tavern haunting, 41–42, 83; censorship of, 42, 175–176; representation of critical public in, 176; in public houses, 177–180; effect of, on collective drinking, 179; oral transmission of, to illiterate, 180–181, 180n; criticism of royal government in, 181; and weakening of drink regulation, 186; culture of, on King Street, 233; and lack of public knowledge, 239; use of, in taverns

Rawson, Rev. Grindal: on need for reformation, 65

Reading: and drinking, 42, 179; as private activity, 314–315

Religious revivals, 151, 226–227

Republican virtue: and active citizenry, 242–243; lack of, in England, 244–245; of crown appointees, 245, 248, 277; decline of, in colonies, 245–248; need for revival of, 253–254; and Sons of Liberty, 266–267, 284–285, 306–307; in American Republic, 30, 313–314; and reading, 315

Republics: lessons of ancient, 232, 242, 243–247, 259, 282; consumption in, 249, 254, 284–285, 307; creation of, in Massachusetts, 301; and print culture, 314–316

Resistance: and reformation, 243, 250; and clarifying values, 300

Retailers: of drink, 37, 38; and dramshops, 117, 122, 154. *See also* Public houses

Revere, Paul, 260, 289

Revolution: impact of, on drinking, 314–322; and Puritanism, 321

Rowley, 275

Royal Exchange Tavern (Boston), 233, 289

Royal government: introduction of, 60, 159–160; intemperance of members of, 160; manipulation of Assembly by, 201–202, 216–218, 268–269; conflict over powers of governor of, 231; as source of vice, 245, 248, 251–253, 277; growing weakness of, 271–272, 275, 287–292. *See also* Assembly of Massachusetts; Justices

Rulers: ideal character of, 157–158, 162, 185; voters' dialogue with, 206–207

Rum: criticism of, 10, 68, 74, 144–146, 161–162; expansion of trade and production of, 38, 61–62; excise taxes on, 62; to fortify laborers, 68, 247; expansion of consumption of, 68, 74, 119–121, 141, 144–145, 152–155; sale of, in taverns, 73–74; popularity of, 85–86; and public virtue, 96, 230, 242, 244; abstinence of gentlemen from, 161–162; new criticism of, after 1765, 245, 247, 249; muffling of criticism of, 260–262

Salem, 14, 58, 70

Saltonstall, Nathaniel: on number of public houses, 63

Selby, Thomas (Boston tavernkeeper), 73–74, 89–95, 125, 132, 161–162, 177–179

Selectmen: power of, to approve licenses, 36, 159, 184, 191–192; and reduction of licenses in Boston, 67–68, 141–142, 183; and objections to renewal of licenses, 71; and restrictive licensing policy in Boston, 80, 116, 170–172; and licenses for poor in Boston, 108–115; election of Elisha Cooke to board of, in Boston, 170–171; and crowd actions in Boston, 183–184; and public houses in country towns, 189–190, 193, 195, 199; and licenses in country towns, 193, 197–199; and reforms in Boston, after 1765, 250; and petitions to accommodate troops, 255; as Sons of Liberty, 257

Sewall, Samuel; use of taverns and drink by, 13, 19–21, 160; portrait of, 15; as figure of authority, 17–18; distribution of sermons by, 21; on Anglican ecclesiastical calendar,

215; in militia elections, 247–248, 257, 307

Turner, John (Boston tavernkeeper), 14, 18, 47, 92–93, 102

Voluntarism: of Puritans, 30–31; expansion of, after Revolution, 316

Wadsworth, Rev. Benjamin: on use of taverns and drink, 50, 74–76, 82; on licensing of poor, 100, 110–111, 114, 115–116, 129; on addiction, 144

Wallis, William (Boston tavernkeeper), 57, 71, 160

Waltham, 292–293

Wardell, Frances (Boston tavernkeeper), 135–138

Weston, 153, 280–281, 296

Weymouth, 209–210

Whig opposition ideology: origins of, in England, 231–232; influence of, in Massachusetts, 232–234, 236; and more vocal political participation, 242, 309; and intemperance, 242–243, 248, 260; as basis for resistance, 258–260, 273, 282–283; and Puritanism, 298–299

Whiskey, 313–314

Willard, Rev. Samuel: on disruption of hierarchy, 61; on restraint of vice, 66

Williams, Col. Abraham (Marlborough tavernkeeper), 297, 304

Williams, William: on popularity of taverns, 84, 115

Wilmington, 193–194

Wines: in taverns, 37, 93, 119, 121

Winge, John (Boston tavernkeeper), 102

Women: legal position of, 103–104, 131–132; in resistance, 283; and new role in Republic, 320. *See also* Female drinksellers; *individual female drinksellers*

Worcester, 154, 281–285

Worcester County: increase of public houses in, 192; election of drinksellers to Assembly in, 222–224; book-owning drinksellers in, 234; licenseholding representatives of, 324

Workhouses: in England, 101; in Massachusetts, 107–108, 140

Wormall, Sarah (Boston tavernkeeper), 73, 87, 109, 112, 121–122, 130–131, 180

Yeamans, John: and Elisha Cooke, Jr., 172–173